ANTHROPOLOGICAL PAPERS OF
THE UNIVERSITY OF ARIZONA
NUMBER 81

Oysters in the Land of Cacao:

Archaeology, Material Culture, and Societies at Islas de los Cerros and the Western Chontalpa, Tabasco, Mexico

Bradley E. Ensor

THE UNIVERSITY OF
ARIZONA PRESS

TUCSON

The University of Arizona Press
www.uapress.arizona.edu

Printed in the United States of America.
25 24 23 22 21 20   6 5 4 3 2 1

ISBN-13: 978-0-8165-4108-9 (paper)

Editing and indexing by Linda Gregonis.
InDesign layout by Douglas Goewey.

Library of Congress Cataloging-in-Publication Data
Names: Ensor, Bradley E., 1966– author.
Title: Oysters in the Land of Cacao : Archaeology, Material
    Culture, and Societies at Islas de Los Cerros and the
    Western Chontalpa, Tabasco, Mexico / Bradley E. Ensor.
Other titles: Anthropological papers of the University of
    Arizona ; no. 81.
Description: Tucson : The University of Arizona Press,
    2020. | Series: Anthropological papers of the University
    of Arizona ; number 81 | Includes bibliographical
    references and index.
Identifiers: LCCN 2020012106 | ISBN 9780816541089
    (paperback)
Subjects: LCSH: Indians of Mexico—Mexico—Chontalpa.
    | Coastal archaeology—Mexico—Tabasco (State) |
    Chontalpa (Mexico)—Antiquities.
Classification: LCC F1219.1.T13 E67 2020 |
    DDC 972/.6301—dc23
LC record available at https://lccn.loc.gov/2020012106

About the Author

DR. BRADLEY E. ENSOR (Ph.D. 2003, University of Florida)
is a professor of anthropology at Eastern Michigan University
(2003-present) in Ypsilanti, Michigan, where he teaches
archaeology, social anthropology, and physical anthropology.
His research addresses US Southwest, Southeast, Great Lakes,
and Mesoamerican prehistory; theory and methodology in
archaeology, bioarchaeology, and ethnology; and daily social
dynamics in ancient lives envisioned through the intersections
of political economy, kinship, and gender. His previous
publications include *Crafting Prehispanic Maya Kinship*
(University of Alabama Press, 2013) and *The Archaeology
of Kinship* (University of Arizona Press, 2013); articles in
multiple journals including *American Antiquity* and *Current
Anthropology*; and contributions to edited volumes including
The Oxford Handbook of Caribbean Archaeology (Oxford,
2013), *Modes of Production and Archaeology* (University
Press of Florida, 2017), and *Time and History in Prehistory*
(Routledge, 2018).

Cover photo: South end of El Bellote: platform deposits
containing oyster shell within mangrove setting (photo by
author taken August 18, 2007).

Contents

Preface and Acknowledgments...................... vii

1. Introduction 1
    Themes and Contributions............................ 2
    The Chontalpa Region, Islas de Los Cerros,
        and Chronology..................................... 3
    The Chapters 4

2. The Islas de Los Cerros Archaeological Project 8
    Previous Research in the Chontalpa Region.......... 8
    Preliminary Research 12
    2001... 12
        Methods...................................... 13
        Outcomes 13
    2004... 14
        Methods...................................... 14
        Outcomes 15
    2005... 16
        Methods...................................... 17
        Outcomes 17
    2007... 18
        Methods...................................... 18
        Outcomes 18
    Thermoluminescence Dating Experiment, 2011..... 19
    Synopsis... 19

3. Environment and Political Ecology 21
    The Environmental Setting........................... 21
        Climate 21
        Hydrology and Geomorphology.................. 21
        Flora 23
        Fauna 24

        Ecological Synergy 25
    Political Ecology..................................... 26
        Settlement.................................... 26
        Subsistence................................... 28
        Commercial Development 31
    Old and New Impacts to Archaeological
        Resources 32

4. The Sites 34
    Previous Site Records 34
    Survey and Feature Classification 36
    Isla Boca Grande (E 15A-79-27-038) 37
    Isla del Campo (E 15A-79-27-075)..................... 41
    Isla Santa Rosita (E15 A-79-27-073) 41
    Isla Dos Bocas Nuevas (E15 A-79-27-074)............ 42
    Isla Chablé (E15 A-79-27-039) 42
        The Southwest Group 46
        The South Group.............................. 47
        Nonresidential Features........................ 48
        Artifacts at Isla Chablé 48
    La Islita (E15 A-79-27-078) 48
    El Canal (E15 A-79-27-079) 48
    El Bellote (E15 A-79-27-076) 49
        The Northeast Group.......................... 49
        The North-Central Group 54
        The Northwest Group 54
        The Central Group............................ 54
        The South Group.............................. 56
        Artifacts at El Bellote 56
    Summary 56

5. **The Features** 58
  Questions and Hypotheses.................. 58
    When Were the Features Built? 58
    How Did the Features Function? 59
    What Is the Construction Sequence? 60
    Size: Occupation Duration or Labor
      Investiture? 61
  Residential Platforms and Mounds 61
    Discrete Platforms 61
    Discrete Mounds....................... 64
    Mounds-on-Platforms 68
    Multilevel Mounds..................... 71
  Ceremonial Mounds 83
    General Characteristics 83
    Descriptions 83
    Summary............................. 87
  Specialized Features..................... 88
    Feature 92 89
    Features 89 and 122.................... 89
    Feature 176........................... 91
    Feature 155 92
    Summary............................. 92
  Pits and Thermal Features................. 92
    Pits 93
    Thermal Features...................... 93
    Summary............................. 94
  Conclusions 94
    Formative and Late Classic Deposits......... 95
    Function............................. 96
    Construction Sequence 98
    Size: Occupation Duration or Labor
      Investiture? 98

6. **Pottery** 100
  Pottery Classification.................... 100
  Function, Suitability, and Performance.......... 102
  Identities: Symbolic Display, Foodways, and
    Food Sharing 104
  Formative Period Types 105
    Formative Types of Known Period
      Affiliation 105
    Formative Types of Unknown Period
      Affiliation 108
  Late Classic Period Types................. 112
    Late Classic Period Coarse Paste Types........ 112
    Late Classic Period Fine Paste Types 121

Types of Unknown Period Affiliations 125
  Bellote 125
  Type X 125
  Unclassified Pottery..................... 127
Regional Comparisons..................... 127
A Late Classic Pottery Frequency Sequence?....... 128
A Thermoluminescence Dating Experiment 132
Conclusions 133

7. **Other Artifacts and Materials** 135
  Re-Used Sherds and Other Ceramic
    Artifacts 135
  Bitumen............................... 135
  Stone Tools 137
    Obsidian............................. 137
    Chert................................ 138
    Ground Stone 138
    The Functions and Paucity of Stone Tools 138
  Waterworn Stone 140
  Vertebrate Remains....................... 141
    Aggregated Results..................... 141
    Screen Mesh Size Effect 141
    Capture Techniques 143
    Comparison with Comalcalco 143
    Dating Vertebrate Remains 143
  Invertebrate Remains 144
  Architectural Materials 145
    Mortar or Plaster 145
    Brick................................ 147
    Daub................................ 148
    Clay 148
  Summary 148

8. **The Formative Periods** 150
  The Western Chontalpa.................... 150
    Coast 151
    Lower Mezcalapa Delta 151
    Middle Mezcalapa and Terrace
      Valleys........................... 153
    Conclusions.......................... 153
  ILC's Formative Settlement History.......... 153
  Probable Features....................... 156
  Subsistence 157
  Activities and Technologies................ 158
  Social Relations 160
  Synopsis.............................. 163

9. The Late Classic Period 165
   The Western Chontalpa 165
     A Chontalpa Early Classic Settlement Hiatus? .. 165
     Regional Integration 166
     Settlement Patterns 167
   ILC's Late Classic Settlement History 170
   Political Economy, Classes, and Identities 173
     Political Economies of Western Chontalpa
      States 174
     Ceremony, Power, and Elite Identities 175
     Classes at ILC 178
     Internal Class Differentiation 184
   Kinship, Identities, and Social Memory 191
     Approaches and Problems 191
     Mid-Level Theory 191

     Kinship at ILC 193
     A Tapestry of Kinship, Identities, Histories,
      Ancestors, Space, and Time 195
     Kinship in the Broader Western Chontalpa 196
   Gender and Age Relations 198
   Foodways and Feasting 201
     Foodways 202
     Feasting and Food Sharing 204
   Synopsis 205

References Cited 209
Index 229
Abstract 235
Resumén 235

TABLES

4.1. Summary of Features at Isla Boca Grande,
Isla del Campo, and Isla Santa Rosita. 39
4.2. Summary of Features at Isla Dos Bocas Nuevas
and Isla Chablé. 44
4.3. Summary of Features at El Bellote. 51
5.1. Residential Feature Sizes. 62
5.2. Surface Collections at Residential Features 63
5.3. Stratigraphic Distribution of Artifacts in Unit 4,
Feature 40. 65
5.4. Feature 157 Strata. 68
5.5. Stratigraphic Distribution of Artifacts in Unit 1,
Features 77 and 78. 71
5.6. Multilevel Formations: Sizes. 72
5.7. Feature 32-34-35 Strata and Artifactual
Contents. 74
5.8. Stratigraphic Distribution of Artifacts from
Unit 5, Features 75 and 76. 78
5.9. Stratigraphic Distribution of Artifacts from
Unit 3, Feature 92. 90
5.10. Stratigraphic Distribution of Artifacts from
Unit 2, Feature 122. 92
5.11. Percentages of Pottery by Period and Excavation
Level at Aguacatal. 96
6.1. Pottery Types Defined for the PAILC. 101
6.2. Formative Vessel Morphologies and Orifice
Diameters. 109
6.3. Late Classic Coarse Paste Types and Varieties. 114
6.4. Late Classic Coarse Paste Vessel Forms. 114

6.5. Late Classic Coarse Paste Vessel Morphologies
and Orifice Diameters. 116
6.6. Fine Paste Vessel Morphologies and Orifice
Diameters. 123
6.7. Types of Unknown Periods: Vessel Morphologies
and Orifice Diameters. 126
6.8. Unclassified Vessel Morphologies and Orifice
Diameters. 127
6.9. Stratigraphic Distribution of Late Classic Types
in Percentages by Level. 129
6.10. Numeric Distribution by Strata of Late Classic
Sherd Varieties with Plastic Decoration. 130
6.11. Stratigraphic Distribution of Late Classic Sherds
Based on Vessel Morphology. 131
7.1. Obsidian Artifacts. 137
7.2. Chert Artifacts. 139
7.3. Ground Stone Artifacts. 139
7.4. Waterworn Stone. 140
7.5. Vertebrate Remains by Recovery Technique. 141
7.6. Comparison of Faunal Specimen Recovery by
Context. 142
7.7. Comparison of Vertebrate and Crustacean
Remains from ILC and Comalcalco. 143
7.8. Characteristics of Mortar or Plaster Samples. 146
7.9. Characteristics of Brick Fragments Sampled
from the Top of Feature 196. 147
8.1. Comparison of Pottery from Surface Collections
and Excavations or Profiles. 154

8.2. Comparison of Formative Vessel Forms in Percentages by Location. 160

9.1. Estimated Maximum Numbers of Late Classic Conjugal Family Dwellings by Stages. 174

9.2. Comparison of Late Classic Pottery and Other Materials from Surface Collections and Excavations or Profiles. 180

9.3. Artifacts, Materials, and Pot Forms by Social Class. 183

9.4. Percentages of Fine Paste Pottery Types by Class. 184

9.5. Materials and Pot Forms by Feature Type: Resource-Deprived Commoners. 185

9.6. Materials and Pot Forms by Feature Type: Resource-Accessing Commoners. 189

9.7. Materials and pot forms by Group: Ceremonial Elites. 189

FIGURES

1.1. Map of Central and Western Tabasco. 5

2.1. Map of sixteenth-century Chontal provinces. 11

3.1. Map of the Lower Seco River and Mecoacán Lagoon. 22

3.2. The ILC environment. 24

3.3. Coconut ranch on South Group of Isla Chablé. 27

3.4. A recently built house platform. 27

3.5. Saint's day procession. 28

3.6. Oyster harvesting techniques. 30

4.1. Maps of previously recorded sites at and adjacent to ILC. 35

4.2. Mound and platform categories. 38

4.3. Map of Isla Boca Grande, Isla del Campo, and Isla Santa Rosita. 39

4.4. Map of Isla Dos Bocas Nuevas, Isla Chablé, La Islita, and El Canal. 43

4.5. Map of the Northeast, North-Central, and Northwest Groups of El Bellote. 50

4.6. Photos and profile of Feature 196, vaulted substructure beneath mound Feature 202. 53

4.7. Map of the Central and South Groups of El Bellote. 55

5.1. Plan view and profile of Feature 40. 64

5.2. Plan view and profile of Feature 97. 66

5.3. Plan views and profiles of features 156 and 157. 67

5.4. Plan views and profiles of features 77 and 78. 70

5.5. Photo, plan views, and profiles of Feature 32-34-35. . . 73

5.6. Plan view and profile of features 73–76. 77

5.7. Plan view and profile of multilevel mound features 93 and 94. 79

5.8. Plan view and profile of features 160–163. 79

5.9. Plan view, profile, and photos of features 150, 158, 159, and 167. 81

5.10. Plan views and profiles of features 95–96 and 98–99. 82

5.11. Plan view, profile, and photo of features 166 and 185. 85

5.12. Plan view and profile of Feature 151. 87

5.13. Plan view and profile of Feature 100. 88

5.14. Plan view, profile, and photo of Feature 92. 90

5.15. Plan view, profile, and photo of Feature 122. 91

6.1. Morphological classification of pottery. 103

6.2. Orifice diameters of various vessel shapes. 106

6.3. Formative era pottery. 107

6.4. Late Classic coarse-paste types: Centla, Cimatán, and Mecoacán. 113

6.5. Other coarse-paste types: Bellote, polychrome orange, Y, Z (polychrome and incised), and unclassified. 120

6.6. Late Classic fine paste types: Paraíso, Copilco, Comalcalco, Negro-Café Pulido, Jonuta, and Huimangillo. 122

7.1. Miscellaneous artifacts and materials. 136

8.1. Formative settlements in the Western Chontalpa. . . 152

8.2. Percentages of Formative pottery in surface collections. 155

8.3. Distribution of Black and White and Sierra Red pottery. 156

9.1. Late Classic settlements in the Western Chontalpa. 169

9.2. Percentages of Late Classic pottery in surface collections. 171

9.3. Distribution of occupation duration categories. 173

9.4. Comparisons of Late Classic site structures in the Western Chontalpa. 177

9.5. Interpreted social classes at ILC. 181

Preface and Acknowledgments

This book is the culmination of archaeological research at Islas de Los Cerros—the first systematic investigation of coastal sites in the understudied Chontalpa of Tabasco. It reports on the analysis of the local material culture with comparisons to other Western Chontalpa areas for regional synthesis. It delves into the heart of the Chontalpa to balance past perspectives drawn mostly from historical accounts and speculation from outside with new data on actual prehispanic materials and developments within the region. The book brings long overdue focus to this portion of the peripheral coastal lowlands (Parsons 1978), enabling linkages within and beyond as called for by Ochoa (2003) and Pérez Suárez (2003). It addresses the ancient peoples east of the Olman who were not Olmec, Tehuantepequeños, Soconuscanos, Veracruzanos, or traditional Maya. The book focuses on a non-agricultural coastal community—an emphasis generally absent in Gulf Coast archaeology—and challenges stereotypes of Mesoamerican subsistence and domestic activities. Unlike so much Mayanist archaeology, it is not elite-focused but, instead, emphasizes all class relations that form a local community. It is presented from the perspectives and experiences of an archaeologist outside the somewhat restrictive North American circles of Mayanist and broader Mesoamericanist scholarship but with experience negotiating both and beyond. One result of that context is the infusion into the book of some ideas and perspectives from outside Mayanist and broader Mesoamericanist scholarship while also striving to give more attention to Mexican scholarship than usually occurs in North American publications on Mesoamerica.

The Islas de Los Cerros Archaeological Project was a low-budget, "low intensity," and challenging multiseason investigation. Nevertheless, it was a pioneering project for coastal Tabasco that was meant to address that void within the state and, through regional comparisons, to begin filling a "black hole" in broader Mesoamerican archaeology (after Demarest 2009:258–259), for which discussions have been misdirected for lack of data. Whereas long-term research at the better-known site of Comalcalco has advanced knowledge on monumental architecture and the ruling nobility, this book seeks to characterize the materials and lives of the variably situated actors in Western Chontalpan societies from the Formative to Late Classic periods.

Why a book? Because the project was the first modern investigation of a coastal set of sites in Tabasco, the presentation of the material culture may be the most lasting contribution to the archaeology of the region, useful for supporting, overturning, or casting in new light my interpretations with future regional data and changing theoretical perspectives. To fulfill that responsibility and to adequately address questions and preconceptions, extensive description and analyses to test interpretations on materials are necessary. This single, substantial monograph will make those data more accessible to other researchers. Whereas postprocessualist discourse frequently glosses over methods and data, or simply presents data in accordance with the interpretation, the traditional book monograph empowers readers to fully evaluate the interpretations and to equip them for alternative perspectives. Such objectives are less achievable in today's academically demanded articles and short chapters that compel more theoretical or topical significance than completeness of data scattered across numerous venues (Demarest 2009:261–262). The book also affords the opportunity to give greater substance to treatments of the

Formative and Late Classic societies. In addition, readers will find discussions of data to address a range of themes of interest to a broad spectrum of Mesoamerican scholars: classification, chronology, feature and artifact functions, formation processes, subsistence and ecology, intra- and interregional interaction, sociopolitical organization, lifeways, feasting and foodways, and discussions on class, gender, practice, agency, social memory, and identities. The book is organized by material categories and their analyses to address these themes and provide syntheses by period. It includes a history of the project, to provide readers with a strong sense of the challenges, changes, surprises, and disappointments. In it I also hope to give new professionals some measure of guidance and inspiration. Through patience and endurance, even projects with low funding and challenging obstacles can make satisfying contributions. I also include a chapter on environment and contemporary political ecology that are critical for understanding archaeological features and their synergetic relationships to people and the environment.

The book's title is taken from conference and colloquia presentations made during the infancy of the project (at the University of Florida in 2001 and the University of Michigan Museum of Anthropology in 2004). The Chontalpa region once conjured images of a prehispanic heartland for cacao export (Millon 1955; Scholes and Roys 1968). More recently, literature on the antiquity of cacao emphasized its protohistoric and prehispanic production, exchange routes, spouted vessels, and ritual uses from the perspectives of other Maya regions—from the Soconusco, across the Petén, and to the Bay of Honduras (Caso Berrera and Aliphat Fernández 2006; Henderson et al. 2007; Joyce and Henderson 2010; Mariaca Méndez and Hernández Xolocotzi 1992; McAnany and Murata 2007; McNeil 2006). Cacao's spread, domestication in southeast Mesoamerica, and diversity have been researched through genetic ancestries (e.g., Ji and others 2013; Motilal and others 2010), while its lexical origins are sources of historical linguistic debates over Nahua intrusions into Mixe-Zoquean language areas (Dakin and Wichmann 2000; Kaufman and Justeson 2007; Hernández Treviño 2013; Macri 2005; Macri and Looper 2003). Though cacao was and is widespread across southeastern Mesoamerica, the Chontalpa was the focus for the cash crop's production under early Spanish rule (along with leather and lumber) until commercial plantations were expanded elsewhere, most notably to Venezuela and then Africa. Within the Chontalpa, the indigenous populations of the Mezcalapa Delta—having the highest population densities before and after the Spanish incursion—were

the focus of that tribute (West, Psuty, and Thom 1969). Tabasco is still the producer of nearly three quarters of Mexico's 37,000 annual tons of cacao by more than 40,000 growers (SAGARPA 2013), where chocolate production spans the artisanal to the industrial, and where the cultigen has become a major tourist attraction competing with images of the ubiquitous petroleum industry.

Within that context, the focus of this book involves a prehispanic Chontalpa coastal community—Islas de Los Cerros—where oysters and their shells were instrumental resources in the development of Formative and Late Classic period societies; a noticeable material in mounds, mortar, and stucco; and the subject of past archaeological speculation. They remain an important resource for the local community today. Therefore, oysters have a prominent place in the descriptions, analyses, and interpretations throughout this book, while cacao—the stereotyped resource for the region—does not.

In this volume, the term Maya is traditionally used as a noun and adjective in reference to people (e.g., the Chontal Maya), their regions, and their material culture. The term Mayan is used to refer to language only, while the term Mayanist refers to scholars of the Maya.

The different seasons of the Islas de Los Cerros Archaeological Project were funded by a series of small grants. The 2001 season was made possible by a Tinker Foundation grant and multiple small graduate student travel grants from the University of Florida. The 2004 season was funded by a Provost's New Faculty Research Award from Eastern Michigan University. Financing for the 2005 and 2007 seasons was provided through grants from the Foundation for the Advancement of Mesoamerican Studies, Inc. (FAMSI #05024 and #07019). The 2011 season was funded by an Eastern Michigan University Provost's research support award.

All seasons were conducted under permits from the Consejo de Arqueología of Mexico's Instituto Nacional de Antropología e Historia (INAH) following its regulations and dispositions for conducting archaeological research. The project could not have initiated or continued successfully without the members of the Centro INAH Tabasco, especially through guidance of Rebecca González Lauck, but also José Romero Rivera, former director Juan Antonio Ferrer, Ricardo Armijo Torres, and the Centro INAH Tabasco secretarial staff.

Most of all, the project is indebted to the Grupo PAILC, with whom I had the immense pleasure of sharing field euphoria, the daily trips on launches in spectacularly beautiful settings, and the tastiest oysters to be found anywhere.

Gabriel Tun Ayora provided valuable field experience in multiple seasons, produced the field drafts for most of the profiles presented herein, and served as a coauthor on reports, presentations, and other publications. Concepción Herrera Escobar also brought, with remarkable energy and enthusiasm, excellence in fieldwork and coauthorship to reports, presentations, and other publications. It has been a great honor to have worked with both. Other project participants included Keiko Teranishi Castillo, Socorro Pilar Jiménez Alvarez, Elspeth Geiger, Tracy Knoeller, Alexandra Boughton, and Shandra McGuire. From the El Bellote community, Florencio Pérez Ventura, Marcos Wilson Peréz, and Carlos Jaime de Dios de la Cruz provided launches, had intimate knowledge of the lagoon, served as gatekeepers to the community, provided logistical information, and assisted with various needs in the field and lab. Appreciation goes to all those with whom we had frequent interactions for their sincere friendliness and hospitality. I thank Todd Grote for his review of the geomorphic coverage in Chapter 3. I wish to thank Anne Stokes who granted work leaves to initiate the project and past mentors who prepared me along the road to the project, including Barbara Stark, Lynette Heller, Margerie Green, David Doyel, Heather McKillop, Paul Farnsworth, Anthony Andrews, William Keegan, Kenneth Sassaman, and John Moore. I thank the anonymous reviewers of earlier drafts for their comments, even if the condition of some materials prevented addressing some desires. Finally, I thank Allyson Carter, Abby Mogollon, and Leigh McDonald at the University of Arizona Press for enabling a smooth process, T. J. Ferguson at the UA School of Anthropology, Doug Goewey for his InDesign layout work, and especially Linda Gregonis for diligence in the editorial process. Of course, I alone take responsibility for the interpretations and any omissions, errors, or misrepresentations in this book.

CHAPTER ONE

Introduction

Not long ago, the Chontalpa region of Tabasco, Mexico, was viewed as pivotal in prehispanic Mesoamerican developments. For decades, the region conjured images of the possible origins of the Itzá who migrated, conquered, or otherwise influenced much of Mesoamerica. Collective wisdom suggested that the Chontal influenced an emerging political economy in the Epiclassic period (ca. CE 800–950) when mixed Mexican-Maya iconography appeared at regional centers in both macroregions, when fine-paste pottery radiated out from the Gulf Coast, and where cacao was an assumed principle trade crop. The Chontal Maya have been interpreted as having expansionary Omaha segmentary groups (Fox 1987). The region was long believed to be the origin of the Spanish-era Putún merchants (Putún meaning "carriers"; Izquierdo 1997), who in the Postclassic period (ca. CE 950–1500) came to control coastal commerce southeast of the Mexica (Aztec) Empire (Morley, Brainerd, Sharer 1983:157; Sabloff and Rathje 1975; Scholes and Roys 1968; Vargas Pacheco 1992; West, Psuty, and Thom 1969:102). The legendary port and market city of Xicalango inspired ethnohistorically based models for prehispanic commerce and market systems. In addition, the Western Chontalpa—the focus of this book—was where the battle of Centla took place. There the province of Potonchán was defeated by Cortés and his Acalán allies and "La Malinche" (Doña Marina, Malinalli) was given to Cortés. Yet little of the ethnohistorically derived assumptions about the prehispanic Chontalpa—cacao, ports of trade, markets, and the origins of the Itzá/Putún—and how they developed had been well-investigated archaeologically. Although archaeological investigation abounds in the neighboring states of Veracruz, Oaxaca, and Campeche and Olmec research is focused on the extreme west edge of Tabasco, very little research other than royal contexts at Comalcalco and surficial documentation elsewhere, has taken place in the heart of the Chontalpa itself.

In this book I synthesize data from a multiyear investigation of Islas de Los Cerros (ILC), a coastal site complex in Tabasco. It provides the first modern, systematic descriptions and analyses of material culture. These data challenge preconceptions while providing new perspectives on cultural developments from the Formative to Late Classic periods through regional comparisons and contemporary theoretical trends. The goal of the Proyecto Arqueológico Islas de Los Cerros (PAILC) was to build a more adequate understanding of material culture to create a clearer picture of coastal Chontal society and regional political economy. The project was the first to thoroughly survey the mangrove islands at the north end of the Mecoacán Lagoon. It has provided a comprehensive inventory of features and their spatial distributions. Together with surface collections, the inventory has allowed for the interpretation of chronology, function, and settlement pattern. Subsequent excavations and other activities were the first to document formation processes, confirm feature functions, and address a range of additional questions. As the culminating publication on the project, the descriptions and empirical analyses in this book are designed to address alternative hypotheses about the material culture and to update, clarify, and synthesize interpretations leading to an improved characterization of prehispanic developments in the region. Through the information presented here, Mesoamerican archaeologists can begin to balance the speculation on the Chontalpa region with an emerging picture of actual social and cultural developments during and after the Olmec Horizon, before the Itzá-Putún of legend, and long before the sixteenth-century Spanish depictions.

THEMES AND CONTRIBUTIONS

Within the book, readers will find data, discussions, and interpretations on a number of themes important to Mesoamerican archaeology. Though not presented in this order, these themes include (1) classification, analyses, and descriptions of features, artifacts, and faunal remains; (2) feature formation processes; (3) chronology; (4) settlement patterns; (5) multiscalar comparisons to contextualize ILC within the Western Chontalpa, the broader Chontalpa, and the broader Gulf Coast; (6) regional to interregional integration and exchange; (7) political economic perspectives on classes, kin groups, genders, and age groups; and (8) postprocessual perspectives on practice, agency, multilayered identities, and social memories embodied in material culture and landscapes.

When first setting out to conduct the project at ILC, one archaeologist commented that any work there would make important contributions because so little was known about coastal Tabasco. Going far beyond that expectation, this book makes numerous contributions to Chontalpa archaeology, Gulf Coast archaeology in general, and, more broadly, perspectives in Mesoamerican archaeology. As introduction to what the reader can anticipate, the various contributions can be subsumed under four broad categories.

First, the detailed presentation of material culture at coastal Tabascan sites should provide a lasting contribution to the archaeology of the region. Moreover, the presentation of material culture goes far beyond qualitative and quantitative description. New classification strategies are presented for features and artifact categories. Poor sherd conditions and the nature of the pottery made it difficult to use traditional Mayanist culture historical complex-group-type-variety classifications. As a result, I present an alternative classification system that has been used with relative success to address a range of topics such as intra- and interclass integration, intra- and interregional integration, activity analyses, political economy, and practice/agency perspectives on gendered experiences, foodways and feasting, identities, and social memories.

Hypotheses also guide the analyses to evaluate a range of questions leading often to new understandings and treatments of material culture at ILC, with applicability to the broader Chontalpa and Gulf Coast regions. The project's testing of alternative hypotheses in regard to residential feature formation processes have overturned some common assumptions about functions and class affiliations and have led to the development of cultural models on construction sequencing and durations. These models are applicable to settlement history, kinship analyses, and interpretations on status negotiation, identities and social memories. They can also be applied elsewhere in the Gulf Coast region. In addition, the book presents analyses that can guide future research strategies. For example, this first presentation of coastal vertebrate remains—including relative abundance, capture techniques, and comparisons with Comalcalco—also addresses screen mesh-size recovery effects and optimal mesh sizes for different contexts. Finally, assumptions about the collections are also tested. As one example, the representativeness of low- to high-yield surface collection in relation to subsurface deposits was tested before the surface collections were used in distributional analyses; similar evaluations could benefit broader Gulf Coast archaeology.

Second, the book contributes newly revised knowledge on the Chontalpa. It examines the nature of previous data, why and how it was collected, making explicit how those characterizations developed. It also convincingly overturns some characterizations through newly contributed, patterned empirical observations. Much of the knowledge on Chontalpa sites comes from work in the mid-twentieth century. Even today archaeologists are dependent on that earlier information, which has seen few updates and revisions. Many influential projects involved only brief visits to sites yet continue to color characterizations and faulty assumptions. Perhaps because there have been so few academic projects in the Chontalpa apart from Olmec studies around La Venta, there was insufficient accumulation of information that would otherwise have corrected those perpetuated ideas until now. Prior assumptions about material culture are not just demonstrated to be problematic at ILC but at other locations within the Chontalpa, enabling revised interpretations elsewhere. For instance, ILC has been used to characterize the Tabascan coast's earliest (pre-Olmec) societies and it was widely believed that the Chontalpa was depopulated in the Late Formative. The data gathered for this book demonstrates, however, that (1) the earliest and smallest occupation at ILC was in the Middle Formative, (2) that ILC and the region experienced population growth in the Late Formative, and (3) that the long-interpreted Formative *concheros* (shell middens) at ILC and elsewhere are actually residential mounds constructed in the Late Classic.

Although focusing on ILC, the book brings together regional data for new multiscalar comparisons and synthesis, providing new observations on regional patterns in Formative to Late Classic periods in the Western Chontalpa. The resulting synthesis leads to new understandings of the region's patterns and variation in settlement history, settlement patterns, political economy, ecology, exchange, and interaction. For example, though settlement patterns, site structure, and elite ceremonial organization were routinely viewed through normative lenses, the book's comparisons illustrate variation both among and within different areas. There is no single pattern for the Western Chontalpa.

Third, the book makes theoretical contributions to Mesoamerican archaeology by contextualizing past knowledge and by explicitly linking data, theory, and interpretation throughout. The history of research is described not just in chronological sequence but by contextualizing influential projects and publications into theoretical genres and associated trends in methods and data. The book makes explicit linkages between theory, data, and interpretation throughout so that readers can judge the interpretations based on the evidence and analyses. This reflection is often absent in much of today's postprocessualism. In terms of Trigger's (2006) distinctions on levels of theory, although interpretation is guided by mid-level theory (factual correspondence between low-level generalizations and ethnographically-observed behaviors), the book also contributes the low-level theory (generalizations on empirical patterns in material culture). Finally, interpretation is perceived through high-level theory (abstract models of how things are and how they change). Mid-level interpretations on behavior from empirical patterns in material culture are made using cross-culturally tested generalizations, though untested analogy (including direct historical analogy) and untested logic-based interpretations are sometimes explicitly introduced (see Ensor 2013b, 2017e, and Peregrine 1996 for problems with analogy and the direct historical approach). The book takes a pragmatic approach to high-level theories and their associated methods, selecting those that best address a topic with the data at hand. Much of chapters 4, 5, 6, and 7 provide the low-level material patterns at ILC but also link those to mid-level interpretations used to arrive at higher-level interpretations in chapters 8 and 9. In terms of high-level theories, political economic theory provides the variable social contexts (structure) for understanding ecology, social organization, domestic versus public activities, gender and age relations. These are the social experiences and conditions of variably situated actors through which practice

and agency on identity, status, social memory, and more can be inferred, thus enabling interpretation of motives and meanings behind social experiences. Among various labels, "processual-plus" seems the most appropriate (Hegmon 2003).

Fourth, the book's new perspectives address problems and debates in broader Mesoamerican literature. Whereas literature tends to overemphasize nobility, this book emphasizes both vertical and horizontal practice and agency for all classes. Early in the book, the contemporary political economy is shown to influence the variably situated actors involved in the preservation and destruction of archaeological features, which in turn have a synergetic relation among the people and the environment that is ILC. Later, the prehispanic settlement patterns, states, and power relations within the Western Chontalpa are similarly explained through a political ecological perspective that bridges political economic and processualist themes while resolving problems with the latter. Another contribution is that "domestic activities" are not assumed, but rather, illustrated to vary by political economic contexts. Furthermore, classes are defined by political economic relations of production, not by "status goods." Thus, distributional analyses within and across classes of symbolic material culture contribute new perspectives on vertical and horizontal integration, identities, and intra-class agency—an approach that could resolve disputes on how classes and their relationships can be observed in Mesoamerican archaeology. Applications of empirical analyses of kinship using well-tested cross-cultural mid-level theory (Ensor 2013a, 2013b) are expanded for ILC and to additional areas within the Western Chontalpa, which have implications on gender and age relations in addition to status, identities, settlement history, ceremony, foodways, and feasting. As another example, the book treats cultural identities as layered and non-homogeneous, but certainly not as "ethnicity," through multiple sources of material culture and their vertical and horizontal social distributions. This perspective could provide a much-needed alternative to longstanding debates on how to envision culture and identities in broader Mesoamerica.

THE CHONTALPA REGION, ISLAS DE LOS CERROS, AND CHRONOLOGY

The Chontalpa is a region variably described as along the Gulf of Mexico coast and adjacent interior zones roughly conforming with the historical distribution of Chontal Mayan speakers. Although communities, but probably only elites, were multilingual, Chontal Mayan was generally distributed across central Tabasco to southwestern Campeche in the early sixteenth century (Izquierdo 1997; Inchaustegui 1987). The linguistic-based culture area was surrounded by a mosaic of equally multilingual Eastern Nahua that may have been introduced to the Gulf Coast in the late Early Classic or early Late Classic period (Macri 2005; Macri and Looper 2003); Nonoalco and Popoloca in western Tabasco, also widely referred to as the multilingual Ahualulcos region (Herrera Escobar 2004; Ortega Peña 1999); Zoque in south-central Tabasco; and Yucatec in Campeche. This culture area definition, based on sixteenth-century language distributions, perpetuates a "flat" view of history.

Geographic cultural historical trends changed significantly from the Middle to Late Formative, in the Late Classic, and then again to the culturally non-uniform, and unevenly distributed Chontal Mayan-speaking populations in the sixteenth century. For the purposes of this book I use a geographic definition for the Chontalpa—the lowland stoneless alluvial plains, rivers, swamps, and lagoons of the Mezcalapa, Grijalva, and Lower Usumacinta deltas (Figure 1.1). This definition excludes the upland Pleistocene and mountainous Tertiary zones to the south, the Middle Usumacinta, and the limestone peninsular formations of Campeche.

An important note should be made on historical hydrographic changes to the Mezcalapa River and Delta—the Western Chontalpa. The Upper Mezcalapa is currently named the Grijalva River from central Chiapas to Cárdenas, Tabasco. The Lower Mezcalapa through the delta past Comalcalco to its mouth at Dos Bocas and Laguna Mecoacán, where ILC is located, is currently named the Seco River. This is because the course of the Mezcalapa was diverted around 1675 into distributaries eastward from Cárdenas, cutting off water to its main delta distributary, hence the name "Seco" (West, Psuty, and Thom 1969:133, 171–173). Since then, the eastward distributaries join others in the Villahermosa area to form the Lower Grijalva. For this reason, the Upper to Lower Mezcalapa (from Chiapas to the Gulf) referred to throughout this book differs from contemporary naming to correspond with the prehispanic river's course that linked ancient communities from ILC to Chiapas.

Islas de Los Cerros is the local reference to the concentration of mangrove islands and the peninsula of El Bellote at the north end of the Mecoacán Lagoon along the Gulf of Mexico coast, where the Seco River (the once main distributary of the Mezcalapa River) reaches the coast after winding past Comalcalco. The ILC had the largest coastal prehispanic occupation in the Western Chontalpa, and perhaps all of coastal Tabasco. The oyster reefs surrounding the islands and the ubiquitous oyster shells within the archaeological features are prominent characteristics that are most noticeable from the water.

ILC's importance can be seen through the ways prior descriptions guided interpretations on the region. Though undated sites are situated along the coast, no other Formative coastal sites had been identified. When those who briefly stepped off a boat at the most easily accessible mounds at Isla Chablé interpreted them as Formative period *concheros* (shell middens), that characterization of ILC became a generalization for Formative Coastal Tabasco—indeed for the earliest occupants of Tabasco (e.g., Fernández Tejedo and others 1988:51). Visitors to the adjacent site of El Bellote described only Late Classic temple mounds and the site's architectural and ceramic similarities with Comalcalco (e.g., Berlin 1953b; Blom and La Farge 1926; Charnay 1888; Stirling 1957). This led to assumptions that ILC was a regional trade port commanded by Comalcalco, supporting the depictions of sixteenth-century mercantilism. This book demonstrates that ILC indeed had in important role in the region but for neither of these reasons.

Readers will note early in the book that despite multiple seasons' attempts, the project failed to produce an improved ceramic microchronology. This was doubly problematic because neither the surrounding Mexican nor Maya macroregions provide a period framework that makes perfect sense for the Western Chontalpa. So, a combination was adopted. The Middle Formative pertains to the duration of Olmec La Venta. The Late Formative corresponds to that in Mexican frameworks. However, rather than the Mexican Early Classic, Middle Classic, and Epiclassic periods, there is an Early Classic (ca. CE 100/200–600) and a Late Classic period (ca. CE 600–800), which is Maya-like but overlaps the Mexican period dates. A Terminal Classic period also makes sense since ILC and other sites in the Western Chontalpa appear to have been abandoned by CE 900.

THE CHAPTERS

The chapters progress from context to low- and mid-level interpretation to increasingly higher levels of interpretation. Chapter 2 presents a history of the PAILC. Each season's origins, goals, and methods are described. Most seasons had multiple objectives. Some questions remained poorly addressed, leading to alternative strategies in the

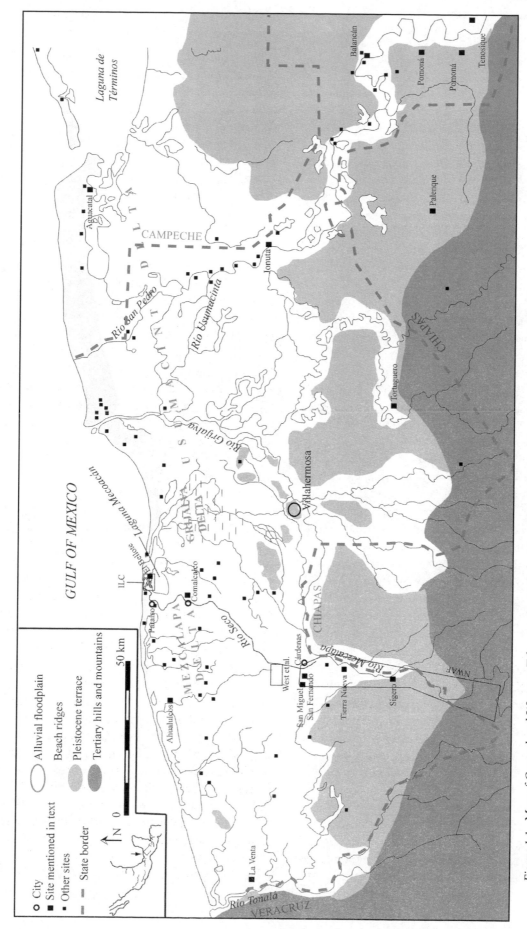

Figure 1.1. Map of Central and Western Tabasco. Compiled and redrawn by the author from West, Psuty, and Thom 1969: Figures 15–17, 28–29 and Piña Chan and Navarrete 1967: Figure 1.

following seasons. The chapter concludes with a description of the project's major accomplishments and unaddressed problems.

Chapter 3 contextualizes ILC within the natural and social environments. Climate, hydrology and geomorphology, flora, and fauna are described. The modern uses of the lagoon and the human relationships to the features are summarized. The environment, features, and modern human activities all mutually influence one another through synergetic relationships. Preservation versus destruction of the features is best understood through a political ecological perspective that contextualizes different social actors. These interrelations are important because they influence possible observations and the availability of different types of data.

The individual sites comprising ILC are described in Chapter 4. The problems with prior site records are first discussed. Once they were better documented by the project, eight archaeological sites were defined. The feature classifications that developed are presented here. For each site, the environment, size, numbers of features, feature types, their distribution, artifacts, and modern uses or impacts are described in summary fashion. The chapter concludes with general observations on the site complex, leading into the analyses in subsequent chapters.

Chapter 5 describes and provides analysis of the features and their formation processes. Guiding the chapter are five major issues, each with alternative hypotheses generated by preconceptions or observations made early in the project. These were tested using the surface collections, the excavations, and opportunistic profiles of cuts from disturbance (sediment mining or shoreline erosion). The first issue involves the co-occurrence of Formative and Late Classic pottery where only Formative *concheros* were previously interpreted at Isla Chablé and only Late Classic features were previously interpreted at El Bellote. The second regards the interpretations of feature functions based on morphology, specifically to infer residential, ceremonial, and other uses. Interpreting residential functions requires consideration of variation in what constitutes domestic activities. The third issue is whether the discrete platforms and mounds, and multilevel formations represent a sequence in residential occupations. The fourth, a related issue, is whether the sizes of residential features signify a longer duration of occupation. Finally, hypotheses were tested on the initial interpretations of specialized features for collectivized activities at ILC. After outlining these questions and their associated alternative hypotheses, the bulk of the chapter provides analyses and descriptions of each feature category: residential (discrete platforms, discrete mounds, mounds-on-platforms, and multilevel mounds); ceremonial mounds; specialized features; and subsurface features within these (e.g., pits and thermal features). The descriptions include summary statistics on shapes, sizes, and surface collection data, followed by descriptions of stratigraphy for the individual features where excavation or opportunistic profiling was conducted. The empirical patterns for each category are used to evaluate the hypotheses for the five issues.

Chapter 6 provides the first published descriptions and interpretations of pottery from the project. The classification system and its rationale are described. Although unconventional for Mayanist traditions designed for area-period culture historical frameworks, the paste-based classification and formal attributes were tailored to the specific challenges and materials at ILC. Morphological and technological functional suitability is considered for evaluating vessel performances. The use of pottery for symbolic display—identity negotiation, gifting, or feasting—is also considered. The resulting 17 types and their attributes, including morphologies, are presented. A limited stratigraphic analysis seeking diachronic frequency trends among the Late Classic types is presented. An experiment using surface collections for thermoluminescence dating is also discussed. The chapter ends with an overview of the results and how these inform analyses and discussions in chapters 4, 5, 8, and 9.

Other ceramic artifacts, stone tools, faunal remains, architectural materials, and possible manuports are described and discussed in Chapter 7. Nonpottery ceramic artifacts include sherds reworked into fishing net sinkers, possible ornaments, and a figurine fragment. There was limited bitumen. Stone tools—chipped obsidian and chert, and ground stone—are described along with discussion on their likely geological sources and uses. Unmodified stones are also described, alongside speculation on their origins and possible uses. The paucity of stone tools and the implications of their scarcity at ILC are discussed. The relative abundance of vertebrate remains is analyzed using numbers of individual specimens (NISP) to characterize subsistence at ILC and the results are compared with data from Comalcalco. In addition, the results of an analysis on the effects of screen mesh-size on recovery by contexts is presented. This analysis guided subsequent excavations at ILC, leading to recommendations for other coastal projects in the region. The architectural materials classifications for mortar, plaster, brick, daub, and clay are described along with interpretations on their uses and manufacturing origins. The chapter includes observations on material distributions across ILC that inform the interpretations on the local Formative and Late Classic communities in chapters 8 and 9.

Whereas Chapters 4 to 7 mostly deal with low- to mid-level theory, mid- to high-level theory is more prominent in Chapters 8 and 9. These two culminating chapters to the book are syntheses geared toward describing the prehispanic societies and lifeways at ILC. Chapter 8 addresses the Formative periods. Given that there were no intact Formative deposits at ILC, this objective was challenging, to say the least. Nevertheless, by assuming that the displaced deposits and artifacts are in the general vicinities of their original Formative uses, spatial analyses of surface pottery—after a test of subsurface representativeness—enable some interpretations on settlement growth from the Middle to Late Formative periods. Observations on the displaced deposits, along with some reasonable speculation, enable a normative depiction of what features may have existed. Assuming exploitation of available resources coupled with evidence on subsistence, a range of potential activities characterizing daily life are also discussed in a normative manner. Three settlement scenarios are discussed, with alternative implications on social relations from culture historical, functionalist, and agency perspectives. The favored model to explain differences in Formative material culture across ILC suggests that there were two principal groups occupying ILC who established rights to the resources and used pottery associated with broader interaction spheres for symbolic displays. Other small, dispersed groups lacking affinity with them were more impoverished and had differences in pottery form frequencies. Little could be concluded on Formative ritual or ceremony at ILC or on gender relations.

In contrast, the fact that all extant features at ILC date to the Late Classic period enables better social contextualization of material culture, facilitating a wide range of the mid- to high-level interpretations discussed in Chapter 9. First, the chapter contextualizes ILC within the Western Chontalpa, suggesting a probable Early Classic hiatus across the broader Chontalpa with varying Late Classic intraregional and interregional integration when viewed through material traits. Settlement patterns, rather than conforming to one model as previously assumed, vary across three states occupying different environmental zones in the Western Chontalpa. Unlike other coastal sites, ILC had a unique position in the regional settlement hierarchy of the more powerful state—headed by Comalcalco—that commanded greater resource diversity and access to trade than the other states. ILC's settlement history is analyzed through two approaches with converging results.

The perspective on layered cultural identities and constructed social memories embodied in features and artifacts—and approaches toward these—is best exemplified in Chapter 9, which provides a postmodern perspective on the insights from all prior chapters. Data and interpretations on social classes and identities across the Western Chontalpa are presented, along with observations on differences between royalty and lesser elites in ceremony, power, and identity. Interpretations on classes at ILC, though previously presented (e.g., Ensor 2013b), are reinforced through additional analyses that enable a more detailed understanding of local class relations and identities. Classes are defined by their social relations of production within the tributary political economy. Rather than basing classes on status differences, the distribution of material culture related to status and symbolic display is analyzed for interpretations on practice and agency forging vertical (interclass) and horizontal (intraclass) integration and differentiation. Class-based kinship practices, introduced elsewhere (Ensor 2013b, 2016b, 2017e), are expanded upon, leading to new interpretations on kinship, identity, and social memory embodied in the cultural landscape. New interpretations on class-based kinship relations are also provided for the broader Western Chontalpa. The mid-level interpretations extend to gender and age relations (including children and childhood). Finally, the class, kinship, and gender contexts interpreted through mid-level theory enable new interpretations on foodways and on feasting or food-sharing, providing further insights on vertical and horizontal relations, identities, and social memories embodied in cuisine, places, and artifacts.

CHAPTER TWO

The Islas de Los Cerros Archaeological Project

After a prelude on previous research in the Western Chontalpa, this chapter provides a history of the Proyecto Arqueológico Islas de Los Cerros (PAILC). Most research on the Formative periods involved Olmec archaeology in the La Venta area in Western Tabasco and Southeastern Veracruz, and most of the post-Olmec research in the Western Chontalpa had focused on Comalcalco. Comalcalco headed a major state in the region during the Late Classic period and ILC likely served an important role in the regional political economy and was a presumed port for Comalcalco. The initial research orientation for the PAILC was to produce a better understanding of the relationship with Comalcalco, and with that a better perspective on the social, political, and economic precursors to the famous Terminal Classic to Postclassic Chontal cultures believed to have influenced trends in broader Mesoamerica. Another goal was to provide new regional data on the Formative period occupations at ILC.

Before models could be made for the relationships between ILC, La Venta, and Comalcalco, foundational data on the coastal complex needed to be established. Each season's objectives built toward the higher-level goals. Neither Formative period affiliations nor contemporaneity with Comalcalco had yet been confirmed. The Comalcalco ceramic chronology and classification system needed substantial revisions. There was limited information on the features and artifacts present at coastal sites in Tabasco. A systematic ground reconnaissance was needed to identify the range of features present, determine their functions, and to define the settlement patterns. There was no evidence, other than the location of the complex and the oysters, with which to interpret issues of trade and subsistence. Formation processes needed to be understood.

Although some of these questions were addressed early on, each season's results begged more questions or suggested alternative strategies for subsequent seasons. For these reasons, the project is best explained in a season-by-season sequence. For a comprehensive bibliographic record, references are included for all reports, publications, and presentations developed from the project.

PREVIOUS RESEARCH IN THE CHONTALPA REGION

This section focuses on previous archaeological research in lowland Tabasco, with emphasis on ILC and the Mezcalapa River and Delta. The first archaeological descriptions of sites were by Desiré Charnay (1888). His expedition was antiquarianist in nature, and he sought evidence of "Toltec" migrations to Yucatán. Charnay's brief visit to El Bellote while en route to Comalcalco, provided the earliest description of ILC:

> Two hours' steady rowing brings us to Bellote Islands, when, stowing our boats on the sand, we hail the first man we see, and under his escort make for the *cuyos*, pyramids, walking by the shore of the island, the water of which is so transparent as to enable us to spy at the bottom of the lagoon a quantity of oyster-shells; presently we come upon a giant bank of them measuring several miles, by more than twelve feet high, *kjœkkenmœdings*; the whole ground around is composed of these broken shells, over which a magnificent vegetation luxuriates.
>
> The pyramids, which are the object of our visit, are three in number, from 195 to 325 feet at the base, by 37 to 43 in height. The temples which once stood on the summit are but a mass of ruins. Thanks to excavations

made by the owner of the rancho, one side of one of the pyramids has been cleared of the vegetation and now a good view can be obtained, enabling us to perceive that it is identical in all respects with those at Tula and Teotihuacan, save that this is much smaller, the baby pattern, so to speak, of those we have hitherto visited. On the terrace crowning the pyramid a fragment of wall on an incline is still standing, covered with hard cement. This facing was composed of four layers of lime and mortar, each coating representing figures and characters in bas-reliefs, modelled in the lime coating. On removing one of these the next was discovered, almost invariably at the cost of nearly the whole bas-relief. We were fortunate in taking away intact the fragment shown in our plate, a head with retreating forehead resting on the instep of a foot which lies on a cushion. The notable feature of this profile is its similarity with those on the bassi-rilievi at Palenque, proving in my opinion the unity of civilisation of the two countries, save that priority of date must be awarded to Bellote. Besides these reliefs we found a vast quantity of broken arms, hands, ex-votos, pottery, etc.

It should be mentioned that these pyramids, unlike those at Teotihuacan, were built with shells and mud, and that baked bricks were only employed in the partition walls and those of the temples. That such materials should have been used was natural in a region where even gravel is unknown. [Charnay 1888:187–188]

Nearly three decades later, Frans Blom and Oliver La Farge (1926) followed in Charnay's footsteps, with antiquarianist visits to El Bellote and then Comalcalco, in addition to Jonuta. Their descriptions focused on the pyramid temples, their architecture, and their stucco images. Charnay's and Blom's and La Farge's travels predated the development of culture historical archaeology in the region. They provide little insight on the ages of sites yet appear to assume contemporaneity or simply exemplify a late nineteenth to early twentieth century belief that nonwestern societies were static.

The first culture historical work in the region was by Heinrich Berlin (1953a, 1953b, 1954, 1955, 1956). He also visited El Bellote and Comalcalco, providing notes on the pyramid mounds and their architecture. Comparing these with the earlier descriptions, it becomes clear that the temple structures and stucco at El Bellote experienced significant erosion and vandalism over the course of those seven decades. The primary purpose of Berlin's fieldwork was to collect pottery to develop his broader ceramic chronology. Excavations and opportunistic surface collections—primarily from the Usumacinta area but also near Huimanguillo in the Mezcalapa area—informed his horizons. Sisson (1976:5) mentions an excavation at El Bellote by Berlin but this was not described in the latter's published field reports. Based on his resulting ceramic chronology, Berlin considered El Bellote to date to the Classic and Postclassic periods. Farther east, near Frontera, Tabasco, Berlin (1956) also documented a small cluster of small sites on both sides of the mouth of the Grijalva River.

Matthew Stirling (1957) also visited El Bellote and several other sites in the region. His descriptions were equally limited. Stirling (1957:231) described a central group of mounds, the largest of which was estimated to be 75 feet tall, surrounded by numerous smaller mounds. Both Berlin's and Stirling's work inspired the belief that the Tabasco lowlands was an origin of fine paste pottery, which at the time was also believed diagnostic of Postclassic periods.

As culture historical archaeology progressed, the early dates of what are now known as Olmec sites and material culture became apparent, shifting much of the attention to those earlier centers. Before having visited El Bellote, Stirling's (1943) previous work at La Venta documented the mound complexes, imported stone monuments, elite burials, drainages, mosaics, and a wide range of artifactual material culture. Coe's and Diehl's (1980) investigations at San Lorenzo, Veracruz led to further refinements in chronology and elaborations on the Olmec Tradition and Horizon concepts. González Lauck (1988) was the first to map La Venta, and her long-term Proyecto Arqueológico La Venta has provided the spatial contexts for numerous studies at that site. While Gulf Coast archaeology for much of the mid- to late twentieth century emphasized the Olmec, research on the later Chontal Maya was largely based on ethnohistoric sources.

Apart from Olmec archaeology in the Tonalá region to the west, the attention of Chontalpa archaeologists focused on Comalcalco's monumental architecture, paralleling interests at Palenque, Chiapas, to the southeast. Surveys of the ceremonial district documented the architecture and brick, along with descriptions of the more unusual artifacts (Andrews 1967, 1989; Littman 1957; Martinez Guzman 1973; Navarette 1967; Pérez Campos and Silva 1992; Romero Molina 1987). Of these, Andrews' surveys produced the most comprehensive studies on the growth and development of Comalcalco to date. Littman's (1957) test confirmed the reliance on oyster shell for the thousands of tons of mortar and plaster for Comalcalco's monumental architecture, the closest source being ILC. Attempts to revise the chronological framework resulted in new pottery classifications, yet the group-type-variety approach (e.g., Boucher 1981; Peniche Rivero 1973) was later found to be problematic. Meanwhile, additional Tabasco sites were investigated along the Usumacinta River including Trinidad (Rands 1969), Pomoná (López Varela 1994), and Jonuta (Alvarez A. and Casasola 1985; Sanchez Caero 1979), the latter gaining attention for its figurines. Interest in El Bellote waned, and no similar projects were undertaken there.

There were few surveys in the Western Chontalpa from the 1950s to 1980s. One of the first New World Archaeological Foundation (NWAF) projects involved a 1953 survey using aerial photos in a study of the Grijalva River in Tabasco and Chiapas. As a reminder, in this book that river is the Mezcalapa, which fed into the Seco River until its course was diverted eastward around 1675 to become the Grijalva River (West, Psuty, and Thom 1969:133, 171–173), thus separating it from the Seco (see Figure 1.1). The Seco River is where Spanish-era Chontal populations and tributary resources such as cacao, lumber, and cattle were concentrated. A partial report, with a culture history framework, was published by Piña Chan and Navarrete (1967). Sanders (1962), who participated in the fieldwork, used personal observations to provide the first interpretation of settlement patterns in the Chontalpa, concluding that small states were laid out in a "solar" pattern. Sisson (1976) conducted the most extensive survey (using aerial photography and site visits) of the Western Chontalpa. He documented sites that were rapidly being destroyed as a result of the Grijalva Commission's Plan Chontalpa, which drained the vast marshlands for agriculture, expanded petroleum infrastructure, and increased looting. Sisson also visited ILC. Though providing brief descriptions of all sites visited, his research focus and excavations emphasized the Formative culture history and settlement patterns. Much later, von Nagy's (1997) survey along a western Mezcalapa distributary concluded that Preclassic to Postclassic occupation changes corresponded to hydrological and geormophological changes.

West, Psuty, and Thom's (1969) historical geography of Tabasco included a chapter that compiled and analyzed the distributions of known prehispanic sites. Their work produced the most comprehensive state-wide map of site locations (Figure 1.1). Although aerial photography was first used in the NWAF survey (Piña Chan and Navarrete 1967), the project run by West and colleagues was the first to use the technique at the Mecoacán Lagoon (Chapter 4). They also used aerial photos for a sample survey west of the Seco River in the Mezcalapa Delta where they identified mounds along banks of deteriorated distributaries (West, Psuty, and Thom 1969:93–94). The Atlas Arqueológico projects by the Instituto Nacional de Antropología e Historía (INAH) relied heavily on West and colleagues' compilation and earlier studies that were supplemented with other sources and sometimes brief visits. For example, visits to Isla Chablé led to the interpretation of early concheros, which became a generalization for early coastal adaptations (Fernández Tejedo et al. 1988:51).

The 1990s saw intensified activities at Comalcalco through tourism-generating excavations and consolidation of monumental architecture (Armijo Torres and Millán Ruíz 1995; Armijo Torres 1997, 1999a, 1999b; Armijo Torres, Gallegos Gómora, and Zender 1999; Armijo Torres, Fernández Martínez, Zender, Gallegos Gómora, and Gómez Ortiz 1999). These excavations provided new epigraphic discoveries, the documentation of the urn burials in the palace of the acropolis, and the first study of the faunal remains (Armijo Torres and Hernandez Sastre 1998, Hernandez Sastre 1997). In addition, the first studies of domestic features at Comalcalco were conducted (Gallegos Gómora 1994, 1995, 1997, 1998). Romero Rivera's (1995) survey indicated dispersed mounds from the north side of Comalcalco to the Mecoacán Lagoon. Interregional exchange was investigated through obsidian sourcing (Lewenstein 1995; Lewenstein and Glascock 1996, 1997). More recent investigations included new efforts to revise the ceramic chronology; it focused on fine paste types (Armijo Torres, Gallegos Gómora, and Jiménez Alvarez 2005). The decades of research at Comalcalco solidified the interpretation that the center was a city surrounded by a sprawling agrarian population during the Late Classic period. Interestingly, no areas for the production of the massive amount of brick, mortar, and stucco have been found at Comalcalco.

In an unpublished report, Zender (1998) describes epigraphic evidence from brick, sculpted stone, pottery, and incised bone at Comalcalco. He observed that Comalcalco's emblem glyph was "Holy Lord of Hok'Chan" or "he of Hok' Chan" and suggested that Comalcalco's patron deity was a manifestation of Chak. Also significant were probable references to El Bellote on two of three bone artifacts in burial Urn 7 of Temple IIIa. Those texts suggested that Comalcalco and El Bellote initiated but lost a war with Tortuguero, resulting in the establishment of the larger kingdom of Bakal in CE 649, the capital of which was located at Comalcalco. If so, this would imply that there were a number of smaller kingdoms prior to consolidation into a regional state. The epigraphy names Chan-Chuwen,

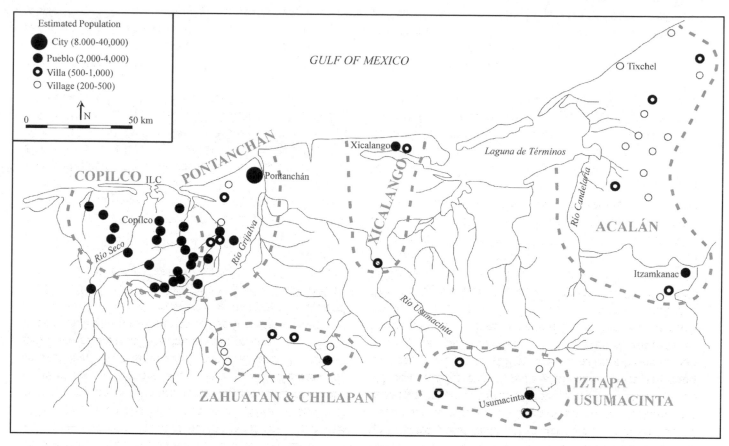

Figure 2.1. Map of sixteenth-century Chontal provinces. Compiled and redrawn by the author from Izquierdo 1997.

or "Four Monkey/Sky Artisan," a subordinate ruler from the site of Peten-Ti' ("Island at the Edge"—assumed to be El Bellote) who, along with Ox Balam, ruler of Comalcalco, was captured by Balam-Ahau, the ruler of Tortuguero, on 20 December, CE 649. Chan-Chuwen's name is repeated on a Tortuguero sarcophagus. Other epigraphic data from Comalcalco indicate rulers with origins at Tortuguero, who in turn originated from Palenque (Arellano 2006; Bíró 2011, 2012). Zender (1998) also provided a history of dynastic succession at Comalcalco: Chan Tok' I/II (late sixth to early seventh century CE), Ox Balam (early seventh century to 649 CE), K'in-Nik (650–680 CE), Chan Tok' II (680–750 CE), K'inich Ol (705–745 CE), Uh Chan (746–760 CE), and El Kinich (760–768+ CE).

Meanwhile, ethnohistoric research emphasized sixteenth-century political geography, settlement patterns, and demography (Cabrera Bernat 1997; de la Garza et al. 1983; Gallegos Gómora 1997; Gerhard 1991; Jiménez Valdez 1989, 1993; Ochoa 1997). Izquierdo's (1997) ethnohistoric reconstructions of sixteenth-century provinces, towns, and population sizes are perhaps the most thorough. Both

she and Ochoa and Vargas (1987) demonstrate that the site of Xicalango and the province of Acalán—famous from Cortes' mischief and from Scholes and Roys' (1968) descriptions—could only have been minor Chontal polities. Instead, the provinces of Copilco and Potonchán in the Comalcalco-ILC area (Figure 2.1), were more populated and powerful (Izquierdo 1997) (Figure 2.1), which corresponds with West and colleagues' (1969:Figure 31) compilation of sources on sixteenth-century town locations (Izquierdo 1997; Roys 1957).

Pottery from a 2002 salvage project directed by Romero Rivera on the west side of the mouth the Grijalva River was analyzed by Chávez Jiménez (2007). He concluded that occupation of the area spanned Late Formative to Colonial times and that trade wares came from Veracruz to the eastern Yucatán. However, the article was oriented toward the search for the port of Potonchán and no data on settlement or settlement size for the periods were provided.

To conclude, much of the archaeology in western Tabasco emphasized Olmec sites (to the west in the Tonalá Delta) and elite zones of Comalcalco. Although nineteenth- to mid-twentieth-century archaeological explorations in the region included the site of El Bellote, very few have visited ILC since. All investigations at ILC were brief, producing little documentation. The NWAF and Sisson surveys, though limited in different ways, were more informative. Within this context I began the PAILC, which became the first systematic, multiseason archaeological investigation of a coastal site complex in Tabasco.

PRELIMINARY RESEARCH

I first visited ILC in 1993 while volunteering on Rebecca González Lauck's La Venta project. In my one-hour visit to El Bellote, I immediately recognized that it was a large site with a complex spatial organization. At the time, I was studying for my master's in anthropology at Louisiana State University, working on my thesis on Postclassic Maya pottery from Heather McKillop's project at Wild Cane Cay, Belize (Ensor 1994). Robert West, also at LSU, showed me the aerial photos from his 1960s historical-geographical research in the area (West, Psuty, and Thom 1969) and shared his reminiscences of that project. After completing my master's degree I worked in cultural resource management archaeology in Arizona from 1994 to 1998. ILC fieldwork remained at the back of my mind for a potential doctoral dissertation.

During my doctoral studies at the University of Florida, I took a more serious interest in ILC, recognizing the region as a niche that very few archaeologists had explored, and which happened to be in a region figuring prominently in speculation about the Epiclassic transitions across broader Mesoamerica. In a return visit in March 2000, permitted by the Centro INAH Tabasco, I identified 13 prehispanic mounds along the northern side of Isla Santa Rosita where West, Psuty, and Thom (1969) had documented only six mounds with the air photos, but no ground archaeological survey had documented features. Having identified more than twice the number of previously recorded mounds in that one location, I realized that the prehispanic settlement of the islands was denser than expected. During the same trip and afterward, I began to collect literature on the archaeology, ethnography, history, ethnohistory, and linguistics on the local area and on Chontal culture in general. The PAILC emerged.

2001

The first season was in 2001, funded by a small, predissertation Tinker Foundation grant and multiple small graduate student travel grants from the University of Florida. The work was permitted by the Consejo de Arqueología of INAH. The overambitious goal was to situate ILC within the broader contexts of the Chontalpa region by (1) evaluating hypotheses on how the capital at Comalcalco influenced the coastal settlement's population growth and roles in the regional political economy and (2) documenting any Formative materials in the process. The objectives were to characterize the occupation history and settlement patterns, feature functions, commerce, and resource exploitation. The fieldwork involved a systematic pedestrian survey of the islands that included surface collections. The goals were to produce a complete inventory of the features and obtain artifactual data with which to address the objectives. The fieldwork excluded the site of El Bellote.

Four hypotheses were developed on the settlement history (Ensor 2002b). First, I hypothesized that ILC's population grew gradually beginning prior to the Late Classic. This might indicate that the settlement was already established but grew to accommodate Comalcalco's developmental needs for coastal resources or port facilities. The second hypothesis was that there was punctuated population growth early in the Late Classic related to the growth of Comalcalco. The third hypothesis was that settlement density remained unchanged from before and after the early Late Classic. This would indicate that Comalcalco had little influence on settlement at ILC. In the fourth hypothesis, I suggested that the settlement population declined in the Late Classic. This would indicate that ILC was marginalized when Comalcalco's population expanded.

The 2001 season included the development of a feature classification system. Previous research across the Gulf Coast Lowlands, the Maya macroregion, and the Chontalpa region, along with my prior visits, provided some expectations for features. Residential and ceremonial mounds similar to those in the broader Gulf Coast region had been recorded in the Chontalpa (Armijo Torres 1997, 1999; Armijo Torres and Millán Ruíz 1995; Berlin 1953b, 1954; Fernández Tejedo et al. 1988; Gallegos Gómera 1995, 1997; Piña Chan and Navarrete 1967; Sanders 1962; Sisson 1976; Stirling 1957). However, mounds previously recorded at Isla Chablé had also been interpreted as Formative shell middens or *concheros* (Fernández Tejedo et al. 1988:51).

Trade and seaports were major subjects in 1980s and 1990s Mayanist archaeology (Andrews 1987, 1990; Folan, Morales, and Tiesler 2002; Gallareta Negrón et al. 1989; McKillop 1996; McKillop and Healy 1989). Ethnohistoric research suggested that Postclassic sites in the Chontalpa had important roles in commercial trade (e.g., Jiménez

Valdez 1989, 1993; Ochoa and Vargas 1987; Scholes and Roys 1968; Vargas Pacheco 1992:291). The attention to trade extended to ethnohistorical research using sixteenth-century Potonchán and Xicalango as examples of seaports (Jiménez Valdez 1989, 1993; Ochoa and Vargas 1987; Vargas Pacheco 1992:291). Given the archaeological attention to Comalcalco, coinciding with a growing interest in trade and ports, El Bellote was speculated to have been a port for the inland capital like Xelhá for Cobá, Isla Cerritos for Chichen Itzá, Canbalám for Chunchucmil, Emal for San Fernando, and Marlowe Cay for Altun Ha (Andrews 1990:166–167). The protected location of ILC along the coast, only 12 km downriver from Comalcalco, made it an ideal place for a port. If not a port, then it could be concluded that trade was directly controlled by Comalcalco, bypassing ILC—a model later interpreted for Late Classic Cancuen (Demarest et al. 2014; Martínez Paiz and others 2017).

Four hypotheses were established on the commercial role of ILC (Ensor 2002b). First, it was hypothesized that ILC was a specialized trading port, in which case there would be port facilities or locations with dense accumulations of long-distance trade goods (e.g., Andrews 2008; Pendergast 1981; McKillop 1996). The second hypothesis was that ILC and Comalcalco precipitated the Epiclassic Gulf Coast trade focus for the Mexican macroregion to the south and west and the Maya macroregion to the east. If so, commodities from long-distance sources in the Mexican as well as Maya macroregions would be present. The third hypothesis stated that sources of long-distance trade goods at ILC shifted along with the changes in the Late Classic-Epiclassic commercial transformation. This suggests that Comalcalco and ILC did not precipitate those changes. The fourth hypothesis was that ILC was not a port. This hypothesis implies that Comalcalco directly controlled coastal trade, bypassing the coastal community altogether.

The 2001 season also sought to produce evidence on resource exploitation through a preliminary analysis of faunal and macrobotanical remains. Interpretations of resource use were very limited, however, as surface observations were biased toward larger, more visible elements and species.

Methods

During the survey stage, the project rented an unused house in Puerto Ceiba for field accommodations and hired a retired fisherman for daily launch transportation. Later, a house in the town of El Bellote was rented, which in addition to cutting transportation time was better suited for the washing, labeling, and sorting of the surface-collected artifacts. For the survey, I crossed each island in parallel transects that were spaced at 20-m intervals and recorded elevated features and artifact concentrations (e.g., Stark 1991, 2006; Stark and Heller 1991). No artifact concentrations were observed except on the elevated features. A Silva brand compass, accurate to 1 degree, was used for navigation, feature orientations, and feature elevation estimates. The locations, sizes, and orientations of features were plotted to scale on survey maps and aerial photo maps (INEGI E15A79B, Paraíso, 1:20,000 scale). Distances and feature lengths were estimated by pacing. Feature numbers were assigned in sequence of documentation. A register was made that included the feature number, location (island), form, size, height, and condition of each feature. Each feature was photo-documented. Surface collections were made using 10- by 10-m units. Some features had no collections due to low surface visibility (Ensor 2002b). The collected artifacts were catalogued, washed, labeled, and recorded. Wrapping up the season, the collection was stored at the Centro INAH Tabasco in Villahermosa.

Outcomes

One hundred twenty-two features were identified on five of the six islands. Feature sizes, morphologies, arrangements, and construction materials were used for classificatory purposes. The overwhelming majority of features did not include shell in their construction, contradicting the previous literature. The feature categories and their combinations described in Chapter 4 were created: platforms, mounds, mounds-on-platforms, multilevel mounds, multilevel mounds-on-platforms, and possible mounds (severely eroded).

The 68 surface collections led to unexpected results. In general, there were low numbers of artifacts within the units (often fewer than 30 items) although some units yielded far more. Fourteen isolated diagnostic artifacts were collected opportunistically outside of collection units. The overwhelming majority of artifacts were rim sherds: 705 in total. The pottery was in poor condition, with highly eroded surfaces. The recording system attempted to follow the groups and types previously developed at Comalcalco (e.g., Boucher 1981; Peniche 1973), but it became clear that this system was problematic for ILC. The surface paint was routinely missing, and some plastic decoration and rim styles were associated with very different groups. As a result, I switched to attribute recording of paste, thickness, surface treatment, decoration, and form. Some attributes not recorded at Comalcalco were observed. Apart from Sierra Red pottery, no extraregional imports were present.

Obsidian, prevalent at sites across Mesoamerica and present at Comalcalco, was completely absent—not a single piece was observed. Only three pieces of chert were found. A poor-quality plaster, made from lime and crushed shell temper, was observed at six features (samples were collected from four). Only 21 faunal specimens were found, 17 of which were pieces of turtle shell. The remainder were from large fish (including shark). No human remains were identified. Eroded pumice stones were present and sampled at several features. Shell was not collected but recorded where present: oyster (*Crassostrea virginica*), quahog (*Mercenaria campechiensis*), and whelk (*Busycon* sp.) were identified, in decreasing order of frequency (Ensor 2002b).

Nearly all surface collections yielded both Formative and Late Classic pottery. There was no Early Classic or Postclassic pottery. Without stratigraphic data I could not evaluate whether or not the features were Formative constructions re-occupied in the Late Classic. Nevertheless, the project results tentatively supported the hypothesis of punctuated population growth in the Late Classic, suggesting that settlement at ILC was associated with Comalcalco's development (Ensor 2002b, 2003b).

Most features shared similar morphologies and sizes with residential mounds described in the broader Gulf Coast region. With few exceptions, the features were widely dispersed, suggestive of small domestic groups (e.g., nuclear households or small extended households). This was not the expected pattern, as *plazuelas*—dwellings surrounding small plaza spaces indicating patrilocal extended residential groups—were broadly touted as a normative Maya pattern. Two locations where dispersed residential features were linearly arranged suggested the presence of canals that have long since filled to obscurity. Two locations on Isla Chablé had aggregated residential features. The Southwest Group of Isla Chablé comprised two residential platforms and two multilevel mounds overlying a large basal platform. The South Group of Isla Chablé included one *plazuela*, two small mounds on a platform, two additional mounds and a severely disturbed larger mound—all of which were constructed of shell and earthen deposits—over an extensive low earthen platform.

Three nonresidential features of kinds not previously reported in the region were documented (Ensor 2002b). Two large deposits of crushed shell, which does not occur naturally, were identified (features 89 and 122). These, in combination with the plaster containing crushed shell temper and the enormous quantities of oyster shell used in the mortar and stucco at Comalcalco signaled that oyster-shell processing for construction materials was an important

local industry. Although there were no obvious port facilities, there was an unusual 4- to 5-m wide shoreline platform (Feature 92), which originally may have reached 600 m in length. This was tentatively interpreted as a probable landing for either collective fishing or commercial port activities. Unfortunately, the entire length of the platform was covered in dense grass, preventing surface collections. Otherwise, the near absence of imported commodities throughout the insular sites suggested that ILC had little involvement in long-distance trade.

In addition to the report to INAH (Ensor 2002b), the season provided updated site data for the Registro Público de Monumentos y Zonas Arqueológicos of INAH. The results were disseminated in a conference presentation and one published article (Ensor 2002a; 2003b). Both emphasized the settlement patterns, chronological data, feature descriptions, and the possibility of a port function or resource extraction role in the regional political economy. I was unsuccessful in obtaining grants to return in 2002 or 2003. Rather than delay my Ph.D., I changed my dissertation topic to another project already nearing completion, which postponed the second season.

2004

The second season was in 2004, funded by a Provost's New Faculty Research Grant at Eastern Michigan University where I began as an assistant professor in 2003, and with a permit from the Consejo de Arqueología of INAH. The same house was rented for field and lab accommodations. Gabriel Tun Ayora contributed to the fieldwork, analyses, and report, and later contributed to project research. A student volunteer also assisted with the screening, washing, and labeling of artifacts. The objectives of this season were to (1) confirm the feature function interpretations made in 2001, (2) refine the ceramic chronology for a more detailed understanding of the settlement history, (3) determine if the residential groups and the dispersed residences were contemporaneous, (4) model mound construction and determine the relationship between Formative and Late Classic deposits, and (5) better characterize subsistence. To address these issues, the season included stratigraphic excavations at a variety of features at the islands and creating profile drawings of erosional cuts and sediment mines in the South Group of Isla Chablé.

Methods

The stratigraphic excavations took place at three residential features: a platform, a mound-on-platform, and a multilevel mound-on-platform. As an alternative to excavations at the South Group of Isla Chablé, profile drawings were made of cuts from sediment mines and erosion, which provided stratigraphic information with which to address these same four themes. Excavations also took place at one of the crushed shell deposits and at the long shoreline platform to better identify their functions and formation, and to evaluate their contemporaneity with the residences.

Small test units were used for stratigraphic sampling. As with all excavations at ILC, the units were excavated in 10-cm arbitrary levels, but we switched to cultural levels if stratigraphic changes occurred in less than 10 cm. In this way, artifacts and other contents of upper and lower portions of strata more than 10 cm thick could also be separated. At the same time, the levels enabled the easy detection of subsurface features. Feature fill was also sampled in controlled levels. The level forms, feature forms, and a number of additional forms for the project were initially developed in this season. Subsurface floors and pits were left *in situ* after documentation. They were pedestaled if excavation continued. Excavation in a unit was terminated if a feature occupied most of its area. Upon completion, plastic bottles with cards identifying the project inside them were placed in the four corners of the unit at different depths as the units were backfilled with the screened sediments. All sediment excavated in 2004 was screened through ⅛-inch (3-mm) mesh to recover potentially small faunal and botanical remains (Ensor and Tun Ayora 2004). The smaller mesh size cost an enormous amount of field time, in addition to allowing for fewer excavated units, but led to interesting, useful observations.

The residential features selected for test units represented a range in morphological types. One low residential platform (Feature 40) was selected for a 1- by 2-m unit on Isla Santa Rosita. One mound-on-platform combination (Features 77 and 78, respectively) was selected at Isla Chablé. That unit was originally a 2- by 2-m unit. After encountering a poorly preserved clay floor in one half, the other half was used to continue the excavation (1- by 2-m). A multilevel mound-on-platform (Features 73 through 76) was selected at Isla Chablé. A smaller 1- by 1-m unit was used to sample stratigraphy there. A 2- by 2-m unit sampled Feature 92, the linear shoreline platform of Isla Chablé. Another 2- by 2-m unit sampled Feature 122, the crushed shell deposit on the southeast corner of Isla Chablé. A theodolite was used to produce contour maps of these features (Ensor and Tun Ayora 2004).

Near-vertical cuts from sediment mining and shoreline erosion at the South Group of Isla Chablé were cleaned and profiled. Alarmingly, one mound with only two small mining pits in 2001 (Ensor 2002b) had since been mined extensively, leaving only two-thirds of the mound intact (Ensor and Tun Ayora 2004). In each location, the cuts were profiled to document the mound construction sequence, search for subsurface features, and stratigraphically collect artifacts. A contour map of the entire group was produced (Ensor and Tun Ayora 2004).

The artifacts collected in the excavation levels and from strata documented in the profiles were catalogued, washed, and labeled. After consulting the Comalcalco Archaeology Project on its evolving pottery classifications, some modifications were made for ILC. Poor preservation of sherd surfaces and the attribute emphasis on paste, plastic decoration, and form made for inconsistencies between the two projects. At the end of the season, the collection was delivered for storage to the Comalcalco Museum Laboratory.

Outcomes

The season's results contributed a significant advance toward understanding the mound and platform construction, in identifying a range of subsurface features, and in contributing information on subsistence and commerce. Little progress was made in refining the ceramic chronology, however, which complicated the settlement history analysis.

In all strata sampled, Late Classic pottery was mixed with Late Formative pottery. These results provided conclusive evidence that each deposit, even in the lowermost observed, was associated with the Late Classic. In other words, earlier Formative deposits had been removed from their contexts and reused to build the Late Classic mounds and platforms. Furthermore, nearly all pottery in the shoreline platform (Feature 92) and the crushed shell deposit (Feature 122) were Late Classic types and, by association, the other artifacts from those contexts had Late Classic affiliations. At this point the project could confidently associate all of the extant features with the Late Classic (Ensor and Tun Ayora 2004). This limited the potential to understand the Formative occupations.

The excavation and profile data indicated that the platforms and mounds were built in multiple episodes. Occupation surfaces were often separated by multiple strata, however, indicating that building episodes sometimes included more than one fill deposit. The thickness of mound construction deposits varied considerably, and the taller mounds did not have more construction episodes than lower platforms and mounds, indicating that greater mound height was not an indicator of longer use life (Ensor and Tun Ayora 2004).

The season produced new information on domestic architecture and other buried features (Ensor and Tun Ayora 2004). Although no intact features were present in the excavation at platform Feature 40, highly eroded nodules of poor-quality mortar, along with few pieces of daub, were present in the fill deposits. Near the base of the large mound (Feature 75) and overlying the top of its underlying platform (Feature 76), the 1- by 1-m unit encountered a portion of a burned structure with a decomposed plaster floor and a clay wall segment. Eroded nodules of poor-quality plaster were in the overlying fill. A small kitchen having an earthen pedestal was observed over the surface of platform Feature 78. Daub was found in the overlying fill. Although no structures were identified in cuts profiled at the South Group of Isla Chablé, occupation surfaces associated with pits were observed in one multilevel mound.

The functions of the specialized features were clarified. The excavation at the linear shoreline platform (Feature 92) revealed two earthen strata with a high density of faunal remains overlying the natural mangrove sediment. No imported commodities were present, leading to more doubts about a trade-related function. It was more likely a fishing-related landing (Ensor and Tun Ayora 2004). The excavation at Feature 122 revealed one thick deposit of crushed shell. There was no evidence for a lime kiln. Included with the small shell fragments was a high density of small faunal specimens and very small, severely eroded sherds (Ensor and Tun Ayora 2004). These additional materials may also have been crushed and included with the shell for construction materials.

The season expanded information on the range of artifacts at ILC. A total of 4,739 were collected. The majority were pottery sherds (76.13% of the assemblage). All nine fishing net sinkers were modified sherds. Fauna represented the next largest category of artifacts (20.26%), nearly all of which came from nonresidential locations. Small nodules of highly eroded mortar were encountered in two residential contexts. The season yielded only five pieces of obsidian and seven pieces of chert, confirming that stone cutting tools were infrequent. One fragment of a basalt metate was collected at the South Group of Isla Chablé—the first piece of ground stone identified at ILC. Also collected were small unmodified stones (Ensor and Tun Ayora 2004).

Limited progress was made for interpreting subsistence. The season demonstrated that, aside from the shell used to form mounds, faunal remains (both vertebrates and invertebrates) were characteristically absent or occurred in very low frequencies at the earthen residential platforms and mounds—the majority of the features on the islands. Few vertebrate remains were observed in the mounds at the South Group of Isla Chablé, although shell was found in some strata in those mounds. The overwhelming majority of vertebrate remains came from two contexts: the linear shoreline platform and the crushed shell deposit. These discrepancies were the first indications of collective fishing activities at the shoreline platform, with perhaps only deboned and de-shelled animals brought to residential contexts. The limited taxonomic classification of the vertebrate remains relied on numbers of individual specimens (NISP) for evaluating relative abundance (Chapter 7). After their field collection using ⅛-inch (3-mm) mesh, the vertebrate remains were passed through ¼-inch (6-mm) mesh in the lab to compare recovery results and their impacts on taxonomic NISP percentages (Chapter 7).

Although the 2004 season was unsuccessful in refining the ceramic chronology, several advancements were made. The results cast further doubts about port facilities but provided good information on feature construction, expanded the range of material culture documented, and enabled a general characterization of fauna exploitation. These results were disseminated in a report and a conference presentation (Ensor and Tun Ayora 2004; Ensor 2004a).

2005

The third season, in the summer of 2005, was funded by the Foundation for the Advancement of Mesoamerican Studies, Inc. (FAMSI #05024), under a permit from the Consejo de Arqueología of INAH (Ensor 2005a). Collaborating in this season were Concepción Herrera Escobar (Universidad Veracruzana), who also contributed to subsequent project research; Socorro Jiménez Alvarez (Universidad Autónoma de Yucatán); and Keiko Teranishi Castillo (Escuela Nacional de Antropología e Historia). The same house was rented for field and lab accommodations. The same laborer from 2004 provided launch transportation and assisted in the field. Three supervised volunteer students also participated.

The goal of the 2005 season was to refine the ceramic chronology while also producing more information on mound construction and domestic activities. Because the 2004 investigations indicated that mound building involved mixing of earlier and later deposits, this season's objective was to use the contents of stratified Late Classic features, rather than the mound fill, for pottery sequencing. The 2004 results at two locations indicated that multilevel mounds-on-platforms were constructed in a platform, inferior mound, superior mound sequence, rather than platforms developing around existing mounds. This generalization was also tested with the 2005 excavations. The 2001 and 2004 results also indicated a near absence of chipped stone, ground stone, and faunal remains at residences, which differs from elsewhere in Mesoamerica. This observation begged the question of what encompassed "domestic" activities at ILC. The 2005 excavations would provide more data for modeling the range of domestic activities and their spatial relationships.

Methods

Whereas the 2004 season used test units to sample mound stratigraphy, this season's objectives called for broader horizontal excavations at a mound formation that should have multiple occupation surfaces. The goals were to identify subsurface features and their spatial relationships and to sample stratified features. Features 32, 34, and 35, comprising one multilevel mound-on-platform formation near the northeast corner of Isla Santa Rosita, were selected. Feature 32 was a small circular superior mound overlying the east end of Feature 34 (a larger elliptical inferior mound), which, in turn, was situated on top of Feature 35 (a low platform). Blocks of adjacent 2- by 2-m units were placed over the small superior mound and over the western end of the larger inferior mound. A 1- by 1-m unit was positioned between the two blocks to test for continuity in strata between the two locations. An additional 2- by 2-m unit was placed over a surface artifact concentration on the platform to test for midden deposits there (Ensor and others 2006).

As in 2004, the units were excavated in 10-cm arbitrary levels, switching to cultural levels when encountering sediment changes in less than 10 cm. Within each block, one level was excavated in adjacent units, then cleaned with a leaf blower to identify the faintest of sediment differences and the outlines of subsurface features. Feature fill was also excavated in controlled levels. Once excavated and documented, the features were pedestaled, and the next level was excavated around them. Because the 2004 season confirmed that few faunal remains were present at the earthen residential features, and because those few fauna specimens were large, ¼-inch (6-mm) mesh was used for screening. The excavations were slow-going due to the extreme compactness of the clay sediments. Upon completion, plastic bottles containing cards identifying the project were placed within excavations at different depths as the units were backfilled with the screened sediments (Ensor and others 2006).

The 1,880 recovered artifacts were catalogued, washed, and labeled. The vast majority were sherds (94.31% of the assemblage). Jiménez Alvarez was able to correlate several of the Late Classic ceramic types from ILC with those from Comalcalco, although some differences were also noted. We established a revised descriptive classification for the Formative pottery while reclassifying the 2004 collections. Afterward, I used the resulting system to classify the 2005 collection. Despite the changes, the project maintained the full range of attribute recording for each sherd. Pumice stone made up the next largest artifact category (3.51%). Thirty-seven chunks of clay were collected. The estimated 22.40 square meters of excavated sediment in the blocks and other units yielded only four pieces of obsidian, again confirming the near absence of these imported materials at the earthen residential features. The excavations did not yield fauna in any form (not even shell), or any additional artifact categories (Ensor and others 2006). At the end of the season, the collections were stored at the Comalcalco Museum Laboratory.

Outcomes

The excavations confirmed the platform, inferior mound, superior mound sequence in mound formation (see Chapter 5). Two small mounds were built over the platform that were later joined through filling to create the large inferior mound, over which the smaller superior mound was added. Meanwhile, a midden accumulated over the platform. Three successive occupation surfaces were observed. Each was associated with small pits and one had a portion of a poorly preserved clay floor.

Unfortunately, every one of the subsurface features lacked *in situ* use-related fill or artifacts. Their fill was always the overlying mound construction fill that contained mixed Formative and Late Classic pottery. Once again, the fieldwork produced highly useful data for some purposes but not for refining the ceramic chronology.

Nevertheless, the pottery classification system evolved to its current form (see Chapter 6). The 2004 interpretations of multilevel construction sequences was confirmed, and a sequence of occupation surfaces was documented. The relative poverty in the range of artifacts at earthen residential features were by this time a well-documented pattern, which challenges stereotypes of diverse activities including craft manufacturing at Mesoamerican households (Hirth 2012). In addition to the reports to FAMSI

(Ensor 2005a) and INAH (Ensor et al. 2006), the season contributed additional information to synthesize in three conference presentations (Ensor 2005b, 2007; Ensor et al. 2005) and one article (Ensor and others 2006).

2007

The fourth season, in 2007, was dedicated to the site of El Bellote. It was funded by the Foundation for the Advancement of Mesoamerican Studies, Inc. (FAMSI #07019) under a permit from the Consejo de Arqueología of INAH (Ensor 2008b). The director of the Centro INAH Tabasco made arrangements with the ranch owner. Concepción Herrera Escobar collaborated on the proposal and report to INAH. Gabriel Tun Ayora took part in the fieldwork and collaborated on the report. The same house was rented, and a new local laborer assisted in the field and lab and provided launch transportation.

The objectives were to document the occupational history and produce information on elite material culture and spatial organization for comparison with the insular sites to complete the picture of Late Classic society and social organization, and to investigate the possibility for Formative deposits. El Bellote was already known to have monumental architecture (Charnay 1888; Berlin 1953a, 1953b, 1954; Stirling 1957) and my 1993 visit suggested a range of additional features including, potentially, elite residences and specialized features. El Bellote was the last possible location for port facilities at ILC. The investigation of the site would provide the opportunity to contrast elite residential material culture and domestic activities with those at the insular residences. The objectives were to (1) produce the first contour map of El Bellote, (2) collect surface artifacts from features, and (3) profile mounds cut by erosion or past sediment-mining for stratigraphic data on mound construction and functions.

Methods

The aggregated and well-bounded nature of the site allowed an initial walk-over and sketch map for planning purposes. The surrounding mangrove was inspected at intervals to confirm the boundary. The site mapping, surface collections, and profiles took place simultaneously. The surface collections used the same 10- by 10-m units as in the 2001 survey of the islands. Profiles documenting the strata and any subsurface features were drawn wherever erosion or sediment mines left near-vertical cuts in the features, using the same methods described for the 2004 season. Visible artifacts were collected from those strata.

The artifacts collected at El Bellote were catalogued, washed, and labeled in the same manner as in previous seasons. In addition to recording the 2007 collections, the 2001, 2004, and 2005 collections were brought from Comalcalco to the field house. The reclassification of the 2004 ceramic collection, initiated in 2005, was completed, as was the reclassification of the 2001 pottery collection. Once the pottery from all four seasons was classified and recorded consistently with the revised system, those data were ready for the analyses presented in Chapter 6. At the end of the field season, the entire PAILC collection was housed at the Centro INAH Tabasco office in Villahermosa, facilitating access for future research.

Outcomes

The season recorded 43 platforms and mounds arranged in five spatial groups (Ensor, Tun Ayora, and Herrera Escobar 2008). In addition to at least six large ceremonial mounds, there were residential mounds, large and small nonresidential platforms, and other features with unidentified functions. Unlike the majority of insular residences, all at El Bellote occurred in groups, with each placed over its group's basal platform. Although most features were constructed of shell and earth deposits, some features were earthen-only. There was severe decades-old damage to some larger ceremonial mounds and extensive shoreline erosion where mangrove was absent. One such location exposed a large hearth and plaster-lined pit. A significant amount of information was gained on the site structure with which to interpret Late Classic social organization.

One of the initial project questions was finally answered. No trade facilities were identified at El Bellote (Ensor, Tun Ayora, and Herrera Escobar 2008). Although documenting a trade port function would have been interesting, establishing the absence of such a role in the regional political economy was equally interesting and challenging to explain. Like other aspects of ILC, the findings at El Bellote differed considerably from prevailing assumptions.

Not only did the 2007 season produce the first map and systematic collections at El Bellote, but the information gained also provided perspective on ILC as a whole (Ensor 2008b; Ensor, Tun Ayora, and Herrera Escobar 2008). Now observable were three categories of residential mound arrangements: mound groupings associated with ceremonial features, mound groupings associated with production-related features, and the dispersed mounds across most of ILC (Ensor and Tun Ayora 2008; Ensor, Tun Ayora, and Herrera Escobar 2008; Ensor, Herrera Escobar, and Tun Ayora 2008). Predictably, sherds (89.5%)

made up the majority of the 3,076 artifacts recovered. Some pottery attributes at El Bellote were absent at the insular sites. The only pottery that may be diagnostic of the Middle Formative was found at El Bellote. There was also a small percentage of pottery imported from the Laguna de Términos and Usumacinta regions, again found only at El Bellote. Other collected materials included 122 vertebrate faunal specimens, 11 pieces of obsidian, 6 pieces of chert, 10 pieces of ground stone (metate and mano fragments), 34 clay chunks, and samples of mortar, stucco, brick, and unmodified stone (Ensor, Tun Ayora, and Herrera Escobar 2008). Although low, these numbers are significantly higher than those from all seasons at the islands. Plaster was plentiful at residences (and of far better quality than at the insular sites). *In situ* floors were documented in several contexts. Brick and mortar architecture was also present, including one vaulted arch exposed by disturbance (Ensor Tun Ayora, and Herrera Escobar 2008).

As elsewhere at ILC, Late Formative and Late Classic pottery were found together in the surface collections (Ensor, Tun Ayora, and Herrera Escobar 2008). The same was observed in the stratigraphic collections from the profiled locations, indicating the same pattern of Late Classic feature construction where earlier deposits were recycled. A very small quantity of possible late Middle Formative diagnostics were present at El Bellote (absent at the insular sites).

Many of the confusing observations of previous seasons now fell into place providing a more coherent picture of settlement patterns, trade, and subsistence practices. With a more complete view of ILC, the four seasons of data were ready for synthesis, culminating in a book on class-divergent kinship and gender (Ensor 2013b); additional articles (Ensor 2014a, 2014b, 2016, 2017e; Ensor and Tun Ayora 2011); a book chapter (Ensor 2017d); and conference presentations (Ensor 2008a, 2011a, 2015, 2016b, 2017c, 2018b, 2019; ; Ensor and Tun Ayora 2008; Ensor, Herrera Escobar, and Tun Ayora 2012, 2018b). The project data also contributed to Tun Ayora's (2010) master's thesis.

THERMOLUMINESCENCE DATING EXPERIMENT, 2011

With the failure to refine the Late Classic ceramic sequence using stratigraphic relationships, the project needed an alternative solution. In the summer of 2011, I experimented with thermoluminescence dating of pottery from the 2001 surface collections. Because the 2004 and 2005 excavations did not collect sediment samples adjacent to recovered sherds, the only feasible approach, without further

excavations, was to collect sediment associated with the previously collected pottery from the surface collection unit locations after 10 years. Following discussions with James Feathers at the Luminescence Dating Laboratory at the University of Washington, the decision was made to use a small sample as an experiment to see if sherds could be accurately dated in this manner. The study was funded by a small award from the Eastern Michigan University Provost's Office and authorized with permits from the Consejo de Arqueología of INAH.

From the collection curated at the Centro INAH Tabasco, one sherd representing each of four types known to date to the Formative and Late Classic and one sherd of a type defined by the project were selected for the analysis. The sediment samples from the 2001 surface collection unit locations were obtained in a day trip to the islands. The permit and small grant also enabled radiometric dating of one charcoal sample from the burned floor encountered in the 2004 excavations—the best *in situ* charcoal associated with a buried feature—and of one fauna specimen from El Bellote.

The results generally conformed with expectations. Thermoluminescence dates generally corresponded with the known period affiliations for four sherds. The charcoal confirmed a Late Classic affiliation for the structure and the bone was dated to the Late Formative. However, the fifth sherd's thermoluminescence results suggested a much earlier date than could be accepted, suggesting potential problems with the use of surface sediments (see Chapter 6; Ensor 2011b, 2013c).

SYNOPSIS

The PAILC successfully achieved several of its goals toward understanding Late Classic material culture, society, lifeways, and regional relationships (Chapter 9) and to a lesser extent the same themes for the Formative periods. Contemporaneity with Comalcalco was established. The surveys provided the information with which to address settlement patterns, social organization, and settlement growth. Feature morphologies, associated artifacts, excavations, and the profile documentation of erosional cuts and sediment mines provided evidence with which to interpret feature functions and formation processes (Chapter 5). Where there was once extremely limited information on the material culture of coastal Tabasco, the PAILC documented a wide range of features and artifacts, including architectural materials, allowing for the descriptions in chapters 4 through 7. Although the location of ILC indicated a fishing subsistence base, the kinds of fauna exploited were better documented, allowing interpretations on capture techniques and social relations in fishing activities (Chapter 7).

Alternative understandings of ILC emerged from the PAILC. In contrast with previous literature, there were no Formative period *concheros*. The features were platforms and mounds, not middens, and all were built during the Late Classic period. There was no evidence supporting the long-held assumption that ILC was a port. More likely, Comalcalco controlled access to long-distance trade in the region and ILC instead served as a location for coastal resource extraction (Ensor 2003b). The unexpected paucity of stone tools indicated that most of the community did not benefit from long-distance trade, and perhaps had little need for stone implements at residences. The general lack of stone tools, vertebrate remains, and invertebrate remains at residences revised assumptions about

"domestic" activities. The analyses in chapters 5 through 7, and the contextualization in chapters 8 and 9 provide social explanations for these unexpected findings.

The greatest limitations involved chronological associations. Because no undisturbed Late Formative deposits were encountered, the ability to interpret those early occupations was limited and required assumptions, normative characterization, and occasional speculation (Chapter 8). Given the mixing of Formative and Late Classic deposits, the project could not associate the stone tools and faunal remains to specific periods. Another major limitation was the failure to produce a refined ceramic chronology, resulting in synchronic depictions of societies at ILC (though an alternative strategy is presented in Chapter 9). Finally, some of the pottery types defined by the project have not had their period affiliations confirmed (Chapter 6). Some of these problems could yet be solved through absolute dating of a considerable number of ceramic, faunal, and stone materials.

CHAPTER THREE

Environment and Political Ecology

This chapter begins with a description of the general environmental context for ILC including climate, hydrology and geomorphology, flora, and fauna. An important aspect of ILC is the mutual influence between environmental factors and the prehispanic features. Contemporary political ecology—how political economy structures the use of the dynamic environment—is also described, as these are related to the varied philosophies, uses, preservation, and impacts on the archaeological features while also providing examples on how resources are exploited.

THE ENVIRONMENTAL SETTING

Sisson (1976:1-4) describes the Chontalpa region as both a tropical hell and a Garden of Eden: a hell for the sweltering heat, humidity, and biting insects and a paradise for its bounty. Swamps abound throughout the coastal plain, and one academic journal on the region is aptly entitled *Tierra y agua* ("Land and Water"). These factors have produced rich and productive ecosystems.

Climate

The climate of the coastal plain of Tabasco is classified as tropical lowland monsoon. After a relatively dry season from mid-March to May (with temperatures around or above 30° C and ca. 35 to 90 mm mean precipitation per month), the Comalcalco-Paraíso region experiences the first of two peaks in precipitation. The summer peak (ca. 214 mm per month) usually begins in June. It is characterized by thunderstorms, fiercest in August, that intensify inland. Most of the summer is hot with daytime temperatures reaching over 40°C, interrupted by the

cooling storms. The long winter season, from September to January, brings far more precipitation (ca. 200 to 400 mm per month). "*Nortes*," south-moving cold air masses that create fronts, are responsible for the lengthy storms and their associated high levels of precipitation and high wind velocities. The nortes cause fluctuations in temperatures, but the means remain in the upper 20s. This is the season when the Tabasco coastal plains are commonly flooded and when ILC and the margins surrounding the entire Mecoacán Lagoon are inundated by up to a meter of water (West, Psuty, and Thom 1961:5–17).

Hydrology and Geomorphology

Traveling north from the savanna-covered Pleistocene terraces along the Tabasco-Chiapas border, one enters a vast lower, more recent sedimentary floodplain that has occasional Pleistocene terrace remnants. Closer to the coast, the remnants disappear and are replaced by a broad flat landscape. No rock is present on these floodplains. Two major deltaic regions characterize the lower fluvial expanse: the Usumacinta delta in eastern Tabasco and the Mezcalapa delta to the west where the Mecoacán Lagoon is situated (Figure 1.1). Up to 70 percent of these deltas are prone to flooding (West, Psuty, and Thom 1969:37). Where the Mezcalapa River enters the fluvial plain it meanders and has created natural levees (5–6 m high and up to 2 km wide). These decrease in size toward the coast as the river passes through lower marshland zones (West, Psuty, and Thom 1969:42). Several distributaries radiate out from the Mezcalapa seaward. Closer to the Gulf, the river channels become braided from high sediment loads, creating low, shifting islands. The Grijalva River forms another delta between the Mezcalapa and Usumacinta systems (Figure 1.1).

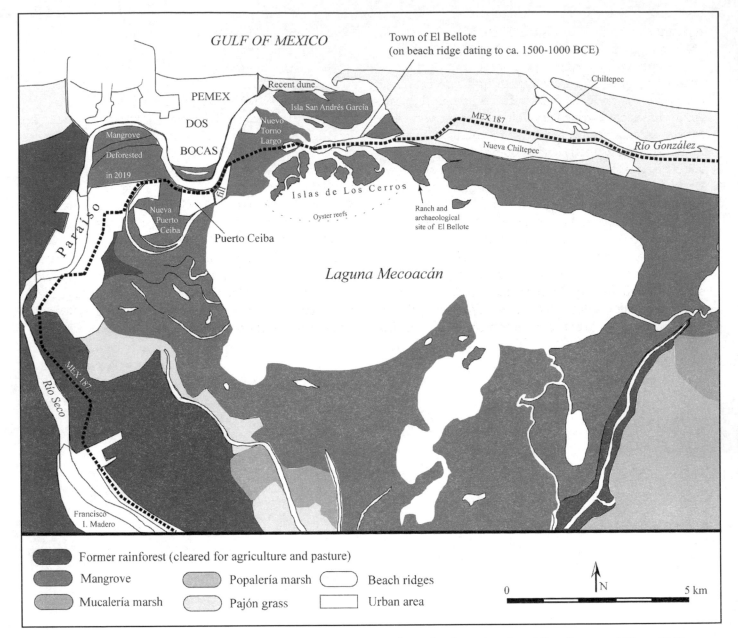

GULF OF MEXICO

Town of El Bellote
(on beach ridge dating to ca. 1500-1000 BCE)

Chiltepec

Recent dune

PEMEX

Isla San Andrés García

MEX 187

DOS

Nuevo
Torno
Largo

Nueva Chiltepec

Río González

BOCAS

Mangrove

Deforested

in 2019

Islas de Los Cerros

Oyster reefs

Ranch and
archaeological
site of El Bellote

Nueva
Puerto
Ceiba

Puerto Ceiba

Laguna Mecoacán

Paraíso

MEX 187

Río Seco

Francisco
I. Madero

Former rainforest (cleared for agriculture and pasture)

Mangrove   Popalería marsh   Beach ridges

Mucalería marsh   Pajón grass   Urban area

0   N   5 km

Figure 3.1. Map of the Lower Seco River and Mecoacán Lagoon. Redrawn by the author from West, Psuty, and Thom 1969: Figure 30.

The Seco River was the main channel of the Mezcalapa River until it was diverted in the seventeenth century and was the transportation artery linking Comalcalco and ILC. It is now an inactive distributary. Comalcalco, Paraíso, and other towns in the area are located on the low levee of the Seco River. To the north and west of Paraíso, the river is braided, with a very narrow levee on its south side until its main channel encircles the large island of San Andres García, at the mouth of the Mecoacán Lagoon (Figure 3.1).

Sediments are carried to the Gulf of Mexico where coastal processes create dunes and beach ridges (West, Psuty, and Thom 1969:47). Although more permanent beach formations are present west and east of the Seco River's channel, sandy formations at the mouth are constantly shifting. The mouth of the river is, in fact, named Dos Bocas. Over the course of the PAILC, the characteristics of the mouth have changed dramatically. West and colleagues (1969: Figure 21) show a single mouth north of the center of Isla San Andres García. In 2001, there was one wide mouth on the west and a smaller mouth on the east. By 2006, only the western mouth was present, but it was much narrower, as if closing. The shifting sediment entirely blocked the eastern mouth. The uninhabited north side of Isla San Andrés García had more dunes than previously, and the east end of the island appeared to be expanding. In recent years, the western mouth was blocked by a substantial dune deposit stretching all the way across the retreating northern side of Isla San Andrés García, and the only mouth was on the east. Meanwhile, the inhabited southern side of the island appeared stable.

The beach ridges on the seaward sides are the youngest, developing normally through progradation (Tamura 2012). The ridges paralleling them further inland are older and higher as a result of aeolian processes. Psuty (1967) concluded that the ridges along the Tabasco coast generally have low seaward slopes, steeper gradients forming berm crests in the center, and broad, gently sloping landward sides. The nortes are an important force in beach ridge formation. They cut into the seaward sides of the ridges and deposit that material over the crests and landward sides through washover. Thus, the ridges are retreating landward and increasing in height as new dunes form along the coast. As they migrate inland, they can expose buried mangrove stumps and clay organic deposits while creating new niches for the spread of mangrove vegetation between the shoreline and the retreating ridge (Psuty 1967:38–41).

Two beach ridges are currently present near the mouth of the lagoon (Figure 3.1). One is the low younger shifting formation along the shoreline at the Seco River's mouth. The older, and much larger one (up to 4 m in height), is on the south bend of the river. It frames the north side of the lagoon and is the location for most houses in the area—the modern town of El Bellote. The highway also runs along the crest and a bridge built in the 1970s crosses the mouth of the lagoon. The mouth of the lagoon cuts through the ridge to join the braided channels of the river that encircle Isla San Andrés García. Broad zones of mangrove have formed on the lagoon side of the older beach ridge and between the that ridge and the shoreline beach.

The Mecoacán Lagoon is classified as an elongated barrier lagoon. It was created when the older beach ridge on the north side of the project area dammed the area (West, Psuty, and Thom 1969:24–27). The lagoon is approximately 51 km² with an east-west orientation (ca. 12 by 4 km) and its depth averages 2.0 m (West, Psuty, and Thom 1969:Table 2). The areal extent and depth varies with the seasons.

The ILC environment developed during the Early Formative period and stabilized by the Middle Formative period. A portion of the world's longest beach ridge sequences—that of the Grijalva-Usumacinta deltas, which began forming ca. 2500 years ago—lies only a few kilometers east of the project area (Muñoz-Salinas and others 2017; Nooren and others 2017). The beach-ridge dune that frames the north side of the Mecoacán Lagoon is part of a zone of dunes to the east that date between ca. 1800 BCE and 150 CE (Nooren and others 2017). It most likely developed closer to the earlier bracket, around 1500 to 1000 BCE, placing the incipient formation of the lagoon within that time-frame. The mangrove forests found on the islands, the south edge of the barrier dune, and along the margins of the river north of the barrier dune are relatively stable and can respond to sedimentation, progradation, and gradual sea-level rise. Modern infrastructure and settlement can, however, create "coastal squeeze," which exacerbates sea-level rise (Osland and others 2018). Most likely, and despite sea-level rise, there was marine regression due to sedimentation until the seventeenth-century diversion of the Mezcalapa, which also suggests stability in the mangrove formations around ILC. Since the diversion of the river, we could expect subsidence (for which there are no data), transgression, and coastline retreat to have caused mangrove migration over time if it were not for the coastal beach protecting the zone of mangrove between it and the lagoon's barrier dune. The dune protected the mangrove to its south, though that beach was probably wider than its eroding condition today.

Flora

The Tabasco plain has extensive mangrove formations, which predominately surround coastal lagoons and inland sides of beach ridges (West, Psuty, and Thom 1969:69). At the Mecoacán Lagoon (Figure 3.1), red mangrove (*Rhizophora mangle*) and black mangrove (*Avicennia nitida*) are the most common species. Black mangrove is found in wide bands around the west, north, and northeast sides of the lagoon and on the islands as well as on the El Bellote peninsula. On the beach ridge framing the north side of the lagoon was a semideciduous forest, where grasses, native palms, and various trees (including bellote [*Sterculia apetala*]) were located. That forest has been replaced by housing, coconut palms, and the highway. The beach ridges to the west and east of the lagoon also had semideciduous forest, which has largely been replaced by extensive zones of coconut palms, cacao trees, other tree crops, settlement, and commercial development. Mixed mangrove formations are on the south side of the lagoon, while black mangrove dominates along the inland side of the

Figure 3.2. The ILC environment: (A) island edge, (B) northern Isla Santa Rosita in dry season, (C) interior of Isla Dos Bocas, and (D) interior of Isla Chablé. Photos by the author.

northern margins of the lagoon. To the southeast of the lagoon are vast marshes (*popolerías*) dominated by tall broad-leafed *quentó* (arrowroot, *Thalia geniculata*). There were vast stretches of rain forest along the Seco River's levees between the lagoon and Comalcalco, but most of the forest has been cleared for ranching and settlement (West, Psuty, and Thom 1969:Figure 25B).

On the western islands that form ILC, black mangrove forms a broad shoreline ring around the islands that blocks breezes. The inundated interiors are exposed to sunlight creating a sauna effect. These interiors have low, succulent and salt-tolerant *Batis maritima* ("saltwort" or "turtleweed"; Figure 3.2). The central island, Isla Santa Rosita, ranges from open, sunlit spaces with saltwort bisected by mangrove forest to areas of continuous black mangrove forest. The interior of the eastern island, Isla Chablé (Figure 3.2D), seems a world apart from those to the west. This largest island is covered in dense, tall, black

mangrove forest that provides. shade but less visibility and more difficult foot travel around the prop roots that rise from the inundated sediments. On the east, the peninsula of El Bellote has a protected band of black mangrove along its western shoreline, a patch of red mangrove on the northwest side of the archaeological site, and dense black mangrove (similar to the interior of Isla Chablé) on the eastern third of the peninsula.

Fauna

The area is rich in fauna. West and others (1969:79–88) describe seven major faunal areas for Tabasco, three of which are at ILC: the freshwater marsh association, the lagoon association, and the mangrove swamp association. Added to this are the marine fauna of the adjacent Gulf. The freshwater marsh association pertains to the Seco River and nearby marshes. The lagoon association characterizes the waters surrounding ILC. The mangrove swamp association characterizes the edges of the Mecoacán Lagoon, the islands, and the El Bellote peninsula.

The freshwater association includes a variety of mojarras (Cichlidae), a variety of catfish (Pimelodidae), small topminnows (Poeciliidae), mullets (Mugilidae), the famous Tabascan *pejelagarto* (*Atractoseus* sp.), slender gars (*Lepisosteus* sp.), snapping turtles (Chelydridae), the mud turtle or *pochitoque* (*Kinosternon leucostomum*), water snakes (*Nerodia* sp.), a great variety of frogs and salamanders, native fulvous whistling ducks (*Dendrocygna bicolor*) and Muscovy ducks (*Cairina moschata*), migratory ducks (*Anas, Aythya, Mareca,* and *Oxyura* spp.), geese (*Chen* spp.), coots (*Fulica* spp.), pelicans (Pelecanidae), herons and egrets (Ardeidae), roseate spoonbill (*Ajaia ajaja*), and a variety of mammals (e.g., otter, rice rat, and agouti) (West, Psuty, and Thom 1969:84–85). Species once common to the freshwater association but nearly or completely hunted out by the last quarter of the twentieth century include manatee (*Trichechus manatus*), Morelet's crocodile (*Crocodylus moreletii*), and spectacled caiman (*Caiman sclerops*). White-tailed deer (*Odocoileus virginianus*) are claimed to have occasionally wandered into these ecosystems.

The lagoon association that surrounds ILC is home to an abundance of fishes and shellfishes thanks to the converging fluctuations in fresh, marine, and brackish waters. Commonly exploited fish include mullet (*Mugil cephalus*), a variety of snapper (*Lutjanus* spp.), robalo (*Centropomus* spp.), sea mojarras (Gerreidae), tarpon (*Megalops atlanticus*), and pompano (*Trachinotus* spp.). The abundant oysters (*Crassostrea virginica*) that form the oyster reefs, or *ostionales*, are the most apparent resource to the visitor. Southern quahog (*Mercenaria campechiensis*) and at least two types of whelks (*Busycon* sp.) are also plentiful. The oyster beds are found around the mouth of the lagoon, on either side of the tidal channel, between some islands, between the islands and the north side of the lagoon, along the west shore of the El Bellote peninsula, and in an extensive zone on the south side of the islands. Older local informants claim that the oyster beds were once so extensive that one could walk across portions of the lagoon on them. Although rarely spotted today, marine turtles (*Eretmochelys imbricata* and *Chelonia mydas*) were once plentiful, feeding on lagoon grasses. The crew came across the remains of one poached sea turtle in 2005. Manatee are no longer present in the lagoon. Small rays are frequently observed, though sharks are absent. The Tabascan lagoons function as nurseries for marine shrimp, which are captured in the current between the north side

of the lagoon and the eastern, larger islands (West, Psuty, and Thom 1969:86–87, Figure 30).

The mangrove association, by contrast, appears far less diverse in fauna. Nevertheless, it is a habitat for crustaceans and mollusks, a crucial filter for water quality, and a critical nursery for many fish species (Osland and others 2018). The most important of these for humans are the land crab (*Cardisoma guanhumi*) and the fiddler crab (*Uca mordax*). Root and tree crabs (*Goniopsis cruentata* and *Aratus pisonii*) are abundant. As one walks through the mangrove interiors of the islands, thousands of tiny crabs scamper away, giving the illusion of a vibrating surface. Oysters (*Crassostrea virginica*), the hooked mussel (*Brachidontes recurvus*) and the acorn barnacle (*Balanus* sp.) attach themselves to the mangrove prop roots. The underlying mangrove sediments are home to a variety of small clams. Herons, pelicans, and other waterfowl flourish. Insects are abundant. West and colleagues' summary of the sounds is apt: "the mangrove swamp is characterized by its extreme silence, broken only by the occasional hum of insects and the click of closing clam shells in the soft mud" (West, Psuty, and Thom 1969:85).

ECOLOGICAL SYNERGY

The ILC environment is best viewed as a synergistic convergence of geomorphological, hydrological, floral, faunal, and archaeological features. The rich flora and fauna of the area are conditioned by the hydrology that produced the interactions of the floodplain, lagoon, and braided river with the coastline. The beach ridge supports the semideciduous forest and protects the northern side of the lagoon with its mangrove islands and associated biota. That protected area within the resulting ecosystem attracted prehispanic settlement as early as the Middle Formative and still does today. In addition to creating the freshwater association and semideciduous forest along its levee, the Seco River was an important avenue of transportation between ILC and the Upper Mezcalapa region.

The prehispanic features built by the ancient occupants affected the environment. For example, wherever mounds are close to the shorelines, they provide a buffer against erosion of interior sediments that support mangrove forest. Indeed, along the southern shoreline of Isla Chablé, the large platform supporting the mounds of the South Group, a long narrow platform extending east and west from there, and a long deposit of crushed shell on the southeast corner of the island are preventing the erosion of the island's sediments and mangrove. Without them, the island would retreat northward, providing less mangrove habitat in the lagoon. Where erosion has broken through these lower features, or where there were no features, the shoreline pushes inward or forms miniature bays. Although at the same time eroded by waves, the southernmost mounds at El Bellote are essentially preserving the southern tip of the peninsula, which would retreat without those features. In this way, the islands and the features have a synergetic relationship, which in turn influences the floral and faunal regimes.

The distribution of flora is influenced by ancient and modern human activities. Wherever mounds or platforms are present, so too are grasses and trees that create miniature habitats for the semideciduous forest, except where these have been cleared and replaced with tree crops. Because those tree crops are used by people, the features are preserved. The historical ranch of El Bellote has seen a century and a half of tree cropping over the extensive mounds and platforms at the site. Wherever boat landings are found, mangrove has been removed to provide access to the shoreline. The few residences on the islands also have cleared small areas of shoreline mangrove. These locations are also where one finds evidence of shoreline erosion. From the sizes and shapes of the islands to the floral and faunal associations, ILC is an ancient, yet ongoing product of the interactions among varied natural processes, the archaeological features, and modern agents.

POLITICAL ECOLOGY

"Political ecology" is a concept defined by Eric Wolf (1972) to describe how cultural political economies mediate human interaction with natural environments. Whereas other ecological perspectives focus on how humans use or are influenced by environmental resources, political ecology contextualizes social conditions and vulnerabilities among variably situated actors within the political economies that shape how humans interact with their environment (e.g., Campbell 1996; Ensor, Ensor, and De Vries 2003; M. Ensor 2009; Oliver-Smith and Hoffman 1999). For example, colonial and post-colonial global capitalism favors forest clear-cutting and displacement of peasant farms for large commercial plantations that grow cash crops using low-wage labor for profits in international markets. Although widely recognized as environmentally and socially harmful, international political economy structures the motives for such land use. Because peasant farming is pushed into more marginal lands like hillsides, the political economy promotes mudslides and other types of erosion. Other peasant farmers often cannot compete in markets that import subsidized grains from developed nations, so they convert farm plots to other uses or abandon farming altogether. Aquatic resources, like those at the Mecocán Lagoon, are equally influenced by political economic forces. The communities in and around ILC rely on the lagoon's resources but there are a variety of ways in which those resources are exploited and preserved. Profit-driven commercial uses of the area have different environmental impacts than the majority of the local family-based or cooperative-based practices. The various agents also differ in ideologies regarding conservation. Furthermore, the competing ways in which the environment is used influences cultural resource preservation, that is, the conditions of the archaeological features at ILC. This section focuses on the ways different actors with divergent motives use the resources at ILC and how those customs and strategies differentially impact the environment and the prehispanic features. As an archaeologist, I did not conduct an ethnography but assembled the following from interactions and observations in the local community over decades.

Settlement

The modern town of El Bellote (not to be confused with the ranch and archaeological site of El Bellote on the peninsula) stretches along the beach ridge, which is the only well-drained elevated landform protected from inundations (Figure 3.1). Having only two narrow lanes with speed bumps in this location, Highway 187 follows the crest of the beach ridge through the town (crossing the bridge over the channel between the lagoon and the Seco River). On both edges of the road are houses, the few restaurants for travelers, and fishing cooperatives' landings, docks, and packing facilities.

Traditional circular houses had wood planks for walls and tall conical thatch roofing to cool interiors. Although wood-plank houses are still common, today they are rectangular and roofed with slanting corrugated fiberglass covered in tar. These types of houses are found on the gently sloping lagoon side adjacent to the mangrove or the lagoon edge. Most of the houses along the roadsides are concrete-block, with flat concrete roofs, which, although considered more modern and longer-lasting than wood, have less ventilation and hotter interiors. Only one house in the community has more than one floor. It was owned by a family with a ranch and other businesses outside the local community. Patri-neolocality—immediate postmarital residence with the husband's father until a couple can establish a neolocal home nearby (Sandstrom

Figure 3.3. Coconut ranch on South Group of Isla Chablé. Photo by the author.

Figure 3.4. A recently built house platform. Photo by the author.

2000)—is the residential norm in the area. With crowding from increased settlement on the beach ridge, however, there are now few gaps remaining for new housing without filling what remains of low-lying, inundated locations. The demands for housing space, the rising costs of living, and the low wages available to many make neolocality difficult, extending the durations of patrilocality.

Private landownership is now the norm. A collective ejido, which included the islands and surrounding waters, was disbanded after the revisions to Article 27 of the Mexican Constitution under the Salinas Gortari administration in the 1990s. Plots on the islands are now owned by individuals or families. Two large insular areas are privately owned. One encompasses the majority of Isla Santa Rosita. It was owned by what was once a large matrilocal family. It

has now become an ambi-lineal descent group as numerous granddaughters and grandsons are also remaining after marriage, residing in a hamlet at the north end of the island. The other includes the southern two-thirds of Isla Chablé where a private coconut ranch is owned by a resident of the beach ridge (Figure 3.3). Smaller plots on the islands have been acquired by individuals. These have a variety of uses today, new homes and beekeeping among them. In most cases, these recent uses involve constructing new platforms with fill to raise the homes or work areas above inundation levels (Figure 3.4). East of the islands is the Rancho El Bellote, which contains the archaeological site of El Bellote (Figure 3.2). It was a family-owned hacienda before the Mexican Revolution and has since been a private commercial ranch.

Figure 3.5. Saint's day procession. Photo by the author.

The highway enables efficient transport of commodities to and from the community and there are private automobiles and public transports of various kinds including collective taxis, buses, and most recently taxi-vans and motorcycle-powered rickshaws that replaced the bicycle versions. Nevertheless, much of the population still travels frequently by water. For those living at Isla San Andrés García and on the islands within the lagoon, boat travel is the only option. For this reason, most houses on the islands are located by the shores. Residences not along the shores usually have canals leading to them through the mangrove for launches and canoes.

Although neoliberal privatization has increased residence and other uses of the islands, this is by no means new. Residences were present on the islands in the past and the survey documented the occasional decades-old,

abandoned house location. What appears to be taking place today is a shift to island settlement by a few new families and an intensification in commercial exploitation of insular areas.

Subsistence

The lagoon is essential to most of the community's livelihoods, which influences ideology. Community events, even religious processions on saints' days that involve flotillas of decorated fishing launches accompanied by music and singing illustrate a traditional religious connection and collective identity with the lagoon (Figure 3.5). Geographical cognition is shaped by waters, not by landforms. Shorelines are the edge of the water (not the edge of the land) and locations and directional references use channels or currents, not peninsulas or islands as used in this book.

Even the islands are unnamed and those used herein are merely references to distinguishing characteristics that may vary among local respondents and change over time, rather than formal, static place names.

As in the past, the modern community exploits a wide range of aquatic resources at ILC and the surrounding areas. Fishing and shell fishing are the principle economic activities. Each morning just before sunrise, fortified with *pozol,* men leave town in pairs or larger groups on motor-powered launches heading to the Gulf waters for net fishing. They return in the afternoons to clean and ice their catch, sell it fresh to merchants arriving in trucks, and tend to their nets. During the fishing day, women are usually the only adults present in the households, as domestic chores dominate their gender roles. Children are away at school, and young women and men commute daily or weekly for school or jobs in cities. In the afternoons, women often shuck oysters and process the fish for family consumption or for sale along the highway. Women and children also operate small roadside seafood stands. Closer to the bridge that crosses the mouth of the lagoon, children commonly peddle bags of shucked oysters, clams, and occasionally crabs to automobile travelers, especially on weekends. Men who do not fish can be found working in the restaurants or commuting for wages elsewhere. Increasingly, young men and women are leaving the community for work and educational opportunities.

Exploitation of the lagoon resources is said to be restricted to members of cooperatives or those with private property. Young and elderly men bring small launches and canoes, occasionally traditional dugouts, into the lagoon primarily to harvest oysters and other shellfish but also to fish with small hand-thrown nets. Another fishing strategy is to place mangrove branches in shallows. The mangrove leaves attract fish, which congregate and are easily captured by raising the nets around the surrounding poles. Shrimping also takes place in the lagoon as well as in Gulf waters. One method is to stretch nets among poles placed at intervals across a channel.

Marín-Mézquita and others (1997) estimated that an average of 10,000 tons of oysters per year were harvested in the Mecoacán, Carmen, and Machona lagoons. At ILC, there are two ways that oysters are collected (Figure 3.6). The most common method today is to submerge oneself in the water wearing a diver's mask. After hand-removing the oysters, they are inspected and placed in a floating basket—usually a plastic produce carton with soda bottles or styrofoam tied to their edges as floats. The oysters are then transferred to the canoe or small launch (Figure 3.6A). The older method, less often seen but apparently favored by older men, involves the use of two rake-like devices. The person stands in the canoe, holds the two rakes so that they cross at the middle forming an "X." After pushing down onto the oyster reefs the tops of the poles are pulled together, which enables the bottom rakes to grasp a cluster of oysters that are pulled up and dumped into the canoe (Figure 3.6B). I once witnessed an elderly man fill a dugout canoe in less than half an hour using this technique.

Most of the fishing is done by members of cooperatives. With the disbanding of the local ejido, cooperatives took over as the major collectivized source of incomes. Because the fishing launches cost the equivalent of an automobile and because most families have modest incomes, the cooperatives have been important institutions for obtaining not only rights to fishing but also access to boats, gasoline, and other equipment. The cooperatives also market their catches to distributors. The demand for fish and shellfish in nonlocal markets, as well as the growth of the local restaurant industry, has seen an increase in the exploitation of the lagoon and adjacent waters. As a result, some cooperatives have invested in additional resources. The most notable are the former ejido's cement posts seen rising out of the water between Isla Chablé and El Bellote. These rows of cement posts, spaced at 2- to 3-m intervals, protect and encourage the growth of the oyster populations (Figure 3.6C). Newer nurseries are fashioned with wooden posts with cross-beams from which fishing lines are tied (Figure 3.6D). The oysters are then pulled up by the fish lines on which a cluster is attached, allowing their growth to be monitored until they are harvested (Figure 3.6E). Most of the cooperatives' fish, shellfish, and shrimp are sold to the commercial buyers who distribute them regionally and internationally. There are also several restaurants of varying sizes that either purchase locally or are operated by the cooperatives using their own fish and seafood. At the larger restaurants, most of the workers are men. Along the road, some cooperatives also have small tables or bins with fish and shellfish for sale to passersby; these may also be set up by other community members. The locations of the cooperatives along the beach ridge and highway also seem to promote residential clustering of members.

Tree-cropping is another important economic activity. Apart from the beach ridge and highway where the population is concentrated, practically all locations with sediment elevated above the inundated mangrove mud are used for productive trees. Of course, the only formations

Figure 3.6. Oyster harvesting techniques: (A) by hand, (B) with rakes, (C) an older cement-post nursery, (D) a newer wood-built nursery, and (E) oyster clumps from the wood-built nursery. Photos by the author.

that are elevated above the mangrove floor are the prehispanic platforms and mounds, which makes those features' preservation important for subsistence today. The most common tree crop in the area is coconut, while more cacao is grown farther inland. Although not all mounds and platforms have coconut palms, the presence of those trees indicates the presence of those features. The entire site of El Bellote is densely covered by coconut, cacao, and other tree crops. The extensive platform and overlying mounds in the South Group of Isla Chablé are similarly covered in coconut palms (Figure 3.3). On a smaller scale, and in addition to coconut and the rare cacao tree, some families use mounds and platforms for domestically consumed crops such as plantains, mamey, guayaba, papaya, and hibiscus.

Farther inland, cattle historically and today are a major livestock industry, but none are kept in the modern community. The mangroves are not conducive to livestock, save for backyard fowl (chickens, turkeys, and ducks) and a few pigs located in households on the beach ridge. The only exception are the goats kept at the privately owned El Bellote ranch, the only location with dry land from archaeological deposits broad enough to support them.

Over the past decades, consumption and production has increasingly been market-oriented. Imported regional commodities are limited but trips to regional markets are frequently necessary for anything not produced locally. Two family-owned stores were operating on opposite sides of the highway in 2001. One has since closed. The other remains as the only local source for purchasing fruit, vegetables, canned goods, and dry-goods. Purified water is sold at the store, but it is more commonly purchased from the delivery trucks that pass daily. The community has always been well connected with Puerto Ceiba and

Paraíso, the former accessible by boat but more often today by bus, taxi, or automobile. Families with automobiles frequently shop and bank in Paraíso and even Comalcalco. With recent improvements to Tabasco's highways, some wealthier families with automobiles make regular trips as far as Villahermosa for bulk shopping at large national and multinational retailers. As in the rest of Mexico, wireless communication is omnipresent.

Commercial Development

The large PEMEX (Petróleos Méxicanos) petroleum port and refining plant at Dos Bocas is currently the largest commercial industry in the area (Figure 3.1). However, few people from the community work at Dos Bocas. At least one of the facility's two tall flame booms seems always lit, producing a roaring sound that can be heard from the coast to the mouth of the lagoon. At night, these light up the sky in the entire surrounding area. Most of the employees have family origins in the state of Veracruz, where there is a longer history of oil production (the Tabasco oil boom began as recently as the 1960s). Many live in a sprawling PEMEX colony on the northeast side of Paraíso and in other exponentially growing neighborhoods. Many of these families now have three generations living in the area. Very few migrants reside in the town of El Bellote. Some local informants argue that Dos Bocas is a source of contamination of local waters. Others argue this is the fault of local boat operators with leaky motors, as well as those who used to dump oil cans in the lagoon. To explain the 1990s oyster population reductions in the Mecoacán Lagoon, Marín-Mézquita and others (1997) identified trace metals in oysters and sediments related to petroleum (but much less than along US coasts), salinity declines caused by Dos Bocas, sedimentation from river mismanagement, and violations of seasonal harvesting regulations.

Since 2004, a new commercial port facility was constructed adjacent to the PEMEX port of Dos Bocas. Associated with that expansion, a significant amount of highway construction has taken place between Villahermosa and Puerto Ceiba. Travel time from Villahermosa to ILC in the early 1990s took nearly three hours by automobile and more than four hours by bus with two connections. Now that trip only takes an hour and a half. Meanwhile, the population has expanded exponentially between Paraíso and Puerto Ceiba. Areas that once were long stretches of coconut and cacao, broken by semideciduous forest or mangrove, have now been taken over by expansive residential areas interspersed with small stores and large

retailers. The first hotel east of Paraíso was constructed by 2011 between Puerto Ceiba and El Bellote. One concern about rapid commercial development was an increase in the cost of utilities.

The most dramatic development has been a new rapid expansion of PEMEX refining facilities and administrative buildings at Dos Bocas in the past two years between Paraíso and Puerto Ceiba, west of the lagoon. Associated with that construction, a vast area of mangrove north of Paraiso and northwest of Puerto Ceiba has been destroyed. Those losses gained international attention (de Haldevang and Wolfe 2020) and are likely to impact the whole area's ecosystems and fishing and shellfishing livelihoods.

The demographic growth extending from Paraíso, the improved highway, and the growth in commercial industries associated with Dos Bocas has also increased the numbers of day visitors to the lagoon. Although weekend tourists from Villahermosa are by no means new to the area, they seem to have increased since the 1990s and early 2000s. The scenery is one attraction. The waterside restaurants owned and operated by the local cooperatives are another. Some come to fish on weekends using sport rods, at times placing themselves on small platforms that connect the supports of the bridge that crosses the mouth of the lagoon. To get there, they typically hire a local launch operator. Several of the cooperatives' restaurants also own small tour boats—fishing launches outfitted with padded seating, a shade canopy, and life preservers. The restaurants closest to the bridge are the largest and appear to have the greatest number of customers, as these are the first ones encountered when traveling east from Paraíso. As of 2011, tourism had not yet posed environmental impacts. How its future growth will impact resources, including the archaeological sites, remains to be seen.

While the petroleum industry, new port facilities, highway improvements, and population growth to the west of the lagoon have indirectly influenced the cost of living and the development of a light tourism industry in the community, globalization has also made its mark in another way. By 2004, a limited number of young men were being recruited for work as crab harvesters in the United States. According to some local informants, more leave each year for seasonal harvests there, which is discussed with excitement but also trepidation given the political climate they face there. Nevertheless, their remittances may mitigate some of the rising costs of living (felt throughout Mexico). This trend may reverse, however. Anti-immigrant measures in the United States have dramatically reduced

H-2B guestworker visas, causing a shortage of experienced women crab pickers from Mexico, threatening the US crab industry, and presumably impacting migrant harvesters from Tabasco (Dance 2018; National Public Radio 2018).

OLD AND NEW IMPACTS TO ARCHAEOLOGICAL RESOURCES

In my experience with the community at ILC, people have always expressed concerns over the quality of the local environment. Although few trash dumps are present on some of the islands, no new ones have been observed since the inception of the project. Trash floating in the lagoon is common, especially after storms, yet is scorned. Most view the cutting of mangrove as bad for the maintenance of the ecosystem they so greatly depended upon.

In contrast to this environmental consciousness, there seems to be little concern for the archaeological features for heritage-based purposes. Instead, the mounds and platforms are *resources* and their preservation has more to do with traditional uses of those features for houses and for tree crops and even gardens. Occasional pits are noted here and there. Most are not looter's pits, but rather small mines for sediment. In fact, sediment mining appears to be the primary threat to the mounds and platforms apart from shoreline erosion. Despite the need for sediment for fill at homes—one resource lacking on the islands that would otherwise need to be purchased—the scale of sediment mining is fortunately limited in most cases.

Commercial uses of the area have caused the greatest damage to the environment and archaeological resources. Most of the severe damage to features on the islands and at El Bellote is associated with sediment or lime mining in mounds. According to some community members, the mostly destroyed largest mound at the South Group of Isla Chablé was mined for the lime in its shell deposits several decades ago. Also, several elders said the extensive disturbance to the temple mounds at the site of El Bellote was due to excavating fill for the construction of the highway in the 1970s. Although scoured around its sides, one mound there was saved from further mining when the local occupants objected to its destruction. The mound had a supernatural rooster dwelling inside it, which is occasionally heard, and its destruction would have released evil upon the community. The severe disturbance to mounds at the site of El Bellote is obviously several decades old, and despite being a commercial ranch dedicated to tree crops, far less disturbance can be attributed to the ranch's commercial activities.

The most severe case of recent sediment mining in mounds is at the South Group of Isla Chablé. Since 2001, that privately owned location has seen the construction of a warehouse and dock to facilitate coconut harvesting on the mounds and other features on the south half of the island. The sediment needed for this construction was taken primarily from one mound. These activities resulted in the disappearance of at least one half of that large, multilevel mound and disturbance to the bases of at least two additional mounds. The same ranch also clearcut a large area of mangrove on the adjacent interior of the island between 2004 and 2005, which exhibits signs of subsidence and retreat.

The northwest side of the lagoon has seen significant manipulation. The mangrove on the northwest shoreline was entirely replaced by an immense platform for a private park with miniature replicas of prehispanic and historic monuments. Local people claim the filling blocked the path of seasonal crab migrations. Nearby, an area of mangrove was clearcut and sediments were manipulated into a waffle pattern of ponds. The new hotel is on the opposite side of the highway, which required filling of another large area of mangrove. Any archaeological features that may have been in these areas obviously would have been destroyed.

Old looter's pits are present in some of the mounds. I was told stories of treasure-hunters coming to the area, although looting seems to be minimal compared to many other sites in the region and elsewhere in Mesoamerica. As will be seen, most of the residential features at ILC appear impoverished compared to many Mesoamerican sites. There is simply little "treasure" in the form of figurines, whole painted vessels, burials, or other items to be found at ILC. This lack of valuable objects may be the reason for so little looting activity at the site complex.

In casual discussions with community members, the notion that the preservation of the sites could bring tourism to the area is certainly present. Both positive and negative attitudes for this prospect have been expressed. My impression is that archaeologically based tourism and development seemed distant compared to the more immediate uses of the mounds and platforms as resources for tree crops and the occasional house sites, which has thus far led to their preservation.

Other major impacts to features are indirectly related to human activity and are less intentional. The most common is associated with the few sections of protective mangrove that have disappeared at landings on the south shoreline of Isla Chablé, at the South Group, and on the west shoreline of El Bellote. In those locations, where platforms and mounds are exposed to the stronger waves of the lagoon (the north side of the islands see less wave action) significant portions of those features have been eroded. Two mounds at the southern end of El Bellote, for instance, have been reduced by approximately one third to one half their original size. This is entirely due to the loss of mangrove in that location. Immediately adjacent mounds, protected by only a thin zone of mangrove, by contrast, have experienced practically no similar erosion from wave action.

Still other impacts appear to be purely natural in origin. For instance, sediment from the upper portions of nearly all earthen mounds can be found eroding down the sides of the mounds, but gently and slowly over centuries rather than rapidly and severely. Around the base of each earthen mound where eroding sediments accumulate, the slope is much less steep. These processes are the result of precipitation and seasonal inundation of the islands.

In sum, different agents have impacted the archaeological features in varied ways. Most in the community maintain a concern for the preservation of the environmental resources and use the waters for fishing and shell fishing along with use of the mounds for tree cropping. These activities have minor impacts on the mounds, which are essentially an agricultural resource. Clearing of mangrove is usually limited to small areas for landings near homes. Individuals as well as the local cooperatives are also concerned with the preservation of mangrove, which ensures natural nurseries. Mangrove preservation is also critical to the preservation of the archaeological features. Where it is absent, mounds and platforms are eaten away by erosion. Tourism, due to its current small scale, has had no significant impact on the environment or the archaeological features. In contrast, more severe impacts to the environmental and cultural resources are activities at the larger, privately owned areas in the northwest side of the lagoon, in the south half of Isla Chablé, and at El Bellote.

The archaeological data collected by the PAILC is influenced by these different impacts. Given the destruction of the mangrove on the northwest edge of the lagoon, any features there were destroyed, which may influence the interpretations of settlement patterns and social organization. In other areas, the large-scale mining for sediments, and the severe shoreline erosion from mangrove removal, has severely impacted features. At the same time, the PAILC project made use of vertical cuts from mining and erosion to document stratigraphy and make artifact collections. These impacts are ongoing, however, and for some features documentation by this project may be all that remains.

CHAPTER FOUR

The Sites

This chapter describes the defined archaeological sites at ILC. The content is based on the 2001 survey data from the islands (Ensor 2002b, 2003b) and the 2007 season at El Bellote (Ensor and Tun Ayora 2011; Ensor, Tun Ayora, and Herrera Escobar 2008). The first section describes the previous site records, which documented fewer features at each location. Different projects had conflicting descriptions, requiring redefinition using the PAILC data. In the second section, the survey methods are described, along with the feature classification developed by the PAILC. After the 2001 documentation of features (the first complete record of these features on the islands), consultation with the Registro Publico de Monumentos y Zonas Arqueológicos of INAH led to the decision to treat each island with features as a site. Eight sites were defined: Isla Boca Grande, Isla del Campo, Isla Santa Rosita, Isla Dos Bocas Nuevas, La Islita, Isla Chablé, El Canal, and El Bellote. These are presented in a sequence from west to east. For each, there is a description of the island, features and their spatial relationships, their interpreted functions, observations from artifact collections, and notes on disturbance. The feature categories are analyzed in Chapter 5. Although summary references to artifacts are made here, the collections are described and analyzed in chapters 6 and 7, and their distributions are presented in chapters 8 and 9.

PREVIOUS SITE RECORDS

As described in Chapter 2, Charnay (1888:183–193), Berlin (1953b, 1954), and Stirling (1957) previously visited El Bellote, providing brief text descriptions of temple mounds. No maps were produced. West, Psuty, and Thom (1969) documented and plotted mounds on the islands and surrounding areas using aerial photos but most lacked field verification and dense mangrove and tree crops obscured many features. Sisson's (1976) visit relied on air photos accompanied with some visual inspection of features along shorelines.

INAH's Registro Público de Monumentos y Zonas Arqueológicas had records for six sites at ILC (Figure 4.1). I could not find information on which project documented those sites, although it is assumed the data were collected as part of the Atlas project. Some of this information appears to have been used by Fernández Tejedo and colleagues (1988). Those site locations were along shorelines, suggesting field reconnaissance by boat. In some cases, however, the number of mounds listed suggested that the recorder(s) did disembark and saw more than shoreline features. Only the location of each site was indicated but no site plans showing feature distributions were available.

The site of El Bellote had two site numbers (E 15A-79-27-041 and E 15A-79-27-076). The first record (E 15A-79-27-041) indicated 15 mounds having heights from 2 to 5 m. The site size was recorded as being only 1.00 hectare. The West, Psuty, and Thom (1969: Figure 30) map showed a larger area with more features. Sisson (1976:677), who visited in 1968, stated that the "site has been almost completely destroyed for road construction material since Berlin worked there in 1953." In my own very brief visit in 1993, it was apparent that El Bellote was not completely destroyed and was larger and had more mounds than were recorded in all prior descriptions. However, no mounds over 5 m in height, as described by Charnay (1888:183–193), Berlin (1953b, 1954), and Stirling (1957), were recorded in the archival data. Despite the previous attention to El Bellote, each source differed in the size and number of mounds, underestimating both, and no map had yet been produced.

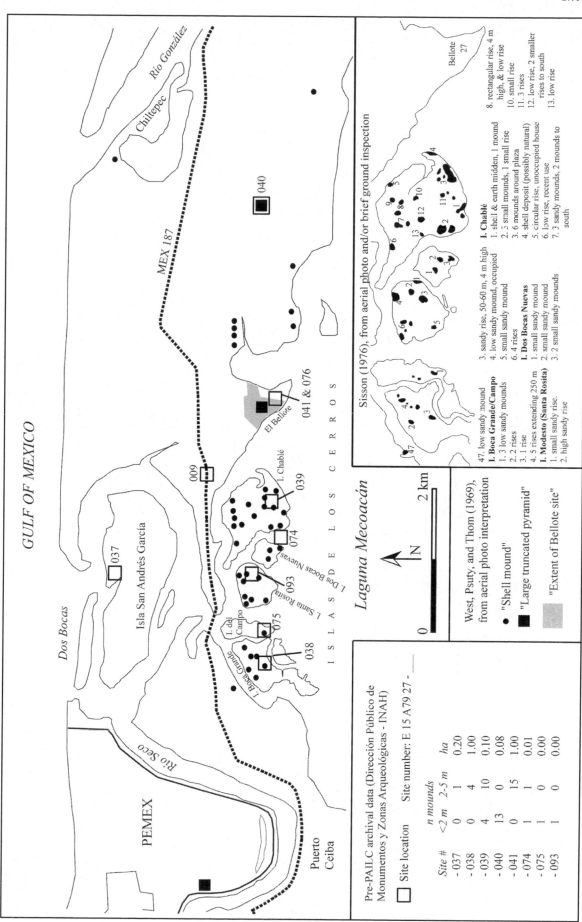

Figure 4.1. Maps of previously recorded sites at and adjacent to ILC. The larger map is based on aerial photo interpretation, the smaller inset from aerial photo and/or brief ground inspection. Redrawn by the author from West, Psuty, and Thom 1969: Figure 30; inset map based on Sisson 1976: 645, 677, 682–691, 814, 775–779.

The INAH registry recorded Isla Chablé as E 15A-79-27-039. The record only refers to one location, now identified as the South Group of Isla Chablé. The record listed four mounds less than 2 m in height and 10 mounds between 2 and 5 m in height. In this case, the number of mounds recorded exceed the number now known to be at the South Group, suggesting that surrounding mounds on the interior were probably included. However, the site size was recorded as only 0.10 hectare, which is excessively small. Given the shell deposits with Formative period pottery in this location, the site was characterized as comprising Formative period *concheros* (shell middens) and was used as an example to make generalizations about coastal occupations (Fernández Tejedo and others 1988:51). Meanwhile, the West, Psuty, and Thom (1969: Figure 30) map indicated that there were 15 mounds distributed throughout the island, rather than being restricted to the south side. Sisson (1976:683) recorded more features: 14 mounds, 11 "rises," one midden, and one shell deposit. What is now known as the South Group was stated to have six mounds surrounding a plaza, which was not mentioned by other sources. Thus, the number of mounds and their distribution was unclear from these three sources of information.

The INAH registry also indicated one site (E 15A-79-27-074) having a mound less than 2 m in height and one mound between 2 and 5 m in height located in the channel between Isla Chablé and Isla Dos Bocas Nuevas. These records begged the question of where exactly the site was located. That site might pertain to three mounds at Isla Dos Bocas Nuevas indicated on the map by West, Psuty, and Thom (1969: Figure 30), which Sisson (1976:688–690) recorded as four mounds.

The fourth site in the INAH registry was located at the northeast portion of Isla Santa Rosita (E 15A-79-27-093). According to that record the site consisted of one mound less than 2 m in height. In contrast, the West, Psuty, and Thom (1969: Figure 30) map identified eight mounds across the island, concentrated in the north. Sisson's map (1976:645) shows nine "rises" and mounds across the island, with a concentration in the northeast. As with the other site records, the area, number of mounds, and spatial distribution of features was unclear given these discrepancies. In my brief, preliminary visit in 2000, I observed 13 features on just the north end of the island, indicating that the aerial photos could not be relied upon to identify all features, even in open areas with high visibility.

On the south end of Isla del Campo, the INAH archives registered another site that was comprised of only one mound less than 2 m in height (E 15A-79-27-075). This matched the only mound identified on that island by West, Psuty, and Thom (1969: Figure 30). Sisson (1976:645) identified one mound in the area described for site E 15A-79-27-075, but also identified two mounds to the north of that site, another discrepancy.

The sixth site in the INAH registry was assigned to four mounds between 2 and 5 m in height at the south end of Isla Boca Grande (E 15A-79-27-038). The site was described as being 1.00 hectare in size. The West, Psuty, and Thom(1969: Figure 30) map indicated six mounds distributed throughout the island (a much larger area). Sisson (1976:645) recorded eight "rises" distributed throughout much of the island that were, instead, concentrated in the north. Again, the discrepancies created an unclear picture of the site size, number of features, and their distributions.

What became clear from comparing the INAH registry with the maps made by West and coworkers (1969) and Sisson (1976), is that there is a potentially extensive zone of prehispanic features at ILC. Due to the discrepancies between the three sources, however, the project could not rely on those data. In addition, the visit in 2000 revealed that the aerial photos did not show all of the features. There was an obvious need for a systematic pedestrian survey of the islands to more accurately identify and document features and to replace the previous site records. The 2001 survey provided the information used by the Registro Publico de Monumentos y Zonas Arqueológicos of INAH for the current site definitions, whereby each island with features was designated as a site. Rather than producing new site numbers, which could cause further confusion, I was given the previous site numbers. The site names are based on local references to the islands at the time and those indicated on maps of the Instituto Nacional de Estadística Geografía e Informática.

SURVEY AND FEATURE CLASSIFICATION

Although described in Chapter 2, a review of the survey methods is warranted before proceeding to the site descriptions. Each island was traversed in parallel transects, spaced at 20-m intervals, to search for elevated features and artifact concentrations. No artifacts were observed away from the elevated features. A Silva brand compass, accurate to 1 degree, was used for navigation and plotting feature locations on maps. Distances were recorded by pacing. A register was made that included the feature number, island, form, size, height, and condition. Feature heights were estimated using the compass' level feature. Each feature was photographed. Surface collections in sampling units of 10- by 10-m were made at 68 features. It was not possible to make collections at some features due to dense grass. Feature numbers were assigned in the sequence by which they were identified. The 2007 field mapping at El Bellote provided the locational and distributional data for features at that site.

After the 2001 survey, the sizes, morphologies, and construction material data were used to classify features. Most were constructed with sediments lacking shell. Though Sisson (1976) recorded "sandy" mounds and rises, earthen deposits were clays and silts. Some features included shell deposits (but not exclusively shell). Six morphological categories were created: platform, mound, mound-on-platform, multilevel mound (small superior mounds on top of larger inferior mounds), multilevel mound-on-platform, and possible mound or platform (severely eroded) (Figure 4.2.). The ceremonial mound category was added after the 2007 season at El Bellote.

Feature numbering assumed a construction sequence for multilevel formations. Different feature numbers were assigned to the apparent platforms and mounds overlying them. Likewise, different numbers were assigned to inferior mounds and superior mounds. The rationale for distinguishing these as separate features was guided by the assumption that they represented a sequence of features built upon earlier larger features (see Chapter 5). With few exceptions, most of the mounds and platforms were interpreted as residential features. Their morphologies conformed with the shapes and sizes of residential features in the Gulf Coast, Maya regions, and Chontalpa (Hall 1994; Piña Chan and Navarrete 1967; Sanders 1962; Santillán 1986; Stark 1991; Tourtellot 1988). This interpretation was also supported by surface collections that yielded enough pottery to observe the diverse functions characteristic of domestic trash, as opposed to specialized use locations with a low diversity in artifact functions (Chapter 5).

ISLA BOCA GRANDE (E 15A-79-27-038)

Isla Boca Grande is the westernmost island at ILC; it has an approximate total area of 10.5 hectares. The island has an outer ring of black mangrove surrounding an interior with few stands of mangrove amidst broad open areas with low-growing saltwort. The surface seems always inundated with at least a few cm of standing water. Most features at Isla Boca Grande were situated in the open areas, or at the interior edge of the island-bordering mangrove (Figure 4.3). Grasses covered each mound and platform; some

had dense wild trees and foliage. When the lagoon water is low, Isla Boca Grande joins a smaller island to the south and the passage between it and a second small island on the southeast disappears. No features were identified on these adjacent smaller islands.

The site comprised 16 features: one platform, six mounds, two mound-on-platform formations, two mounds sharing the same platform, and two low features that are either mounds or platforms (Figure 4.3; Table 4.1). The platforms are elliptical or crescent-shaped and have a mean length of 47.5 m. All are approximately 0.5 m in height. The mounds are circular or oval in shape, with a mean length of 23.5 m and mean height of 0.9 m. The three mounds overlying platforms are also circular or oval, with mean lengths of 15 m and an average height of 0.7 m. All features have morphologies expected for residences elsewhere in the Gulf Lowlands (see Chapter 5).

There is one cluster of features (the Northeast Group); the rest are dispersed. The Northeast Group includes a mound-on-platform (features 7 and 12), a second mound-on-platform (features 10 and 124), two small mounds (features 8 and 9), a relatively large platform (Feature 13), and a small possible platform (Feature 14). Compared to the feature groups at Isla Chablé and El Bellote, the Northeast Group of Isla Boca Grande is less compact—having wider spaces among the features—and unlike those at Isla Chablé and El Bellote, these features lack a large group, basal platform. The Northeast group has a linear distribution, possibly indicating features located along a canal that disappeared long ago. Similar interpretations have been given for alignments of features across mangrove islands elsewhere (Stark 1989) and are present at ILC today, though not the large-scale canals found east of Laguna de Términos (Ochoa 2003). The remaining features—two mounds on one platform (features 1, 2, and 11), four mounds (features 3, 4, 5, and 6), and a possible mound (Feature 15)—are scattered across the site. No shell deposits were identified. All of the features are earthen constructions.

In general, the features had low to moderate densities of surface artifacts. Both Formative and Late Classic pottery types were recovered in the surface collection units. The overwhelming majority are Late Classic types. Feature 5 had a higher density of surface artifacts, which included the only pieces of chert found on the islands, along with a shell that may have been engraved. This was the only possible evidence for domestic craft manufacturing found at ILC. A small fragment of poor-quality plaster was found at Feature 1, indicating the presence of a structure. An unmodified piece of pumice was found at Feature 3.

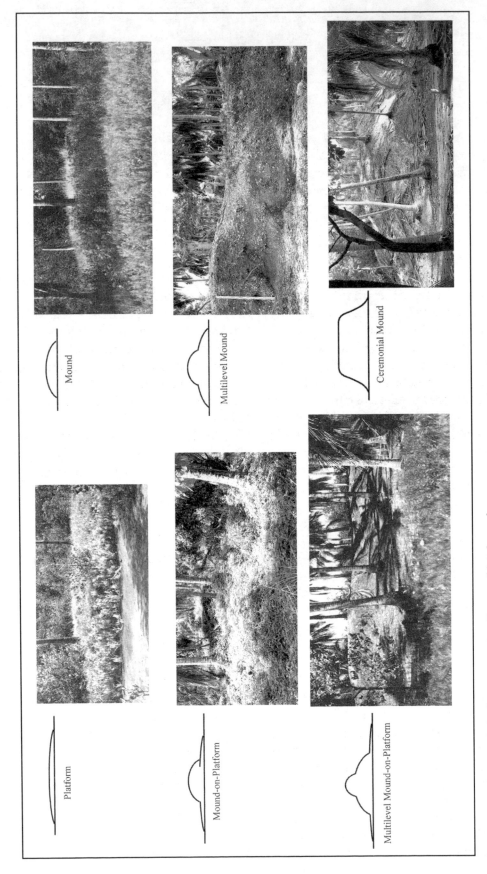

Figure 4.2. Mound and platform categories. Prepared by the author.

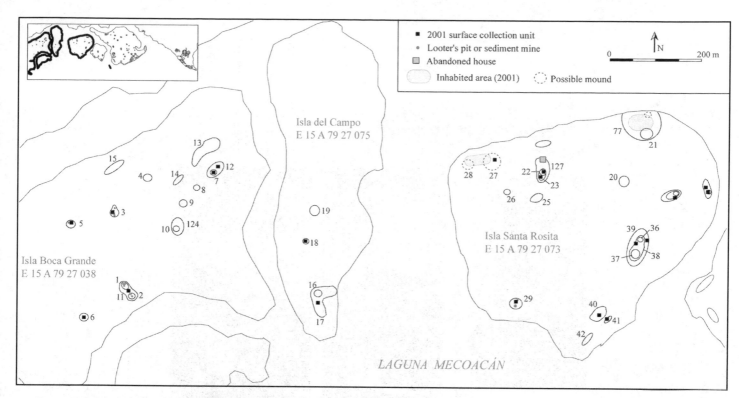

Figure 4.3. Map of Isla Boca Grande, Isla del Campo, and Isla Santa Rosita. Prepared by the author.

Table 4.1. Summary of Residential Earthen Features at Isla Boca Grande, Isla del Campo, and Isla Santa Rosita

Site	Feature Number	Function	Type	Sub-Type	Fill	Shape	Size (m)	Height (m)
Isla Boca Grande (E 15A-79-27-038)	13	Residential	Platform	—	Earthen	Crescent	70 x 25	0.50
	15	Residential	Platform	—	Earthen	Elliptical	70 x 22	0.50
	3	Residential	Mound	—	Earthen	Oval	40 x 20	2.00
	4	Residential	Mound	—	Earthen	Circular	20	1.00
	5	Residential	Mound	—	Earthen	Circular	27	1.00
	6	Residential	Mound	—	Earthen	Circular	25	0.50
	8	Residential	Mound	—	Earthen	Circular	17	0.50
	9	Residential	Mound	—	Earthen	Circular	20	0.50
	14	—	Probable mound		Earthen	Elliptical	20 x 18	1.00
	11	Residential	Mounds-on-platform	Platform	Earthen	Elliptical	50 x 25	0.50
	1	—	—	Mound	Earthen	Oval	20 x 18	1.00
	2	—	—	Mound	Earthen	Circular	15	0.50
	12	Residential	Mound-on-platform	Platform	Earthen	Elliptical	45 x 32	0.50
	7	—	—	Mound	Earthen	Circular	15	0.75
	124	Residential	Mound-on-platform	Platform	Earthen	Elliptical	25 x 15	0.50
	10	—	—	Mound	Earthen	Circular	10	0.50

continued

Table 4.1. (continued)

Site	*Feature Number*	*Function*	*Type*	*Sub-Type*	*Fill*	*Shape*	*Size (m)*	*Height (m)*
Isla del Campo (E 15A-79-27-075)	18	Residential	Mound	—	Earthen	Circular	15	0.50
	19	Residential	Mound	—	Earthen	Elliptical	20 x 18	0.50
	17	Residential	Mound-on-platform	Platform	Earthen	"L"	115 x 20	1.00
	16	—	—	Mound	Earthen	Circular	15	0.75
Isla Santa Rosita (E 15 A-79-27-073)	24	Residential	Platform	—	Earthen	Elliptical	30 x 18	0.25
	40	Residential	Platform	—	Earthen	Oval	45 x 23	0.60
	41	Residential	Platform	—	Earthen	Elliptical	16 x 17	0.25
	42	Residential	Platform	—	Earthen	Elliptical	40 x 10	0.25
	25	Residential	Mound	—	Earthen	Oval	30 x 20	2.00
	26	Residential	Mound	—	Earthen	Circular	15	0.50
	29	Residential	Mound	—	Earthen	Circular	30	2.00
	27	—	Possible mound	—	Earthen	?	?	0.50
	28	—	Possible mound	—	Earthen	?	?	0.50
	31	Residential	Mound-on-platform	Platform	Earthen	Elliptical	45 x 20	0.25
	30	—	—	Mound	Earthen	Circular	10	1.00
	77	Residential	Mound-on-platform	Platform	Earthen	Circular	90	1.00
	21	Residential	—	Mound	Earthen	Circular	30	1.50
	38	Residential	—	Mound	Earthen	Circular	10	0.50
	127	—	—	Platform	Earthen	Irregular	65 x 40	0.25
	23	Residential	Multilevel mound-on-platform	Inferior mound	Earthen	Elliptical	30 x 20	1.00
	22	—	—	Superior mound	Earthen	Circular	20	0.50
	35	—	—	Platform	Earthen	Oval	45 x 37	0.75
	34	Residential	Multilevel mound-on-platform	Inferior mound	Earthen	Oval	35 x 20	1.50
	32	—	—	Superior mound	Earthen	Circular	20	0.50
	39	—	—	Platform	Earthen	Elliptical	85 x 45	0.50
	38	—	—	Inferior mound	Earthen	Pinched elliptical	60 x 35	1.00
	36	Residential	Multilevel mound-on-platform	Superior mound	Earthen	Circular	10	0.50
	37	—	—	Superior mound	Earthen	Circular	25	0.75

Multiple small pits or sediment mines intruded into features 1 and 3. Features 2 and 5 each had one small pit. Otherwise, the features are well preserved. An old trash dump is present on the south side of the island, which has not seen additional dumping since 2001. The site appears to be less visited by people compared to others.

ISLA DEL CAMPO (E 15A-79-27-075)

Isla del Campo is the next island east. Like Isla Boca Grande, it has an outer ring of black mangrove surrounding an interior with low-growing saltwort interspersed with few small stands of mangrove. The surface is usually inundated with at least a few cm of standing water. The site area, restricted to the south half of the island, is approximately 2.1 hectares. The features are in the open areas at the interior edge of the mangrove (Figure 4.3). Grasses cover each mound and platform, and the largest had a stand of wild trees and bushes.

The features include two small mounds (features 18 and 19) and an L-shaped platform with a superior mound (features 17 and 16, respectively; Table 4.1). None are in close proximity to one another. All are earthen constructions that match the morphologies of residential features (Chapter 5). L-shaped platforms that form monumental and smaller residential features like the one on Isla del Campo have been found near Comalcalco (Romero Rivera 1995:21) and as far west as Central Veracruz (Stark 1999) but only one other occurs at ILC (at Isla Dos Bocas Nuevas). The two mounds are circular and elliptical in shape, have lengths of 15 and 20 m, and are 0.5 m in height. The L-shaped platform is 115 m in length and varies from 0.5 to 1.0 m in height. The circular superior mound is 15 m in diameter and 0.75 m tall.

According to a local informant, the island's informal name is derived from the northern end, which is a few cm higher in elevation, and less inundated in the dry season, where soccer games took place in the past. Sisson (1976:645) observed two mounds in that location and an informant claimed that a mound there had been removed. No features or artifacts were observed in that location by this project.

Very few artifacts were observed due to the dense grass cover on the features. Only three sherds were present in the collection unit on the L-shaped platform and only one sherd was collected from Feature 19. All of these are Late Classic types. No other artifacts were observed or collected, except for one unmodified piece of pumice at Feature 18.

All of the features identified were in good condition, save for natural erosional processes. The east arm of the L-shaped platform extended to the shoreline where the protective boundary of black mangrove is absent. There, the roots of a large tree were occasionally used for seating by rare tour groups viewing the lagoon.

ISLA SANTA ROSITA (E15 A-79-27-073)

Isla Santa Rosita is approximately 23 hectares in size. Dense black mangrove forest covers most of the island, but large portions of the southeast and north sides have less mangrove where the dominant vegetation is saltwort. The island surface is usually inundated with a few cm of water. The hamlet housing a large extended family is on the north side of the island, where surrounding areas are clear of mangrove. Most of the mounds throughout the island were cleared of wild trees and grass and are used for a variety of tree crops. The southernmost mounds and platforms, which are farthest from the modern settlement, are covered in dense grass.

Twenty-four features were identified by this project (Figure 4.3; Table 4.1). These included seven mounds (features 20, 25, 26, 27, 28, 29, and 40), three platforms (features 24, 41, and 42), and five multilevel features. Most of the platforms are elliptical in shape but vary considerably in size. The average platform length is 57.1 m and the average height is 0.5 m. The mounds are circular and oval, have an average length of 30 m and an average height of 1.3 m. At two multilevel mound-on-platform formations, the inferior mounds are elliptical, have lengths of 35 and 60 m, and an average height of 1.25 m. The superior mounds on those and on mound-on-platforms, are circular, with a mean diameter of 19.3 m and height of 0.8 m.

At the northwest corner of the island are two possible mounds (features 27 and 28). Both are severely eroded and flattened. West, Psuty, and Thom (1969:Figure 30) show three mounds in that location and Sisson (1976:779) describes four "rises." In 2001, the location had a small modern settlement with three pole-and-thatch structures, which was abandoned by 2004 but re-occupied by 2018. Proceeding east on the north half of the island is a cluster of features including two mounds (features 25 and 26), one crab hole-ridden low platform (Feature 24), and a multilevel mound (features 22 and 23) overlying a platform (Feature 127). An abandoned cement-block house and modern trash deposit is on the north end of platform Feature 127.

The modern hamlet occupies a large prehispanic earthen platform (Feature 77) with at least two mounds on its surface (Features 21 and 38). Due to the growing number of structures on that platform, however, the original shapes of these mounds could not be discerned. There may have been a third small mound at one time. The earthen platform was circular in 2001 but shells were being deposited around its edges, extending its size and altering its shape over time.

South of Feature 77 is a mound (Feature 20) and two multilevel formations. One is a multilevel mound over a platform (features 32, 34, and 35) where block excavations were conducted in the 2005 season (Chapter 5). A short trench from sediment mining was cut into the east end of the inferior mound and the platform. Otherwise, this formation was in good condition and was being used for tree crops. Along the east shoreline is a mound-on-platform (Features 30 and 31), which is severely eroded due to a loss of protective mangrove.

The largest feature is in the central-east portion of the island. This is comprised of one small and one larger superior mound (features 36 and 37) overlying a 60-m-long inferior mound (Feature 38), which in turn overlays an 85-m-long platform (Feature 39). Though Sisson (1976:687) estimated a 4 m height, the multilevel formation reached an estimated height of 2.25 m. Despite its size, the morphology and artifact collections suggest a residential function. As the home to Africanized bees after the 2001 season, it was not further investigated.

A small concentration of features was found at the southern tip of the island including platform features 40 and 41 (later found to have been one feature bisected by erosion) and Feature 42 (a severely eroded possible platform). Feature 40 is the only earthen residential feature on the islands where vertebrate faunal specimens were encountered. A test unit was excavated in Feature 40 in the 2004 season (Chapter 5).

Feature 29 is the only feature identified in the southwestern quarter of the island. This is a tall mound (2.0 m in height) with dense wild trees covering its steep sides. Two deep looter's pits had dislocated fragments of thin delicate plaster with crushed shell temper and a polished surface, suggesting a floor or wall surface.

The dense, tall grass on some of the southern features prevented surface collections. On other features, there were low densities of surface artifacts. In several, less than 10 sherds were recovered. The majority of the pottery was Late Classic, though several units also yielded low numbers of Formative pottery. There was one exception to this pattern: 62 percent of the pottery from the collection unit at Feature 23 was Formative.

ISLA DOS BOCAS NUEVAS (E15 A-79-27-074)

Isla Dos Bocas Nuevas lies between Isla Santa Rosita and Isla Chablé (Figure 4.4). Most of the island is covered in dense, tall, black mangrove. There is one large open space with low saltwort in the southwest corner of the island, framed by several features and a shoreline band of black mangrove. The site area, covering the southern half of the island, is approximately 3.75 hectares. Dense grass covered most of the features and native trees covered three multilevel formations. Coconut palms grew on most features. The island is usually inundated with at least a few cm of water.

Eleven features were identified (Figure 4.4, Table 4.2). In the southwest corner, forming an arc along the interior edge of the mangrove bordering the island, are four platforms (features 45, 46, 52, and 53). These are elliptical and rectangular in shape and have mean lengths of 41.3 m. Widths range considerably (from 10 to 40 m) due to the erosion of features 52 and 53. All are approximately 0.5 m in height. At the opposite edge of the open area is one mound-on-platform (features 43 and 44). At the southeast corner of the island is a mound over a 0.25 m-high, 80 m-long "L"-shaped platform (features 47 and 48). Close by is a multilevel mound-on-platform (features 49–51). The circular and elliptical superior mounds, overlying the inferior mound and the L-shaped platform, average 25 m in length or diameter and 1.25 m in height.

In general, the features are widely scattered across the south half of the island. The arc of platforms and features 43 and 44 bound an extensive open space, which tempts the observer to perceive a plaza. These features are very widely spaced, however, unlike other residential groups at ILC.

The dense grass on most of the features limited the surface visibility, resulting in low numbers of artifacts collected. Most units yielded more than 6 sherds, but the maximum was only 11. Nearly all features had Late Classic pottery. Two features (44 and 46) each had one Formative period sherd as well. No other artifact categories were observed.

The only major disturbance to the features appears natural. The island has a healthy mangrove edge that prevents erosion but two of the platforms (features 52 and 53) have severe erosion on their sides and surfaces. The platforms closest to the edge of the island also have abundant crab holes.

ISLA CHABLÉ (E15 A-79-27-039)

Isla Chablé is the largest site at ILC, both in area and number of features. The site covers approximately 64 hectares. Nearly the entire island is covered by black mangrove forest. The only exceptions are small, open, saltwort-covered spots (less than 0.5 hectare, each) on the north end of the island and one in the southwest portion of the island.

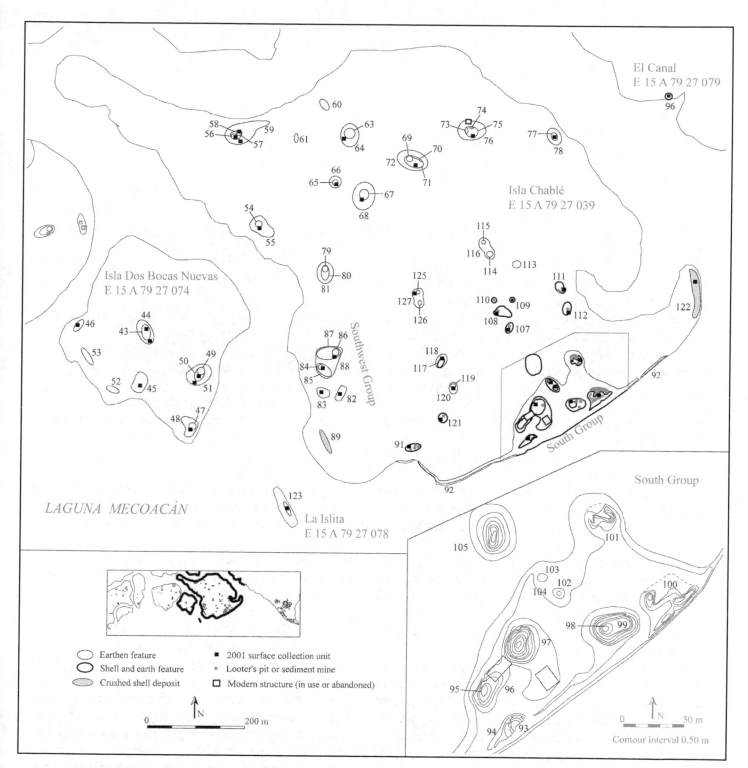

Figure 4.4. Map of Isla Dos Bocas Nuevas, Isla Chablé, La Islita, and El Canal. Prepared by the author.

Table 4.2. Summary of Features at Isla Dos Bocas Nuevas and Isla Chablé

Site	Feature Number	Function	Type	Sub-Type	Fill	Shape	Size (m)	Height (m)
Isla Dos Bocas Nuevas (E15 A-79-27-074)	45	Residential	Platform	—	Earthen	Rectangular	40 x 30	0.50
	46	Residential	Platform	—	Earthen	Elliptical	28 x 12	0.5
	52	Residential	Platform	—	Earthen	Elliptical	35 x 10	0.50
	53	Residential	Platform	—	Earthen	Elliptical	45 x 10	0.50
	44	Residential	Mound-on-platform	Platform	Earthen	Elliptical	55 x 40	0.50
	43	—	—	Mound	Earthen	Elliptical	35 x 25	2.00
	48	Residential	Mound-on-platform	Platform	Earthen	"L"	80 x 30	0.25
	47	—	—	Mound	Earthen	Circular	20	1.25
	51	Residential	Multilevel mound-on-platform	Platform	Earthen	Oval	55 x 40	0.50
	50	—	—	Inferior mound	Earthen	Elliptical	35 x 22	1.50
	49	—	—	Superior mound	Earthen	Circular	20	0.50
Isla Chablé (E15 A-79-27-039): Southwest Group	82	Residential	Platform	—	Earthen	Rectangular	40 x 18	0.5
	83	Residential	Platform	—	Earthen	Oval	30 x 25	0.50
	85	Residential	Multilevel mound	Inferior mound	Earthen	Elliptical	35 x 20	0.25
	84	—	—	Superior mound	Earthen	Circular	12	0.50
	88	Residential	Multilevel mound-on-platform	Platform	Earthen	Oval	65 x 35	0.25
	87	—	—	Inferior mound	Earthen	Oval	55 x 35	3.00
	86	—	—	Superior mound	Earthen	Elliptical	20 x 18	0.75
Isla Chablé South Group	97	Residential	Mound	—	Shell & earth	Oval	35 x 30	4.00
	101	Residential	Mound	—	Shell & earth	?	32 x 28	2.00
	105	Residential	Mound	—	Shell & earth	Elliptical	45 x 35	3.00
	94	Residential	Multilevel mound	Inferior mound	Shell & earth	Oval	45 x 20	1.00
	93	—	—	Superior mound	Shell & earth	Elliptical	20 x 18	1.00
	96	Residential	Multilevel Mound	Inferior mound	Shell & earth	Oval	40 x 30	1.50
	95	—	—	Superior mound	Shell & earth	Oval	25 x 20	0.75
	99	Residential	Multilevel Mound	Inferior mound	Shell & earth	Oval	45 x 30	2.25
	98	—	—	Superior mound	Shell & earth	Circular	20	0.50
	104	Residential?	Mound-on-Platform	Platform	Earthen	Elliptical	30 x 20	0.25
	102	—	—	Mound	Earthen	Circular	10	0.25
	103	—	—	Mound	Earthen	Circular	7	0.25
	100	Ceremonial	Disturbed Mound Base	—	Shell & earth	?	65 x 40	2.50

Table 4.2. (continued)

Site	Feature Number	Function	Type	Sub-Type	Fill	Shape	Size (m)	Height (m)
Isla Chablé: Specialized Features	89	Shell crushing	Deposit	—	Crushed shell	Elliptical	45 x 10	0.25
	92	Landing	Shoreline platform	—	Earthen	Linear	600 x 5	0.50
	122	Shell crushing	Deposit	—	Crushed shell	Curvilinear	78 x 7	0.35
Isla Chablé	60	Residential	Platform	—	Earthen	Elliptical	25 x 15	0.25
	61	Residential	Platform	—	Earthen	Elliptical	12 x 10	0.25
	91	Residential	Mound	—	Shell & earth	Elliptical	32 x 20	1.50
	107	Residential	Mound	—	Shell & earth	Elliptical	20 x 18	1.50
	108	Residential	Mound	—	Shell & earth	Irregular	30 x 25	2.00
	109	Residential	Mound	—	Shell & earth	Circular	10	0.50
	110	Residential	Mound	—	Shell & earth	Circular	10	0.50
	111	Residential	Mound	—	Shell & earth	Oval	30 x 25	2.00
	112	Residential	Mound	—	Shell & earth	Elliptical	30 x 20	1.75
	113	Residential	Mound	—	Earthen	Circular	15	0.50
	121	Residential	Mound	—	Shell & earth	Circular	20	1.50
	55	Residential	Mound-on-platform	Platform	Earthen	Oval	55 x 35	0.50
	54	—	—	Mound	Earthen	Circular	15	0.50
	64	Residential	Mound-on-platform	Platform	Earthen	Oval	60 x 55	1.00
	63	—	—	Mound	Earthen	Circular	25	1.00
	66	Residential	Mound-on-platform	Platform	Earthen	Circular	25	0.50
	65	—	—	Mound	Earthen	Circular	15	0.50
	68	Residential	Mound-on-platform	Platform	Earthen	Elliptical	60 x 50	1.00
	67	—	—	Mound	Earthen	Elliptical	25 x 20	1.50
	78	Residential	Mound-on-platform	Platform	Earthen	Elliptical	40 x 27	0.25
	77	—	—	Mound	Earthen	Elliptical	20 x 15	0.50
	116	Residential	Mound-on-platform	Platform	Earthen	Pinched elliptical	50 x 25	0.50
	114	—	—	Mound	Earthen	Circular	16	1.25
	115	—	—	Mound	Earthen	Circular	11	0.50
	118	Residential	Mound-on-platform	Platform	Earthen	Elliptical	35 x 20	0.25
	117	—	—	Mound	Earthen	Elliptical	25 x 18	1.50
	120	Residential	Mound-on-platform	Platform	Earthen	Elliptical	20 x 15	0.50
	119	—	—	Mound	Earthen	Circular	10	1.50
	127	Residential	Mound-on-platform	Platform	Earthen	Pinched elliptical	35 x 20	0.25

continued

Table 4.2. (continued)

Site	Feature Number	Function	Type	Sub-Type	Fill	Shape	Size (m)	Height (m)
Isla Chablé (continued)	125	—	—	Mound	Earthen	Circular	10	1.25
	126	—	—	Mound	Earthen	Elliptical	10 x 8	1.00
	59	Residential	Multilevel mound-on-platform	Platform	Earthen	Irregular	80 x 50	0.25
	58	—	—	Inferior mound	Earthen	Oval	25 x 22	0.25
	56	—	—	Superior mound	Earthen	Circular	10	1.00
	57	—	—	Superior mound	Earthen	Circular	10	0.75
	72	Residential	Multilevel mound-on-platform	Platform	Earthen	Elliptical	70 x 45	0.50
	71	—	—	Inferior mound	Earthen	Elliptical	45 x 28	1.00
	69	—	—	Superior mound	Earthen	Circular	20	0.50
	70	—	—	Superior mound	Earthen	Crescent	25 x 7	0.50
	76	Residential	Multilevel mound-on-platform	Platform	Earthen	Oval	60 x 55	0.50
	75	—	—	Inferior mound	Earthen	Oval	35 x 28	1.25
	73	—	—	Superior mound	Earthen	Elliptical	10 x 5	0.25
	74	—	—	Superior mound	Earthen	Elliptical	6 x 4	0.25
	81	Residential	Multilevel mound-on-platform	Platform	Earthen	Elliptical	45 x 38	0.50
	80	—	—	Inferior mound	Earthen	Elliptical	30 x 16	0.50
	79	—	—	Superior mound	Earthen	Circular	15	1.00

Most of the features had grasses, trees, coconut palms, and occasionally other tree crops growing on them. Mounds constructed of shell have little grass but dense coconut palms and shrubs. Those mounds are on the southern portion of the island.

Sixty-nine features were recorded at Isla Chablé. They include 4 residential platforms, 13 residential mounds, 7 single-mound-on-platform formations, 3 twin-mounds-on-platform formations, 3 multilevel mound formations, 5 multilevel mound formations on platforms, 1 large mound that was too damaged to define, and 3 nonresidential features (Figure 4.4, Table 4.2). Those in and around the South Group were built of both shell and earth, while the majority of the features were constructed with earthen deposits only.

Most features at Isla Chablé have the same morphologies as residential mounds and platforms elsewhere at ILC and throughout the region. Residential platforms have an average length of 26.8 m and average height of 0.4 m. Platforms supporting mounds are much larger, with a mean length of 47.9 m, but have a similar mean height of 0.5 m. Mounds are circular, elliptical, or oval in shape. Mounds have a mean length of 25.8 m and mean height of 1.8 m. Those situated on platforms are smaller: averaging 16.6 m in length and 1.0 m in height. Superior mounds overlying inferior mounds are similar in size, with a mean length of 16.1 m and height of 0.7 m. The inferior mounds supporting them are large, averaging 39.4 m in length and 1.2 m in height. Most residential features at Isla Chablé are widely dispersed in a *ranchería* settlement pattern and do not form groups. There are, however, two groups present on the south side of the island: the Southwest Group and the South Group.

The Southwest Group

The Southwest Group is a concentration of seven earthen features near the southwest corner of the island and is surrounded by dense black mangrove. The group includes two low residential platforms (features 82 and 83) separated by a small open area with saltwort. On their north side is a large platform (Feature 88) supporting two multilevel mounds. Feature 84 is a low (0.50 m high) superior mound overlying a larger inferior mound (Feature 85) that is also relatively low in height (0.25 m). On the north side of platform Feature 88 is a large multilevel mound with a 3.0 m tall inferior mound (Feature 87) on top of which is a 0.75-m tall superior mound (Feature 86). The top of Feature 86 is the highest extant point on the island; standing there, one's eye level is at the top of the mangrove forest's canopy. As elsewhere at ILC, the platforms are covered in grass and the mounds have small trees and bushes. Coconut palms grow on all of the features.

The South Group

The South Group of Isla Chablé includes 13 features, 12 of which are situated on an extensive low, earthen platform (the basal platform for the group). The linear shoreline platform (Feature 92) is comprised of shell and earth deposits only where it passes the group's basal platform. For most of its length, however, Feature 92 is formed of earthen deposits. Due to the absence of mangrove along the shoreline, the basal platform and eroded deposits in front of the South Group were heaped upward by waves, forming a dune crest. Also, in the absence of mangrove, several of the group's mounds are clearly visible from the water, even from the site of El Bellote across the channel.

The mounds of the South Group were previously thought to be Formative *concheros* or shell middens (Fernández Tejedo and others 1988:51) but the PAILC determined that they were Late Classic residential mounds (Chapter 5). Rather than being midden accumulations, they were intentionally constructed as dome-shaped mounds. At least half of the pottery collected from them is Late Classic. The 2004 profiles documented alternating deposits of shell and earth (the latter was more common) to form the mounds, with mixed Formative and Late Classic pottery in many strata. Occupation surfaces were also seen. For these reasons, it became clear through the PAILC investigations that these were not *concheros* but rather, Late Classic residential mounds built with earlier deposits. There may once have been Formative *concheros* on the island but none were identified at the site or anywhere else at ILC.

The large earthen basal platform averages 0.25 m in height (Figure 4.4). On its west half are two multilevel mound formations (features 95 and 96 and features 93 and 94) and one large mound (Feature 97). A fourth mound

may have been located where a modern cement-brick structure is located. These residential mounds—all of earth and shell—form a rectangular *plazuela*. The multilevel mound including features 93 and 94 had moderate shoreline erosion in 2001. By 2004 one-third of the formation had been removed by sediment mining. In 2005, more sediment had been taken, at which point only one half of the formation remained. This was also around the time when a new cement-block storage warehouse was constructed between the bases of features 96 and 97.

Several features surround an open space or plaza on the east half of the large basal platform. One is a multilevel mound with earth and shell fill (features 98 and 99). A low, elliptical earthen platform (Feature 104) on the north side of the basal platform supports two very small earthen mounds (features 102 and 103). Another earth and shell mound (Feature 101), severely damaged by mining activity, is at the northeast corner of the basal platform. On the south edge of the basal platform is Feature 100: the remains of a very large mound that was destroyed in decades past. In 2001, only three large irregularly shaped remnants of Feature 100 remained from the extensive mining (for lime, according to one informant). Although the large base suggests a square shape, it, too, was severely disturbed and its fill may have been redeposited from the mining activity. The base was also being cut by shoreline erosion where mangrove was absent. An elder told me the mound was once about 5 m in height. It is tentatively interpreted as a ceremonial mound due to its estimated base-size, although no brick was observed.

Another large mound (Feature 105), with little disturbance, is situated off the north side of the group's basal platform. It is considered to be part of the South Group due to its close proximity. Farther north, other shell and earth mounds are present, but these are not considered part of the South Group as they were more distant and widely dispersed.

For decades, the South Group has been the central hub of a coconut ranch that also includes the other more dispersed features and the shoreline platform in the south half of the island. All of the features, including the large basal platform, have an abundance of coconut palms and other tree crops growing on them. Older aerial photos and maps sometimes show white lines radiating north from the South Group—these were modern shell-laid paths for hauling coconuts through the inundated mangrove to the South Group. Several hectares of that mangrove-forested area were clear-cut between the summers of 2004 and 2005, precipitating erosion of that portion of the island.

Nonresidential Features

Three features found on the island are clearly nonresidential in function. Features 89 (50 × 10 m) and 122 (75 × 15 m), located at the southeast and southwest corners of the island, are 0.3-m high deposits of crushed shell. Sisson (1976:683) made note of Feature 122 but considered it to be a natural oyster bank. However, all of the shell is crushed; this does not occur naturally. Moreover, amidst the small pieces of crushed shell are small, highly eroded sherds and small bone fragments (fish and turtle). Both deposits are interpreted as processing locations for construction material (temper for mortar and plaster). Lime kilns may have been present but there was no evidence for them on the surfaces or in the 2004 excavation at Feature 122.

Feature 92 is unique. To my knowledge, no similar feature has been reported for the Mexican and Maya Gulf Coast regions. Feature 92 is a linear, earthen platform along the south shoreline of the island that appears to have been overlooked by all prior archaeologists visiting ILC. The platform is estimated to have been 600 m in length, averaged 0.3 m in height, and ranged from 2.5 to 5.0 m in width. The platform extends southwest and northeast from the South Group to the general locations of both crushed shell deposits. It was interpreted as a landing thought to have had a commerce- or fishing-related function. The dense grass on it prohibited surface collections. The 2004 excavation (Chapter 5) yielded dense faunal remains. With no indication of trade-related imports or large-scale storage vessels associated with the platform, it was interpreted as a landing for collective fishing-related activities. Although impacted by erosion in some locations, Feature 92 protects the interior of the island against erosion.

Artifacts at Isla Chablé

Like most of the earthen residential features at ILC, earthen features at Isla Chablé—the majority on the island—had high percentages of Late Classic pottery and low percentages of Formative pottery. In contrast, the fewer features constructed of shell and earth deposits had higher frequencies of Formative types (nearly half of the ceramics from those features). One Formative ceramic figurine fragment was recovered from Feature 100.

Other artifact categories appear to be associated with the features constructed of shell and earth. Faunal remains, rarely seen at residential features, were present at many of the residential mounds that included shell deposits. This does not necessarily indicate that the vertebrate remains date to the Formative; they were also present at

exclusively Late Classic contexts. Higher quality plaster floors or walls (from the Late Classic period) were more commonly associated with residential features constructed of shell and earth, though poorer quality plaster was found at some earthen residential features. The only piece of ground stone from the insular sites was recovered from Feature 97 in the South Group. Although no obsidian was recovered from any of the surface collection units at the insular sites, several were found in the 2004 profiles at the South Group. The overall impression is that the residential mounds constructed of shell and earth have a greater diversity of artifacts than the earthen residential features. These could date to either the Formative or Late Classic periods, or both.

LA ISLITA (E15 A-79-27-078)

The site of La Islita is a single 20- by 5-m, northwest-southeast oriented earthen deposit (Feature 123) in the lagoon, approximately 100 m off the southwest corner of Isla Chablé (Figure 4.4). In the dry season, the feature is about 0.25 m above the lagoon level, which is less than 0.50 m deep between it and the island. A narrow strip of black mangrove formed around the deposit. The feature experienced severe erosion and is said to be submerged in the winter. The feature was likely a mound on Isla Chablé that was separated by island erosion. Five eroded sherds were collected at Feature 123. Four are of Late Classic types. One is Formative. The small island formed by the feature is often used to secure the canoes of oyster harvesters working nearby in the lagoon.

EL CANAL (E15 A-79-27-079)

El Canal is a second single feature site, located along the north shoreline of the lagoon, opposite Isla Chablé (Figure 4.4). Feature 106 is a low circular mound (20 m in diameter and 0.50 m in height) constructed of shell and earth deposits. The mound is bounded by black mangrove on the west, north, and east, and by the shoreline on the south where the edge of the feature is eroding. Five sherds were collected: four of Late Classic types and one Formative type. A relatively wide canal (5 to 7 m in width) was cut through the mangrove on the east side of the mound, leading to the modern houses on the south side of the dune. The canal, after which the site is named, is used to transport boats between the houses and the lagoon. After 2001, large nursery ponds were created to the east of the site.

EL BELLOTE (E15 A-79-27-076)

The site of El Bellote is compact compared to the insular sites. El Bellote had 43 mounds and platforms covering approximately 16 hectares (Ensor, Tun Ayora, Herrera Escobar 2008). The distribution of features indicates five spatial groups: Northeast, North-Central, Northwest, Central, and South. All but the Northwest Group are joined by basal deposits (extensive platforms of just earth or of shell and earth on which the mound groups were constructed). Residential mounds are the most common features. Nine discrete earthen residential mounds average 28.1 m in length and 1.9 m in height. The 12 discrete residential mounds including shell average 30.8 m in length and 3.0 m in height, though they are quite variable in size. There are few discrete platforms, mounds-on-platforms and multilevel mounds. Except for Feature 100 in the South Group of Isla Chablé, El Bellote is the only site at ILC with ceremonial mounds. Among the nine ceremonial mounds at El Bellote, the six with recordable dimensions average 48.3 m in length and 3.4 m in height. There is also one large platform with an uninterpreted function. The site is surrounded by mangrove on the east, north, and northwest. The western shoreline of the peninsula has less mangrove; features there are eroding from wave action.

The Northeast Group

The Northeast Group is the largest, comprising 19 mounds (Figure 4.5, Table 4.3). This group was subdivided into three internal subgroups. Each subgroup is comprised of ceremonial and residential mounds. Subgroups A and B have mounds surrounding plazas. Subgroups A and C share the same basal deposits of earth and shell fill. Subgroup B is on a very low earthen basal platform.

Subgroup A

Subgroup A is a *plazuela* comprised of seven ceremonial and residential mounds on the west side of the Northeast Group. The subgroup is situated on a 1.0- to 1.5-m high basal deposit of shell and earth. From the southwest corner, moving clockwise, are a pair of steeply sloped residential mounds constructed of shell and earth, a pair of broader earthen residential mounds, a pair of large flat-topped shell and earth mounds with steep sloping sides, and a very large but severely damaged mound of shell and earth (Figure 4.5).

The morphologies of mound features 168, 169, 183, and 184 resemble residential mounds elsewhere at ILC. Features 168 and 169 are built of shell and earth deposits and have conical shapes, similar to residential mounds of the Southern Groups at both El Bellote and Isla Chablé. Both have eroding chunks of plaster for floors or walls. Features 183 and 184 are earthen residential mounds that appear to be deflated due to erosion. They lack evidence of plastered architecture.

Features 165, 166, and 170 are interpreted as ceremonial mounds. Feature 165 was badly disturbed several decades ago by machine removal of fill. This mound is suspected to have been the 75 foot-tall (ca. 23 m) pyramid described by Stirling (1957). It is probably the same mound where Charnay (1888:183–193) and Blom and LaFarge (1926) described the remains of a temple. A small oval mound (Feature 185) with brick and mortar fragments sits on the flat surface of Feature 166. Feature 166 had three decades-old trenches on its north side. Feature 170 has a rectangular shape and a sloping flat surface.

Subgroup B

Subgroup B is a second *plazuela* on the east side of the Northeast Group. These mounds were constructed on a lower earthen basal platform that has a surface elevation of 0.50 to 1.00 m. The identified features include six residential mounds and one ceremonial mound (Figure 4.5).

Five mounds in the *plazuela* are small to large residential mounds. Feature 187 is a small mound on the northwest corner of the plaza. Feature 191 is a second small mound on the southwest corner. Three larger mounds (features 188–190) frame the east side of the plaza. Only Feature 188 includes limited shell deposits, the other four are earthen. Feature 189 is the largest residential feature in the subgroup. Feature 190 is a smaller, more steeply sloped conical mound, half of which has been removed by sediment mining. Although located south of the *plazuela*, Feature 192 was an earthen residential mound that shares the same low basal deposits with the rest of the subgroup and is considered to be an additional residential mound in Subgroup B. Plaster chunks were observed only at two of the larger residential mounds (features 188 and 189).

The interpretation of steep sided, relatively flat-topped mounds as having ceremonial functions is supported by observations about Feature 196 (Figure 4.6). Feature 202—built of shell and earthen fill—is a square mound with rounded corners. It has steep slopes and a relatively flat top. A decades-old trench was cut from its northeast corner to its center. Although the trench walls are eroded, a ceiling and vaulted arch of a substructure (Feature 196) is visible in the southeast and southwest sidewalls. The substructure's

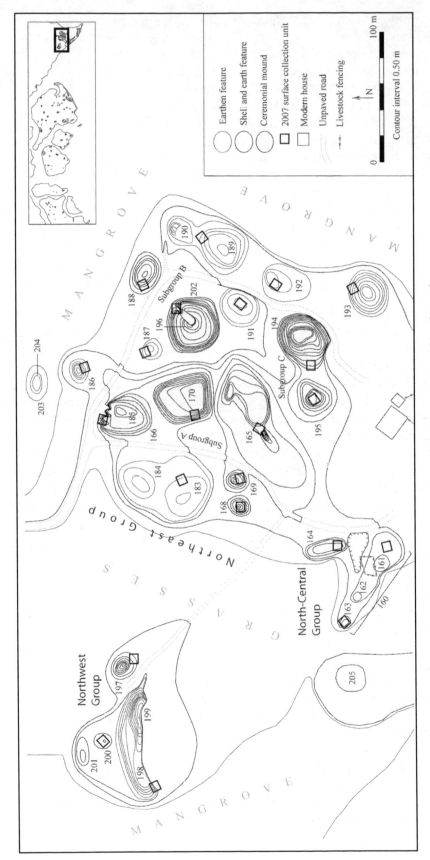

Figure 4.5. Map of the Northeast, North-Central, and Northwest groups of El Bellote. Prepared by the author.

Table 4.3. Summary of Features at El Bellote

Group	Feature Number	Function	Type	Sub-Type	Fill	Shape	Size (m)	Height (m)
Northeast	168	Residential	Mound	—	Shell & earth	Circular	19 x 17	2.70
	169	Residential	Mound	—	Shell & earth	Circular	20 x 19	2.60
	183	Residential	Mound	—	Earthen	Oval	34 x 26	0.90
	184	Residential	Mound	—	Earthen	Elliptical	27 x 20	1.00
	186	Residential	Mound	—	Earthen	Oval	18 x 15	2.40
	187	Residential	Mound	—	Earthen	Circular	15	1.40
	188	Residential	Mound	—	Shell & earth	Oval	32 x 21	2.90
	189	Residential	Mound	—	Earthen	Oval	37 x 34	2.50
	190	Residential	Mound	—	Earthen	Oval	23 x 20	2.20
	191	Residential	Mound	—	Earthen	Circular	28	1.50
	192	Residential	Mound	—	Earthen	Oval	36 x 27	1.40
	195	Residential	Mound	—	Shell & earth	Oval	33 x 29	3.10
	193	Residential	Mound	—	Earthen	Elliptical	35 x 30	3.80
	203	Residential	Mound-on-platform	—	Earthen	Elliptical	35 x 25	0.70
	204	—	—	Mound	Earthen	Elliptical	22 x 15	0.90
	165	Ceremonial	Mound	—	Shell & earth	?	97 x 42	2.60
	170	Ceremonial	Mound	—	Shell & earth	Trapezoidal	45 x 35	3.70
	194	Ceremonial	Mound	—	Shell & earth	Pentagonal	45 x 36	6.10
	166	Ceremonial	Multilevel mound	Inferior mound	Shell & earth	Oval?	41 x 34	2.80
	185	—	—	Superior mound	Shell & earth	Oval	17 x 9	1.00
	202	Ceremonial	Mound	—	Shell & earth	Square	38 x 37	3.50
North-Central	160	Residential	Multilevel mound	Inferior mound	Shell & earth	Linear	80 x 20	0.90
	161	—	—	Superior mound	Shell & earth	Oval	13 x 11	0.90
	162	—	—	Superior mound	Shell & earth	Circular	6	0.30
	163	—	—	Superior mound	Shell & earth	Oval	9 x 7	0.60
	164	Ceremonial	Mound	—	Shell & earth	Elliptical	34 x 15	1.80
Northwest	197	Residential	Mound	—	Shell & earth	Oval	21 x 17	3.30
	200	Residential	Mound	—	Shell & earth	Oval	19 x 12	1.10
	201	Residential	Mound	—	Shell & earth	Elliptical	22 x 12	1.00
	198	Ceremonial	Multilevel mound	Inferior mound	Earthen	Elliptical?	86 x 20	2.70
	199	—	—	Superior mound	Earthen	Elliptical? w/ramp	45 x 14	2.50
Central	152	Residential	Platform	—	Shell & earth	Curvilinear	50 x 11	0.80
	153	Residential	Mound	—	Shell & earth	Oval	20 x 12	0.80
	178	Residential	Mound	—	Shell & earth	Elliptical	13 x 8	1.30

continued

Table 4.3. (continued)

Group	Feature Number	Function	Type	Sub-Type	Fill	Shape	Size (m)	Height (m)
Central (continued)	177	Residential	Mound remnant?	—	Shell & earth	Curvilinear?	65 x 12	1.40
	167	Residential	Multilevel mound	Inferior mound	Shell	Rectangular?	38 x 35	0.80
	150	—	—	Superior mound	Shell	Elliptical?	8 x 4	0.30
	151	Ceremonial	Mound	—	Shell & earth	?	34 x 27	4.30
	179	—	Erosional remnant	—	Shell & earth	Oval	13 x 10	0.80
	180	—	Erosional remnant	—	Shell & earth	Oval	7 x 6	1.00
	181	—	Erosional remnant	—	Shell & earth	Oval	7 x 4	0.90
	182	—	Erosional Remnant	—	Shell & earth	Oval	8 x 4	0.80
South	154	Residential	Mound	—	Shell & earth	Oval	62 x 24	2.20
	156	Residential	Mound	—	Shell & earth	Oval?	23 x 10	3.70
	157	Residential	Mound	—	Shell & earth	Oval?	51 x 28	3.20
	175	Residential	Mound	—	Shell & earth	Elliptical	48 x 26	2.20
	173	Residential	Mound-on-platform	Platform	Shell & earth	Trapezoidal	52 x 33	0.90
	174	—	—	Mound	Shell & earth	Oval	34 x 22	2.20
	155	Collective?	Mound-on-platform	Platform	Shell & earth	Oval	70 x 40	0.80
	172	Residential	—	Mound	Shell & earth	Circular	11	0.50
	176	Fishing-related	Platform	Platform	Shell & earth	Elliptical	21 x 16	0.60
	205	Residential	Platform	—	Shell & earth	Oval	25 x 22	0.40

walls and vault are constructed of brick and mortar, with heavily plastered wall and ceiling surfaces in at least four layers (Figure 4.6). The top of Feature 196, where its brick and mortar are exposed, protrudes 1.6 m above the top surface of Feature 202. The trench may have been from sediment mining or looting. Another possibility is that this was the excavation by Berlin in the 1950s mentioned by Sisson (1976:5) and was never backfilled. The vaulted substructure is presumed to be a tomb.

Subgroup C

This subgroup is comprised of two adjacent mounds on the south side of the Northeast Group (Figure 4.5). Subgroup A and Subgroup C share the same taller basal platform constructed of shell and earthen deposits. Feature 195 is an oval residential mound constructed of earthen deposits with a limited amount of shell. Sediment mining has impacted the uppermost eastern portion. The southeast base has been affected to a lesser extent by a small livestock pen.

The dominant mound is Feature 194—the tallest extant mound in the Northeast Group. This mound has an unusual pentagonal shape with rounded corners caused by slumping (Chapter 5). The mound summit is relatively flat. Fill deposits are primarily densely packed shell, which provides stability to all but one side. The western slope has experienced slumping and erosion. Given the mound height, steep slopes, and flat top, Feature 194 is thought to be a ceremonial mound. There are thick stucco fragments on the feature, indicating that there was a substantial structure associated with its upper deposits.

Additional Mounds in the Northeast Group

Three additional mounds associated with the Northeast Group were not incorporated into subgroups A through C. Feature 193 forms the southeast corner of the group. It is situated on very low earthen deposits at the edge of the mangrove. This tall earthen mound has an oval base and a conical morphology. The mound is larger than most

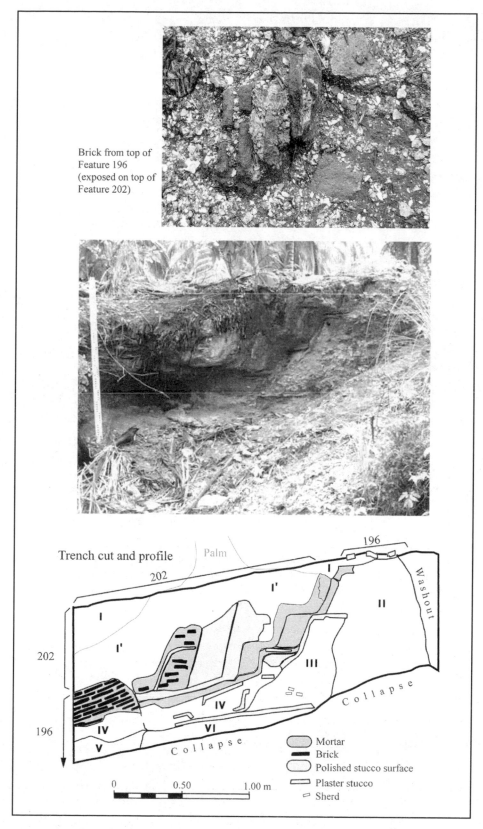

Brick from top of
Feature 196
(exposed on top of
Feature 202)

Trench cut and profile

Palm

196

202

202

196

Washout

I

I'

II

I'

III

I

IV

IV

VI

V

Collapse

Collapse

Collapse

Mortar
Brick
Polished stucco surface
Plaster stucco
Sherd

0   0.50   1.00 m

Figure 4.6. Photos and profile of Feature 196, vaulted substructure beneath mound Feature 202. Prepared by the author.

residential features, yet smaller and less formal than the ceremonial mounds.

The remaining features in the Northeast Group also have morphologies common to residential features at ILC. Feature 186 is a small earthen mound on the north side of the group. This mound is off and below the large platform for Subgroup A, immediately adjacent to the edge of the mangrove.

An additional mound-on-platform is spatially associated with the Northeast Group. Surrounded by mangrove at the north end of the site, Feature 203 is an earthen platform with a base elevation 0.20 m below lagoon level. Feature 204 is a small earthen mound on top of Feature 203.

The North-Central Group

The North-Central Group is a small concentration of mounds situated on an extension of the basal platform for subgroups A and C of the Northeastern Group, but spatially separated from the Northeast Group (Figure 4.5, Table 4.3). Feature 160 is an 80 by 20 m, 1.1-m high northwest southeast-oriented linear mound supporting three small superior mounds (features 161, 162, and 163), each less than 1.00 m in height, resembling typical residential mounds. Three superior mounds are unusual for multilevel mounds at ILC. Feature 164 is an elongated elliptical mound with steep slopes and a flat top. It is 34 m in length, 15 m in width, and 1.80 m in height. The flat top and steep slopes suggest a ceremonial function. All features in the North-Central group were constructed with earth and shell fill.

The Northwest Group

The Northwest Group was the only one with basal deposits not connected to those of other groups (Figure 4.5). This group was situated on a 0.50-m high platform of earthen and shell deposits bordered by low, inundated grassy areas on the north, east, and south, and by dense mangrove on the west. The group includes one multilevel ceremonial formation and three residential mounds (Table 4.3).

Feature 198 is a large, flat-topped earthen mound that supports a superior mound (Feature 199) on its east summit. From the base of Feature 198 to the top of Feature 199, the multilevel mound is 6.50 m in height. This had been the tallest remaining prehispanic formation anywhere at ILC. Unfortunately, however, the south half was removed several decades ago. The estimated original size of the large inferior mound (Feature 198) is 40 by 86 m. It could have accommodated a ceremonial space or structure on its western summit. The superior mound (Feature 199) was situated on its eastern summit and is estimated to have been approximately 25 by 45 m. The superior mound has steep sides on the north and east, but a more gently sloped western side, suggesting a ramp from its summit to the flat top of the large inferior mound.

Three additional mounds conformed in size and shape with residential mounds at ILC. Feature 197 is a conical mound constructed of earthen and shell deposits on the east side of the large multilevel ceremonial formation. Two lower residential mounds—features 200 and 201—are north of the ceremonial formation. Both have earthen and shell deposits. A few pieces of mortar and plaster were found eroding from Feature 197, suggesting a more substantial building than on the two low mounds.

The Central Group

The Central Group was a large area of disturbed deposits with six mounds and other feature remnants located along the western shoreline of the peninsula (Figure 4.7, Table 4.3). It probably contained a *plazuela* that was severely disturbed by more than a century of hacienda and later ranch activities, by shoreline erosion from a lack of mangrove, and historical-modern use as a landing. With the exception of Feature 151, all features and their basal deposits included shell and earth fill.

The most prominent mound is Feature 151 at the center of the disturbed deposits (Figure 4.6). This mostly earthen mound has decades-old mechanical digging scars around its sides. According to informants, it was spared from total destruction by the community because it has a supernatural rooster dwelling within. Given the large size of the mound, it is more likely nonresidential in function—presumably another ceremonial mound.

Several features (178 to 182) are situated on the south and southeast sides of Feature 151. A small residential mound (Feature 178) is adjacent to Feature 151. Along the shoreline, an additional possible mound (Feature 177) is protected by a thin stand of mangrove. In an eroded area to the southeast of Feature 151 are four small remnant deposits (features 179–182) where palms prevented complete erosion from a century and a half of ranch activities.

To the southwest of Feature 151, along the shoreline, is a low broad mound (Feature 167) with a remnant of a smaller mound on top (Feature 150). Surface erosion exposed a plaster floor (Feature 171) on top of superior mound Feature 150 (Figure 4.6). Waves had cut a near-vertical face in Feature 167 exposing two buried features: Feature 159, a large circular plaster-lined pit, and Feature 158, a large thermal pit or possible *chultún* with thick oxidized clay

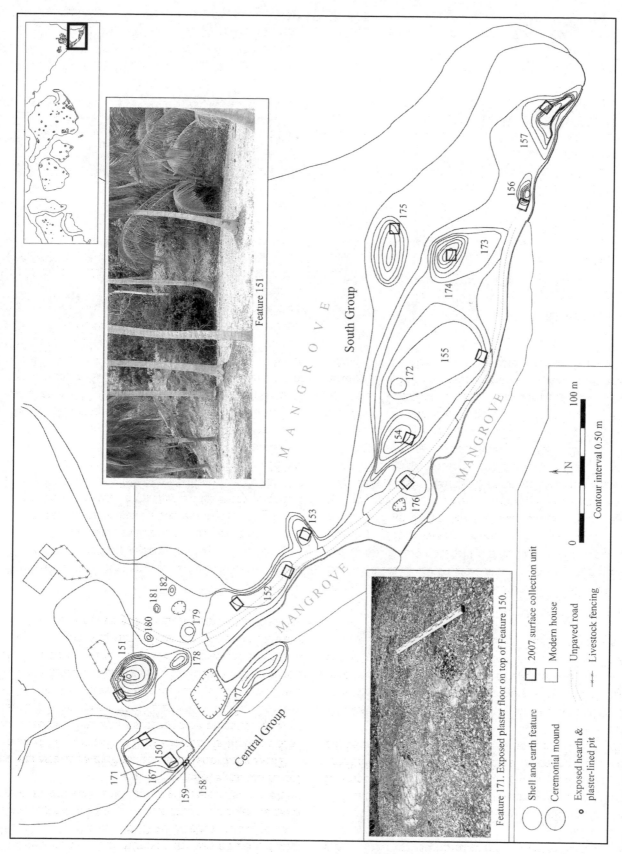

Feature 151

Feature 171. Exposed plaster floor on top of Feature 150.

Central Group

South Group

MANGROVE

MANGROVE

MANGROVE

151
150
167
171
159
158
178
177
179
180
181
182
152
153
176
154
155
172
174
173
175
156
157

○ Shell and earth feature
○ Ceremonial mound

◦ Exposed hearth &
plaster-lined pit

☐ 2007 surface collection unit
☐ Modern house

⋯⋯ Unpaved road
–•– Livestock fencing

N

0   100 m

Contour interval 0.50 m

Figure 4.7. Map of the Central and South Groups of El Bellote. Prepared by the author.

walls (Chapter 5). Because these were buried under the multilevel mound, they cannot be linked to the activities associated with that formation.

A linear, low basal deposit extends southeast from the Central Group, which supports two residential features. One is a curvilinear platform (Feature 152). The second is a small mound (Feature 153).

The South Group

The South Group is a somewhat linear concentration of basal deposits and nine platforms, mounds, and mounds-on-platforms creating the southern end of the peninsula (Figure 4.6, Table 4.3). All are constructed of shell and earth. Although the only group at El Bellote without a ceremonial mound, the residential group is associated with fishing, fish-processing, and unspecified collective activities on a distinctively large platform.

Feature 176 is a small eroded platform on the west end of the basal deposits along the shoreline. This feature is distinct for its combination of surface artifacts. Ten of the 11 net sinkers from El Bellote came from the South Group. Eight of those were recovered from Feature 176, along with a high density of vertebrate remains and obsidian, which suggests that it was a specialized fishing-related platform.

East of Feature 176 are several prominent features including a distinctively large northwest-southeast-oriented platform (Feature 155) that has a small residential mound on its northwest end (Feature 172). Unfortunately, the large platform is covered by dense undergrowth that prevented surface collection. The collection unit placed over the south edge of the platform did yield another fish-net sinker in a collection that otherwise lacked distinction. Morphologically, however, Feature 155 appears to have been suited for large-scale collective activities.

The remaining features on the large basal deposit share the general morphology of residential mounds elsewhere at ILC. Feature 154 is a well-defined oval residential mound situated between the small and large platforms. A relatively tall, steep-sloped residential mound-on-platform (feature 173 and 174) is located on the east end of the large basal deposit. The collection unit on this mound also yielded one fish-net sinker.

Three additional residential mounds range from 2.50 to 4.30 m in height. Features 156 and 157 are severely eroded due to a lack of protective mangrove along the southern tip of the peninsula. The erosional cut into Feature 157 demonstrated successive mound construction deposits and house constructions with high quality plaster and clay flooring (Chapter 5).

Artifacts at El Bellote

As with the island sites, the most abundant artifact category at El Bellote was pottery. Interestingly, El Bellote is the only context at ILC with nonregional Late Classic pottery. Though found in low quantities, El Bellote is also the only site at ILC with late Middle Formative to early Late Formative pottery of the Olmec Horizon.

Several materials are far more frequent at El Bellote than at the island sites. Although there are low quantities of chipped stone artifacts at El Bellote, there are far more there compared to those at the insular sites. No obsidian was observed on the surfaces of the 122 island features; only very few pieces have been recovered from the islands in excavations or profiles of cuts from erosion or sediment mining (Ensor 2002b; Ensor and Tun Ayora 2004; Ensor and others 2006). In contrast, 11 pieces of obsidian and 5 pieces of chert were recovered from the surface collections at El Bellote. Ten ground stone artifacts (all basalt metate and possible mano fragments) were recovered at El Bellote whereas only one piece was found on the islands (at the South Group of Isla Chablé). Eleven fish-net sinkers were collected from El Bellote, mostly from the South Group. Bones (all nonhuman and unmodified) were also present in greater quantities than in residential contexts at the insular sites. Architectural debris from the surface collections and profiles included loose chunks of clay, loose pieces of mortar (denser and thicker than where present on the insular sites), thick plaster fragments (absent at the island sites), and brick (also absent at the insular sites).

SUMMARY

Prior archival records for ILC included portions of six sites. These typically identified fewer numbers of mounds than are actually present and were biased toward mounds observable from the lagoon. The previous documentation also included conflicting numbers or descriptions of features at the sites recorded. In addition, the greater focus on the shell deposits at Isla Chablé and at El Bellote gave an inaccurate impression of the more typical construction materials. The combination of shell and Formative pottery at the South Group of Isla Chablé led many to mistakenly interpret the shell middens as being Formative in age. Using aerial photos, West, Psuty, and Thom (1969: Figure 30) identified more mounds scattered throughout the islands, including their interiors. These identifications were confirmed by Sisson (1976). However, a preliminary inspection of one area indicated that there are far more mounds and platforms than were detectable from air photos.

Eight sites were defined by the PAILC's systematic ground reconnaissance survey. Five of the islands were designated as individual sites: Isla Boca Grande, Isla del Campo, Isla Santa Rosita, Isla Dos Bocas Nuevas, and Isla Chablé. El Bellote is a separate site. One feature that forms its own tiny island (La Islita) was defined as a site. Another single-feature site is El Canal. Two of the mangrove islands on the south side of Isla Boca Grande lack features.

Distributed across the eight sites are a total of 165 platforms and mounds. These occur as solitary features (platforms or mounds), as mounds-on-platforms, as multilevel mounds, or as multilevel mounds-on-platforms. Most conform with morphologies and sizes of residential mounds and platforms elsewhere in the Gulf Coast and Maya lowland regions. Most features were built with sediments, but shell deposits were included with earthen deposits at most of the features in the South Group of Isla Chablé, and at 72 percent of features at El Bellote.

Most residential features are widely scattered across the islands in a *ranchería* settlement pattern that extends throughout the interiors, not just at the shorelines. Though dispersed, some linear arrangements of features may indicate that there were prehispanic canals. Elsewhere, a linear arrangement of features across mangrove islands may be the result of residences placed along canals (Stark 1989). On Isla Boca Grande, one such canal may have been flanked on one side by features 8, 9, and 12 and on the other by features 13 and 14 (Figure 4.3). Other features were in compact groupings: the Southwest and South groups of Isla Chablé and the five groups comprising El Bellote.

Nonresidential features were identified at Isla Chablé and El Bellote. Ceremonial mounds are defined as those features with large sizes, steep slopes, and/or large flat surfaces, several of which also had brick and mortar architectural materials. The long shoreline platform along the south shore of Isla Chablé was eventually defined as a landing, presumably for collective fishing-related activities but not as a commercial port facility. One large oval platform at El Bellote was also documented but its function is unknown. Isla Chablé also had two deposits of crushed shell, thought to be processing locations for mortar temper and, potentially, for lime production. The two crushed shell deposits, in combination with the use of crushed shell in mortar and plaster for ceremonial structures at El Bellote and Comalcalco suggest that there was a major industry focused on the exploitation of the extensive oyster beds surrounding the islands. This, in turn, illustrates the primary role of ILC in the regional political economy headed by the nobility at Comalcalco. The area was not a trade port for the inland capital, but instead was a resource-extraction zone (Ensor 2003b).

The morphological and pottery data indicate that all of the identified extant features were constructed during the Late Classic period. The mixed Formative and Late Classic pottery found at the sites indicate that the platforms and mounds were constructed using recycled deposits. This assertion is demonstrated by the analyses in Chapter 5. None of the features can be interpreted as Formative in age or as shell middens. Despite the displacement of Formative deposits in the Late Classic, however, some observations on Formative occupations can be made (see Chapter 8).

The conditions of the features varied considerably. Although centuries of gradual natural erosion affected all of the features, historical and modern human impacts, particularly for commercial uses, have caused the most severe disturbance. Wherever shoreline mangrove was removed, adjacent features experienced greater erosion, in some cases leaving tall vertical erosional cuts. Small-scale mining of sediment from the mounds was also common. Looters' pits were less common.

CHAPTER FIVE

The Features

The descriptions of the platforms and mounds at ILC presented in Chapter 4 were informed by the PAILC's scrutiny of morphological and stratigraphic data to address questions on (1) the relationship between Formative and Late Classic deposits, (2) feature functions, (3) construction sequence, and (4) whether residential mound size variation indicates differences in the duration of occupation or investment of labor. These questions developed either from previous interpretations or from observations made during the 2001 season. Alternative hypotheses for these four questions are outlined in the first section of this chapter. The feature descriptions, surface collections, and excavation and profiling data used to test the hypotheses are then presented. Those are followed by description and analysis of the specialized production features, as well as various pits and thermal features. Finally, the results are discussed to address the four main questions. As the first empirical analyses on the nature of the features in the coastal Chontalpa, the results overturned some prior assumptions and significantly advanced interpretations on ILC.

QUESTIONS AND HYPOTHESES

The 2001 survey of the islands identified platforms and mounds, combinations of the two feature types that suggested building sequences (Figure 4.2), and size variation among the features. The surface collections yielded both Formative and Late Classic pottery. Several questions immediately emerged that needed to be addressed in subsequent seasons: How were the features constructed; when were they constructed; and what is the significance of size variability? The following sections describe these questions and the alternative hypotheses for each.

When Were the Features Built?

As described in previous chapters, one long-held assumption about ILC is that the mounds with large quantities of oyster shells were Formative *concheros*. This characterization, based on the South Group of Isla Chablé, was used as a generalization for early human occupations in Tabasco (Fernández Tejedo and others 1988:51). That depiction ignores the age of the lagoon, the presence of Late Classic pottery, and the morphological similarities to residential mounds found elsewhere in the Gulf Coast region. Meanwhile, the depictions of El Bellote as a Late Classic ceremonial center (Berlin 1953b, 1954; Blom and La Farge 1926; Stirling 1957) ignored the Formative pottery associated with those shell mounds. At any rate, the 2001 surface collections at earthen features also yielded both Late Formative and Late Classic pottery, suggesting that the relationship between those periods' deposits applies to all features, not just those with shell.

The first hypothesis speculated that Late Classic features were built over Formative deposits. If so, then mound-on-platform combinations—if demonstrated to be platforms overlain by mounds—should have Formative pottery on platforms and the mounds on them should have only Late Classic pottery. Or, perhaps the lower strata were Formative deposits and Late Classic occupants added more deposits over those. In this case, there should be a stratigraphic Formative-Late Classic pottery sequence within features. In addition, in the case of the South Group of Isla Chablé and at El Bellote, if Formative *concheros* were leveled in the Late Classic to create the extant basal platforms on which the Late Classic mounds were constructed, then the mounds should only have Late Classic materials. Support for this hypothesis would be ideal: it would consist of in-situ Formative period material culture with which to base chronological associations with other artifacts, faunal remains, structures and pits, and for spatial analyses to interpret the social organization of those earlier societies. This would imply that the settlement patterns seen in the Late Classic components were a byproduct of Formative settlement patterns.

The second hypothesis speculated that the extant features were built entirely during the Late Classic by removing and redepositing earlier Formative deposits. This possibility first developed when pottery from both periods were seen on the surfaces of both mounds and platforms in mound-on-platform combinations. In addition, Piña Chan and Navarrete (1967:5–7, 11) describe mound fill with both Classic and Formative pottery at San Miguel, suggesting that the mixing occurred through the recycling of earlier deposits. If this was the case at ILC, then the stratigraphic data should indicate pottery from both periods in each fill stratum, from the lowermost to the uppermost. As stated previously, this hypothesis was supported by the data. The significance is that no in-situ Formative deposits remained. This severely limits interpretations on the earlier occupations and prevents the dating of other artifacts and faunal remains through stratigraphic association.

How Did the Features Function?

Many of the project's interpretations of the Late Classic period at ILC assumed that the majority of the mounds and platforms were residential features (Ensor 2003b, 2013b, 2016a, 2017d, 2017e; Ensor, Herrera Escobar, and Tun Ayora 2012). These assumptions were based on morphological conformity with residential features identified elsewhere in the Gulf Coast (Hall 1994; Piña Chan and Navarrete 1967; Santillán 1986; Sanders 1962; Stark 1991, 2001) and Maya regions (Masson 1997; Tourtellot 1988; Webster and Gonlin 1988:174). Near Comalcalco, Gallegos Gómora (1995) assumed that low platforms were used for processing cacao but instead found that they were used for residential activities. At ILC, the larger, taller mounds with flat surfaces and steep sides were assumed to be ceremonial mounds, that is, structures reserved for public religious activities and ancestral associations. The surface collections from the various features, accompanied by excavation data and opportunistic profiles of existing cuts, were used to test these assumptions.

Mesoamerican archaeologists typically expect a wide range of artifacts and features at residences, based on generalizations from ethnographic and ethnoarchaeological research on "household archaeology," which was developed in the 1980s and 1990s (Netting, Wilk, and Arnould 1984; Wilk 1984). One problem with those is the universalizing of ethnographic accounts from the 1980s. Another is that the generalizations are biased toward agrarian land-owning or land-possessing peasant populations of the modern period. By definition, peasant household groups own parcels of land, and their domiciles thus contain not only food processing refuse but also agricultural tools and storage features. And, in the case of 1980s Mesoamerica, many peasant households augmented their subsistence and monetary incomes through small-scale craft production (petty commodity production), which also led to generalizations that ancient Mesoamerican households *should* involve craft production (Hirth 2012). While this generalization may be supported by some instances in Classic-Postclassic central and southern Mexico it cannot be universal. As contemporary markets for household-produced crafts are undermined by cheap, factory-produced crafts and imports, peasant household craft production has declined since the 1980s. In short, broad political economic factors influence what "domestic activities" entail, as demonstrated historically for Guatemalan petty commodity production (Smith 1984). This applies to the prehispanic past as well. Changes in household production activities have been related to changing political economic structures in prehispanic Oaxaca (Joyce, Hendon, and Lopiparo 2014). Furthermore, in contrast to peasants, historic and contemporary plantation wage laborers are less likely to have agricultural tools and features at their homes. Analogous segments of prehispanic societies lacking rights to resources should similarly lack production-related tools and features at their dwellings.

The generalizations made from observations of 1980s peasant agrarian populations may not apply well to the expected range of activities in coastal fishing households. Political economic contexts structure who has access to fishing waters or shellfish beds. Where associated tools are located is also dependent on the political economy. As described in Chapter 3, not all residents in the town of El Bellote today have rights to fishing or shellfish harvesting. These rights are restricted to members of the cooperatives. Previously, they were restricted to members of an ejido. Historically, the surrounding resources were owned by the hacienda at El Bellote. Therefore, we cannot assume that "domestic activities" among prehispanic residents within the tributary, class-based political economy of Comalcalco would have included tools and waste byproducts from fishing and shell fishing. Storage of tools and discard from processing activities in a public rather than household context may, in part, explain the paucity of stone cutting tools, fishing tools, and faunal remains at most residential features.

Nevertheless, certain minimal expectations for domestic activities can be made. Dwellings and hearths should be present. Diverse sherd rim forms suggest residential activities, as opposed to one or few forms, which suggest specialized activity locations (Ensor and Doyel 1997:75; Santillán 1986). If foods were processed outside of residential areas, then pottery for at least limited storage (*tecomates* and jars), cooking (ollas/bowls/wide-mouth *tecomates* for wet foods or *comales* for dry foods), and serving purposes (bowls/dishes and plates) can be expected at residential contexts. The surface collections were used to test the first of these expectations. As surface artifacts are subject to post-depositional formation processes (Arnold and Stark 1997:320; Hendon 1992; Lewarch and O'Brien 1981:299-319, 332), stratigraphic sampling from excavations and profiling of sediment mines and erosional cuts provided additional pottery for this purpose.

This minimal evidence for domestic activities might be accompanied by tools and byproducts of fishing and craft manufacturing. Fishing-related tools at some residences may indicate which groups had rights to those activities (i.e., group specialization). Likewise, if the byproducts of craft production—formal tools, debitage, and unfinished lapidary items—are also associated with minimal evidence for domestic activities, then craft manufacturing may also be considered a specialization for some groups (Charlton 1993; Feinman and Nicholas 1993). But these should not be assumed criteria for interpreting domestic locations.

Common morphologies for earthen ceremonial mounds in the Gulf Coast Lowlands include steep-sided conical mounds with circular bases and steep-sided square or rectangular mounds with flat surfaces (Fernández Tejedo and others 1988; Piña Chan and Navarrete 1967; Sanders 1962; Stark 1999). The same range of ceremonial architectural features can be found at Comalcalco and other sites in the central Chontalpa region, which also feature brick architectural substructures or overlying temples and palaces along with mortar and stucco (Andrews 1989; López Varela 1994). The interpretation of features as having ceremonial functions was also tested with surface collections and opportunistic profile data.

One initial hypothesis, based on prior assumptions about ILC, was that the coastal community functioned as a trade port for the inland capital of Comalcalco. Feature 92, the unusual linear platform along most of Isla Chablé's southern shoreline was tentatively interpreted in 2001 as a landing for either trade or fishing-related purposes. The former was discounted after not finding trade goods, but the latter was supported by the high density of vertebrate remains. One additional feature (176), located in the South Group of El Bellote, may have been a specialized fishing-related platform, based on an unusual concentration of net sinkers, chipped stone, and vertebrate remains found there.

Local materials processing was also hypothesized. Near Comalcalco, Gallegos Gómera (1995) suggested that platforms were used for tributary cacao processing. Instead, she found evidence for residential activities and possibly brick manufacturing. To date, there is no additional evidence at Comalcalco for shell processing or brick manufacturing. The PAILC therefore hypothesized that one of ILC's roles in the regional tributary political economy was to process oyster shell at the source. Features 89 and 122, at the southwest and southeast corners of Isla Chablé, had dense accumulations of crushed shell, providing evidence for local processing of construction materials.

What Is the Construction Sequence?

As described in Chapter 4, mounds and platforms occur alone (discrete), in mound-on-platform combinations, and as multilevel mounds (Figure 4.2). It was hypothesized that these represented a pattern of sequential construction whereby platforms were the first features occupied. In this model, inferior mounds were built over the platforms, and smaller superior mounds were built over the inferior mounds. Alternatively, the platforms surrounding mounds may have been constructed around the bases of existing mounds. Another possibility was that the assumed platforms were formed by erosion of mounds, wherein sediments accumulated around mound bases, rather than being human-built features.

These alternatives were tested with excavations in three locations: at one mound-on-platform formation and two multilevel formations. If the excavations in mounds-on-platforms revealed living surfaces or features on the tops of platforms beneath their mounds, then the assumption of a platform and overlying mound sequence would be supported. Likewise, if excavations in multilevel mounds revealed occupation surfaces and features on the tops of inferior mounds beneath superior mounds, then that sequence of first-built inferior and second-built overlying superior mounds would be supported. If not, then the alternative hypotheses that the platforms were later additions built around existing mounds, or that they are actually the product of mound erosion could be entertained. Evidence supporting the postulated sequence of platform, then mound, then superior mound would also suggest the mounds-on-platforms and multilevel mound formations were long-term occupations and that the discrete platforms and discrete mounds were occupied more briefly (and reflect early stages in longer-term occupations).

Size: Occupation Duration or Labor Investiture?

The 2001 survey indicated significant variation in size, particularly height, of the mounds at the insular sites. In addition, in multilevel formations, inferior mounds were typically much larger and taller than discrete mounds. Given these observations, another early hypothesis for the project was that the size variation represents occupational duration, whereby the larger and taller mounds were built up over longer periods of time and would have more numerous occupation levels (Hall 1994). Elsewhere in the Chontalpa, residential mounds were observed to have been built-up through a sequence of occupation layers (Piña Chan and Navarrete 1967:30; Sanders 1962). Alternatively, the platforms and low mounds may represent the residences of the poorest occupants or lowest ranking class (Webster and Gonlin 1988). Builders may also have negotiated status through mound size; that is, they symbolically manipulated social differences using residential feature size through labor mobilization.

To test these alternatives, the PAILC examined the construction episodes within platforms, mounds, and multilevel formations using the excavation and profile data at residential features. More numerous fill strata and occupation surfaces in larger mounds would support the first hypothesis, while fewer but thicker fill strata with fewer occupation surfaces in larger mounds would indicate a desire and command of labor for a taller feature relative to others.

RESIDENTIAL PLATFORMS AND MOUNDS

The assumed residential features include discrete platforms, discrete mounds, mounds-on-platforms, and multilevel mounds (Figure 4.2). If the extant features were built using recycled Formative period deposits, then both Formative and Late Classic period pottery should be present in each fill stratum. Alternatively, if these were Late Classic features built over Formative deposits, then only Late Classic pottery should be present in overlying mounds or upper fill strata in discrete features. To confirm

residential functions, diverse vessel forms should be present, along with dwellings, hearths, and pits. If the multilevel formations represent a sequence of features built over earlier ones, then there should be evidence for surfaces, architecture, or hearths and pits on the original surfaces of the platforms beneath the inferior mounds, and on the original surfaces of inferior mounds beneath the superior mounds. Alternatively, the occupants may only have built the mounds, and the erosion of these created the appearance of a surrounding platform. Another possibility is that the low platforms were built around the bases of existing mounds. If the larger mounds reflect status differences, rather than longer occupation durations, then there should be few construction episodes with thick fill strata.

Morphological, surface collection, excavation, and profile data from the 2001, 2004, 2005, and 2007 seasons (Ensor 2002b; Ensor and Tun Ayora 2004; Ensor and others 2006; Ensor Tun Ayora, and Herrera Escobar, 2008) were compiled to test the various hypotheses. Tables 5.1 and 5.2 provide summary data from the survey and surface collections. These, along with stratigraphic data from excavations and profiles of cuts from disturbance are discussed in the following subsections.

Discrete Platforms

The "discrete platform" category refers to platforms without mounds over them. All have sloping sides but relatively flat or slightly domed surfaces. These morphologies are illustrated in their low height to length ratios (Table 5.1).

Size

There are nine platforms and six possible platforms. The platforms varied in shape from circular, oval, to elliptical. Possibly due to erosion, some have indentations that create a crescent shape. Although having a considerable standard deviation in base sizes, most are less than 40 m long and all have low heights compared to mounds (Table 5.1). They were relatively uniform in width (ranging from 8 to 22 m, with a mean of 11.7 m) and in height. All nine platforms were earthen constructions. None had shell deposits. The possible platforms had irregular narrow, curving elliptical shapes and were severely eroded.

Surface Collections

Unfortunately, too few artifacts could be observed at discrete platforms because dense grasses limited surface visibility. Table 5.2 shows surface pottery associated with the Formative and Late Classic, along with the vessel forms indicated by rims. Three platforms had both Formative

Table 5.1. Residential Feature Sizes

	Number	Base Length/Diameter (m)			Height (m)			Height/Length Ratio		
		Range	Mean	Standard deviation	Range	Mean	Standard deviation	Range	Mean	Standard deviation
DISCRETE FEATURES										
Possible Platforms (earthen)	6	15–70	37.5	19.7	0.25–0.50	0.4	0.1	—	—	—
Platforms (earthen)	9	12–70	35.6	16.2	0.25–0.50	0.4	0.1	0.01–0.02	0.01	0.01
Mounds (earthen)	22	15–40	25.1	8.0	0.40–2.50	1.3	0.9	0.02–0.13	0.05	0.03
Mounds (w/shell)	19	10–62	28.2	13.9	0.50–3.70	2.0	0.9	0.04–0.16	0.08	0.03
MOUNDS ON PLATFORMS										
Basal platforms (earthen) [1]	18	20–60	41.9	12.6	0.25–1.00	0.5	0.2	0.01–0.03	0.01	0.01
Mounds (earthen)	21	10–35	16.1	6.7	0.50–1.25	1.0	0.4	0.03–0.15	0.07	0.03
Basal platforms (w/shell)	2	20–52	36.0	22.6	0.25–0.90	0.6	0.5	0.01–0.02	0.02	0.01
Mounds (w/shell)	4	7–34	19	12.7	0.25–2.20	1.1	1.0	0.03–0.07	0.05	0.02
MULTILEVEL FORMATIONS										
Basal platforms (earthen)	9	45–85	66.7	14.4	0.25–0.50	0.4	0.1	0.003–0.01	0.01	0.003
Inferior mounds (earthen)	10	25–60	38.5	11.3	0.25–1.50	0.9	0.5	0.01–0.40	0.02	0.01
Superior mounds (earthen)	14	6–25	15.9	6.2	0.25–1.00	0.6	0.2	0.03–0.10	0.04	0.02
Inferior mounds (with shell)	6	38–80	48.5	15.8	0.50–1.50	1.2	0.5	0.01–0.04	0.02	0.01
Superior mounds (with shell) [2]	8	6–30	12.7	6.1	0.30–1.50	12.7	6.1	0.02–0.07	0.05	0.02

Notes: 1. Base lengths and height/length ratios are based on 16 platforms, after removing lengths from two "L"-shaped platforms. One of the earthen platforms (Feature 118) supported a mound constructed with shell deposits (Feature 117).

2. Lengths and height/length ratios are based on seven superior mounds, after removing one with an unusual narrow but long curvilinear shape.

and Late Classic pottery. Three had only Late Classic pottery. One had only Formative pottery. Three had no visible artifacts. The pooled rim data suggest an emphasis on *tecomates* during the Formative occupations and a variety of functions during the Late Classic occupations including serving and storage but primarily for cooking moist foods. Thin, friable fragments of plaster with shell temper for structures were observed on Feature 82 (Isla Chablé). This is the only surface evidence for architecture on the platforms.

Feature 40 Excavation

One platform (Feature 40 on Isla Santa Rosita) was selected for excavation. Unit 4 was a 1- by 2-m test unit (Unit 4) placed in the center of the platform (Figure 5.1; Ensor and Tun Ayora 2004:61–63). The platform was selected for testing because the 2001 surface collections yielded a slightly higher number of sherds and had vertebrate remains (Table 5.3). As with all excavations at ILC, this unit was excavated

in 10-cm arbitrary levels, switching to cultural levels when sediment changes were encountered in less than 10 cm. All sediments were screened through 3-mm mesh. Five levels were excavated. Only half the unit was used for the fifth level near the platform's water-logged base (Figure 5.1).

The platform was constructed with two earthen deposits. The first (Stratum II) was a compact, dark grayish-brown clay. There was a gradual transition zone with the upper stratum comprised of a compact, medium-brown clay. The artifact densities (n artifacts/volume of excavated sediment) were generally high but were lighter in Stratum II (480 and 425 artifacts per m^3 in levels 5 and 4, respectively). The artifact densities in levels 3, 2, and 1 (Stratum I) were 585, 554, and 1,199 per m^3, respectively. The highest density in the uppermost level may indicate that sediments eroded from the top of the platform, leaving artifacts behind.

No subsurface features were present within the unit. Included in all levels of both strata were 26 eroded nodules of a poor-quality calcium-based plaster with very fine sand

Table 5.2. Surface Collections at Residential Features

Total Sherds		Formative Pottery							Late Classic Pottery							Other Artifacts*
Number	%	%	J	O	T	B	D	P	%	J	O	T	B	D	P	
DISCRETE PLATFORMS (7)																
33	4.7	20.1	–	1	2	–	–	–	79.9	1	11	–	1	–	1	5F, M2
DISCRETE MOUNDS—EARTHEN (16)																
531	33.2	23.4	1	4	3	4	3	3	76.6	6	23	1	4	4	3	36F, 5GS, 3CS
DISCRETE MOUNDS—SHELL FILL (16)																
486	30.4	60.9	7	8	7	10	14	7	38.8	1	9	1	3	2	5	32 F, 1 GS, 5 M¹, 1CS
MOUNDS-ON-PLATFORMS—EARTHEN Mounds (14)																
106	7.6	11.8	–	1	2	1	1	–	80.8	1	42	3	3	3	10	2 M²
Platforms (9)																
33	3.7	21.8	–	1	–	–	–	–	78.2	1	13	–	1	–	1	
MOUNDS-ON-PLATFORMS—WITH SHELL (Mounds only) (4)																
111	27.8	70.0	1	3	1	3	4	2	30.0	1	2	1	–	1	–	2 F
MULTILEVEL MOUND FORMATIONS—EARTHEN Superior Mounds (7)																
19	2.7	13.7	1	1	–	–	–	–	86.3	–	23	1	1	1	1	
Inferior Mounds (7)																
169	24.1	12.0	1	2	5	–	–	–	88.0	2	102	5	2	1	3	
Platforms (5)																
31	6.2	2.2	–	–	–	–	–	–	97.8	–	20	–	–	–	2	2 M²
MULTILEVEL MOUND FORMATIONS—WITH SHELL Superior Mounds (4)																
33	8.3	54.5	1	1	2	–	3	1	45.5	–	2	1	–	–	–	6 F, 4 M¹
Inferior Mounds (4)																
347	86.8	51.5	1	8	1	2	8	1	47.3	2	1	2	2	7	3	9 F, 2 M¹

Key: J = jar; O = olla; T = *tecomate*; B = bowl; D = dish; P = plate; F = vertebrate fauna specimens; GS = ground stone; M¹ = mortar/plaster, high quality; M² = mortar/plaster, low quality; CS = chipped stone.

* = The number of artifacts recovered precedes the letter indicating the category of artifact.

or sand and shell temper (see Chapter 7). The plaster was used for floor or walls, indicating that a razed Late Classic structure had been recycled for platform fill. Some of the vertebrate remains also had mortar or plaster adhered to them. The lack of a distinct break between the two strata and the presence of plaster nodules through both strata suggest that the platform was constructed in one episode using two deposits of material.

The platform was built in the Late Classic period. Both strata consisted of reused deposits that contained a mixture of Formative and Late Classic pottery. Stratum II had a higher percentage of Late Classic pottery. In Stratum I, the percentage of Formative pottery was higher than in Stratum II, indicating that reused Late Classic deposits mixed with Formative deposits were placed over Stratum II (Table 5.3).

Two sherds of Sierra Red were recovered from levels 1 and 3, indicating a Late Formative occupation associated with the recycled fill. The Formative period rim sherds from all levels represent bowls, *tecomates*, and (most common) ollas, suggesting the deposits were associated with residential functions. The Late Classic rim sherds exhibit a wider range of vessel forms, with ollas more common in levels 1 through 4, which better suggests a residential association.

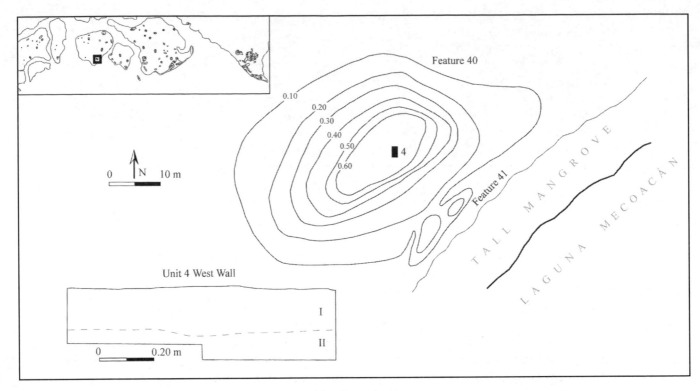

Figure 5.1. Plan view and profile of Feature 40. Prepared by the author.

Summary

The few artifacts from the surface collections suggest that platforms were either built in the Formative or the Late Classic, although nearly half had pottery from both periods. The unit in Feature 40 illustrated that mixed deposits were used in two layers during one construction episode in the Late Classic period. This included using the destroyed and displaced remains of a structure with low-quality plaster. The rim sherds from the surface collections and from the unit in Feature 40 suggest a wider range of vessel forms used in the Late Classic, with a greater emphasis on ollas, but that both the Formative and Late Classic deposits came from residential contexts.

Discrete Mounds

There were 41 discrete mounds that lacked platforms beneath them. These were assumed to have residential functions based on their morphologies. They were dome-shaped with circular, oval, or somewhat elliptical bases.

Size

The mounds typically had smaller base lengths than the platforms. However, they were generally taller, and hence steeper, as illustrated by the height to length ratios (Table 5.1). There were 22 discrete mounds built only with sediments and 19 built with shell and earthen deposits.

The 22 earthen mounds were found throughout the islands and in the Northeast Group of El Bellote. Although having a range in base sizes, they were less variable than among the discrete platforms (Table 5.1). Unlike platforms, the mounds made with earthen deposits had greater variation in heights (Table 5.1).

Mound height roughly correlates with base size. Among the six mounds with heights 2 m or greater, five had base lengths of at least 30 m. In contrast, among 11 mounds with heights of less than 1 m, the mean base length was 20.1 m (18.6 m if ignoring one mound that was severely "deflated" from disturbance).

The 19 mounds built of earth and shell deposits were in the south of Isla Chablé and in the Northeast, Northwest, and South Groups of El Bellote. These had greater variation in base sizes and in heights than their earthen counterparts but were generally steeper, taller, and more conical, as illustrated by the height to length ratios (Table 5.1). One explanation for this difference is that the shell deposits erode less easily than earthen deposits, making the latter more squat in shape. As with earthen mounds, their heights also correlate with base sizes. The three mounds

Table 5.3. Stratigraphic Distribution of Artifacts in Unit 4, Feature 40

Stratum	Level	Elevation (m)	Number of sherds	Formative Pottery							Late Classic Pottery							Other Artifacts			
				%	J	O	T	B	D	P	%	J	O	T	B	D	P	F	M^1	M^2	CS
I	1	0.56–0.46	237	37.6	–	1	–	2	–	–	62.0	–	2	1	–	–	–	26	–	14	–
	2	0.46–0.32	144	43.8	–	3	2	–	–	–	56.3	–	2	1	1	–	–	9	–	2	–
	3	0.32–0.22	102	42.2	–	2	1	–	–	–	52.0	–	3	–	–	2	1	8	–	2	–
I–II (trans)	4	0.22–0.12	59	18.6	–	3	–	–	–	–	72.9	–	1	–	2	–	–	9	–	6	3
II	5	0.12–0.02	40	22.5	–	1	–	–	–	–	77.5	–	–	–	–	–	–	6	–	2	–

Key: J = jar; O = olla, T = *tecomate*; B = bowl; D = dish; P = plate; F = vertebrate specimen; M^1 – mortar/plaster, high quality; M^2 = mortar/plaster, low quality; CS = chipped stone.

with heights of only 1 m or less had a mean base length or diameter of 14 m. The seven with heights greater than 2 m had a mean base length of 36 m.

Surface Collections

There were higher percentages of Late Classic pottery on the earthen mounds than on those that included shell (Table 5.2). The one exception is Feature 183: a severely deflated earthen mound in Subgroup A of the Northeast Group of El Bellote. Higher percentages of Formative pottery occurred on that feature.

The surface-collected pottery and other artifacts suggest residential functions. Both the Formative and Late Classic rim sherds illustrate the wide range of forms. In addition, ground stone and a good quantity of vertebrate remains (mostly turtle but also shark and other fish) occurred on those with shell deposits, although these cannot be associated with specific periods. Architectural plaster, which is associated with the Late Classic, was only observed on surfaces at mounds with shell deposits.

Profiles

No excavations were made in the discrete mounds. Profiles were made at three: one with a vertical cut from past sediment mining and two with vertical cuts from shoreline erosion. Each included shell, but rather than being just shell deposits, as previously characterized, the profiles demonstrate that the mounds were constructed with layers of shell, sediment only, and sediment with shell.

Feature 97 (Figure 5.2) was the largest mound in the South Group of Isla Chablé, having a maximum height of 4.00 m. A small sediment mining pit was on the northern, lower edge of the mound. After cleaning the sidewall, two strata were documented (Ensor and Tun

Ayora 2004:43–44). Because the pit was at the lower edge of the mound, these strata were presumed to be late deposits over earlier mound fill strata. No subsurface features were identified. Stratum II was a very compact brown clay with little shell. Stratum I was a lightly compact brown silt with a moderate density of shell. Most of the artifacts came from the collapsed sediment that accumulated at the base of the mine and could not be associated with specific strata. These included 36 sherds: 4 (11.1 percent) are Late Classic types and 32 (88.9 percent) are Formative types. Seven sherds were associated with Stratum II: two are Late Classic types and five are Formative types. This suggests that the mound construction fill involved the removal and redeposition of earlier Formative deposits sometime in the Late Classic period. Among the Formative sherds were six rims representing three bowls, one *tecomate*, and two ollas. This diversity suggests a residential origin. Two Late Classic rims were from a bowl and an olla.

Feature 156 is a 3.7-m tall mound in the South Group of El Bellote. Approximately half the mound was lost to shoreline erosion due to a loss of mangrove, leaving a vertical cut from the summit to near the base of the mound (Ensor, Tun Ayora, and Herrera Escobar 2008). Six strata were observed (Figure 5.3). Stratum VI was a compact, light brown, fine sand with a high density of whole shell. Underlying and overlying deposits were not visible due to collapsed sediments from the cut. Stratum V consisted of whole shell, broken shell, and small fragments of plaster. There was no in-situ floor or wall observed, and the mixing of the plaster with the shell throughout the deposit indicates reuse of materials from a razed Late Classic structure. Stratum IV had whole shell with light brown, fine sand (similar to Stratum VI). Stratum III consisted of whole shell mixed with crushed shell and light

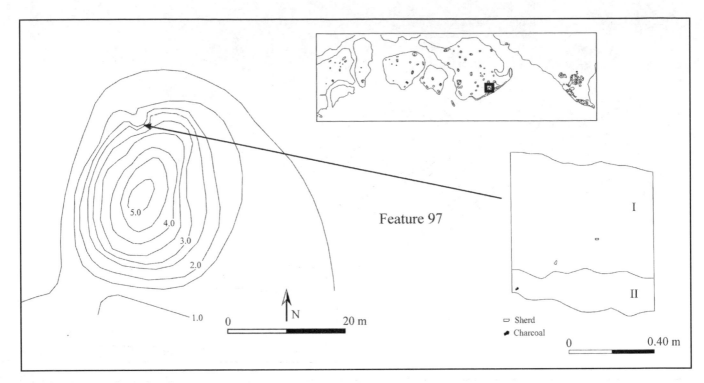

Figure 5.2. Plan view and profile of Feature 97. Prepared by the author.

brown sand. Stratum II was a deposit of light brown, fine sand that lacked shell. The last deposit, Stratum I, was a humic layer of dark brown sand and clay with whole and broken shells. Only three sherds were collected: one of a Late Classic type from the collapsed sediment, another of a Late Classic type from Stratum III, and one of the Sierra Red type (Late Formative) in Stratum I. The presence of a Late Classic type in Stratum III and a Formative type in the latest stratum indicate recycling of earlier deposits for Late Classic mound construction.

Feature 157 was a large mound adjacent to Feature 156 (Figure 5.3). Shoreline erosion from the lack of mangrove left a long vertical cut across the south half of the mound. Most of the upper deposits collapsed across the cut but a 5 m-long section was cleaned and profiled revealing 26 construction fill deposits along with architectural remains (Table 5.4). Most, but not all strata contained shell but there were differences among the strata. Some had whole shells, others had shell fragments, still others had crushed shell that were further distinguished by the sizes of shell particles. Several strata had combinations of shell in various stages of fragmentation.

The profile may indicate that there were few construction episodes. Remnants of an early mound's fill overlaid by a plaster floor are indicated by strata XVIII and XIX (Figure 5.3). Mostly overlying, but also undercutting, the plaster floor is Stratum XVII—a major mound construction fill deposit. Whatever second occupation surface was on top of Stratum XVII was later destroyed and numerous deposits of fill were added to increase the height of the mound. Several of these included fragments of plaster and clays from razed structures. Stratum V then capped those multiple deposits and may be associated with the plaster floor shown in the upper portion of the east side of the profile, which was also associated with a large block of adobe-like clay. This is a possible third occupation zone. Finally, the mound was again capped mostly by Stratum III but also by strata II and I in the west side of the profile. A fourth and final occupation surface presumably eroded off of the surface.

The subsurface structure remains (e.g., in-situ floors) and structural debris indicate residential functions for the mounds, assuming these were for dwellings and not other types of structures. The flooring materials were a high-quality dense calcium-based plaster with crushed shell temper. Some of the clay floor materials were well sorted, dense, and broken into hard red blocky fragments. Other clays were used for the adobe-like material, presumably a lower portion of a wall. None of the poorer-quality plasters were observed at Feature 157.

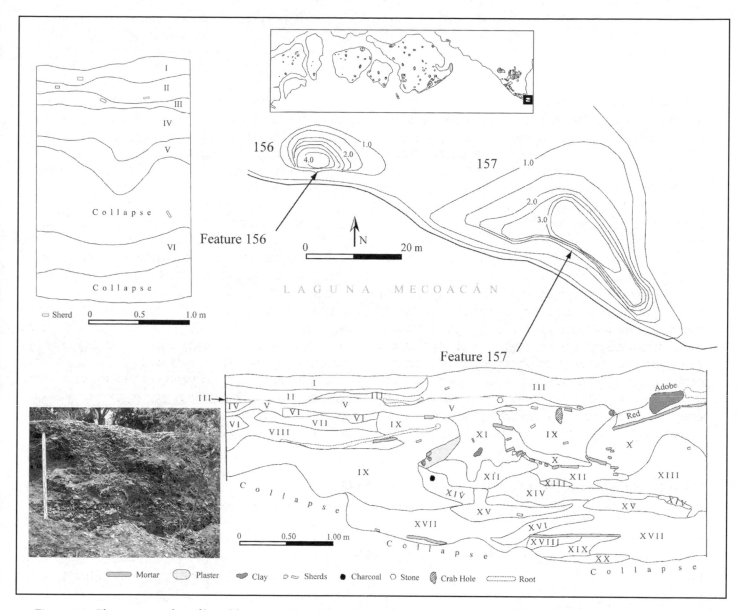

Figure 5.3. Plan views and profiles of features 156 and 157; photo of Feature 157. Prepared by the author.

Twenty-four sherds were collected from the profile. Eleven were from the collapsed sediment: 7 were Late Classic types and 4 were Formative types. One Late Classic sherd was recovered from Stratum X. Stratum IX had a Late Classic sherd and another of a Formative type. One Late Classic sherd was retrieved from Stratum V. From Stratum II, there were four Formative sherds and one Late Classic sherd. Two Late Classic sherds were recovered from Stratum I. Although 77 percent of the 33 sherds from the surface collection at Feature 157 were of Formative types, this stratigraphic information indicates mixing of Formative with Late Classic deposits.

Summary

Discrete earthen mounds generally had higher percentages of Late Classic pottery than those that included shell, which generally had higher percentages of Formative pottery (Table 5.2). Among the latter, the profiles of cuts from sediment mining and erosion indicate that mound-fill strata included some deposits with dense shell (whole and/or fragmented) and some earthen deposits with few to no shell inclusions. This observation further supports the interpretation that the obviously shaped extant mounds are not shell middens. Although the surface collections had higher percentages of Formative pottery, the stratigraphic

Table 5.4. Feature 157 Strata

Stratum	Description
I	Lightly compact, dark brown, humic sediment with shell fragments
II	Light brown silt with shell fragments
III	Lightly compact, dark brown, humic sediment with whole shell
IV	Compact, light brown silt with crushed shell (0.5–1.0 cm)
V	Compact reddish clay
VI	Compact light brown clay with dense whole shells and crushed shell (1.0–3.0 cm)
VI'	Compact light brown clay with dense whole shells and crushed shell (1.0–3.0 cm)
VII	Compact reddish-brown clay
VIII	Compact light grayish brown clay and whole shells with a fragment of floor plaster
IX	Semi-compact gray clay
IX'	Semi-compact dark brown silt with crushed shell (0.5–2.0 cm) and plaster fragments
X	Semi-compact dark brown silt with whole shells and red clay nodules
X'	Semi-compact reddish-brown sand and fragments of floor plaster
XI	Semi-compact reddish-brown silt
XII	Semi-compact dark brown silt with a light density of whole shells
XII'	Compact reddish-brown clay
XIII	Semi-compact gray clay
XIV	Compact dark gray silt with crushed shell (0.5–1.0 cm)
XIV'	Compact dark gray silt with whole shells and charcoal
XV	Compact light brown clay
XVI	Compact light brown clay
XVI'	Compact dark brown silt
XVII	Compact whole shells
XVIII	Lightly compact light brown silt
XIX	Light brown silt with crushed shell (0.5–1.0 cm)
XX	Lightly compact gray fine sand

information indicates that Formative deposits were redeposited to form the mounds during the Late Classic. The mixed deposits were subsequently redeposited to increase mound heights later in the Late Classic. The range of vessel forms suggest the pottery came from residential contexts in the Formative and Late Classic. The evidence for small structures with plaster and other floor/wall materials within Feature 157 does suggest Late Classic residential functions. The Feature 157 profile suggests at least four mound-building episodes (each with multiple fill strata) and four sequential occupations.

Mounds-on-Platforms

There were 18 earthen platforms with mounds that appear to overly them. Fourteen had only one mound. Four supported two mounds. Most were earthen constructions.

Size

Table 5.1 lists the similarities among platform base sizes, heights, and height-to-length ratios. The number of mounds on the tops of platforms did not influence the sizes. The four platforms that support two mounds have a mean length of 42.5 m and a mean height of 0.4 m. These are similar to the platforms with only one mound and those with no mounds. The similarity in platform sizes, regardless of presence or number of mounds over them, may indicate that discrete platforms were an initial stage in long-term occupations, whereby mounds were added later. Nevertheless, excavation and profile data are used to evaluate the alternative: that the platforms were built around mounds or were accumulations of eroded mound sediments.

The earthen mounds on earthen platforms were generally smaller and lower than the discrete mounds that lacked platforms, but they had similar height-to-length ratios (Table 5.1). The low standard deviations suggest more uniformity than among discrete mounds. Where two mounds occupied the same platform, the mounds' base sizes were generally smaller than solitary mounds on platforms but had similar heights (having a mean length or diameter of 12.8 m and a mean height of 1.0 m). As such, they had a slightly higher mean height-to-length ratio (0.08).

Mound-on-platform combinations that include shell deposits are rare. Most mounds containing shell were in mound groups built over their group's basal platforms. Mound Feature 174 on top of platform Feature 173 in the South Group at El Bellote is similar to the earthen mound-on-platform formations. In the South Group of Isla Chablé, mound features 102 and 103 are unusually small mounds over an unusually small platform (Feature 104); these had sediments containing less shell than most in that group. In southern Isla Chablé, Feature 117 was an average-sized mound with shell deposits but it was on top of an earthen platform (Feature 118). Given their rarity and variability (Table 5.1), size comparisons with their earthen counterparts are difficult to make and possibly without relevance.

However, the fact that less-erodible mounds with shell were rarely associated with platforms was one reason to consider that the platforms among the earthen mounds-on-platforms could be a product of mound erosion.

Surface Collections

Due to low surface visibility, the surface collections at mounds-on-platforms generally yielded few artifacts. In nine cases, surface collections were not attempted due to the dense grass, bushes, and trees. Mound Feature 174 (on platform Feature 173 at El Bellote) was an exception: 82 sherds were recovered there. Despite this problem, the low numbers of artifacts collected at mounds-on-platforms illustrate the same patterns observed for discrete mounds. As illustrated in Table 5.2, the percentages of Late Classic pottery were much higher at the earthen mounds-on-platforms compared to those with shell. The only exception was mound Feature 30 on platform Feature 31 at Isla Santa Rosita, where only 3 sherds were collected from the mound and only one from the platform. Platforms had slightly higher percentages of Formative pottery than the mounds overlying them, which might suggest that the mounds were built in the Late Classic over Formative period platforms. The opposite occurred at the few mounds-on-platforms with shell. Among those three, two had higher percentages of Formative pottery on the mounds and one had an equal percentage of Late Classic and Formative pottery.

Formative pottery rim sherds illustrate a wide range of vessel forms. No particular form category (plates, dishes, bowls, *tecomates*, ollas, or jars) was dominant. Those among the Late Classic types also represent a wide range of vessel forms, though 56 percent of rims were from ollas, suggesting an emphasis on cooking moist foods. No mortar or plaster, and few vertebrate remains, were found at these features.

Feature 77–78 Excavations

One mound-on-platform was stratigraphically sampled through excavation. Feature 77 was a broad, dome-shaped mound (0.75 m in height) that appeared to overlay platform Feature 78 (0.25 m in height) along the northeast shoreline of Isla Chablé (Figure 5.4). Unit 1 was 2 by 2 m, but was reduced to 1 by 2 m as the excavation proceeded to preserve a clay floor or surface in its east half. Afterward, that clay floor was determined to be modern. The resulting 1- by 2-m unit was excavated to below the elevation of the mound base. The excavation yielded a large sample of artifacts from six strata and revealed an oven feature and a small hearth (Ensor and Tun Ayora 2004:52–56).

The earliest fill deposit observed was Stratum VI—a dark brown silt with sand with a moderate artifact density of 456 per m³. Within Stratum VI was a small, elliptical informal hearth (Feature 134) in the southwest corner of the unit (Figure 5.3). The hearth was associated with the projected elevation for the top of platform Feature 78, beneath the mound. Partially overlying the hearth, was a 1.35-m wide, 0.30-m tall, east-west oriented platform (Feature 133) made from a reddish-brown clay. It contained a hearth (Feature 132) that was 0.09 m deep with a very dark grayish brown clay with dense charcoal staining and moderate artifact density (500 per m³). Features 132 and 133 were interpreted as a small elevated oven on the surface of platform Feature 78 (Figure 5.4). No postholes or additional architectural characteristics were observed. The oven was buried when the mound was created. Stratum V, on the north side of the oven, was a lightly compact brown silt and sand with a moderate artifact density (400 per m³). Stratum IV, overlying Stratum VI on the south side of the oven, was a lightly compact brown fine sand with a low artifact density (111 per m³). Observed in the south half of the unit, Stratum III—a moderately compact dark yellowish-brown silt with sand with an extremely high artifact density (1,254 per m³)—was deposited over Stratum IV and a good portion of Feature 133. Observed in the northern two-thirds of the unit, Stratum II—a moderately compact yellowish-brown silt with a low artifact density (200 per m³)—was later deposited over Stratum V, the north side of Feature 133, and Stratum III. An animal burrow extended from the top of Stratum II into a portion of features 133 and 132. Stratum I—a moderately compact light yellowish brown silt—was the final mound construction deposit observed, which overlay Stratum II in the north, partially filled the animal burrow in the center, and overlay Stratum III in the south. Midway into Stratum I, a 5-cm-thick floor of compacted dark yellowish-brown clay was found in the east half of the unit (Feature 130) with a chunk of burned clay on its southern edge (Figure 5.4). Beneath Feature 130, Stratum I had a moderate artifact density (113 per m³) but above the floor there was an extremely low artifact density (54 per m³). Both above and below the floor, modern glass and metal artifacts were found along with the prehispanic artifacts, indicating that both Stratum I and Feature 130 were modern additions to the mound. Stratum I was also associated with 6.1 liters of oyster shell, which was unusual in the prehispanic deposits at earthen features and was likely from modern use.

Formative and Late Classic sherds were combined in all strata and in each features' fill, indicating reuse of

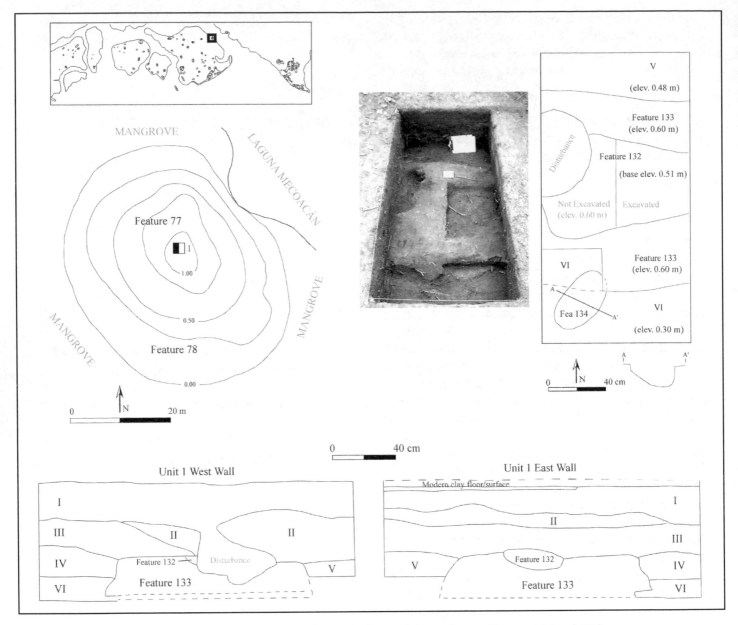

Figure 5.4. Plan views and profiles of features 77 and 78 with photo of elevated oven (features 132 and 133). Prepared by the author.

Formative deposits for the construction and use of features 77 and 78 in the Late Classic (Table 5.5). Of note are higher percentages of sherds of Formative types in Feature 78-associated fill and in the fill of features 132 and 134 compared to those in the overlying mound-fill deposits. Those suggest that more Formative deposits were reused for platform Feature 78 and its associated features than for mound Feature 77, which supports the observations from surface collections that more Formative pottery is associated with the platforms than the mounds, despite

both having been constructed in the Late Classic. Although rare at ILC, there were five chipped stone artifacts and six fish-net sinkers (made from Late Classic sherds) from Stratum III. Although indicating fishing activities, these were from earlier deposits reused for mound fill.

Three Late Classic occupation surfaces can be interpreted. The first was associated with the top of platform Feature 78 where Feature 134 was identified. Later, the oven was added. That was subsequently covered with multiple mound fill deposits (strata V, IV, III, and II) presumably in

Table 5.5. Stratigraphic Distribution of Artifacts in Unit 1, Features 77 and 78

Stratum	Level	Elevation (m)	Number of sherds	Formative Pottery							Late Classic Pottery							Other Artifacts		
				%	J	O	T	B	D	P	%	J	O	T	B	D	P	F	CS	Sinker
I	1	1.14–1.03	16	25.0	–	–	–	–	–	–	75.0	–	–	–	–	–	–	1	–	–
	2	1.03–0.94	15	46.7	–	1	–	–	–	–	46.7	–	1	–	–	–	–	–	–	–
II	3	0.94–0.84	36	36.1	–	–	–	–	–	–	63.9	–	–	–	–	1	–	–	–	–
II/III	4a/4b	0.84–0.74	88	39.8	–	–	–	–	–	–	60.2	–	–	–	–	–	–	–	–	5
III	5	0.74–0.60	149	8.1	–	–	–	–	–	–	88.6	1	–	–	–	–	–	–	5	1
IV	6b	0.60–0.48	4	75.0	–	–	–	–	–	–	0.0	–	–	–	–	–	–	–	–	–
V	6a	0.58–0.46	16	93.8	–	–	1	–	–	–	0.0	–	–	–	–	–	–	–	–	–
F 132	1	0.60–0.51	14	14.3	–	–	–	–	–	–	85.7	–	–	–	–	–	–	–	–	1
F 133	1	0.60–0.37	10	90.0	–	–	–	–	–	–	10.0	–	–	–	–	–	–	–	–	–
F 134	1	0.37–0.26	142	44.4	–	–	–	–	–	–	55.6	–	–	1	–	–	–	–	–	–
VI	7	0.48–0.36	31	41.9	–	–	–	–	–	–	58.1	–	–	–	–	–	–	–	–	–

Key: J = jar; O = olla; T = *tecomate*; B = bowl; D = dish; P = plate; F = vertebrate specimen; CS = chipped stone.

one episode to create mound Feature 77. The latest prehispanic occupation was not observed. Finally, the surface of the mound was manipulated in modern times.

Summary

Compared to discrete mounds, smaller but more uniformly sized mounds were built over platforms. Those platforms were similar in size to the discrete platforms. The surface collections at earthen mounds-on-platforms yielded mostly Late Classic pottery, but the percentages of Formative types were higher on platforms than on the mounds, suggesting that the platforms were earlier, which was supported by the stratigraphic percentages of Formative and Late Classic pottery from the excavation in features 77 and 78. Nevertheless, the assumption that mounds-on-platforms represent a sequence whereby mounds were built over earlier occupied platforms was supported by the observation of features 132-133 and 134 at the projected elevation of the top of platform Feature 78. Formative and Late Classic pottery sherds were found in all strata (and in subsurface features' use-related fill), supporting the hypothesis that the features were Late Classic constructions that recycled earlier deposits. The diversity of surface-collected Formative and the Late Classic rim sherds suggest residential origins for the fill in mounds-on-platforms. The Late Classic rim sherds suggest a greater emphasis on ollas for stewing. Too few rims were recovered from the excavation in features 77 and 78 to corroborate this. However, the presence of the oven over the small hearth on top of platform Feature 78 indicates that domestic activities took place there. Fish-net sinkers found in one mound-fill deposit in Feature 77 also indicates a brief period of fishing activities at this location.

Multilevel Mounds

Sixteen multilevel mounds were documented. These have large inferior mounds over which smaller superior mounds were constructed (Figure 4.2). Ten are earthen, and nine have platforms underlying the inferior mounds. None with shell deposits have underlying platforms, as those were constructed over larger basal platforms for mound groups.

Size

Table 5.1 compares the sizes of multilevel mounds with other feature categories. Where present, multilevel mound platforms were larger than discrete platforms and those under mounds-on-platforms. Inferior mounds were larger than discrete mounds and those at mounds-on-platforms. Superior mounds were the smallest of any mound category. Table 5.1 also indicates that the inferior mounds with shell were usually larger and taller than those of earthen-only deposits, though the largest multilevel formation was earthen (features 36–39 at Isla Santa Rosita). Although the superior mounds with shell had smaller base sizes than their earthen counterparts, they shared similar heights.

The number of superior mounds influenced the sizes of inferior mounds and platforms. Table 5.6 compares the platform and inferior mound sizes by the numbers of superior mounds. In formations with multiple superior

Table 5.6. Multilevel Formations: Platform, Inferior Mound, and Superior Mound Sizes

	Number	Base Length or Diameter (m)			Height (m)			Height-to-Length Ratio		
		Range	Mean	Standard deviation	Range	Mean	Standard deviation	Range	Mean	Standard deviation
EARTHEN: WITH 1 SUPERIOR MOUND										
Basal Platforms	4	45–65	55	8.2	0.25–0.50	0.4	0.1	0.004–0.01	0.01	0.003
Inferior Mounds	4	30–35	32.5	2.9	0.50–1.50	1.1	0.5	0.02–0.04	0.03	0.01
Superior Mounds	4	15–20	18.8	2.5	0.50–1.00	0.6	0.3	0.03–0.07	0.04	0.02
EARTHEN: WITH 2 SUPERIOR MOUNDS										
Basal Platforms	5	60–85	76	10.8	0.25–0.50	0.4	0.1	0.003–0.01	0.01	0.004
Inferior Mounds	6	25–60	42.5	13.3	0.25–1.25	0.8	0.4	0.01–0.04	0.02	0.01
Superior Mounds	10	6–25	14.8	7.0	0.25–1.00	0.6	0.2	0.02–0.08	0.05	0.03
SHELL & EARTH: WITH 1 SUPERIOR MOUND										
Inferior Mound	5	38–45	42.2	3.8	0.50–1.50	1.16	0.6	0.01–0.04	0.02	0.01
Superior Mound	5	8–22	15.3	6.8	0.30–1.50	0.8	0.5	0.02–0.07	0.05	0.02
SHELL & EARTH: WITH 3 SUPERIOR MOUNDS										
Inferior Mound (Feature 160)	1	80	–	–	1.1	–	–	0.01	–	–
Superior Mounds	3	6–13	9.3	3.5	0.30–0.90	0.6	0.3	0.05–0.07	0.06	0.01

mounds, the superior mounds were smaller than any other category of mounds, while their inferior mounds were larger, regardless of the presence or absence of shell in either type of mound. With multiple superior mounds, the platforms underlying inferior mounds (associated with earthen-only constructions) were also larger. Platforms may have been large originally; they may have been enlarged to accommodate the construction of large inferior mounds; or their size may be the product of accumulated trash and sediments eroding from the inferior mounds.

Surface Collections

Although most surface collections on multilevel mounds yielded low quantities of artifacts, several had much higher yields than from discrete features and mounds-on-platforms. Two multilevel formations—features 73–76 and 150/167—had very high surface artifact densities.

As described, earthen features generally had higher percentages of Late Classic pottery whereas those with shell had higher percentages of Formative pottery. This was also the case for the multilevel mounds (Table 5.2). Except for features 22 and 23 on platform Feature 127 (on Isla Santa Rosita), the earthen multilevel formations had much higher percentages of Late Classic pottery. Inferior mound Feature 75 at Isla Chablé—with a dense concentration of surface pottery—had an extremely low percentage of Formative

pottery. In contrast, multilevel formations with shell had high percentages of Formative pottery regardless of numbers of sherds collected. For example, inferior mound Feature 167 (Central Group, El Bellote) had 304 sherds collected, 63 percent (n = 191) of which were Formative types.

The surface collections at multilevel mounds also suggest residential contexts for both periods. Rims of Formative types represent a wide variety of vessel forms without a dominant category (Table 5.2). The Late Classic rims also show a wide range of vessel forms but with a high percentage from ollas. In some collections, the percentage of ollas represented by rims was extremely high: at platform Feature 35 (100 percent); at inferior mound Feature 50 (70 percent); at inferior mound Feature 58 (75 percent); at inferior mound Feature 71 (95 percent); at inferior mound Feature 75 (97 percent); and at superior mound 86 (100 percent). But when pooling all collections from multilevel mounds, the percentages of different vessel forms represented were more evenly distributed.

Feature 32-34-35 Excavations

Features 32, 34, and 35 comprised an earthen multilevel mound on a platform in the northeast portion of Isla Santa Rosita (Figure 5.5). Feature 32 was a small, 0.5-m-tall circular superior mound overlying inferior mound Feature 34. The latter was 35 m in length and 20 m wide. Feature 35

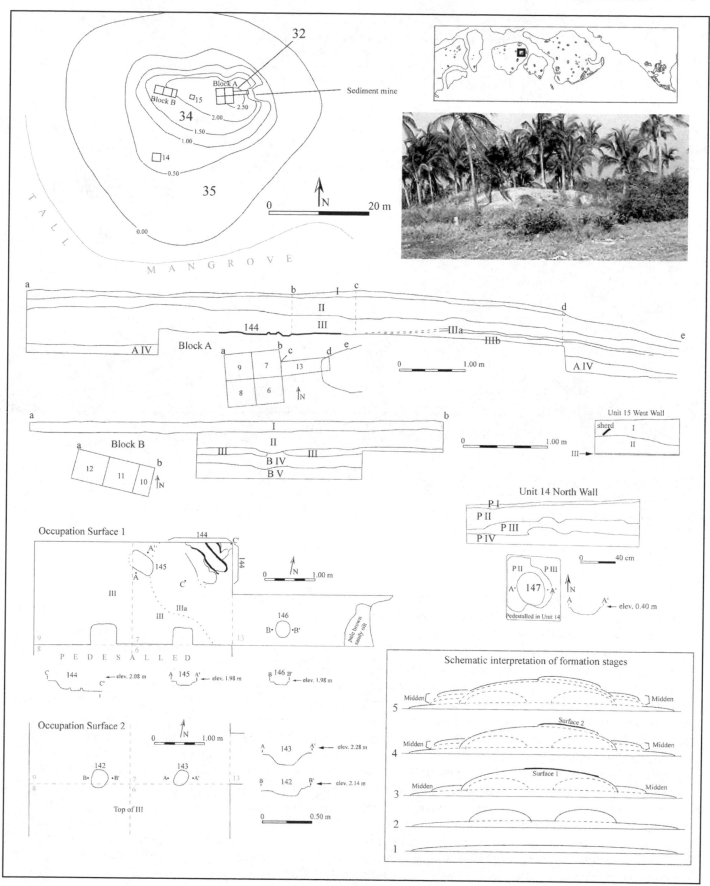

Figure 5.5. Photo, plan views, and profiles of features 32-34-35, with schematic of multilevel mound formation. Prepared by the author.

Table 5.7. Feature 32–34–35 Strata and Artifactual Contents

Stratum	Location	Density*	Number of sherds	Formative Pottery							Late Classic Pottery							Other
				%	J	O	T	B	D	P	%	J	O	T	B	D	P	CS
STAGE 5																		
I	Block A	27.71	64	10.5	–	–	–	–	–	–	81.0	–	–	–	–	–	–	2
	Block B	15.60	17	16.7	–	–	–	–	–	–	66.7	–	–	–	–	–	–	–
	U15	5.00	1	0	–	–	–	–	–	–	100	–	–	–	–	–	–	–
II	Block A	35.58	274	2.6	–	–	–	–	–	–	96.0	–	28	–	–	–	–	1
	Block B	22.96	62	0	–	–	–	–	–	–	96.8	–	1	–	–	–	–	–
	U15	36.36	12	0	–	–	–	–	–	–	100	–	–	–	–	–	–	–
P I	U14	443.39	235	0	–	–	–	–	–	–	100	–	8	–	–	2	–	–
STAGE 4																		
III	Block A	12.78	45	8.9	–	–	–	–	–	–	88.9	–	29	–	–	–	–	–
IIIa	Block A	66.67	2	0	–	–	–	–	–	–	100	–	–	–	–	–	–	–
P II	U14	742.03	512	0	–	–	–	–	–	–	100	–	17	–	–	3	–	–
STAGE 3																		
IIIb	Block A	18.18	2	0	–	–	–	–	–	–	100	–	–	–	–	–	–	–
III	Block B	13.04	6	0	–	–	–	–	–	–	100	–	–	–	–	–	–	–
P III	U14	847.62	533	0.8	–	–	–	–	–	–	99.3	–	12	–	1	–	–	1
STAGE 2																		
A IV	Block A	0.00	0	0	–	–	–	–	–	–	0	–	–	–	–	–	–	–
B IV	Block B	4.76	2	0	–	–	–	–	–	–	100	–	–	–	–	–	–	–
B V	Block B	4.23	3	0	–	–	–	–	–	–	100	–	–	–	–	–	–	–
STAGE 1																		
P IV	U14	87.50	35	0	–	–	–	–	–	–	100	–	1	–	–	–	–	–

Key: * = number of artifacts/excavated volume (m3); J = jar; O = olla; T = *tecomate*; B = bowl; D = dish; P = plate; CS = chipped stone.

was an oval platform that sloped gently from the base of the inferior mound to near-horizontal edges. The 2001 surface collection unit on the slope of the platform adjacent to the inferior mound yielded 11 sherds, all of which were of Late Classic types. Eight rims were from ollas and one was from a plate. The multilevel mound was being used for tree crops and was therefore in good condition except for a sediment mine on the east side of the inferior mound.

Excavations in 2005 were originally conducted to stratigraphically sample the pottery from subsurface features but provided far more evidence on construction sequence (Ensor 2005b; Ensor and others 2006). There were two blocks of multiple, adjacent 2- by 2-m units and two additional units (Figure 5.5). Block A had four units forming a 4- by 4-m square over the west side of the superior mound and the adjacent surface of the inferior mound. Connecting the block to the sediment mine was a 1- by 3.10-m unit

that allowed the project to link the strata in the block to those observed in the mine's sidewall. Block B consisted of two 2- by 2-m and one 1- by 2-m units forming a 2- by 5-m rectangle on the western top of the inferior mound. One 1- by 1-m unit was placed between the two blocks to confirm that the upper strata observed in both blocks were continuous across the inferior mound. One 2-by 2-m unit was excavated on the slope of the platform, within the 2001 surface collection unit.

Five construction stages were defined (Figure 5.5; Table 5.7; Ensor and others 2006). Stage 1 was the platform built with Stratum P IV—a compact brown clay with a low artifact density. All 35 sherds were of Late Classic types. Presumably, there was an occupation surface associated with the platform (not observed).

Stage 2 represents the construction of two small mounds over the platform, one on the west and one on the east, indicated by the distinct, lowermost fill in Blocks A (A IV, a compact brown silt with light charcoal flecking) and B (B V and B IV, an extremely compact yellowish brown clay with a surface inclination to the southeast and moderately compact yellowish brown silt with a surface inclination toward the south, respectively). These fill strata for the two small mounds had extremely low artifact densities. All sherds were of Late Classic types.

Stage 3 was the consolidation of the two small mounds into inferior mound Feature 34, observed with Stratum III—a very compact dark yellowish-brown clay in Block A, Block B, and Unit 15. This fill layer also had a very low artifact density. A chemical analysis comparing a sample of Stratum III with three samples of surrounding mangrove sediments confirmed that the fill was derived from the latter (Ruíz R. 2005). Most sherds were Late Classic types. Only four Formative sherds were recovered from Stratum III in both blocks and Unit 15. In Block A were two layered variations of Stratum III. Whereas Stratum III was present throughout most of Feature 34, Stratum IIIb (mottled with compact yellowish brown and pale brown silt) substituted it only at the eastern edge and slope of Feature 34. Overlying Stratum IIIb were thin laminations of sand, clay, and silt—designated as Stratum IIIa—suggesting a surface exposed to air- and waterborne erosion, with a low artifact density, though higher than Stratum III. Stratum IIIa was designated as Occupation Surface 1: a living surface with an earthen-floored structure and two outdoor pits of unknown function. Feature 144 was a smoothed surface in the top of Stratum IIIa, which had northwest-southeast–oriented vertical clay "lips" that were oxidized—a possible earthen floor edge that had been remodeled and burned. Feature 145 was a small subrectangular pit (0.40 × 0.30 m × 0.09 m) with compact brown clay fill and no artifacts. Feature 146 was a small, shallow circular pit (0.32 m in diameter, 0.06 m deep) with sloping walls and a flat base, and compact grayish brown clay fill with no artifacts.

A midden accumulated on the platform in Stage 3 near the base of the inferior mound around the time of Occupation Surface 1. Stratum P III (a compact yellowish-brown clay) was the first midden deposit, which had a high density of charcoal flecking (that increased toward the northwest corner of Unit 14), a light density of eroded poor-quality plaster, and a high artifact density. Of the 531 sherds recovered, 99.25 percent were of Late Classic types. One obsidian prismatic blade was also recovered. This trash deposit created the slope between the flatter portions of the platform and the lower portions of the inferior mound (that is, the slope was not from erosion of mound sediments).

Stage 4 involved the creation of superior mound Feature 32. The upper portion of Stratum III in Block A—overlying Occupation Surface 1—was 0.50 m thick compared to only 0.10 to 0.15 m thickness in Unit 15 and Block B, which created the inferior mound. Like other mound fill deposits, this stratum had a very low artifact density, with only a few Late Classic sherds. Occupation Surface 2, within the superior mound, was indicated by Feature 142 (a shallow oval pit with in-sloping walls and a concave sloping base measuring 0.36 × 0.30 × 0.08 m) and Feature 143 (a shallow elliptical pit with inclined walls and a flat base measuring 0.32 × 0.28 × 0.12 m). Both had lightly compact, light grayish brown silt fill and each contained one artifact: a Formative sherd in Feature 142 and a Late Classic sherd in Feature 143. There were no indications of earthen floors or compacted surfaces and there were no flat-lying artifacts in proximate areas. Nevertheless, the presence of two pits associated with the top of Stratum III suggested a living surface, presumably an outdoor work area. Around the same time as Stage 4, another trash deposit accumulated on the platform—Stratum P II, a compact pale brown clay (without charcoal flecks) having a high artifact density. All 512 sherds recovered were Late Classic types. Feature 147—an elliptical pit with inclined walls and a concave base—was found midway through Stratum P II. Its ashy fill, and small clay chunks and charcoal at its base suggest an ephemeral outdoor hearth over which Stratum P II continued to be deposited.

Stage 5 involved the deposition of two fill deposits over the superior and inferior mounds. Stratum II—observed in both blocks and between in Unit 15—was a 0.20- to 0.40-m thick layer of compact silty clay ranging in color from grayish brown to pale brown with small eroded nodules of poor-quality plaster and light charcoal flecking (probably from mixing with redeposited earlier platform-associated midden deposits). Although low, its artifact density was higher than earlier mound fill deposits. A chemical analysis also indicated a match to surrounding mangrove sediments (Ruíz R. 2005). Of the 348 sherds recovered, 94.8 percent were Late Classic types. One obsidian prismatic blade was also recovered. Two possible features were associated with Stratum II in Block A: Feature 141 was a small shallow (0.03 m) depression with fill that was barely distinguishable from Stratum II; Feature 140 was a large shallow depression (2.64 × 1.27 × 0.10 m) containing Stratum I fill. Both features appeared to be the result of natural disturbance. Stratum I—also observed in both blocks and between in Unit 15—was a thin surface layer of compact, light brown to pale brown clay with a low artifact density. Two prismatic blades were recovered. Of 82 sherds, 84 percent (n = 69) were Late Classic types. No features were associated with Stratum I because all evidence of the latest occupation surface had eroded away. Associated with Stage 5, the midden over the platform had continued to accumulate with Stratum P I—a 0.09 m thick humic zone with a high artifact density (Table 5.7). All 235 sherds were Late Classic types.

Feature 75-76 Excavation

A small unit was excavated in an inferior mound in the northeast interior of Isla Chablé (Figure 5.6). Feature 76 was a 0.75- to 1.00-m tall oval platform (60 × 55 m) with a sloping surface. It had a projected elevation of ca. 1.50 m at its center, assuming that the inferior mound was built over it. An abandoned modern house indicated by a cement floor and midden were located on the northwest side of the platform. A long canal, made shallow and narrow from sedimentation, led from the northeast shoreline to the platform. Inferior mound Feature 75 was 2.5 m tall and oval, measuring 35 by 28 m. The top of Feature 75 sloped from the north (at an elevation of 3.23 m) to the south (at an elevation of 2.83 m). On its northern side were disturbed remnants of superior mound features 73 (10 × 5 × 0.25 m) and 74 (6 × 4 × 0.25 m). The sloping summit of the inferior mound and a high density of prehispanic pottery exposed on the southern top edge may have been products of disturbance, although no remains of modern structures or holes from digging were identified there. The surface collection at that location yielded 99 sherds, all but 2 of which were Late Classic types. Among the rims, 71 were from ollas, 1 was from a jar, and 1 was from a plate.

A 1- by 1-m test unit (Unit 5) was placed next to that high-density surface scatter on Feature 75. Twelve levels were excavated into four strata until a structure (Feature 137) was encountered at 1.65 m elevation—close to the projected top of platform Feature 76. To preserve the structure, the excavation was halted, documented, and backfilled without subfloor sampling.

The floor of Feature 137 (Figure 5.6) was an undulating calcium-based plaster of poor quality that had decomposed into a powder with small crushed shell inclusions. The floor covered two thirds of the area within the unit and had a clear northern boundary. Extending north from the floor's edge was a 0.27-m tall modeled adobe wall base. No postholes within or adjacent to the wall base were observed. Stacked against the interior wall edge, over the decomposed floor, was a concentration of large sherds from different vessels. Other sherds were found scattered across the floor, where a large ash stain was also

present. Outside the northern floor boundary was a dense concentration of charcoal (dated to cal. CE 660–780 [2σ, cal. 1290–1170 BP], Beta Analytic 299881; Ensor 2011c). Stratum V (lightly compacted brown clay mottled with reddish brown clay) overlaid the floor and had abundant charcoal and ash staining, along with 103 eroded nodules of a poor-quality plaster similar to those from Feature 40. Nine additional nodules were on the floor. Together, these observations indicate that a Late Classic structure was built with poor-quality plaster for flooring, with at least one wall base of adobe and upper walls of perishable materials covered in poor-quality plaster, and that the structure burned and collapsed over the floor.

Stratum IV—a 0.91-m thick deposit of compact brown clay with light charcoal flecking—represents a major episode in the inferior mound's construction. Within it, at 10 to 20 cm above the burned fill of Feature 137, was a 4- to 7-cm thick lens of the same clay material that formed the adobe wall base. Because Stratum IV occurred both over and under this lens, the wall base may have been taller than the portion observed in-situ and was pushed over while Stratum IV was deposited over the structure fill. The artifact density within Stratum IV varied among the nine excavation levels within it but was generally high (having a mean of 537 artifacts per m^3 with a standard deviation of 219 per m^3). Overlying it was Stratum III, a thinner deposit of very compact pale brown clay with a higher artifact density (815 per m^3). Stratum II was a lens of sherds (10,819 per m^3) within a pale brown clay. Stratum I, the surface sediment, was the same but with a lower but also very high (2,196 per m^3) artifact density.

Most sherds recovered in Unit 5 were Late Classic types (Table 5.8). The few Formative sherds suggest that deposits from an earlier occupation in the vicinity were redeposited during the Late Classic to build Feature 75. The rim sherds illustrate a preponderance of ollas accompanied by dishes and few bowls.

Profiles

Profiles of three multilevel mounds with shell deposits at Isla Chablé (Ensor and Tun Ayora 2004) and El Bellote (Ensor and Tun Ayora 2011; Ensor, Tun Ayora, and Herrera Escobar 2008a) also demonstrate that superior mounds were constructed over inferior mounds. In addition, they demonstrate that the "shell" mounds' construction included a significant amount of earthen deposits, not just shell.

Feature 93 was a superior mound overlying inferior mound Feature 94 in the South Group of Isla Chablé

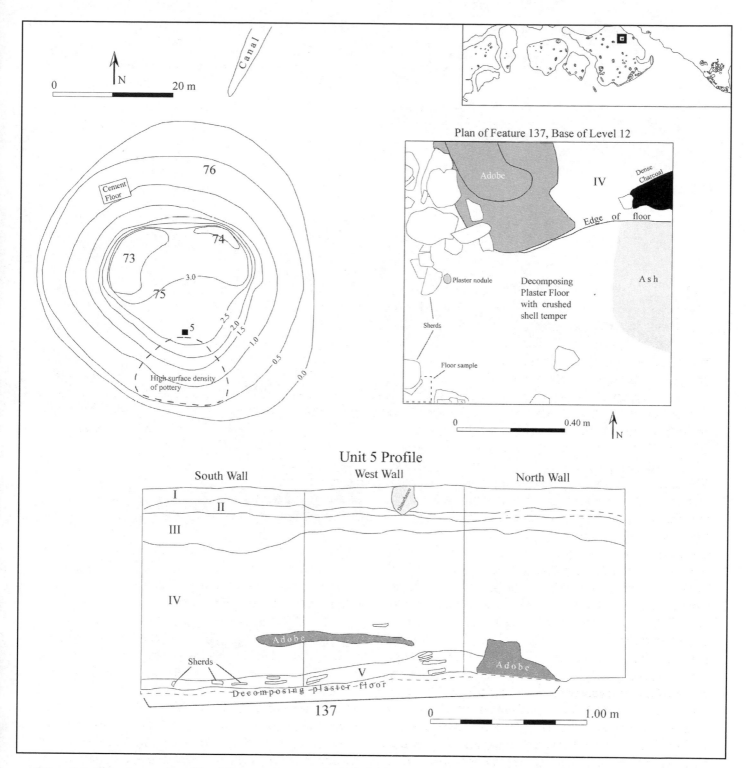

Figure 5.6. Plan view and profile of features 73–76, with inset showing Feature 137. Prepared by the author.

Table 5.8. Stratigraphic Distribution of Artifacts from Unit 5, Features 75 and 76

Stratum	Level	Elevation (m)	Number of sherds	Late Classic Pottery							Other
				%	J	O	T	B	D	P	M²
I	1	2.87–2.74	242	100	–	4	–	–	1	–	–
II	2	2.74–2.67	687	99.7	–	22	–	2	1	–	–
III	3	2.67–2.56	68	100	–	1	–	–	–	–	–
	4	2.56–2.46	36	94.4	–	–	–	–	–	–	–
	5	2.46–2.36	72	100	–	1	–	–	–	–	–
IV	6	2.36–2.26	49	95.9	–	–	–	–	3	–	–
	7	2.26–2.16	64	95.3	–	–	–	–	1	–	–
	8	2.16–2.06	68	100	–	–	–	1	1	–	–
	9	2.06–1.96	82	93.9	–	1	–	–	–	–	–
	10	1.96–1.86	32	100	–	2	–	–	–	–	–
Clay lens		1.88–1.84	11	54.5	–	–	–	–	–	–	–
IV	11	1.86–1.76	39	97.4	–	–	–	–	–	–	–
V – F 137 fill	12a	1.76–1.65	79	100	–	1	–	–	–	–	103
F 137 floor	12c	–	37	100	–	–	–	–	1	–	9
IV	12b	1.76–1.69	2	100	–	–	–	–	–	–	–

Key: J = jar; O = olla; T = *tecomate*; B = bowl; D = dish; P = plate; M² = mortar/plaster, low quality.

Note: No Formative pottery was recovered from these features.

(Figure 5.7). The multilevel mound was intact in 2001 but approximately one-third had been removed as a result of sediment mining by 2004, when it was profiled. Although reported, more mining on its south side occurred afterwards and only half the formation remained by 2005. No further disturbance has been observed since. Just over half (55 percent) of the surface-collected pottery was Late Classic. The lowest strata observed were associated with the inferior mound (Feature 94). Stratum VII was a dark brown sand lacking shell inclusions. Five sherds of Formative types were recovered from Stratum VII. Stratum VI was another mound fill deposit of light brown clay with few pieces of shell. Among nine sherds, five were unclassified, two were Formative, and two were Late Classic types. Stratum V was an occupation surface across the top of the inferior mound: a thin layer of horizontally lying unmodified shell with three horizontally lying Formative sherds. Overlying that surface was Stratum IV—the first mound fill deposit creating superior mound Feature 93. This was a light brown clay generally lacking in shell. Six more Formative sherds were recovered from Stratum IV. The top of Stratum IV was an earlier surface of the superior mound, as

indicated by two pits (features 135 and 138) associated with its top. Stratum III—unmodified shell within a matrix of light brown clay—overlay that surface and filled both pits. Sixteen sherds were recovered, including 9 Formative and 4 Late Classic types. In addition, one Formative sherd was found in Feature 135. Strata I and II covered the surface of the superior mound, were identical to Stratum III but with humus, and included two Formative sherds. The profile demonstrates that (1) the multilevel formation was not a shell midden but an intentionally formed mound; (2) most of its construction involved earthen deposits, despite surface appearances; and (3) although most pottery was Formative in age, Late Classic types were also represented in the inferior mound's fill indicating mound construction in the latter period.

Feature 160 was a narrow 20- by 80-m inferior mound in the North-Central Group of El Bellote. It has three superior mounds (features 161, 162, and 163) (Figure 5.8) and is similar to Central Coastal Veracruz "palaces" (Stark 1999:209). A near-vertical cut from erosion was located on its south side, at the location of superior mound Feature 161. Stratum IV—densely compacted unmodified shell with

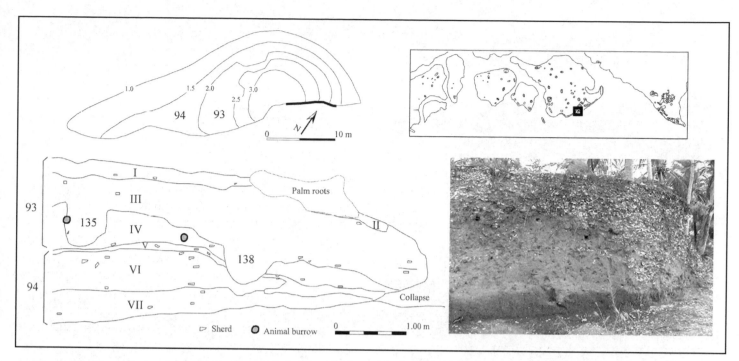

Figure 5.7. Plan view and profile of multilevel mound features 93 and 94. Prepared by the author.

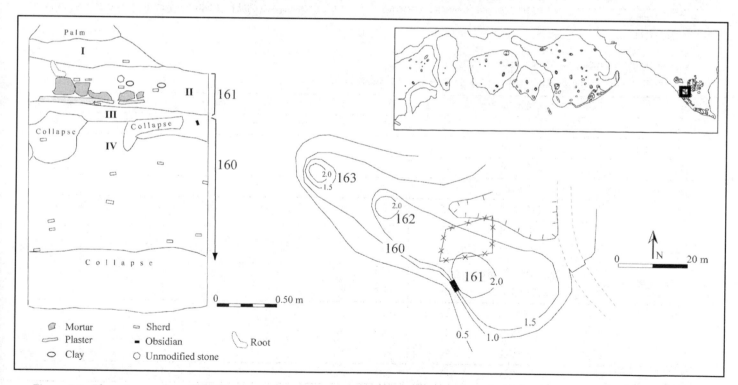

Figure 5.8. Plan view and profile of features 160–163. Prepared by the author.

dark brown silt—was the lowermost observed. It comprised the bulk of Feature 160's mound fill: at least 1.00 m of the 1.10-m tall mound. Eleven sherds were recovered from Stratum IV: five were Formative types and six were Late Classic types. Stratum III was a thinner deposit of compact whole shells in a dark brown clay. One piece of obsidian was collected but no sherds were observed. The top of Stratum III was the surface of the inferior mound associated with an eroding in-situ plaster floor over which chunks of mortar, possibly from collapsed lower walls, were observed. One Late Classic sherd was associated with the structure. Stratum II—a compact dark brown sandy clay with unmodified and crushed shell—overlaid and surrounded the collapsed structure, creating the superior mound (Feature 161). Stratum I was the same but with less crushed shell, more humus, and with dense palm roots. From both superior mound strata, four sherds of possible Formative types and two sherds of Late Classic types were recovered. The inferior mound, the structure, and the superior mounds were Late Classic constructions.

Feature 150 was a superior mound overlying inferior mound Feature 167 in the Central Group of El Bellote (Figure 5.9). Located at the landing that the ranch has used since the nineteenth century, the lack of protective mangrove caused significant erosion to the multilevel formation as a result of storms and flooding, as well as ranch-related activities. One hurricane during the 2007 season eroded more of the inferior mound where a hearth (Feature 158) and plaster-lined pit (Feature 159) were further damaged before they could be documented. Immediately after the hurricane, a composite profile and plan map of the two features were drawn (Figure 5.9) The plaster-lined pit (Feature 159) and the large hearth or roasting pit (Feature 158) were within the lowermost strata (VI and V) observed for the Feature 167, the inferior mound, yet they were partially covered by the collapsed sediments. Stratum VI was a deposit of unmodified shell with small pieces of mortar indicating redeposition from a razed structure. No other artifacts were observed in Stratum VI. Stratum V—the uppermost fill creating the inferior mound—was a deposit of unmodified shell with compact light brown sandy clay. One Late Classic sherd was found in Stratum V. Associated with Stratum V was Feature 158, the hearth or roasting pit. Stratum V' appeared to be the pit wall for Feature 158. Ten sherds were recovered from Feature 158's fill: two Formative, one possible Formative, and seven Late Classic types. Superior mound Feature 150 was constructed with small deposits: Stratum IV, a reddish brown clay with

red clay nodules from a razed structure's floor; Stratum III, a deposit of unmodified and crushed shell with dark brown silt; and Stratum II, a light reddish brown clay with crushed shell. Stratum IV had four sherds of Late Classic types. Stratum II had three sherds of Late Classic types. Over those small deposits, Stratum I was a thick layer of unmodified shell, shell fragments, and dark brown sandy clay. One concentration of charcoal was observed within Stratum I. Four sherds of Late Classic types were recovered from that latest fill deposit. The exposed plaster floor overlay Stratum I (Figure 5.9). The profile, plan view, and associated artifacts demonstrate that the multilevel mound was constructed in the Late Classic.

Two inferior mounds in the South Group of Isla Chablé had mining pits with vertical walls that were profiled. Although they do not illustrate the relationships between the superior and inferior mounds, the profiles document the use of sediments that contain abundant amounts of shell in their construction along with mixing of Late Classic and Formative pottery (Figure 5.10). Feature 96 was an inferior mound (beneath superior mound Feature 95) with a sediment mine on its north side. The cut revealed five mound fill strata. Stratum V, the lowest observed, was a grayish brown clay with charcoal flecking and a light density of unmodified shell, which yielded 13 sherds: 11 Formative and 2 Late Classic types. One turtle bone was recovered from Stratum V. Stratum IV was a deposit of unmodified and crushed shell in a limey, light pale brown clay that yielded one turtle bone, one Formative sherd, and one Late Classic sherd. Stratum III was a light brown clay with abundant unmodified shell. During the cleaning of the wall, 18 sherds were recovered from either Stratum III or Stratum IV: 13 Formative and 5 Late Classic types. Stratum II was a compact deposit of unmodified shell. Stratum I was a dark brown silt with humus and unmodified shell. The cleaning of these upper two strata yielded two turtle bones and four Late Classic sherds. An additional eight sherds were collected from the collapsed sediments at the base of the mine: two were Formative and six were Late Classic types.

The mine in the northeast side of inferior mound Feature 99 revealed three mound fill strata (Figure 5.10). Stratum III, the lowest observed, was a grayish brown clay with a light density of unmodified shell that yielded five sherds: two Formative, one Late Classic, and two that could not be assigned a type. Stratum II was a light brown clay with a moderate density of unmodified shell where five sherds were recovered: two possible Formative and three

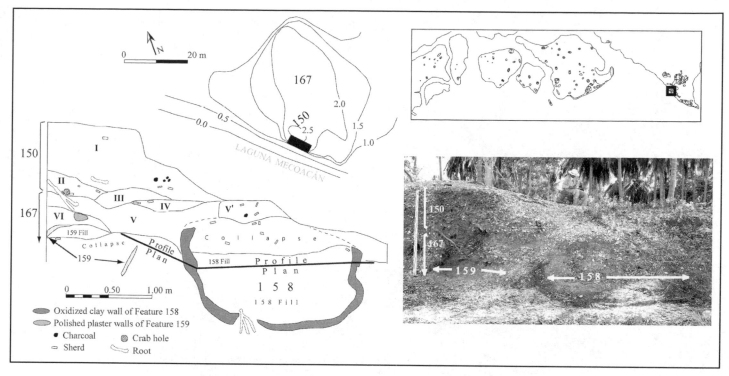

Figure 5.9. Plan view, profile, and photos of features 150, 158, 159, and 167. Prepared by the author.

Late Classic types. Stratum I was a dark grayish brown clay with unmodified shell. No artifacts were recovered from Stratum I. Eleven sherds were collected from the collapsed sediment at the base of the mine: five Formative, five Late Classic, and one possible Formative. Although the profile did not reveal the relationships between the superior and inferior mounds, the profiles of the sediment mines in features 96 and 99 illustrate how sediments with varying amounts of shell were used to construct the inferior mounds. The mixture of Formative and Late Classic pottery in most strata demonstrate construction during the latter period.

Summary

Superior mounds on multilevel mound formations were the smallest of all mound categories. The greater the number of superior mounds, the larger the inferior mounds and underlying platforms. As with other categories, the surface collections at multilevel mounds with shell had higher percentages of Formative pottery and those with earthen-only deposits had higher percentages of Late Classic pottery. Although there was a greater emphasis on ollas among Late Classic rims, the Formative and Late Classic pottery represented a diversity of forms. Residential

function is also supported by structures, their materials, and pits identified in excavations and profiles.

The excavations at features 32-34-35 indicated a sequence of platform, mounds-on-platform, inferior mound, and superior mound construction. Five stages were defined and occupation surfaces were associated with two of those stages. Likewise, the excavation into inferior mound Feature 75 revealed a structure at the expected elevation of the top of its underlying platform, illustrating a similar sequence. Although some Formative sherds were present in fill of these features, the vast majority were Late Classic types, indicating construction during the latter period. Both multilevel formations included thick fill strata, indicating that their heights were achieved in single construction episodes rather than in more numerous occupation layers.

The opportunistically made profiles at multilevel mounds with shell at the South Group of Isla Chablé and the Central and North-Central Group of El Bellote also indicate a sequence of inferior mound construction followed by superior mound construction. In two cases, occupation surfaces were identified over inferior mound surfaces. Superior mound fills were deposited on top of those occupation surfaces. Many of the fill deposits were sediment, rather

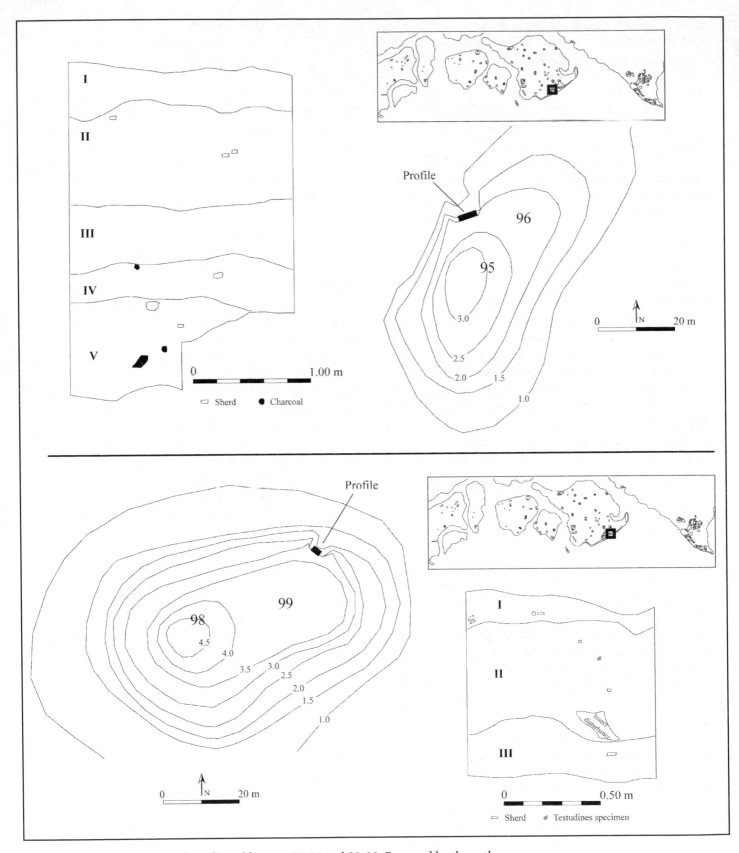

Figure 5.10. Plan views and profiles of features 95-96 and 98-99. Prepared by the author.

than of shell, and most contained Late Classic sherds in addition to Formative types, demonstrating that the features were also constructed in the Late Classic.

CEREMONIAL MOUNDS

Since the nineteenth century, visitors describing El Bellote emphasized the presence of large temple mounds. Charnay (1888:183–193) examined three "pyramids" built of "shells and mud" with brick temples, thick stucco, and bas-reliefs. Blom and LaFarge (1926) described the remains of one temple on a tall mound. Stirling's (1957) description of the tall mounds makes no mention of standing temple wall remnants. The descriptions suggest a deterioration of the structures over time.

Nine mounds were classified by the PAILC as having ceremonial functions based on their morphologies and orientations. All but one was at the site of El Bellote. Five were within the large Northeast Group. Among those, three were in Subgroup A, one was in Subgroup B, and one was in Subgroup C. The largest extant mound at ILC, also classified as ceremonial, was in the Northwest Group. Another, much smaller than these, was in the North-Central Group. One was in the Central Group. The mostly destroyed Feature 100 of the South Group of Isla Chablé was likely a ceremonial mound. Surface collections and profiles of vertical cuts from sediment mining were made where possible to document the chronological affiliation, construction techniques, and functions of these mounds.

General Characteristics

Two defining characteristics distinguished ceremonial from residential features. One was a flat summit with either a horizontal or slightly sloping plane. The second was steep sidedness. Two ceremonial mounds had what at first appeared to be superior mounds built on their summits. In both cases, these were brick substructures that protruded above the eroded surfaces of the mounds built over them. Deposits were placed over the tops of those protruding substructures, creating the appearance of superior mounds. Another did have a superior mound, not the product of a protruding substructure, on its flat summit.

In addition to their flat summits and steep sides, these mounds had quadrilateral shapes with rounded corners. They were generally oriented in cardinal directions (a few degrees west of true north). In contrast, none of the dome-shaped residential mounds had quadrilateral shapes and they shared no common orientation. Corroborating evidence for nonresidential functions was the presence of plastered brick-and-mortar substructures. Brick and mortar were absent at residential mounds.

The ceremonial mounds varied considerably in size. Several were smaller than some inferior mounds of residential multilevel mounds but had greater height-to-length ratios. Of six with identifiable base lengths, there was a range from 35 m to 86 m, with a mean of 48.3 m and a very large standard deviation of 18.9 m, illustrative of the variation in size. Of the five with identifiable base widths, they ranged from 15 m to 37 m, with a mean of 31.4 m and a standard deviation of 9.2 m. The six with identifiable heights range from 1.8 m to 6.1 m, with a mean of 3.4 m and a standard deviation of 1.5 m. The height-to-length ratios ranged from 0.03 m to 0.17 m. Removing one outlier with the low ratio, the mean was 0.09 m with a standard deviation of 0.05 m. Few residential mounds have comparable height-to-length ratios (Table 5.1).

There was no "religious precinct" at ILC. Ceremonial mounds were incorporated into, and shared basal platforms with, residential mound groups. They were constructed in the same manner as residential mounds, even reusing Formative deposits for their construction in the Late Classic.

Descriptions

Features 196 and 202

Included within the Subgroup B *plazuela* of the Northeast Group at El Bellote, and sharing that residential group's low earthen basal platform, Feature 202 was a square, steep-sloped, and flat-topped ceremonial mound with rounded corners constructed with shell and earth fill (Figure 4.5). At its base, it measured 38 by 37 m. Its height was 3.5 m. The small flat summit was largely obscured by the upward protrusion of a substructure but measured approximately 20 m across. The substructure (Feature 196) was a vaulted brick-and-mortar chamber with a vaulted arch and thick layers of stucco. The top of the substructure protruded 1.6 m above the surface of Feature 202 where mound fill, once covering the top of the substructure, eroded to expose the roof bricks (Figure 4.5).

A wide trench from the northeast corner to the center of the mound exposed the interior ceiling of the vaulted substructure (Figure 4.5). Unlike most cases of large-scale sediment mining at El Bellote (reportedly in the 1970s for road construction fill) that entirely removed large portions of mounds, a significant amount of sediment was left behind, filling the base of the trench. This unusual characteristic suggests that the trench may not have been the result of sediment mining, but rather was created by looters or, perhaps, by Berlin (Sisson 1976:5).

The surface collection unit was placed at the northeast corner of the mound where the disturbance left a high density of pottery, presumably from multiple stratigraphic contexts. Of the 63 sherds collected, 14.3 percent (n = 9) were Formative, 6.4 percent (n = 4) were possibly Formative, and 79.4 percent (n = 50) were Late Classic types. Among the Late Classic rim sherds, one bowl, four ollas, and one jar were represented, which is not different from the pattern for residential features. Only four sherds were of fine paste types; most were utilitarian types, which is also similar to collections from residential features. Two Late Classic sherds and one Formative sherd had mortar adhered to them, indicating that they were incorporated in the construction materials used in the substructure. In addition to the pottery, mortar fragments, brick fragments, and one animal bone were collected.

Figure 4.5 shows the profile of the southern trench sidewall. Six strata in addition to the brick, mortar, and stucco were observed (Ensor, Tun Ayora, and Herrera Escobar 2008:32). A significant amount of sediment obscured the base of the substructure. The lowermost deposit observed was Stratum VI—a layer of mortar coated by a layer of plaster. On the east side of that was Stratum V—a compact deposit of unmodified shells and light brown silt. Portions of these two strata were covered by Stratum IV—a dark brown clay with unmodified shells. No pottery was observed in strata VI, V, and IV, all of which represent sequential episodes in the remodeling or filling of the interior of the substructure. Stratum III was a compact deposit of whole and fragmentary shell in a light brown silt matrix. Five sherds were recovered from Stratum III: one Formative and four Late Classic types. Stratum II—a dark brown silt with whole shell inclusions—was interior substructure fill that reached its ceiling. Within Stratum IV, but primarily overlying strata IV, III, and II were sequential layers of stucco and mortar for the roof of the vaulted substructure. Stratum I was the mound fill of Feature 202, which was built over the substructure. It also covered the protruding top of the substructure, giving the false appearance of a superior mound. Stratum I was a dark brown sandy clay with humus. Stratum I′ was the same but with dense palm roots. No artifacts were observed in Stratum I but five sherds—one possible Formative type and four Late Classic types—were recovered from the surface of the mound where the profile was drawn. The substructure's architecture and the pottery demonstrate construction during the Late Classic.

Features 166 and 185

Feature 166 was the northernmost of three ceremonial mounds in Subgroup A of the Northeast Group of El Bellote (Figure 4.5). Constructed of earth and shell fill, the mound appeared to have been rectangular with rounded corners and a north-south orientation. Three short trenches (from sediment mining) with collapsing sidewalls on the north end and erosion on the northeast portion produced a more rounded outline. The extant mound was 41 m in length, 34 m in width, and 2.8 m in height, with steep slopes and a flat summit approximately 35 by 25 m in size. Feature 185 had the appearance of a dome-shaped, 17- by 9-m oval superior mound (1.0 m in height) on the east side of Feature 166. However, brick and mortar fragments were observed on the adjacent surface of Feature 166, suggesting that it is a substructure protruding above the mound summit.

The easternmost of the three small trenches in mound Feature 166 had a near vertical sidewall where five strata were documented (Figure 5.11). Stratum V was a compact light brown silt with unmodified shell. Along with Formative and Late Classic sherds, a flat piece of mortar and one animal bone were observed within Stratum V. Along its west surface was Stratum IV, a small deposit of unmodified shell, where seven sherds were recovered: one Formative, two possible Formative, and four Late Classic types. Stratum III, another deposit of unmodified shell on the west, was mixed with Stratum II—a compact dark brown clay—that partially overlay the former. Recovered from Stratum III were five Formative sherds and two Late Classic sherds. Ten sherds were recovered from Stratum II—four Formative, one possible Formative, and five Late Classic types. Stratum I was a dark brown clay with few shell fragments yielding six sherds: two Formative and four Late Classic types. The mound fill stratigraphy demonstrates several episodes of mound construction that recycled mixed Formative to Late Classic deposits.

Feature 170

This central ceremonial mound on the east side of Subgroup A had a north-south–oriented quadrilateral shape with rounded corners at its base and steep-sloping sides. Whereas the northern and southern ends were approximately of similar lengths (35 and 37 m, respectively) the western side was shorter than the eastern side (38 and 45 m, respectively). The summit–20 m wide, and 34 m and 20 m in length on the eastern and western sides, respectively—was a plane that sloped from 5.3 m on its southern end to 4.2 m in elevation on its northern end. Feature 170 was constructed with earthen and shell fill deposits.

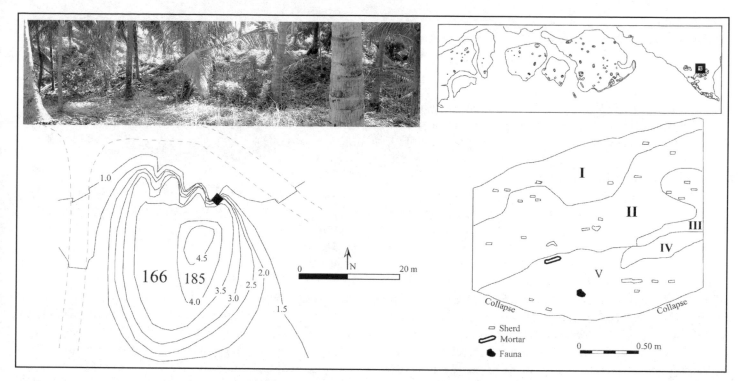

Figure 5.11. Plan view, profile, and photo of features 166 and 185. Prepared by the author.

This mound was not disturbed by looting or sediment mining.

The surface collection on the western side of Feature 170 (from summit to base) yielded 102 sherds, 1 obsidian flake, and 10 animal bones. Among the sherds, 55.8 percent (n = 57) were Formative types, 14.7 percent (n = 15) were possible Formative types, 26.5 percent (n = 27) were of Late Classic types, and 2.9 percent (n = 3) were unclassified. Among the few rim sherds collected, only two dishes and two ollas were represented

Feature 165

Stirling (1957) described the tallest mound at El Bellote as 75 feet tall (ca. 23 m). It was presumably the same mound where Charnay (1888:186–190) and Blom and LaFarge (1929) describe the remains of a temple. No such mound was observed by the PAILC. Feature 165 in Subgroup A of the Northeast Group at El Bellote (Figure 4.5) was severely disturbed, with most of its fill removed reportedly in the 1970s for road fill. It had the largest base and is thus the best candidate for the tallest mound described in these early visits. What remained of mound Feature 165 was an extensive 97- by 42-m zone of disturbed and uneven earth and shell. It was approximately 0.5 m in height but had two higher mound fill remnants. The remnant in the

center of the mound measured only 4 by 10 m in size and 2.6 m in height. A larger (40 × 20 m) but lower (1.8- to 2.3-m tall) remnant of mound fill with pinched sides was immediately to the east of the central mound. Using the height-to-length ratios from other ceremonial mounds in the Northeast Group, Feature 165's original height— assuming an approximated 80 m base length—is estimated to have been between 5.6 and 13.6 m; 8.8 m if using the average (0.11).

A surface collection unit placed between the two mound remnants yielded 124 sherds, 1 obsidian flake, 1 plain but polished slab of stucco, a clay nodule, and six animal bones. Among the sherds, 52.4 percent were of Formative types, 4.8 percent were of possible Formative types, and 42.8 percent were of Late Classic types. Only two dishes and one bowl were represented, which differs from most residential contexts where ollas were predominant.

Feature 194

Feature 194—adjacent to a residential mound in Subgroup C in the Northeast Group of El Bellote (Figure 4.5)—was also constructed of shell and earth fill but displayed morphological irregularities. At its base, five sides with rounded corners could be interpreted on its north, east, south, southwest, and west (Ensor and Tun Ayora 2011). At mid-slope, however, only four sides with rounded corners were apparent. The northern, eastern, and southern sides were steeply sloped. The western side had slumped, extending the mound fill beyond what would have been the western edge of its original base. This created the appearance of a fifth corner at the base, while also creating a concave contour midway upslope when all other sides had slightly convex contours (see Figure 4.5). Taking into account the deformation caused by the slumping on the west, Feature 194 likely had a square shape; each side was approximately 35 m long. Another unusual characteristic was that its flat-topped summit was oval in shape. This was not a result of the slumping because that occurred more than a meter beneath the summit. From base to summit, the mound measured 6.1 m in height, producing a height-to-length ratio of 0.17—the largest of any extant mound at ILC.

A surface collection unit on the lower western slope yielded 127 sherds, four undecorated pieces of stucco (one with a smoothed surface), a mano fragment, and three vertebrate faunal specimens. Among the sherds, 26.8 percent were Formative types, 23.6 percent were possible Formative types, 44.9 percent were Late Classic types, and 4.7 percent were unclassified. Six ollas and one bowl were represented by the Late Classic rim sherds.

Features 198 and 199

Features 198 and 199 formed a multilevel mound in the center of the Northwest Group of El Bellote (Figure 4.5). Unlike the other ceremonial mounds, these were constructed entirely of earthen deposits, were elliptical in shape, and have an east-west orientation. Approximately two-fifths of the southern side of the formation was removed, reportedly also in the 1970s for road fill. Feature 198, the large inferior mound was 86 m long. The width, before the destruction of its southern side, is estimated to be about 40 m. The sides and ends were steep-sloping, although a portion of the northern mid-section had slumped, creating a concave contour at its top and a convex contour beneath. The top of the inferior mound was 2.7 m high and formed a horizontal plane 25 m long on the west side of the superior mound. The superior mound (Feature 199) was conical but with a gradually sloping western side that led down to the flat summit of the inferior mound. That slope appears to have been a ramp (potentially accommodating a staircase) for accessing the top of the superior mound, which was 2.8 m high. Ramps were also observed on ceremonial mounds in the NWAF study area (Piña Chan and Navarrete 1967: Figure 39). At an elevation of 7.0 m, this was the tallest extant human-made elevation observed at ILC.

One surface collection unit placed on top of the collapsing sediment from the disturbed southwest corner of the inferior mound yielded 69 sherds, eight plain pieces of stucco (three of which had smoothed surfaces), and four clay chunks. Among the sherds, 84.1 percent (n = 58) were Formative and 15.9 percent (n = 11) were Late Classic types. The Late Classic rims were few but represented one dish and two ollas.

Feature 164

Within the North-Central Group of El Bellote, Feature 164 was a mound tentatively classified as ceremonial. This was an elliptical mound only 34 by 15 m in size at its base with steeply sloped sides and a low height of 1.8 m. Though smaller than other ceremonial mounds it had a remarkably flat summit and a north-south orientation. Built with shell and earthen deposits, the mound was in good condition.

A surface collection on its southern summit and sloping side yielded 303 sherds, one chunk of clay, and one obsidian blade fragment. No mortar, brick, or stucco was observed. Among the sherds, 69.0 percent (n = 209) were Formative, 10.6 percent (n = 32) were possible Formative, and 20.4 percent (n = 62) were Late Classic types. Represented among the Late Classic rims were one plate, one dish, three ollas, and one jar.

Feature 151

One large mound in the Central Group of El Bellote was classified as a ceremonial mound although it lacked a flat summit, possibly due to disturbance. Feature 151 was in the central clearing in the group (figures 4.6 and 5.12) at the heart of the El Bellote ranch and had been subjected to surface disturbance since the nineteenth century. The subject of local lore, this mound was in the process of being removed for road fill in the 1970s, but people reportedly prevented its destruction because a supernatural rooster dwells within. The vertical scars from mechanical digging circumferentially around its sides were still apparent. Unknown is whether the damage also modified the top of the mound. The resulting mound was oval (34 × 27 m and 4.3 m tall) with a domed top.

A surface collection unit over the disturbed northeastern slope and base yielded 277 sherds, three pieces of mortar and stucco, and one vertebrate faunal fragment. Among the sherds, 68.9 percent (n = 191) were Formative, 5.4 percent (n = 15) were possible Formative, 16.6 percent (n = 46) were Late Classic, and 9.1 percent (n = 25) were unclassified. Very few rims were present and only one olla and two bowls were represented.

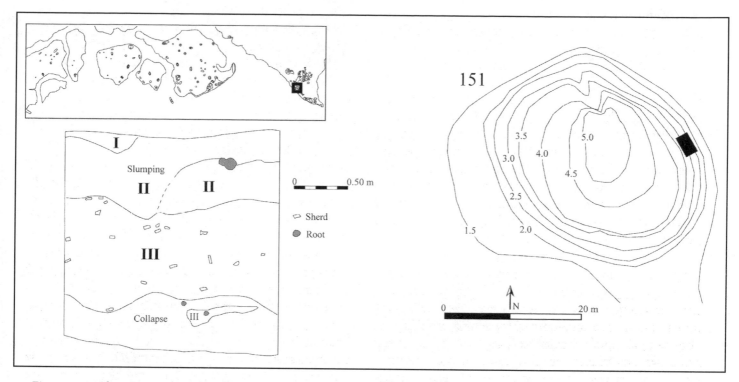

Figure 5.12. Plan view and profile of Feature 151. Prepared by the author.

A profile was drawn of a vertical cut in the lower east slope. Only three strata were observed (Figure 5.12). Stratum III was a thick deposit of very compact light brown clay with unmodified shell. Twenty-two sherds were collected: 1 Formative and 21 Late Classic types. Stratum II was a compact, light brown clay with few shell inclusions. Two Formative sherds and two Late Classic sherds were collected. Stratum I was a deposit of unmodified shell in a humic matrix. No artifacts were observed in Stratum I.

Feature 100

The only possible ceremonial mound not located at El Bellote was Feature 100 in the South Group of Isla Chablé. Feature 100 was on the northeast corner of the extensive basal platform for the mound group (Figure 4.4). The mound was mostly destroyed, having only three steep-sided remnants with uneven surfaces of disturbed fill in-between. According to an elder informant the mound once stood 5 m tall but was quarried for lime in decades past. Lacking protective mangrove, the remnants were also severely eroded. Given the size and cornered shape of the projected mound base, Feature 100 was classified as a possible ceremonial mound. No earthen deposits were observed; all extant fill had dense concentrations of shell.

A surface collection unit in the center of the mound remnants yielded only 12 sherds (3 Late Classic and 9 Formative) and a Formative period figurine fragment. One olla and one jar were represented by the Formative rim sherds; one Late Classic rim sherd was from an olla.

A profile was drawn of a near vertical shoreline erosional cut in a mound remnant. Three strata were observed (Figure 5.13). The lowest, Stratum III, was a compact layer of abundant whole and broken shell lacking sediment. It was partially obscured by roots from an adjacent coconut palm that was also collapsing due to erosion. Stratum II was a fill deposit of abundant whole and broken shell in a brown clay matrix. Strata III and II each had one Formative sherd. Stratum I was a compact layer of whole and broken shell. No artifacts were observed in Stratum I. Between each strata were zones of collapsing fill. The collapsing zone between strata III and II yielded three additional Formative sherds. Although Late Classic sherds were recovered in the surface collection, none were observed in the fill deposits.

Summary

Nine features were classified as ceremonial mounds. All but one (Feature 100) was at El Bellote. Although mortar, stucco, and brick were found at several of these, none of

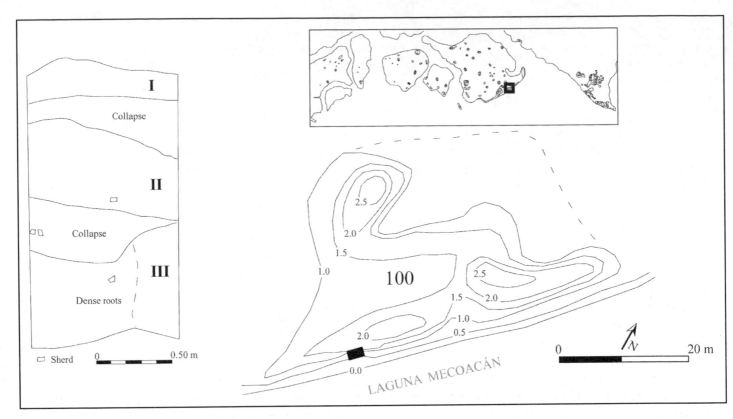

Figure 5.13. Plan view and profile of Feature 100. Prepared by the author.

the temple walls observed and reported by Charnay and Blom and LaFarge were still present. If Berlin did, in fact, excavate at El Bellote, it was likely the trench into Feature 202, where a brick and mortar, thickly plastered, vaulted substructure (Feature 196) was observed. The 75-foot–tall temple mound described by Stirling was not relocated but may have been the destroyed Feature 165 in Subgroup A of the Northeast Group of El Bellote.

Although some residential mounds were larger than some ceremonial mounds, the latter were generally taller, with higher length-to-height ratios. With the exception of those that were significantly damaged, they nearly all had quadrilateral shapes and flat-topped summits. The shapes and flat summits, combined with the presence of brick, mortar, and stucco at many, along with the vaulted substructure indicates their classification as ceremonial. Though the specific ceremonial functions were not identified, all were associated with residential groups, suggesting group-affiliated functions.

All but Feature 198-199 in the Northwest Group of El Bellote were constructed with shell and earth deposits. All had Formative and Late Classic pottery in the surface collection units. The stratigraphic sampling from profiled

cuts confirmed that the sherds were mixed even in lower mound fills, with the exception of Feature 100. This indicates that earlier mixed deposits from residential contexts in the Late Classic were repurposed for fill. Unlike the clay-capped stepping found in Mound 10 at Tierra Nueva in the NWAF study (Piña Chan and Navarrete 1967:30), there was no evidence of capped surfaces and stepped sides at ILC's ceremonial mounds.

SPECIALIZED FEATURES

Motivating the extensive literature on specialized production features and locations in Mesoamerican archaeology is the modeling of political and economic organization at regional to local scales. Much of the literature focuses on class specialization and identifying the contexts for manufacturing (Charlton 1993; Feinman and Nicholas 1993; Haviland 1974; McKillop 1995; Moholy-Nagy 1992; Santley 2004; Shafer and Hester 1983, 1986; Stark and Garaty 2004) and the social dimensions of craft production (Arden and others 2010; Carpenter, Feinman, and Nicholas 2012; Stark, Heller, and Ohnersorgen 1998; Pérez Rodríguez 2006). Often, new categories of features are included, for example, port facilities (Andrews 2008; Barrett and Guderjan 2006), terraces (Feinman, Nicholas, and Haines 2002), and water storage features (Weiss-Krejci and Sabbas 2002). Although many of these studies conclude that production was controlled by households, specialized activity features may also be indicators of community-wide collectivized production, adding another dimension to understanding social relationships. Four features were interpreted as specialized production locations at ILC: Features 89, 92, 122, and 176 (Figures 4.4 and 4.6). Another feature (Feature 155), for which there is little information, may also have had a specialized function.

Feature 92

Although unreported in previous research, one of the more apparent and distinctive features at ILC was the low, narrow platform spanning the southern shoreline of Isla Chablé (Figure 4.4) (Ensor 2003b). Although the edges of the islands and lagoon are typically lined by zones of mangrove, with submerged sediments gradually rising to low inundated flats beneath the tangled arches of mangrove roots, approximately 600 m of the south shore of Isla Chablé is lined by Feature 92. It is a 2.5- to 5.0-m wide, 0.2- to 0.5-m high embankment with a flat, grassy surface that is preventing the erosion of the island's sediments. It is currently used to grow coconut trees.

Where Feature 92 blends into the large basal platform of the South Group of Isla Chablé it is formed of shell and earth deposits that are both eroding and heaped from wave action. Formative and Late Classic pottery was seen on the surface of the feature there. The shell, wave disturbance, and surface visibility gradually diminished 20 m west and east of the South Group's basal platform, where Feature 92 is characterized by a low, earthen construction. The shoreline platform extended approximately 50 east of the South Group, followed by a gap of the same length, followed by another 45- to 50-m remnant, after which no traces were visible. On the west, the platform extended approximately 220 m from the South Group to another gap where the island is eroding, followed by low traces of the platform that gradually disappeared (Figure 4.4).

In 2001, the interpretation of Feature 92's function was based on its morphology alone. No surface collections were possible due to the low surface visibility from dense grass. No similar features have been reported in the region and the only analog elsewhere is a stone-built dock at Postclassic period Isla Cerritos in the Yucatán (Andrews 1987:83, 2008). Smaller but similar embankments are used as landings at or near modern residences. As such, the platform was interpreted as a landing for a collective specialized function such as commerce or fishing (Ensor 2003b:108).

In 2004, one 2- by 2-m unit was excavated 90 m west of the South Group in Feature 92 (Figure 5.14). Three strata were identified (Ensor and Tun Ayora 2004:56–58). The lowermost, Stratum III was sampled in only a 0.5-×-0.5 m subunit. It consisted of the natural sediment under Feature 92 and was below the water table. The stratum was a moderately compact, gray clay with a very low artifact density (Table 5.9). Those artifacts were likely introduced to Stratum III by the burrowing of crabs, which even occurred during the excavation. The platform was constructed with two deposits. Stratum II was a 5-cm-thick, lightly compact brown sand with a light artifact density that included Formative and Late Classic pottery, and eight bones (turtle and one unidentified animal). Stratum I was a 10- to 14-cm-thick, moderately compact grayish brown silt with fine sand and few inclusions of crushed shell with a significantly higher artifact density that included both Formative and Late Classic pottery (Figure 5.9). The sherds were severely eroded; no rims or surface decorations were identifiable. Among the abundant faunal specimens, 50.1 percent were from turtles (Testudines), 26.9 percent were from boney fishes (Osteichthyes), 1.0 percent were from sharks (Lamniformes), and 21.1 percent were from unidentified taxa. Based on the morphological and artifactual observations, Feature 92 was interpreted as a Late Classic landing for collective fishing-related activities.

Features 89 and 122

Features 89 and 122 were dense deposits of crushed oyster shell overlying the mangrove sediments. Included with the crushed shell fragments were very small and severely eroded sherds and small broken and eroded animal bones. Feature 89, near the Southwest Group of Isla Chablé, had an eroded elliptical shape; it measured 15 by 65 m in size and was 0.30 m high (Figure 4.4). Apart from the crushed shell, too few artifacts were observed to warrant a surface collection.

Feature 122 was a larger deposit at the southeast corner of Isla Chablé measuring 78 m in length, 10 m in maximum width, and 0.35 m in height (Figure 5.15). Unlike Feature 89, it was not spatially associated with a residential group. Six sherds were recovered from the surface collection unit, all but one of which were Late Classic types. If Feature 92 extended to this corner of the island before the erosion of that area, then the platform would have connected Feature 122 to the South Group (Figure 4.4). Where Feature 89's edges sloped gradually toward the present mangrove

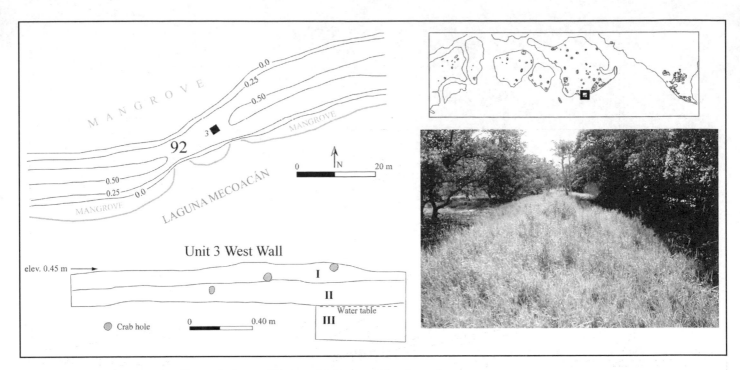

Figure 5.14. Plan view, profile, and photo of Feature 92. Prepared by the author.

Table 5.9. Stratigraphic Distribution of Artifacts from Unit 3, Feature 92

Level	Stratum	Density (per m3)	Vertebrate NISP (%)*					Pottery		
			Number	L	O	T	I	Number	% Formative	% Late Classic
1	I	382.58	104	0.96	26.93	50.96	21.15	96	22.92	69.79
2	II	120.00	8	0	0	87.50	12.50	15	46.67	53.33
3	III	280.00	4	0	50.00	50.00	0	3	0	100
4		142.86	0	0	0	0	0	4	25.00	75.00

Key: L = Lamniformes (sharks); O = Osteichthyes (fishes); T = Testudines (turtles); I = indeterminate vertebrate.

sediment, Feature 122's morphology was more "berm-like" with steep sloping sides due to shoreline erosion (Figure 5.15). Only a thin, interrupted line of mangrove shielded its eastern side from battering by waves. The north end was exposed to a small bay forming in the east side of the island and the south end was exposed to the lagoon's waves. Although at risk of separating from the island, Feature 122 appeared to be a physical barrier that slowed that process, thus temporarily helping to preserve mangrove between the lagoon and the small bay.

Because the crushed shell does not occur naturally, both features were interpreted as specialized locations for processing temper for mortar and plaster. Lime kilns also result in fragmented shell byproducts (Ensor 2003b:108). Either way, mortar (as well as lime) were needed as construction materials at both ILC and Comalcalco. No shell-processing locations have been discovered at Comalcalco, suggesting that shell was not only obtained from ILC, but also processed there.

One 2- by 2-m unit was excavated in the south-central portion of Feature 122 in 2004. Levels 1 and 2 encompassed the 2- by 2-m excavation. To probe 0.19 m below lagoon level, Levels 3 and 4 were excavated as a 0.5- 0.5-m subunit. Although excavated to a total depth of 0.46 cm where the crushed shell became less dense, only one stratum was observed: crushed shell with brown sand (Figure 5.15).

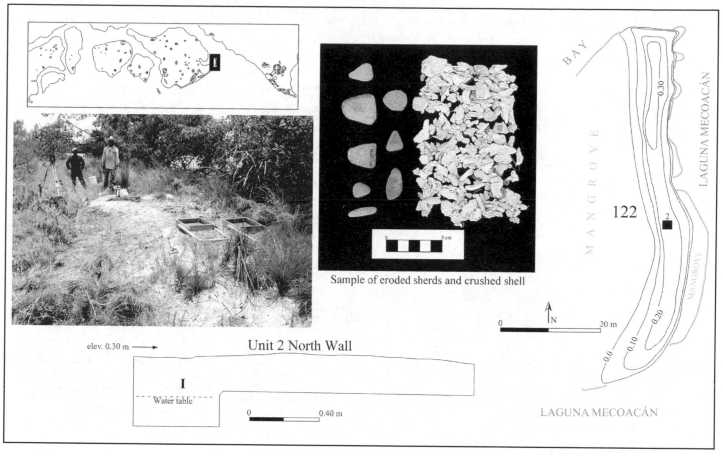

Figure 5.15. Plan view, profile, and photo of Feature 122 and photo of eroded sherds and crushed shell found in the feature. Prepared by the author.

The combined artifact density in the deposit was high and increased from levels 1 to 3 (Table 5.10). The shell particles were rarely larger than 1.0 cm in size and many small fragments fell through the 3-mm mesh screens. A small sample recovered in the screens was collected. In addition to crushed shell, there was a high density of animal bones, a high density of pottery, and four small pieces of chipped stone. No whole or large fragments of shell were observed. The vertebrate remains—primarily fragments less than 1.5 cm in size— constituted 67.65 percent of the non-shell artifacts and were densest in Level 2. In each level, turtle specimens had highest frequencies, followed by fish specimens (Table 5.10). There were low percentages of other taxa. There was a relatively high density of sherds. All were small, most less than 3 cm in size. All were severely eroded, leaving only paste to observe. Only one rim was identifiable. Level 1 had the highest density of sherds, which was the only level having a higher percentage of Formative types. The percentage of sherds of Late Classic types

increased in each successive level (Table 5.10). Although rare at the insular sites, one piece of obsidian and one piece of chert were recovered in Level 1 and another piece of obsidian and chert were recovered in Level 2 (all less than 1.5 cm in size).

The crushed materials match those used as temper in mortar and plaster at ILC and Comalcalco. No burned sediments or charcoal were identified to suggest the presence of lime kilns. Shell crushing for construction materials processing was the interpreted primary activity at Feature 122.

Feature 176

On the west end of the basal platform for the South Group of El Bellote, Feature 176 was a small elliptical platform of earth and shell deposits measuring 16 by 21 m with a maximum height of 0.60 m (Figure 4.6). Although morphologically no different from residential platforms, the artifacts from the surface collection unit suggest a

Table 5.10. Stratigraphic Distribution of Artifacts from Unit 2, Feature 122

Level	Density (per m3)	Vertebrate NISP (%)								Pottery			Chipped Stone
		Number	A	C	L	R	O	T	I	Number	% Formative	% Late Classic	
1	992.54	294	0	1.36	0.68	0.34	29.59	52.72	15.31	252	32.54	67.46	2
2	1,368.18	400	0	0.75	1.25	0	34.25	47.00	16.75	74	21.62	78.38	2
3	3,100.00	55	1.82	0	5.46	0	40.00	40.00	12.73	31	35.48	64.52	0
4	2,320.00	31	0	6.45	0	0	16.13	61.29	16.13	12	0	100	0

Key: NISP = number of individual specimens; A = Aves (birds); C = Crocodylia (crocodiles); Lamniformes (sharks); R = Rajiformes (rays); Osteichthyes (fishes); T = Tesdudines (turtles); I = indeterminate vertebrate.

specialized function. These included 23 Formative (56.09 percent) and 18 Late Classic (43.90 percent) sherds, chunks of clay from hearths or flooring, and vertebrate faunal specimens. Distinct, however, were eight fish-net sinkers, which was far beyond the number found in any other context at ILC. Six were modified Late Classic sherds and one was the only stone sinker found to date at ILC. The eighth was a modified unclassified sherd. The unit also had an unusual concentration of chipped stone—two obsidian prismatic blade fragments and one chert flake. The obsidian was from central Mexican sources (Zaragoza and Pachuca), which is characteristic of the Late Classic in the Chontalpa (Lewenstein 1995; Lewenstein and Glascock 1996, 1997). Given the unusual concentration of net sinkers, cutting tools, and undated vertebrate faunal remains, Feature 176 was interpreted as a specialized fishing-related platform for members of the South Group (Ensor and Tun Ayora 2011; Ensor, Tun Ayora, and Herrera Escobar 2008).

Feature 155

Feature 155 was a large oval platform in the center of the South Group of El Bellote, which shared the same basal platform as the rest of the group (Figure 4.6). Excluding basal platforms for groups and Feature 92, Feature 155 was the largest platform at ILC, measuring 70 m in length, 40 m in width, and 0.80 m in height. The platform had a broad, relatively flat surface, which was covered in dense vegetation that prohibited surface collections. Its southern edge was cut by a ranch road, where a surface collection unit yielded 59 Formative (88.06 percent) and 8 Late Classic (11.94 percent) sherds. Also found were chunks of clay from hearths or flooring. One net sinker was present (a modified sherd of a Formative type). The combination of artifacts was not unusual for residential features in the South Group. The feature's unusual size suggested that Feature 155 had

a collective specialized function, but the type of function was not determined (Ensor and Tun Ayora 2011; Ensor, Tun Ayora, and Herrera Escobar 2008a).

Summary

Two features were interpreted as community-wide collective specialized production locations. Feature 92 was a linear platform along the shoreline that is thought to have been a landing for fishing-related activities. Feature 122 was a deposit of crushed shell (and other materials) for construction materials. Two features were interpreted as residential group-associated specialized production locations. Feature 176 was a small platform used for collective fishing-related activities in the South Group of El Bellote. Feature 89 was a second deposit of crushed shell that was spatially associated with the Southwest Group of Isla Chablé. All four of these were associated with activities geared toward resource exploitation (fishing and shell processing). The activities seen in these features did not occur in most residential locations, signifying an emphasis on collective labor at specialized public locations or, at least, within the two group locations. In addition to shedding light on the organization of production at ILC, the excavations at features 92 and 122 also illustrate the recycling of Formative deposits in the Late Classic—the same pattern found at residential and ceremonial features.

PITS AND THERMAL FEATURES

The range of pits and thermal features has not been previously reported for coastal sites in the region. Seven pits and four thermal cooking features were documented in the 2004, 2005, and 2007 seasons (Ensor and Tun Ayora 2004; Ensor and others 2006; Ensor, Tun Ayora, and Herrera Escobar 2008). Although mentioned previously in relation to stratigraphic contexts in various features, the pits and cooking features are described here.

Pits

Hoping to develop hypotheses on pit functions, the PAILC was prepared with a classification for pits. Plan-view shape categories included circular, elliptical, oval, subrectangular (rectangular with rounded corners), and irregular. Cross-section shapes included depths, bases (basin- and bowl-shaped), walls (insloping, incurving, vertical, outsloping, and outcurving), and bell-shaped. The pits were to be compared to study patterns among sizes, morphologies, and contents. However, only seven pits and two possible pits were identified over the course of the project. These fell into few categories or could not be viewed in their entirety (e.g., only cross-sections in profiles were available). None had fill that could be associated with their uses.

Four pits had shallow, basin shapes with insloping walls (Features 142, 143, 145, 146). All were identified in occupation surfaces 1 and 2 in the Block A excavations within features 32 and 34 (Figure 5.5) and were associated with domestic activities. Despite their similarity in shallowness and cross-section shapes these varied in plan-view shapes. Two were oval (features 142 and 143), one was circular (Feature 146), and one was subrectangular (Feature 145). The mean length was 0.35 m with a standard deviation of 0.04 m. The average depth was 0.09 m with a standard deviation of 0.03 m. Unfortunately, all were filled with overlying strata that contained Formative and Late Classic sherds rather than use-related fill. The small sizes, shallow depths, and flat bases leave their functions open to speculation. If these were pot supports, then one would expect all to be circular. They were too small to have been trash pits. They also seemed too small to have served as storage pits for any useful volume. Fermentation functions within a domestic context also seemed unlikely.

Two deep pits were documented by profiling multilevel mound Feature 93–94 in the South Group of Isla Chablé. This was an elite residential context (Chapter 9). Pit features 135 and 138 were associated with the first surface of Feature 93, the superior mound (Figure 5.7). Feature 135 was a 0.55-m wide, 0.70-m–deep bowl-shaped pit with a western outcurving wall and an eastern vertical, stepped wall. Feature 138 was also a deep bowl-shaped pit but with incurved walls, an observed orifice width of 0.75 m, and a depth (from the upper western rim to the base) of 0.52 m. Whereas Feature 135 was deeper than its orifice, Feature 138 had a wider orifice than depth. Both contained fill from the overlying mound. Within a domestic context,

trash and fermentation functions seemed unlikely, but their morphologies may suggest use for storage.

Only one formally prepared pit was observed at ILC. This was the plaster-lined pit (Feature 159) adjacent to a large formal hearth/roasting pit (Feature 158) exposed by the erosion of inferior mound Feature 167 in the Central Group of El Bellote (Figure 5.9). This was also an elite context. The plaster covering the observed pit walls was 6 to 8 cm in thickness. The eroding interior surface was polished. Before the hurricane during the 2007 season, more of the plaster lining was observable and the pit had a more rounded appearance. After that erosional event, only two portions of the wall were observable: a curved western wall segment and a relatively straight eastern wall segment. The estimated orifice size was 0.90 to 1.00 m. Because the season was not permitted for excavation, the pit's depth and base shape were unknown. A small area of fill was exposed, revealing a reddish-brown silt and sand with few pieces of broken shell. Without excavation, however, it was also unknown whether or not any fill associated with the pit's use was present at the base. At approximately the same elevation as the large formal hearth (Feature 158), Feature 159 may have been used to store or process food or liquid.

Two shallow "depressions" were also identified in the Block A excavations at the Feature 32–34 multilevel mound. Feature 141 was a depression with a subrectangular basin that measured 0.42 by 0.40 m in area but had a depth of only 3 cm. It was filled with material from the overlying mound. Feature 140 was a larger elliptical depression containing fill from the uppermost part of the overlying mound. It measured 2.64 m in length, 1.27 m in width, and 0.10 m in depth. After excavation, these depressions were interpreted as natural disturbance.

Thermal Features

Four thermal features were identified by the PAILC, all of which appeared to have been cooking features. Two were informal hearths in residential contexts on Isla Chablé. One was interpreted as an oven. One was the large formal hearth or roasting pit in the Central Group of El Bellote.

The two informal hearths were simple pits that contained burned sediments, with no wall or base treatments (e.g., clay lining) and barely discernable oxidation to their walls or bases, suggesting minimal use. Feature 134 was associated with the surface of platform Feature 78 (beneath mound Feature 77) on Isla Chablé (Figure 5.4). This elliptical hearth had a vertical eastern wall and a sloping western wall meeting a bowl-shaped base. It measured 0.46 m in length, 0.27 m in width, and 0.11 m in depth. Although small, its artifact density was extremely high. One hundred forty-two sherds were recovered from the hearth: 44.4 percent (n = 63) were Formative and 55.6 percent (n = 79) were Late Classic types; some were lightly burned. Although limited oxidation was observed in the walls and base, the fill was distinct from the overlying strata. It was a very dark, grayish brown clay with dense charcoal staining, suggesting its use as a hearth.

Feature 147 was an informal hearth within the midden over platform Feature 35 in the Feature 32-34-35 multilevel mound on Isla Santa Rosita (Figure 5.5). The pit was elliptical, with incurving walls and a bowl-shaped base. It measured 0.50 m in length, 0.40 m in width, and 0.11 m in depth. The upper fill was a lightly compact, brown silt stained with a light density of ash. The fill contained a few small clay chunks and pieces of charcoal. One sherd lay flat on the base. Because the base and walls were lightly oxidized, it was interpreted as an ephemeral outdoor hearth.

Associated with the top of platform Feature 78 (beneath mound Feature 77), Feature 133 was an earthen oven partially overlying the north side of hearth Feature 134 (Figure 5.4). The oven was constructed with a reddish-brown clay "platform" (1.35 m wide with an average height of 0.30 m). Cut into the center of the "platform" (Feature 133) was a large but shallow hearth-like feature (Feature 132), which was 0.70 m wide and 0.09 m deep, containing a very dark grayish brown clay with dense charcoal staining. Most of the sherds found in its fill were Late Classic types. Although treated as separate features during excavation and documentation, the platform and its internal hearth were interpreted as an oven. Alternatively, this feature could have been an above-ground roasting or grilling feature (assuming the thermal cavity was not covered). Both the platform and its internal hearth were surrounded by and covered by unburned deposits that created mound Feature 77.

Feature 158 was the large formal hearth adjacent to the plaster-lined pit (Feature 159) near the base of multilevel mound Feature 150-167 in the Central Group of El Bellote (Figure 5.9), an elite context (Chapter 9). It was the only thermal feature with formally prepared clay walls. Although having an indentation in the east wall, Feature 158 was generally circular in shape. The diameter was estimated to be 1.80 to 1.90 m. Because the 2007 season was not permitted for excavation, it was not tested, so its depth was unknown. The top of the feature was removed by the shoreline erosion that exposed it and it was further eroded by a hurricane during the 2007 season. The 10- to 14-cm–thick clay wall was highly oxidized and dark red

toward the center of the feature (where it extended beneath the mound fill). The southwest margin of the wall had a very dark gray color indicative of wood fuel or an inconsistent internal heat. The observed fill was a dark brown fine sand, which was presumably deposited after use of the feature. Only one Late Classic sherd was observed in the fill. An alternative interpretation for Feature 158 is that it was the base of a *chultún* that had been prepared with a fired clay lining as observed in a more complete example at Aguacatal (Matheny 1970:72). The large size and formal preparation of the feature suggests use for a large-scale activity beyond domestic purposes. The association with the adjacent plaster-lined pit may indicate a relationship, perhaps with a storage or processing and cooking events prior to the construction of the multilevel mound above it.

Summary

Seven pits and four thermal features were observed. All were dated to the Late Classic period. Four pits (features 142, 143, 145, 146) were small, shallow, basin-shaped pits with insloping walls but with circular, oval, and subrectangular plan-view shapes. Two pits (features 135 and 138) had deep bowl shapes. One was formally prepared with a polished plaster lining. The functions of these pits remain unknown. Two features (78 and 147) were informal outdoor hearths, essentially small pits with limited base or wall oxidation containing burned sediment. One earthen platform enclosed a similar, but larger hearth (Feature 134) that was interpreted as an oven. One large formal hearth, roasting pit, or *chultún* (Feature 158) with highly oxidized clay walls was adjacent to, and probably culturally associated with a plaster-lined pit (Feature 159). The variation in these features is related to their contexts. The small, shallow pits and the small informal hearths, along with the earthen oven, were all found in three residential contexts that lacked significant architectural materials. At the same time, their presence in those contexts support the interpretation that the mounds had residential functions. The deep pits, formally prepared plaster-lined pit, and large formal hearth, roasting pit, or *chultún* were associated with elite contexts.

CONCLUSIONS

This chapter began with four questions and sets of hypotheses regarding the features identified at ILC. First, the association of Formative and Late Classic pottery in surface collections suggested either that Late Classic mounds were constructed over Formative deposits or that the latter were recycled in the Late Classic to build the extant features. Second, the morphologies of features should indicate their functions, requiring additional data to confirm the presence of residential features, ceremonial mounds, and specialized production locations. Third, there was a cultural sequence in feature construction, for example, platforms were built first, then mounds were placed over the platforms, and superior mounds were later constructed over inferior mounds. Alternatively, the platforms were built around existing mounds or were the product of naturally eroding sediments from the mounds. Fourth, residential mound size variation could reflect occupation durations or were the result of differences in labor investment when the mounds were constructed. Data derived from feature and profile mapping provided the relevant evidence to address these research issues, leading to the following conclusions.

Formative and Late Classic Deposits

Previous identification of features as Formative *concheros* at Isla Chablé and Late Classic temples at El Bellote ignored the residential morphologies of most features and the associated, mixed period pottery, as demonstrated by the 2001 survey results. Stemming from those observations, the ideal hypothesis was that Late Classic features were constructed over Formative features. If so, then a stratigraphic sequence of Formative pottery in basal features or in lower mound strata and Late Classic pottery in overlying features or upper mound strata should have been present. The alternative hypothesis was that Formative deposits were removed and redeposited to build the extant features in the Late Classic, implying that no intact Formative features or other deposits remained at ILC. If so, then both Formative and Late Classic pottery should be associated with the lowermost to the uppermost features and fill strata.

The first hypothesis was dismissed, with overwhelming support for the alternative. Apart from the mixing of Formative and Late Classic pottery in most surface collections, the excavations and profiles demonstrated that across ILC and in all categories of features the earliest to the latest construction deposits contained both Formative and Late Classic pottery. This was the case in the excavation in platform Feature 40; the profiles of discrete mound features 97, 156, and 157; the excavation in mound-on-platform Feature 77-78; the excavations and profiles in multilevel mound features 32-34-35, 75-76, 93-94, 95-96, 98-99, 161-160, and 150-167; the profiles in ceremonial mound features 151, 196-202, and 166-185; and the excavations in specialized features 89 and 92. As such, the project can definitively conclude that the extant features at ILC

were built by recycling displaced Formative and earlier Late Classic deposits to construct the features during the Late Classic period. Formative *concheros* and other features may once have existed at southern Isla Chablé and across much of El Bellote but if so they were destroyed to construct the extant features. Further implications are that the settlement patterns are not purely reflective of Formative period settlement and, unfortunately, that the dating of stone artifacts and faunal remains (vertebrate and invertebrate) cannot be done through stratigraphic associations.

The recycling of Formative deposits is not unique to ILC and has broader implications for interpretations throughout the Chontalpa. Aguacatal (at Laguna de Términos, Campeche), for instance, was initially occupied in the Late Formative, had its most substantial occupation in the Late Classic, and had lighter Early Classic and Postclassic occupations (Matheny 1970:120–121). Aguacatal is also commonly cited as a significant Formative era settlement based on the assumption that most of its features were built in the Formative. Late Formative pottery was likely observed on the surface of features, which would give the impression that the features were Formative in age, as occurred at ILC. Yet substantial mixing of Formative to Postclassic pottery in lower to upper strata is evident in most features where excavations were conducted in levels. For example, Table 5.11 shows the pottery recovered from excavation units that Matheny describes as best representing the Late Formative Pinzón Pottery Complex. The pottery percentages by level indicate, however, that features represented by excavation units A-5 and E-3 were constructed during the Postclassic, Unit A-8 was constructed primarily in the Late Classic with the uppermost strata deposited during the Postclassic, and Jilón del Sur was primarily constructed in the Postclassic over a Late Formative deposit (which may or may not have been redeposited). Thus, despite significant percentages of Late Formative pottery, most of the prehispanic features observed at Aguacatal were likely constructed in the Late Classic and Postclassic periods. Similar recycling of earlier deposits to construct mounds was noted at San Miguel in the upper Mezcalapa (Piña Chan and Navarrete 1967:5–7, 11).

At San Felipe, Campo Nuevo, and Limón, none of Sisson's (1976:Chapter 4 tables) excavations were in mounds. The excavated 'rises' illustrate a sequence in Formative stratigraphic development and mixing of Late Classic with Early and/or Middle Formative pottery only occurred in upper levels. This suggests that recycling of earlier deposits was more common for Late Classic mound-building but less so

**Table 5.11. Percentages of Pottery by Period and Excavation Level
in Features with Abundant Late Formative Pottery at Aguacatal**

Level	Excavation at A-5				Excavation at A-8				Excavation at E-3				Excavation at Jilón Del Sur			
	LF	EC	LC	P	LF	EC	LC	P	LF	EC	LC	P	LF	EC	LC	P
I	21	2	56	21	8	7	42	19	39	<1	56	<1	0	10	30	57
II	26	17	40	17	5	21	52	3	49	0	51	<1	4	10	28	58
III	36	7	41	5	30	44	26	0	0	0	0	<1	76	0	24	0
IV	65	9	26	8	11	79	10	0	–	–	–	–	98	0	0	6
V	87	13	0	0	25	67	7	0	–	–	–	–	100	0	0	0
VI	80	0	0	20	41	50	8	0	–	–	–	–	–	–	–	–
VII	–	–	–	–	56	11	33	0	–	–	–	–	–	–	–	–

Compiled from Matheny 1970: tables 45–49.

Key: LF = Late Formative, EC = Early Classic, LC = Late Classic, P = Postclassic (Early and Late combined).

for non-mound deposits. Routine mixing of deposits may even account for some of the problems with Comalcalco's ceramic chronology, which was based on mound excavations. In that chronology the same pottery groups and types were often assigned to more than one chronological complex (Peniche Rivero 1973).

Function

Initial interpretations of feature functions were based on morphological similarities with features reported throughout the lowland Gulf Coast and Maya regions. Pottery form diversity, pits and hearths, and architectural materials were used to evaluate the interpretations based on morphology. The surface collections, excavations, and profiles provided the data for these evaluations.

Residential Features

Guided by the assumption that diverse activities take place in residential contexts, then the numerous platforms, mounds, mounds-on-platforms, and multilevel mounds sharing morphological similarities with residential features elsewhere should have a diversity of pottery vessel forms (represented by rim sherds), hearths and pits, and evidence for dwellings. Acknowledging that the artifact collections were in secondary fill contexts, features like hearths and dwellings were given greater weight in assessing residential functions.

Surface collections from platforms yielded too few rim sherds but pooling the rims from this feature category indicate a variety of vessel functions. The Feature 40 excavation also yielded a range in vessel forms for Late Classic

pottery. Although no pits, hearths, or in-situ dwellings were observed in the small unit, the numerous small eroding nodules of poor-quality plaster indicated the presence of a razed Late Classic structure. Other platforms also had surface evidence for low-quality structural plaster. A wide range of vessel forms also characterized the pooled surface collections from interpreted residential mounds. This was also the case for the Late Classic period rim sherds from fill deposits profiled at features 97, 156, and 157. In addition, the floors documented within features 157 and 160, and the floor Feature 171 on the surface of superior mound Feature 150 suggest the presence of small structures. The surface-collected rims from mounds-on-platforms indicate a variety of vessel functions. Although too few rims were obtained in the Feature 77-78 excavations, the informal hearth on the platform's surface and the oven over that suggest residential contexts. Surface-collected pottery from multilevel mounds exhibit a range of functions for the Late Classic pottery. The excavations at features 32-34-35 and 75-76, the profile of Feature 93-94, and Feature 171 on superior mound Feature 150 indicated that pits and structures were associated with the platforms, inferior mounds, and superior mounds. Together, these observations support the residential interpretations originally based on morphology.

Differences in domestic activities were observed. If domestic activities included fishing-related or shellfish-related processing, then faunal remains and associated tools should be present. As described in Chapter 2 and in the first section of this chapter, however, evidence for or against domestic processing of local food resources proved to not be an indicator of residential functions, but rather, who had access to resources. Because the residential platforms and mounds were constructed using a mix of Formative and earlier Late Classic deposits, it is difficult to associate faunal remains with particular periods. Nevertheless, apart from mounds that included shell, vertebrate and invertebrate remains were noticeably absent to rare at most of the probable residential features, indicating shell and faunal processing was not a domestic activity.

Exceptions to this general pattern were found at El Bellote and Isla Chablé. At the residential mounds and small platform in the South Group of El Bellote, domestic fishing-related activities were indicated by the chipped stone and Late Classic period net sinkers, suggesting that the group had rights to fishing resources. Similarly, ground stone artifacts for processing grains from the interior was absent at most residential features but were found at residential mounds in the South Group of Isla Chablé and at many of the residential mounds at El Bellote, which indicates differences in the acquisition of grains for domestic processing.

If domestic activities included craft manufacturing, then tools and byproducts should also be associated with the residential features. However, most features had no to very few obsidian or chert tools, and essentially no byproducts from craft manufacturing. At most residential contexts, definable domestic activities included only late-stage food storage, preparation, and consumption using a range of vessel forms. The differences in domestic activities are explored further in Chapter 9.

Ceremonial Mounds

The morphological criteria for interpreting ceremonial features are steep-sided conical mounds or steep-sided, flat-topped quadrilateral mounds. These criteria are based on similarities with ceremonial features known elsewhere in the Maya and Gulf Coast regions. Surface collections made from these features should have less diversity of vessel forms and include evidence of more substantial architecture, such as brick-and-mortar constructions and thick plaster stucco. Although they varied considerably in size, the mounds at ILC that were thought to be ceremonial shared quadrilateral shapes, flat summits, steep-sloping sides, and consistent orientations approximating cardinal directions. These were more numerous than indicated by Charnay (1888) and Blom and La Farge (1926). Diverse rim forms from surface collections were suggestive of residential functions, but this was likely due to the reuse of Formative and earlier Late Classic deposits from residential contexts to construct the mounds. Many features did have pieces of high-quality mortar, brick, and chunks of thick plaster (some with smoothed surfaces) suggestive of the major architectural investments expected for temples or substructures. In contrast, brick and mortar were absent from the interpreted residential features. The observed vaulted substructure (Feature 196 beneath Feature 202), which incorporated brick, mortar, and thick plaster layers, is testimony to a nonresidential function for this class of mounds. A similar substructure protruded from the flat surface of Feature 166. The brick and high incidence of high-quality plaster at other features also suggest nonresidential functions involving temples and possible submound tombs.

Specialized Features

The 2001 survey of the islands identified three features that were used for collective production activities. Feature 92—the long, narrow platform along Isla Chablé's southern shoreline—was initially interpreted as a collective landing for trade (signifying a port function) or fishing-related activities. The excavation yielded no evidence for trade, but did produce an unusual amount of vertebrate remains suggestive of fishing or fish processing.

Features 89 and 122—deposits of crushed shell—were assumed to be locations for processing shell for construction materials and possibly for lime. Although the excavation in Feature 122 provided no evidence for lime kilns, there was one thick deposit of crushed shell that matched material found in mortar and plaster. It also included small sherds and vertebrate remains.

The 2007 investigation of El Bellote did not identify a specialized function for Feature 176 based on morphology—it resembled a residential platform—but the surface collection yielded an unusual concentration of chipped stone (likely Late Classic), Late Classic net sinkers, and vertebrate remains. This suggests that it, too, was a fishing-related platform for the South Group of that site. Whereas features 89 and 176 were associated with residential groups, features 92 and 122 were interpreted as locations for community-wide collective activities.

The interpretations based on feature morphology were generally supported. Although residential deposits were repurposed to construct ceremonial mounds, the surface and subsurface structures and architectural materials, along with hearths and pits, supported the residential-ceremonial distinctions. Specialized activities were also supported. Feature morphology thus appears to provide a good basis for interpreting feature functions at ILC and presumably elsewhere in the region.

Construction Sequence

As elsewhere in the Chontalpa and Gulf Coast Lowlands, discrete mounds at ILC developed in a succession of building episodes. Deposits were used to construct the initial mounds for surfaces and structures. Later, those structures were razed, and more fill was added to increase mound heights. Newer surfaces or floor materials for structures were added over the taller mounds. This was most clearly demonstrated at Feature 157 (Figure 5.3).

Nevertheless, a question developed early on as to whether the residential platforms, mounds-on-platforms, and multilevel formations actually represented a cultural sequence in feature construction. If so, surfaces, dwellings, hearths and pits should be present on platform summits beneath mounds in the mounds-on-platforms, and on inferior mound surfaces beneath superior mounds in multilevel mounds. Alternatively, if the platforms were built around existing mounds, there should be no submound platform-associated surfaces, dwellings, hearths, and pits. Another alternative is that the "platforms" were products of natural sediment erosion accumulating around mounds.

Size data lends some support to the first hypothesis. Tables 5.1 and 5.6 shows that discrete platforms, platforms for mound-on-platforms, and basal platforms for multilevel formations with only one superior mound were of similar sizes, which suggests a cultural norm. Likewise, the discrete mounds and the mounds-on-platforms were of similar sizes. This indicates that platforms across all categories were similar but that some had mounds added over them at later stages. The platforms for multilevel mounds with multiple superior mounds were much larger, opening the possibility that those platforms could have been enlarged (if initially they were the same size as other categories) or were partially the product of erosion.

The stratigraphic data from the excavations and profiles support the first hypothesis. Feature 137, a structure within inferior mound Feature 75 was at the projected top of platform Feature 76 (Figure 5.6). Associated with platform Feature 78's surface was hearth Feature 134. The earthen oven (Feature 133) was constructed over the platform's surface and that hearth. Later, mound Feature 77 was built over the oven and surrounding platform surface (Figure 5.4).

Profiles of cuts in multilevel mounds also support the first hypothesis. Inferior mound Feature 94 was constructed with multiple deposits and capped with a surface. The superior mound (Feature 93) was added over that; its first surface had two pits (features 135 and 138) over which more deposits were later added. Likewise, superior mound

Feature 161 was constructed over a structure on the surface of inferior mound Feature 160.

The excavations in one multilevel mound formation—Feature 32-34-35—support the first hypothesis for initial mound-on-platform construction and partially support the second hypothesis for later inferior mound and platform development. Platform Feature 35 was constructed first. Two distinct mounds were built over it but in the third stage, the two mounds were consolidated into one larger inferior mound with a fill deposit between and over both. Also, around this time, a midden was initiated over the platform. Thus, the third stage does not indicate that the platform developed around the mound as predicted by the second hypothesis but, rather, more deposits were added over the existing platform extending its height and possibly its area. In the fourth stage, the superior mound was initiated while the midden over the platform continued to accumulate.

Based on these observations, the first hypothesis is supported. In the case of the mounds-on-platforms, the platforms were first constructed for residential functions and the mounds were later built over those. In the case of multilevel mounds, the inferior mounds were built for residential functions and the superior mounds were added later. The construction of the inferior mounds also involved their expansion or consolidation into one, as in the case of the two mounds built over the platform Feature 35 to create one larger inferior mound. In addition, the midden accumulations over platform Feature 35 demonstrate that deposits were added over the platforms.

The significance of these findings is that there appears to have been a cultural sequence represented by these feature combinations. It also suggests that discrete platforms and discrete mounds were residences that were more briefly occupied than the mounds-on-platforms and multilevel mounds, which represent longer occupations. This observed sequence also contributes to interpreting the settlement history in Chapter 9. Most importantly, these observations indicate that the interpreted platforms were not the result of natural erosion of mound sediments.

Size: Occupation Duration or Labor Investiture?

If the larger, taller mounds were the result of long-term occupations and accretional growth in height, then they should reveal numerous fill deposits and occupation surfaces. But if the larger mounds were constructed in few brief episodes—to achieve a desired mound height—then there should be fewer and thicker mound construction deposits and fewer occupation surfaces. Stratigraphic information from the excavations and profiles of residential mounds were used to evaluate these alternatives.

There is evidence to support both hypotheses but the second is supported in more instances. Some low features, like mound-on-platform feature 77-78 had numerous fill deposits. Some taller mounds, for example discrete mound Feature 156 had numerous fill deposits and multiple occupation surfaces and structures. These instances conform with the explanation that mound heights are related to longer durations of occupation. There are, however, more numerous examples of thick deposits being used to achieve high mound elevations in fewer episodes of mound construction. Nearly half the height of inferior mound Feature 34 was achieved with one thick stratum. Most of the height of inferior mound Feature 75 was achieved with one 1-m–thick deposit. At the South Group of Isla Chablé, only one to two thick mound fill deposits accounted for most of the height of inferior mound Feature 94 and superior mound Feature 93. Features 96, 97, and 99 had one or more fill strata thicker than 0.50 m. At El Bellote, only one fill deposit was observed for inferior mound Feature 160, which was at least 1.00 m in thickness. Even the stratigraphic data from discrete platform Feature 40 suggests it was built in one construction episode. Thus, mound height generally does not correspond with the number of mound-fill deposits or numbers of occupation surfaces and therefore does not predict occupation duration. Instead, most feature heights were achieved with few construction episodes regardless of height differences. These observations open the possibility for status negotiation embodied in residential feature size.

In conclusion, Formative and earlier Late Classic deposits were recycled during the Late Classic period to construct all categories of features. No Formative *concheros* or other in-situ deposits were identified. The excavation and profile data supported the interpretations of feature functions that were initially based only on morphology. Specialized features such as the shoreline landing for fishing-related activities and the deposits of crushed shell for construction material processing were confirmed and thought to be associated with residential groups or larger public community activities. There was a cultural pattern for the sequence of residential feature construction: platforms with mounds later added over them followed by expansion of those mounds into larger inferior mounds supporting the later superior mounds. In general, tall mound heights were often achieved with thick deposits in single construction episodes, as opposed to accretional growth from numerous sequential occupations. An additional outcome was the observation that the distribution of pits and thermal features were influenced by social contexts: small and informal at most of the insular residences, larger or more formal at El Bellote and the South Group of Isla Chablé.

CHAPTER SIX

Pottery

Pottery was the largest category of artifacts collected (8,678 sherds). Ceramics played important roles in understanding feature formation processes and functions in Chapter 5 and contributes substantially to interpretations of regional interaction, social conditions, social integration, identities and social memory, foodways, and food sharing in chapters 8 and 9. The classification system was developed over several seasons and is not the standard culture historical complex-group-type-variety framework that still dominates Maya ceramic research, requiring discussion at the outset. The relationship between morphology and technological properties is discussed as an approach to assess the quality of vessels made available to the occupants of ILC. Also discussed is the use of pottery for symbolic displays such as the expression and manipulation of identity through daily use, foodways, and feasting or food sharing. As the first published descriptions of the pottery assemblage from ILC, much of the chapter is devoted to ceramic descriptions. The descriptions are followed by regional comparisons. Also discussed are the results of a limited stratigraphic analysis to evaluate a possible pottery sequence within the Late Classic and an experiment using thermoluminescence dating on surface collected artifacts. The chapter concludes with the outcomes and implications of the analyses, what research is still needed, and how the pottery data are used in subsequent chapters.

POTTERY CLASSIFICATION

Most Mayanist ceramic analyses continue to emphasize a culture historical framework for classification, for interpreting culture areas and periods with which to interpret regional interaction, trade spheres, or political territories.

"Complexes" represent chronological periods within a given area, each having a list of group-type-varieties. Traditional type-varieties are largely based on decorative categories with subdivisions. These are lumped into groups based on their commonalities. Within the Western Chontalpa, however, little progress was made in defining culture historical area-period complexes, groups, and type-varieties.

The first major effort was by Peniche Rivero (1973). Working with limited stratigraphic excavations at Comalcalco, she defined four complexes: Los Pinos (BCE 800–CE 100), Río Mezcalapa I (CE 800–1000), Río Mezcalapa II (CE 1000–1250), and Cintla I (CE 1250–1350). One problem in her system is that most of the group-type-varieties cross-cut complexes, type-varieties cross-cut groups, and the distinctions between types are often unclear. Boucher (1981) modified the classification of coarse wares but these also evince long spans of time, cross-cutting periods, making them less useful for chronological analyses or defining "complexes." Researchers at Comalcalco increasingly observed that the proposed periods, represented by the complexes, did not conform well with architectural sequences (Andrews 1989). Epigraphic evidence from the 1990s also cast doubts on those periods and pottery assignments. Although advances in the classification of fine paste pottery have been made recently (e.g., Armijo, Gallegos Gómora, and Jiménez Alvarez 2005), fine paste wares constitute only small percentages of ceramic assemblages.

Additional problems occurred when attempting to use the existing classification systems for ILC. Though variable, sherd surfaces in the region are highly eroded, but more so at ILC, limiting the applicability of classifications relying on surface decoration. Elsewhere in Tabasco, Rands (1985) concluded that morphological attributes not typically included in type-variety classification systems are more useful for chronological purposes due to poor sherd surface preservation. For the same reasons, Stark (1989:88–93) found form and paste more useful for chronological purposes at Patarata, Veracruz, which has similar environmental variables as those found at ILC. Arnold (2003) also emphasized the utility of paste-based analysis for Gulf Coast Formative pottery and Wendt (2010) notes that plastic decoration is far more likely to survive than paints or slips. Culbert and Rands (2007) also criticized the culture historical group-type-variety system of classification for the Usumacinta region, instead calling for greater emphasis on paste and technological characteristics.

Given the PAILC's chronological and functional questions, and given the problem of sherd surface erosion, a different pragmatic approach was needed. The system that developed views "types" as paste attributes that conform with technological characteristics. The classification into paste-types had additional utility for comparing technological and morphological suitability. Whenever possible, the paste-type names are based on existing names for "groups" or "types" in prior systems but only when those "groups" or "types" have distinctive pastes. For this purpose, Boucher's (1981) classification of coarse paste pottery provided a useful guide whereas the majority of those "groups" and "types" were not helpful for project purposes. For some resulting categories, no descriptions of similar pastes were described at Comalcalco and were assigned local names (e.g., "Mecoacan" and "Bellote"). Others that did not conform with paste descriptions elsewhere, or that have only a tentatively interpreted similarity to pastes described elsewhere, and which occur in low frequencies were assigned a letter designation (e.g., "X," "Y," and "Z"). For well-known types that were distributed across the Gulf Coast or Isthmus regions (e.g., Sierra Red), the accepted names were used. This was justified because they have specific paste attributes. Table 6.1 lists the resulting types in the PAILC classification system, along with their percentages.

"Varieties" in the PAILC classification were based on vessel surface treatments that primarily involved plastic decoration that is more durable than paints or slips. Some names for the decorative varieties were borrowed from prior culture historical classifications but only if those names specifically refer to a distinct kind of plastic decoration. One major observation of using surface treatment as a variety is that the same Late Classic decorative attributes cross-cut different paste-types. Varieties were thus independent of types. For example, "Fenix" (Boucher 1981) refers to parallel finger-smoothed impressions that are

Table 6.1. Pottery Types Defined for the PAILC

Type Name	Number	% of Period	% of Total
FORMATIVE—KNOWN PERIOD AFFILIATIONS			
Olmec Black and White	43	1.73	0.50
Sierra Red	134	5.38	1.54
FORMATIVE—UNKNOWN PERIOD AFFILIATIONS			
Coarse Paste	1860	74.67	21.43
Sandy Paste	160	6.42	1.84
White Paste	205	8.23	2.36
Unclassified	89	3.57	1.03
LATE CLASSIC COURSE PASTES			
Centla	2295	41.90	26.45
Cimatán	2490	45.46	28.70
Mecoacán	264	4.82	3.04
Orange	41	0.75	0.47
Y	31	0.57	0.36
Z	38	0.69	0.44
LATE CLASSIC SEMI-FINE AND FINE PASTES			
Comalcalco	88	1.61	1.01
Jonuta	113	2.06	1.30
Paraíso	60	1.10	0.69
Huimangillo	20	0.37	0.23
Unclassified	37	0.68	0.43
UNKNOWN PERIOD AFFILIATIONS			
Bellote	318	-	3.66
X	121	-	1.39
Unclassified	271	-	3.12
Total	8678	-	100

found on multiple, distinctive paste-types. "Soyataco" also appears on multiple paste-types. It involves a pronounced external thickening of the vessel wall at the neck-shoulder junction, sometimes accompanied by a thin inward and downward groove. "Trinidad" and "Caobal" both refer to deep incised cross-hatching. In the past, this decoration was considered to be Trinidad when on necks but Coabal if on bodies. The PAILC did away with the distinction. Descriptive names were also applied (e.g., "striated" or "polished"). If there was no evidence of surface treatment, the variety assigned was "plain." Readers should note that the latter does not assume vessels lacked paint or slip but that none was observable. Faint vestiges of paints or slips were rare but also recorded.

Morphological attributes were recorded to develop functional interpretations, a major focus of the pottery analysis. Anatomical portions of vessels were recorded: e.g., base, body, shoulder, neck, and rim. Originally based on Sabloff's (1976:22–27) classification, a long-term standard for Mayanists (Rice 1987:216), this system categorized vessels into primary classes (vessel shapes), divisions (contours), and subdivisions (portions, appendages, and lip forms). Over time, the PAILC tailored the categories to conform with the materials at ILC (Figure 6.1). Form categories include *comales*, plates, dishes, bowls, *tecomates*, ollas, and jars. These were subdivided into shape categories (contours), for example, straight outflaring, straight vertical, outcurved, rounded open, and incurved. Base shapes were described. Orifice diameters were recorded whenever possible. Lip forms (e.g., rounded, flat, beveled, D-shaped, out-turned, etc.) were also coded (Figure 6.1). The specific stylistic expressions of these attributes are shown with profiles in subsequent figures. Due to the severe erosion of the surfaces of sherds, this chapter forgoes the standard surface illustrations, focusing instead on the range of rim profiles, which are more useful for the purposes of this study. Thickness, measured 2 to 3 cm below the lip on rim sherds, was rounded to the nearest tenth of a millimeter. The analysis also included seeking correlations among morphological attributes.

FUNCTION, SUITABILITY, AND PERFORMANCE

Standardized pottery production is apparent in the uniformness of paste characteristics, making types based on pastes practical. For the purposes of activity analysis, the morphological variables were essential. However, additional technological considerations of pastes were considered. Conformity between morphological suitability and technological suitability strengthen interpretations of activities represented by the pottery. At the same time, congruence indicates that pottery was well-made for intended uses (performance). Conversely, a lack of congruence indicates that people lacked access to vessels that performed well.

In my M.A. thesis (Ensor 1994), I compared morphological and technological suitability in Postclassic pottery from Wild Cane Cay, Belize (McKillop 1987). The guiding hypothesis was that potters intentionally manipulated form and paste properties to achieve vessels that would perform well for specific purposes. If so, then morphological categories should correlate to paste characteristics. Proceeding with this line of thought, vessels with appropriate morphologies for cooking should have pastes and tempers that are resilient to failure under the stresses of rapid heating and cooling. Vessels morphologically suitable for water storage in hot climates should be porous to enable evaporative cooling. Conversely, vessels with morphologies appropriate for dry storage or for serving foods should have hard but not brittle pastes and can have surface treatments like paint that do not interfere with these functions. To analyze technological properties, I recorded porosity and hardness following the methods of Simon (1988; Simon and Burton 1989; Simon and Coghlan 1989; Simon, Komorowski, and Burton 1992). Of eight types with sufficient sample sizes, four showed positive statistical correlations between morphological and technological suitability, suggesting manufacture for intended uses. Those without positive correlations were interpreted as having been produced for a range of purposes, regardless of technological characteristics, which would result in variable performance for different uses (Ensor 1994).

In hindsight, the emphasis I placed on intended use by manufacturers seems naive from today's theoretical considerations of social contexts and agency. The ancient potters produced standardized pastes having one set of technological properties but with a wide range of morphologies for a wide range of uses, resulting in unsuitable pastes for some functions. People consuming vessels may have had choices in which forms from which pastes they would select. However, mediating people's choices are the political economies in which they are embedded. For example, in ILC's class-based Late Classic society, we might expect the best performing pots—those with pastes suitable for the uses indicated by forms—to have been consumed by high ranking classes and, conversely, vessels with poor performance provisioned to low-ranking classes.

Morphological suitability implies that form and shape characteristics perform well for specific uses, which are based on ethnographic observation, materials science, and "common sense." Squat vessels with wide necks for hand access to contents and thickened lips are suitable for dry storage (Rice 1987:237, 241; Shepard 1976:228; Smith 1985:271). Small-mouthed *tecomates* ("seed jars" in the United States) having globular shapes and restricted orifices without necks are suitable for storing grains and can easily be sealed. However, Rice (1987) suggests that *tecomates* might also have been used for cooking and transportation. Arnold (1999, 2003) suggests they were multipurpose vessels that combined transportability with effectiveness for storage and cooking. Thus, wide-mouth

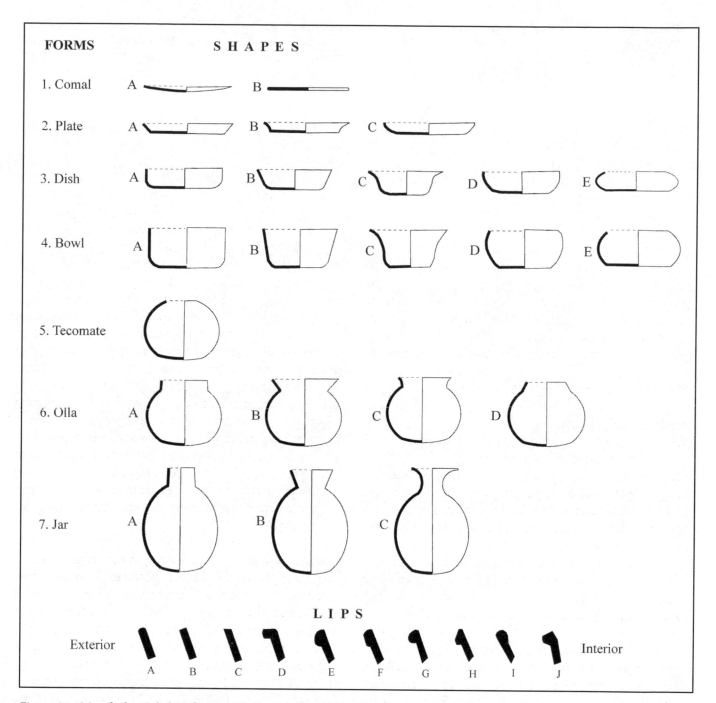

Figure 6.1. Morphological classification of pottery. Prepared by the author.

tecomates with accessible interiors are contrasted with "seed-jars" (small-mouth *tecomates*). Tall jars with restricted necks, small orifices, and flaring rims for pouring and reducing spillage are suitable for liquid storage (Rice 1987:237, 241; Shepard 1976:288; Smith 1985:270–271, 275; Thompson 1958:60, 120–123). An exterior thickened lip prevents the liquid from running down the side while pouring. Ollas—globular bodies with open orifices and low, restricted necks ("necked bowls" or "short-necked jars" outside Mesoamerica)—are suitable for cooking gruels, stews, soups, and also tamales (Rice 1987:237–240; Smith 1985:273). The rounded contours resist breakage during thermal expansion and contraction. However, large deep bowls without necks were also used for cooking in the 1950s Yucatán while ollas, primarily for cooking, were secondarily used for storage (Thompson 1958:60, 113, 120–123). Griddles (*comales*) are obviously suited for cooking tortillas and may secondarily serve as lids (Thompson 1958:62–63). Plates and dishes are suitable for serving dry- and wet-food, respectively (Rice 1987:240; Thompson 1958:61–62).

Technological suitability refers to the paste and temper characteristics that perform well for certain uses. Both dry storage and serving vessels should be hard in order to resist impacts. This quality is achieved with a low-fusing, dense firing clay, or by firing at high temperatures. Such vessels should have small temper particles that create a stronger, less fracturable ceramic body (Rice 1987:362; Shepard 1976:114). Surface treatment of storage and serving vessels has negligible influence on performance. However, serving dishes are typically expected to be plain or highly decorated if used for symbolic displays of identity.

Liquid storage jars may be hard as well. However, water storage jars in hot climates should be permeable (and hence not hard) so that the water penetrates to the exterior and evaporates to cool the interior contents (Shepard 1976:126; Rye 1981:26). Such porosity is achieved through lower firing temperatures and temper particles that are not uniform in size, especially those with angular shapes. Fiber temper that leaves voids after firing and materials like limestone or shell also create porosity (Thompson 1958:146). These vessels should not be painted; that would reduce porosity.

Ollas and other cooking vessels should be resistant to thermal stresses from expansion during heating and contraction during cooling. The body should not be too hard or too soft. Pore spaces also resist thermal stress by allowing expansion of the solid matrix but at the same time promote insulation that reduces conductivity (Rice 1987:367–368; Shepard 1976:126). Abundant, but evenly distributed and generally small temper particles increase conductivity, resisting thermal stress (Rye 1981:26; Simon and Burton 1989:125).

Given what we know of morphological and technological performance, ideal expectations can be made for different functions. Plates, dishes, and small bowls are morphologically suitable for serving purposes and should have hard pastes that are fired at higher temperatures, with small temper particles in moderate densities. Small-mouth *tecomates* for dry storage should have similar paste characteristics. Jars for liquid storage may share these characteristics unless used for water storage, in which case their pastes should be highly porous, which is accomplished through the use of nonuniform and angular particles, fiber, limestone, or shell temper. Ollas and wide-mouth *tecomates*, morphologically suitable for stews, soups, gruels, or tamales, and *comales* for tortillas should have pastes that are moderate in hardness with small, uniformly sized but relatively abundant, and evenly distributed temper particles.

Types with paste characteristics suitable for serving and dry storage should have high percentages of plates, dishes, bowls, and small-mouth *tecomates*. Types with paste characteristics suitable for water storage should be dominated by jars. Types with paste characteristics suitable for cooking purposes should have high frequencies of ollas, wide-mouth *tecomates*, and *comales*. At stake is whether the people who occupied ILC had access to vessels that performed well for their uses or if they had pots prone to failure. The distribution of vessel performance across social contexts is considered in chapters 8 and 9.

IDENTITIES: SYMBOLIC DISPLAY, FOODWAYS, AND FOOD SHARING

Pottery is also essential for studying prehispanic identities, foodways, and feasting or food sharing. Chapter 5 considered mound height investiture to negotiate status identity, which is one form of symbolic display revisited in Chapter 9. Also considered are the uses of pottery as symbolic materials. Apart from chronology, the culture historical perspective generally views pottery in a normative tradition-horizon sense whereby "ethnicities," political territories, or commercial spheres are interpreted through geographic distributions of "complexes" (Ball and Taschek 2003, 2007, 2015; Andrews and Robles Castellanos 1985). Processualism emphasizes symbolism—if unrelated to artifact function—as a mechanism for social cohesion to be contextualized within systems of ecology or social complexity (Binford 1962; Whalen and Minnis 2012). Recent theoretical shifts brought more attention to intra-community distributions of pottery. Some suggest that pottery distributions can be viewed through alliance-building, for example, elite-commoner gifting to maintain support, horizontal commoner gifting, or the importance of having fine serving pottery for feasting (Stanton and Gallareta Negrón 2001). Symbols do not conform well to bounded ethnicities under colonialism, which instead had layered scales of manipulated identities (Hodder 1982; Plog 1978; Voss 2015; Peelo 2011). Postprocessualist and contemporary practice and agency theories emphasize negotiated identities and materiality: the manipulated marking, mediating of, or masking of social difference through gifting, consumption, or production (Clark 2004; Hegmon and others 2016; Joyce et al. 2014; Peelo 2011; Joyce, Hendon, and Lopiparo 2014). These perspectives conform with ethnographic observations that Maya "ethnicities" are not bounded homogeneous cultural or linguistic groupings, but rather, socially manipulated identities with variably situated actors (Alejos García 2006, 2009). In this chapter and in the distributional analyses in Chapter 9 I entertain how certain types may have functioned primarily for symbolic displays of identities in horizontal and vertical relationships. Those should be in lower frequencies because they are less frequently used and as a result have longer use-lives (Straight 2017).

Pottery functions, in addition to subsistence data, lend themselves to understanding cuisine, the manners in which ingredients are selected, processed, and consumed through daily practice, which are commonly interpreted as a form of local to regional identity (e.g., Herrera Flores and Markus Götz 2014; Ochoa 2010; Staller and Carrasco 2010). As such, vessels for cooking and serving, and their performance characteristics, provide insight into daily experiences (practice) that can be analyzed for vertical and horizontal cohesion and differentiation, marking additional layers of identities. Thus, attention is paid here to the ceramic evidence for the ways foods were prepared and served, which also contributes to distributional analyses in Chapter 9.

Hayden (2014) compiled ethnographic, cross-cultural, ethnoarchaeological, and historical information on the importance of feasting. Feasting involves surplus production and adoption of subsistence foods and technologies including domestication and intensified agriculture; a cause for craft production and exchange; reciprocal gifting, along with obligation and alliance building; aggrandizing for status; a leveling mechanism for inequalities; and a means to promote social solidarity. In short, "participating in feasts elevates people from mundane everyday affairs, it panders to the senses, immerses in social intercourse, animates ritual, and fosters fond memories" (Hayden 2014:5). Evidence for feasting can include large structures, large storage facilities and pots, large hearths and roasting pits, symbolic ceramic and lapidary display items, and rapid accumulation of shell mounds or fire-cracked rock (Ensor 2013a, 2017b). Large storage pots are also associated with feasting (Blitz 1993). Although highly decorated and exchanged pottery (typically viewed as a "prestige good") is usually emphasized as socially and symbolically manipulated items, here equal attention is given to coarse-paste large vessels. These would have been used for cooking and communal serving (food sharing) that, in turn, contributed to identities and social memories (Straight 2017; Twiss 2007; Wendt 2010). Such large vessels should occur in lower frequencies because they are used less often and have longer use-lives (Straight 2017).

Figure 6.2 shows the orifice diameter distributions for the different vessel form categories. Orifice diameter can be used as general indicator of vessel size. With the exception of ollas and jars, all form categories had bimodal distributions indicating that small to mid-sized vessels were more abundant. There was a less common subset of larger vessels—as expected for less frequently used, feast-related cooking, storage, and serving pots. Those vessels have orifice diameters over 30 cm, or over 24 cm for jars. Although not bimodal, olla and jar rims also show low percentages of large vessels. Among Formative vessels, bimodality was apparent for all but *tecomates* and ollas, though large examples of those were certainly present (> 30 cm). Somewhat different by comparison, bimodality was apparent for Late Classic plates, dishes, and *tecomates*, but not for bowls, ollas, and jars. Although large bowls and ollas were present, there were no large jars in the Late Classic rim assemblage. These size distinctions are referenced in the following descriptions and are used for analyses in chapters 8 and 9.

FORMATIVE PERIOD TYPES

Formative era sherds comprised 28.7 percent (n = 2,491) of the collection. The majority of Formative types were coarse wares and could not be affiliated with a specific Formative period. Their pastes were identified as Formative by Socorro Jiménez Alvarez, who also recommended and helped create the descriptive categories (Ensor and others 2006). In addition to coarse-paste types, there were a few Olmec Horizon sherds, limited to portions of El Bellote, and a much broader distribution of Late Formative Sierra Red pottery. The Formative types are illustrated in Figure 6.3.

Formative Types of Known Period Affiliation

Types of known period affiliations at ILC are those that are widely distributed through southern Mesoamerica. These include both Middle and Late Formative types. The former is simply labeled Black and White, known from the Olman. Their presence only at El Bellote suggests a small, localized occupation. Diagnostic of the Late Formative is Sierra Red, which is more common and widely dispersed across ILC, indicating a larger occupation during that

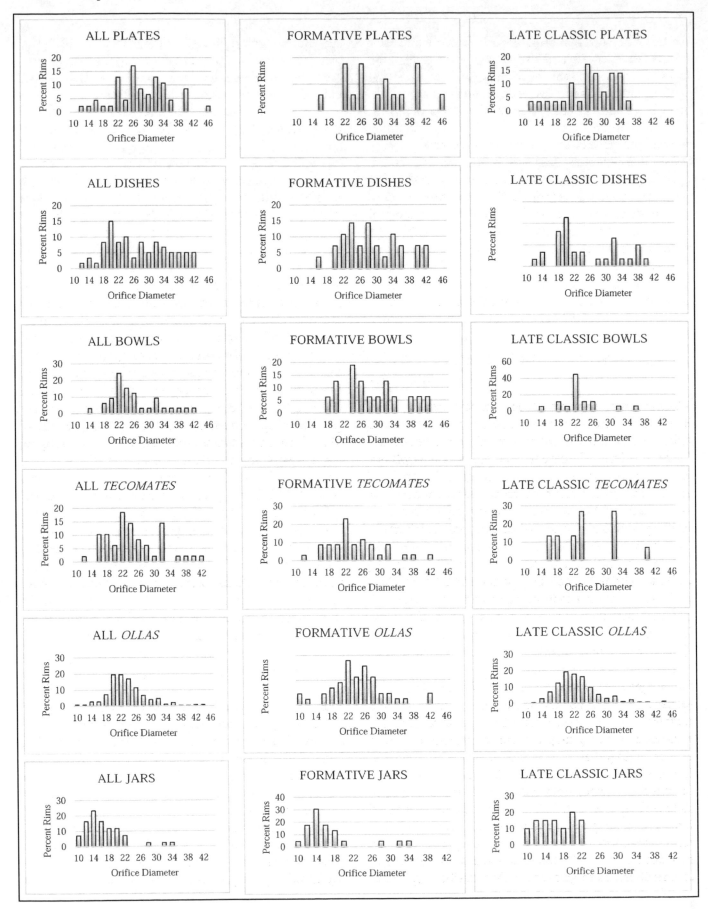

Figure 6.2. Orifice diameters of various vessel shapes. Measurements are in centimeters. Prepared by the author.

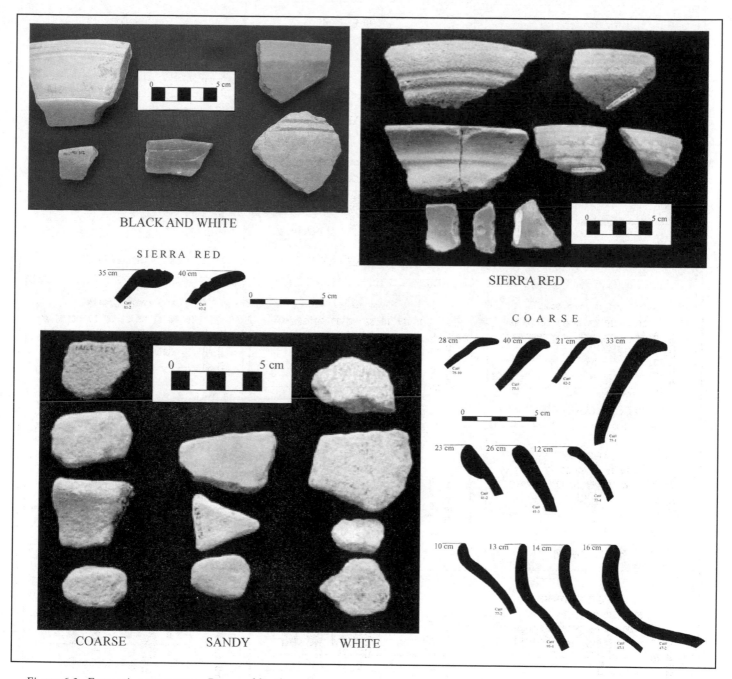

Figure 6.3. Formative era pottery. Prepared by the author.

period (Chapter 8). Both are rare, however, constituting only 7.1 percent (n = 177) of all Formative pottery recovered (Table 6.1).

Black and White

The only pottery associated with the Olmec Horizon of the Middle to early Late Formative found at ILC are white (white-cream) and white-rimmed black (dark gray)

(Figure 6.3; Coe and Diehl 1980). Only 43 sherds of this type were found, all from El Bellote. The paste is hard and has two colors. Seven sherds are entirely white or cream. The remainder are the aptly named "white-rimmed black." Regardless of color, all have the same ash temper. Sherd thicknesses range from 6.6 to 11.3 mm, with a mean of 8.8 mm, a median of 9.0 mm, and a standard deviation of 1.5 mm. Four sherds have characteristic wide grooves on their exteriors. Typically, there are one or two parallel grooves around the circumference of the vessel. On rims, these occur just below the lip, but some body sherds also had grooves. One body sherd also had parallel incisions with a rounded curve at the sherd's broken edge, suggesting a geometric motif.

Nine rim sherds and two bases were found. Vessel form could be identified for seven of the rims: two plates, four dishes, and one bowl. The two plates were large: one had a diameter of 40 cm and another was undetermined but was larger than 40 cm. Both had straight, outflaring sides with rounded lips. The four dishes were also large, ranging from 34 to 36 cm in diameter. Two had straight outflaring sides and two had rounded incurving sides. All had rounded lips. The single bowl rim was also large, having a diameter of 40 cm, and similarly had rounded incurved sides with a rounded lip. Both bases were flat. The paste properties were suitable for a variety of purposes, but the vessel forms represented indicate serving functions only, possibly for symbolic displays in feasts, given the association with a broad interaction sphere (Wendt 2010).

Sierra Red

Sierra Red (of the Chicanel Tradition) is a common Late Formative pottery that is widespread in the Maya and Isthmus regions of Mesoamerica (Figure 6.3). One hundred thirty-four sherds were identified as Sierra Red. The paste is known for being relatively hard, having fine sand temper, and for the inclusion of iron oxide. Other characteristic attributes are red paint, thickened flanged rims, and circumferential grooves on rims. At ILC, the dark orangish brown paste is friable from decomposition. The sand temper particles are 0.7 to 0.8 mm in size and include characteristic iron oxide. Wall thickness was difficult to measure due to the thickened everted rims. Many rims only consisted of those thickened portions, which were over 11 mm thick. Excluding those, the range in sherd thickness is 3.0 to 11.0 mm, with a mean of 7.3 mm, a median of 8.0 mm, and a standard deviation of 2.4 mm. Decoration conforms with what has commonly been ascribed to the type. Circumferential grooves were identified on numerous rim sherds. Only one sherd has a thin incised line. Most of the sherds have remnants of thick red paint.

There are 41 rims and four bases. Vessel forms could be identified for 27 rims: six plates, one plate or shallow dish, five dishes, five dishes or bowls, three dishes, four ollas, and three jars. Seventy four percent (n = 20) of the vessels represented are plates, dishes, and bowls, suggesting a bias toward serving functions. Complete and nearly complete

information was obtained from 17 rim sherds (Table 6.2). The plates are medium to large, had outcurved sides, and rounded lips. The medium-sized dishes and bowl also have outcurved rims and rounded lips. One mid-sized olla has a straight outflaring rim while the others, one of which is large, have outcurved rims. Most of the ollas have rounded lips. One has a beveled lip. The three medium-sized jars have outcurved rims and rounded lips. There are also four bases. Three are flat and one is annular.

Although the moderate original hardness and small evenly distributed temper would have been suitable for cooking, this is also an "average" quality that could perform moderately well for a variety of purposes. The thick red paint would, however, have made the vessels less suitable for water storage or cooking. Although ollas, suitable for cooking, were also present, the one beveled rim suggests that the vessel was covered for storage purposes. Jars, although included in the forms, had rounded lips that would have been less suitable for pouring liquids. Nevertheless, the form distributions within the type indicate a bias toward serving purposes, likely for symbolic display.

Formative Types of Unknown Period Affiliation

Most of the pottery dating to the Formative periods has paste attributes that are found across the Gulf Coast region (Ensor and others 2006). These were categorized into descriptive types: "coarse," "sandy," and "white" (Table 6.1). In their current conditions, each type of paste is soft to medium in hardness and has fine sand temper. Whereas "coarse" and "sandy" are distinguished by the amounts of temper, the "white" paste category is the result of a post-depositional condition. Eighty-nine (3.57 percent) sherds identified as having Formative paste characteristics remain unclassified due to severe erosion, lack of confidence in placing them in one of these descriptive categories, or because they have nondiagnostic attributes.

Coarse Paste

Coarse paste pottery is the most common Formative descriptive type. A total of 1,860 sherds were classified into the type—nearly 75 percent of all Formative pottery. The paste characteristics are uniform: soft to medium in hardness, ranging in color from yellowish brown to reddish brown, and containing small, uniform angular sand temper with particles that are approximately 0.7 to 1.0 mm in size. The paste is friable and would easily crumble off the sherd when scraped. The sherds of this type are highly eroded and rarely have preserved surfaces. Rim sherd thickness ranges from 3.0 to 14.0 mm. The mean and median

Table 6.2. Formative Vessel Morphologies and Orifice Diameters

Type	Morphology				Orifice Diameter (cm)		
	Form	*Shape*	*Lip*	*Number of rims*	*Range*	*Mean*	*Standard deviation*
SIERRA RED	Plate	B	A	4	25–40	33.7	7.8
		B	–	2	26–46	36..0	14.1
	Dish	C	A	2	24–28	26.0	2.8
		C	–	1	26	–	–
	Bowl	C	A	1	26	–	–
	Olla	B	A	1	28	–	–
		C	A	2	42	–	–
		C	C	1	–	–	–
	Jar	C	A	3	12–21	16.0	4.6
	Total number of rims			17			
COARSE PASTE	Plate	B	A	3	22–24	22.7	1.2
		B	D	1	32	–	–
		C	A	4	26–34	30.0	5.7
		C	C	1	32	–	–
	Dish	A	D	2	22–28	25.0	4.2
		B	C	2	42	42.0	0.0
		B	D	5	23–40	29.0	6.5
		B	G	1	40	–	–
		C	A	4	23–30	26.5	4.9
		D	A	1	22	–	–
		D	B	1	–	–	–
		E	A	7	16–36	26.0	7.9
		E	D	2	21–34	27.5	9.2
	Bowl	A	A	1	–	–	–
		B	D	3	21–24	22.5	2.1
		B	E	1	31	–	–
		C	A	2	28–32	30.0	2.8
		C	D	1	42	–	–
		C	E	1	–	–	–
		D	A	2	24–26	25.0	1.4
		D	G	1	21	–	–
	Tecomate	–	A	12	12–38	24.7	7.7
		–	B	1	22	–	–
		–	D	3	18–22	20.7	2.3
		–	E	2	6–32	29	4.2
		–	G	1	28	–	–
		–	I	10	16–32	24.3	4.8

continued

Table 6.2. (continued)

Type	Morphology				Orifice Diameter (cm)		
	Form	Shape	Lip	Number of rims	Range	Mean	Standard deviation
COARSE PASTE (continued)	Olla	A	A	7	10–24	17.7	6.6
		A	B	1	–	–	–
		A	D	1	42	–	–
		A	G	5	13–28	22.3	8.1
		B	A	1	–	–	–
		B	G	1	34	–	–
		C	A	11	16–36	24.2	6.2
		C	C	1	18	–	–
		D	A	1	22	–	–
		D	B	1	24	–	–
		D	J	1	20	–	–
	Jar	A	A	7	12–16	13.9	1.7
		A	C	1	34	–	–
		A	D	2	10–33	21.5	16.3
		A	G	1	18	–	–
		C	A	7	14–28	17.7	5.4
		C	G	1	14	–	–
	Total number of rims			125			
SANDY PASTE	Plate	C	A	1	16	–	–
	Dish	A	A	1	–	–	–
		B	D	1	30	–	–
	Bowl	B	A	1	24	–	–
		D	A	1	34	–	–
	Tecomate	–	D	1	42	–	–
	Olla	B	A	3	20–28	24.0	5.7
		C	A	1	28	–	–
	Total number of rims			10			

See Figure 6.1 for shape and lip keys.

thicknesses are both 8.0 mm, with a standard deviation of 2.2 mm.

Little plastic treatment was observed. The most common is polishing. A total of 251 sherds (almost 14 percent) have polished interior and/or exterior surfaces. Far fewer have other forms of plastic treatment. Seven sherds had oblique incisions. These were presumably from the same vessel and were recovered from the surface collection unit at Feature 174 (South Group of El Bellote). Two rim sherds have circumferential incised lines beneath the lips. Five rim sherds have circumferential "chamfer" grooves on interior or exterior surfaces beneath the lips. Five sherds have striations.

Remnants of surface treatments were observed on only 20 sherds. Fifteen have a buff- to orange-colored slip. Two have vestiges of red paint. Two have black painted interior and exterior surfaces. One has exterior red paint and an interior buff-colored slip.

There are 213 rims and 10 bases. Of these, the basic form category could be determined for 178 rims. They represent 18 plates (10.1 percent), 1 plate or dish, 27 dishes (15.2 percent), 15 dishes or bowls (7.3 percent), 39 wide-mouth *tecomates* (21.9 percent), 46 ollas (25.8 percent), and 19 jars (10.7 percent). Among those, most of the morphological and size attributes could be recorded on 125 sherds (Table 6.2). The nine plates represented were large, with either outcurved or rounded sides. Nearly all have rounded lips. Most of the 25 dishes represented ranged from medium to large, had either straight-outflaring or rounded sides. Lip forms vary considerably and are not correlated to shape. The 12 bowls represented were mostly medium-sized, with some having larger diameters. Shapes vary: straight-outflaring, outcurved, and rounded sides. The bowls also have various lip shapes. The orifice diameters of the 29 *tecomate* rims indicate that the vessels were large. Although lip shapes vary, rounded and D-shapes are more common. Most of the 31 ollas represented were medium to large in size, although two were small (having orifice diameters of only 10 cm). The most common olla shapes have straight-vertical and outcurved necks. The more common lips are rounded and D-shaped. The 19 jars represented were medium to large in size. These either have straight-vertical or outcurved necks. Most lips are rounded. Eight base sherds are flat. One has a concave indentation, and another is indicative of having an annular base.

In general, technological and morphological suitabilities of this type conform with one another. The paste is technologically suitable for cooking purposes. The sand is uniformly small and evenly distributed: a property that resists fracturing from expansion and contraction. The same quality also serves well for serving and dry storage but less so for cool water storage. The vessel forms represented by the rims do suggest an all-purpose intention for the paste: for serving in plates and dishes and perhaps in bowls, for cooking stews in ollas and *tecomates*, and for storage in jars and *tecomates*.

Four sherds have indications of use-related and post-life conditions. One body sherd has bitumen adhered to its interior surface. Another was burned, either from use in cooking or from post-depositional burning. Two sherds are encrusted in mortar, indicating re-use in the Late Classic and one has an oyster shell fragment adhered to it.

Sandy Paste

Another descriptive category, this type was named for its uniform abundance of sand temper. The paste is medium in hardness and has a pale orangish brown color. There is an extremely high density of fine sand (0.7 to 1.0 mm in size), which easily distinguishes sherds of this type from others. Despite the high density of sand temper, this paste is less friable than the coarse-paste type. One hundred sixty sherds were classified into the type. Based only on 19 rim sherds, there is a range in thickness of 6.0 to 9.5 mm, with a mean of 8.3 mm, a median of 8.4 mm, and a standard deviation of 1.6 mm. Compared to many types, these data suggest moderate thickness, with less variation.

Sherd surfaces are highly eroded, leaving few vestiges of plastic or other decoration. Six sherds have polished interior surfaces or are polished on both interior and exterior surfaces. One has black and red paint on its exterior. No other plastic treatment or paint was observed.

There are 21 rim sherds. Vessel forms could be determined for 19 sherds: 1 plate, 2 dishes, 3 dishes or bowls, 2 bowls, 1 *tecomate*, and 10 ollas, illustrating a bias toward the latter. No jar rims were identified. Complete, or nearly complete, morphological and size information was obtained from 10 rims (Table 6.2). The single plate represented was small, had rounded sides, and a rounded lip. The two dishes represented differed in shape. One had straight-vertical sides and a rounded lip. The other was large and had straight-outflaring sides with an everted lip. One bowl was medium-sized, had straight-outflaring sides, and a rounded lip. The other was large and had rounded sides with a rounded lip. The very large wide-mouth *tecomate* had an everted lip that extended vertically from the orifice. The ollas were medium-sized to large. Three had straight-outflaring rims and one had an outcurved rim. All ollas had rounded lips. There were no base sherds.

The technological suitability of the paste and the form suitability are congruous. Although having a high density, the temper particles are uniform in size and are evenly distributed, which would retard thermal fracturing from expansion and contraction. The ollas, suitable for cooking stews, are the predominate form represented. The paste qualities appropriate for cooking are also "average" qualities suitable for serving and dry storage, which are functions reflected by the plate, dishes, and bowls.

White Paste

Two hundred five sherds were classified as the "white paste" type. The paste is the same as the Formative Coarse type (soft to medium in hardness and having a moderate amount of fine sand temper) apart from its white, pink, or pinkish-white color. The color is a result of post-depositional processes, perhaps long-term exposure to water and the absorption of salt and/or calcium. Although often found in shell deposits, these sherds were also found in earthen deposits, suggesting that long-time association with shell did not influence the discoloration. The type was created originally to explore possibilities for correlations in spatial distributions, which might inform on long-term post-depositional processes. Sherd thickness ranges from 4.5 to 11 mm, with a mean of 7.4 mm, a median of 7.7 mm, and a standard deviation of 2.7—like those for the Coarse and Sandy types. Surfaces are severely eroded. Four sherds have polished surfaces, one has vestiges of incised striations, and seven have remnants of red paint on their exteriors.

There are six rim sherds and two base sherds. Vessel forms were identifiable for five of the rims. They represent one dish or bowl, three wide-mouth *tecomates*, and one olla. The dish or bowl (of undetermined diameter) had outcurved sides and a rounded lip. The *tecomates* represented were large, having orifice diameters ranging from 20 to 24 cm. Two have rounded lips and one has a D-shaped lip. The medium-sized olla has an outcurved rim, a rounded lip shape, and an orifice diameter of 26 cm. The two bases are flat.

Unclassified Pottery

Eighty-nine Formative sherds could not be classified, either because of their small sizes, severe erosion, or because of other attributes that did not fit the defined types. Many had faint indications of polished surfaces. One third (n = 29) have incised striations. They came from one provenience (Feature 40 at Isla Santa Rosita) and are likely from the same vessel. One sherd has black paint. There are 10 rim sherds and one base. Vessel forms represented include three bowls of medium to large sizes, one of which was indicated by two rims and a matching base from one provenience (Feature 97 at Isla Chablé), one wide-mouth *tecomate*, two medium-sized ollas, and one small jar with an outcurved rim.

LATE CLASSIC PERIOD TYPES

Over 63 percent (n = 5,477) of the pottery collected at ILC dated to the Late Classic period (Table 6.1). The paste categories can be divided into coarse pastes and fine pastes—the former comprising the vast majority. Other types that were not previously described in regional literature were given local or descriptive names or remain unnamed.

Late Classic Period Coarse Paste Types

There were six coarse-paste types, constituting 94.2 percent of the Late Classic pottery. The most common are regionally known as Centla and Cimatán, which together make up 92.9 percent (n = 4,785) of the coarse-paste types. One coarse-paste type was not described in the regional literature, so it was named for the lagoon (Mecoacán). These three major types are illustrated in Figure 6.4. Some Centla, Cimatán, and Mecoacán sherds have abnormally reddish paste colors and are hard and brittle, indicating over-firing. One type was descriptively named "Orange" for categorization purposes. Two types that occurred in low numbers were given letter designations ("Type Y" and "Type Z"). The following describes each type's paste characteristics, thickness, plastic treatments, surface treatments, vessel form, shape, and size data, and discusses technological and morphological suitability. Table 6.3 presents the varieties associated with the coarse-paste types. Table 6.4 shows the form distributions. High percentages of ollas—suitable for cooking wet foods—were identified. The low percentages of jars, in contrast, suggest there that was little need to store water where there was readily available, if brackish, potable water.

Centla

Centla is a recognized coarse paste type associated with the Late Classic at Comalcalco (Boucher 1981; Peniche Rivero 1973). A total of 2295 sherds were classified into this type. The paste is medium in hardness and orangish brown in color. Few sherds have cores or clouding that suggest a reduced oxygen firing environment. Where darkened cores were present, they were gray in color. One hundred thirty-three sherds (5.8 percent of all Centla) are hard and brittle and are classified as Centla Reddish Paste. Temper is abundant but evenly distributed angular quartzite and mica particles between 0.8 and 1 mm in size. Larger temper particles are extremely rare, which distinguishes Centla from Cimatán. The rims range in thickness from 3 to 13 mm, with a mean of 7.8 mm, a median of 8.0 mm, and a standard deviation of 2.2 mm. The thickness of the reddish variant is similar, having a range from 4.5 to 10.5 mm, with a mean of 7.8 mm, a median of 8.0 mm, and a standard deviation of 1.9 mm.

Although most are plain, plastic decoration varieties include Fenix, polished, Soyataco, striated, and Trinidad/Caobal (Table 6.3), which also occur on other types. Of the 49 sherds with polished surfaces, nearly all have interior burnishing. The Soyataco variety involves a circumferential smoothed-over coil near the union between the neck and shoulder (Boucher 1981) and in this assemblage occurs exclusively on ollas. Striations are usually linear or appearing as deep parallel rough incisions. The Trinidad plastic decorative variety involves deep, 0.3-1.5-mm wide linear parallel and cross-hatched incisions on the rims

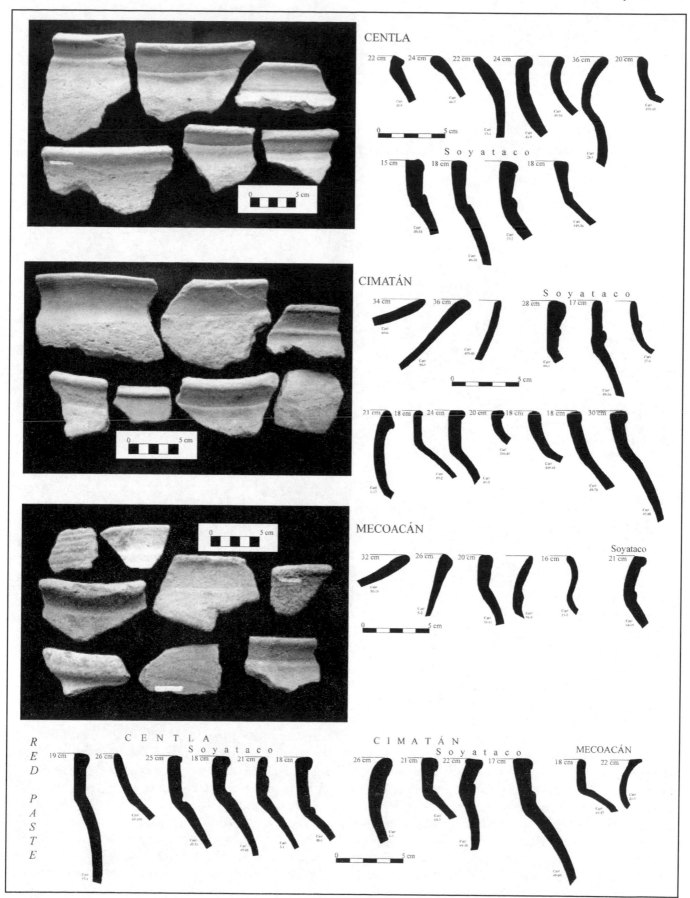

Figure 6.4. Late Classic coarse-paste types: Centla, Cimatán, and Mecoacán. Prepared by the author.

Table 6.3 Late Classic Coarse Paste Types and Varieties

Type	Paste	Plain		Polished		Soyataco		Striated		Trinidad		Fenix		Total	
		number	%	number	%	number	%	number	%	number	%	number	%	number	%
CENTLA	Normal	1978	91.5	48	2.2	22	1.0	63	2.9	7	0.3	48	2.2	2162	94.2
	Reddish	114	85.7	1	0.8	15	11.3	0	0.0	1	0.8	2	1.5	133	5.8
	Total	2092	91.2	49	2.1	37	1.6	63	2.8	8	0.4	50	2.2	2295	100
CIMATÁN	Normal	1445	69.7	74	3.6	62	3.0	6	0.3	481	23.2	4	0.2	2072	83.2
	Reddish	258	61.7	6	1.4	76	18.2	1	0.2	77	18.4	0	0.0	418	16.8
	Total	1703	68.4	80	3.2	138	5.5	7	0.3	558	22.4	4	0.2	2490	100
MECOACÁN	Normal	214	89.9	2	0.8	20	8.4	0	0.0	2	0.8	0	0.0	238	90.2
	Reddish	14	53.9	2	7.7	9	34.6	0	0.0	1	3.9	0	0.0	26	9.8
	Total	228	86.4	4	1.5	29	11.0	0	0.0	3	1.1	0	0.0	264	100

Table 6.4. Late Classic Coarse Paste Vessel Forms (rims only)

Type	Variety	Plate		Dish		Bowl		Tecomate		Olla		Jar		Total	
		number	%	number	%	number	%	number	%	number	%	number	%	number	%
CENTLA	Plain	1	1.0	21	20.8	6	5.9	8	7.9	60	59.4	5	5.0	101	68.7
	Polished	0	0.0	3	60.0	0	0.0	0	0.0	1	20.0	1	20.0	5	3.4
	Soyataco	0	0.0	0	0.0	0	0.0	0	0.0	37	100	0	0.0	37	25.2
	Trinidad	0	0.0	0	0.0	0	0.0	0	0.0	2	100	0	0.0	2	1.4
	Fenix	0	0.0	0	0.0	0	0.0	0	0.0	2	100	0	0.0	2	1.4
	Total	1	0.7	24	16.3	6	4.1	8	5.4	102	69.4	6	4.1	147	100
CIMATÁN	Plain	8	10.3	3	3.8	9	11.5	4	5.1	49	62.8	5	6.4	78	33.8
	Polished	0	0.0	0	0.0	0	0.0	0	0.0	1	100	0	0.0	1	0.4
	Soyataco	0	0.0	0	0.0	0	0.0	0	0.0	138	100	0	0.0	138	59.7
	Striated	0	0.0	0	0.0	1	100	0	0.0	0	0.0	0	0.0	1	0.4
	Trinidad	0	0.0	0	0.0	0	0.0	0	0.0	12	100	0	0.0	12	5.2
	Fenix	0	0.0	0	0.0	1	100	0	0.0	0	0.0	0	0.0	1	0.4
	Total	8	3.5	3	1.3	11	4.8	4	1.7	200	86.6	5	2.2	231	100
MECOACÁN	Plain	12	46.2	1	3.8	0	0.0	1	3.8	10	38.5	2	7.7	26	47.3
	Soyataco	0	0.0	0	0.0	0	0.0	0	0.0	29	100	0	0.0	29	52.7
	Total	12	21.8	1	1.8	0	0.0	1	1.8	39	70.9	2	3.6	55	100

("Trinidad") or on the bodies ("Caobal") (Boucher 1981). The Fenix variety refers to thick, parallel indentations made by fingers across the vessel surface (Boucher 1981; Peniche Rivero 1973). Only 2 percent (n = 50) of the Centla sherds were of the Fenix variety.

As with most of the pottery at ILC, surface slips and paints rarely survived. Only 54 sherds have vestiges of paint. The paint color is red, except for one sherd that has black paint. From what could be observed, the paints originally covered broad areas and were on vessel exteriors. Six sherds have traces of a buff-colored slip on exteriors and/or interiors and one has an orange-colored slip.

There are 160 rims, 5 shoulders, and 16 bases. The shoulders are indicative of necked ollas or jars. The bases are flat or have a slight curvature, some with the upcurved lower portion of the body. Vessel forms were identified for 147 rim sherds, nearly 70 percent (n = 102) of which were from ollas. Morphology and size attributes were recorded for 76 rims (Table 6.5) One medium-sized plate, small and large dishes, mid-sized bowls, large wide-mouth *tecomates*, large *ollas*, and medium-sized to large jars are represented by the sherds. The plate sherd has an everted rim. The 10 rims representing dishes exhibit outflaring straight rims, out-curving rims, and rounded sides without incurving. Those with recordable orifice diameters suggest two size categories: small (18–23 cm) and thinner and large (32–40 cm). Lip forms are predominately rounded although other variations occur. Bowls commonly have rounded sides but straight-outflaring and rounded incurving sides are also present. Orifice diameters are between 22 and 26 cm, although one has a diameter of 32 cm. Lips are typically rounded. *Tecomate* sherds commonly have rounded or D-shaped lips. The *tecomate* sherds represent large vessels, with orifice size categories of 16 to 24 cm, 33 cm, and 40 cm. Ollas are the most common vessel forms represented and are generally large. Those with vertical rims have orifice diameters that are usually less than 25 cm in diameter. Straight-outflaring olla rims typically have orifice diameters over 30 cm. Those with outcurving rims have varying sizes. The most common lips are D-shaped or otherwise thickened or out-turned (65.1 percent; n = 41) and rounded (41.2 percent; n = 26). Jars varied in shape, lip form, and size (11–22 cm).

Centla paste characteristics are most suitable for cooking but could also perform well for other uses. Excluding the reddish paste variant, Centla pastes are moderate in hardness and have small, uniform-sized and evenly distributed temper particles (less susceptible to thermal fracturing). Nearly 70 percent (n =102) of the vessels represented were ollas suitable for cooking moist foods. Rim shapes are generally outcurved (Table 6.5) rather than angled, which would also prevent thermal fracturing from expansion and contraction. Although not facilitating cooking, the D-shaped and other exterior-thickened or out-turned lips on two-thirds of the ollas are ideal for pouring liquids. Nearly 16.5 percent (n = 24) of the rims indicate dishes that are suitable for serving stews. Although other forms are indicated, they occur in very low frequencies. Overall, the Centla type appears best suited for cooking stews, tamales, and/or gruels. One body sherd was smudged on the exterior suggesting use over a wood fire. Ten body sherds were burned; 9 of them belonged to one floor-associated vessel from a burned structure (Feature 137). One body sherd had mortar adhered to it.

Cimatán

Cimatán is another major coarse-paste type that was recovered. It has also been associated with the Late Classic at Comalcalco (Boucher 1981; Peniche Rivero 1973). A total of 2,490 sherds were classified into this type. Cimatán paste is similar to Centla: medium in hardness, orangish brown in color, with angular quartzite and mica temper. Also, like Centla, Cimatán rarely has darkened cores (the few observed were gray) and clouding was extremely rare, indicating that the vessels were fired in a reduced oxygen environment. What distinguishes Cimatán is a greater range in temper particle sizes. Although most are less than 1 mm in size, approximately one third are between 1 and 3 mm in size and are occasionally larger. There are 418 sherds of hard, brittle Cimatán Reddish paste (16.8 percent of the total). Rim sherd thicknesses has a greater range (3-13.5 mm) than Centla pottery but a similar mean of 7.8 mm, a median of 8.0 mm, and a standard deviation of 2.5 mm. The reddish variant had a range of 2.5 to 13.5 mm, a mean of 8.3 mm, a median of 8.5, and a standard deviation of 2.2 mm.

Most Cimatán sherds are plain, although nearly 26 percent (n = 647) have plastic decoration, which includes the Fenix, polished, Soyataco, striated, and Trinidad/Caobal varieties (Table 6.3). Polishing is most commonly found on interior surfaces. The Soyataco circumferential protrusion near the union between the neck and shoulder occurs on 5.5 percent (n = 137) of rim sherds (all from ollas). This is slightly more frequent than in the Centla type. The Trinidad/Caobal variety (parallel and cross-hatched incisions ranging from 0.3 to 1.5 mm in width) is significantly more frequent in the Cimatán sherds compared to Centla. Striated is rare, occurring less in Cimatán than Centla. The finger-made smoothing characteristic of the Fenix variety is also less frequent in the Cimatán type.

Few sherds have surviving traces of paint or slip. Twenty-five have vestiges of red paint (mostly on exterior surfaces), one has black paint on its exterior, and one is polychrome with red and black paint on its exterior. Twenty-nine sherds have traces of a buff-colored slip, most of which are on exteriors. Those with slip are less than 7 mm thick.

There are 242 rims, 9 shoulders, and 1 base. Forms are identified for 231 (Table 6.4). Among those, all or most of the morphological and size attributes could be recorded for 168 rims (Table 6.5). These represent large plates, one medium-sized dish, medium-sized bowls, large wide-mouth *tecomates*, medium-sized to large ollas, and mid-sized to large jars. Among the eight plate sherds, all with rounded lips, seven had straight outflaring rims and one had an upcurved rim. Plate orifice diameters range from 22 to 36 cm. Bowl rims, ranging in orifice diameter from 18 to 36 cm, have straight outflaring sides, rounded sides,

Table 6.5. Late Classic Coarse Paste Vessel Morphologies and Orifice Diameters

Type	Variety	Morphology				Orifice Diameter (cm)		
		Form	Shape	Lip	Number of rims	Range	Mean	Standard deviation
CENTLA	Plain	Plate	A	B	1	24	–	–
		Dish	B	D	1	40	–	–
			C	A	2	–	–	–
			E	A	2	23	–	–
			E	D	1	18	–	–
			E	J	1	–	–	–
		Bowl	B	A	1	–	–	–
			D	A	2	22–24	23.0	1.4
			D	D	1	22	–	–
			E	A	2	22–32	27.0	7.1
		Tecomate	–	A	5	18–40	26.2	9.9
			–	E	1	24	–	–
			–	G	1	16	–	–
		Olla	A	–	1	24	–	–
			A	A	5	18–26	22.0	4.0
			A	G	3	18–24	20.7	3.1
			A	J	2	22–28	25	4.2
			B	A	1	40	–	–
			B	C	1	26	–	–
			B	D	1	36	–	–
			B	G	1	36	–	–
			C	A	5	16–34	26.8	8.3
			D	A	2	22–26	24	2.8
		Jar	A	D	1	11	–	–
			B	C	1	20	–	–
			C	A	1	14	–	–
				Total	46			
	Fenix	Olla	A	A	2	–	–	–
				Total	2			
	Polished	Dish	B	A	1	36	–	–
		Dish	C	A	1	32	–	–
		Dish	E	D	1	–	–	–
		Bowl	D	A	1	26	–	–
		Jar	C	A	1	22	–	–
				Total	5			
	Soyataco	Olla	A	A	5	20–33	23.2	5.5
			–	A	G	16	17–25	21.5	2.6

Table 6.5. (continued)

Type	Variety	Morphology				Orifice Diameter (cm)		
		Form	*Shape*	*Lip*	*Number of rims*	*Range*	*Mean*	*Standard deviation*
CENTLA (continued)	Soyataco (continued)	–	A	J	2	16	–	–
				Total	23			
CIMATÁN	Plain	Plate	A	A	7	22–36	30.9	5.0
			C	A	1	26	–	–
		Dish	B	E	1	22	–	–
		Bowl	B	A	1	26	–	–
			D	A	1	18	–	–
			D	D	1	24	–	–
			D	I	1	36	–	–
			E	G	1	23	–	–
		Tecomate	–	A	2	16–24	20.0	5.7
			–	D	1	22	–	–
			–	E	1	24	–	–
		Olla	A	A	5	16–44	26.4	10.7
			A	G	3	22–32	27	7.1
			A	I	1	26	–	–
			A	J	1	30	–	–
			B	A	1	24	–	–
			B	C	1	28	–	–
			–	–	1	24	–	–
			C	A	2	–	–	–
			C	E	1	–	–	–
			C	I	1	20	–	–
			D	A	1	32	–	–
			D	B	1	18	–	–
		Jar	A	A	1	14	–	–
			B	I	1	20	–	–
			C	A	2	22–23	22.5	0.7
				Total	41			
	Fenix	Bowl	B	A	1	–	–	–
				Total	1			
	Polished	Olla	A	B	1	28	–	–
				Total	1			
	Soyataco	Olla	A	A	30	16–36	24.2	4.9
			A	G	84	15–32	21.8	3.8
			A	J	9	16–32	21.7	5.1
				Total	123			

continued

Table 6.5. (continued)

Type	Variety	Morphology				Orifice Diameter (cm)		
		Form	Shape	Lip	Number of rims	Range	Mean	Standard deviation
CIMATÁN (continued)	Striated	Bowl	B	A	1	22	–	–
				Total	1			
	Polished	Olla	A	B	1	28	–	–
				Total	1			
MECOACÁN	Plain	Plate	A	A	9	26–34	30.4	2.8
			B	A	1	–	–	–
		Dish	E	E	1	28	–	–
		Olla	A	A	3	16–44	29.3	14.0
			A	G	1	21	–	–
			C	A	3	30–34	32.0	2.8
			C	G	1	17	–	–
			C	H	1	22	–	–
			C	I	1	32	–	–
		Jar	C	A	2	16–22	19.0	4.2
				Total	23			
	Soyataco	*Olla*	A	A	2	22	22.0	0.0
			A	G	24	15–32	21.6	4.0
		–	A	J	3	20	20.0	0.0
				Total	29			
Z	Plain	Plate	B	D	1	22	–	–
			C	A	2	30–40	35.0	7.1
		Dish	E	A	2	32–34	33.0	1.4
		Bowl	C	D	1	–	–	–
				Total	6			

See Figure 6.1 for shape and lip keys.

and one had in-curved sides. Bowl lip shapes vary. The few *tecomate* sherds have orifice diameters of 16 to 24 cm. Two have rounded lips, one has an unusual, short everted lip that extends upward from the orifice and the other was D-shaped. Among the 144 olla sherds in Table 6.5, the most common shape is a rounded shoulder with a vertical neck. Soyataco variants have vertical necks. The majority of Cimatán olla sherds have D-shaped or otherwise out-turned lips (70.9 percent; n = 102). Only 24.7 percent (n = 35) have rounded lips. Orifice diameters range from 15 to 32 cm, with only two significantly larger (36 cm and 44 cm). The few jar sherds have rounded shoulders with straight, vertical and outcurved necks, though one has a

straight out-flaring neck. Rounded lips are most common. Three have orifice diameters ranging from 20 to 23 cm whereas one has a diameter of only 14 cm.

Cimatán paste characteristics are suitable for water storage in hot climates. The angular quartzite particles of variable sizes would have made vessel walls porous, functioning to cool the contents, but would have increased susceptibility to failure from thermal expansion and contraction. Nevertheless, ollas—the form most suitable for cooking moist foods—made up 86.6 percent of the Cimatán vessel forms. The discrepancy between technological and morphological suitability of this type suggests that the local population did not receive the most appropriate vessels for that use. One possibility for the dominance of olla forms in the collection is due to their frequent failures. Elsewhere, Straight (2017) found that cooking vessels tend to have the shortest use-lives, which would be compounded at ILC by Cimatán's large angular temper.

Like all the pottery at ILC, the erosion of sherd surfaces prevented observations on use-wear or cause of failure. One body sherd was burned. It was found in a unburned deposit, which may indicate that the burning was use-related. Two body sherds had bitumen adhered to their interior surfaces.

Mecoacán

Mecoacán is a less frequent Late Classic coarse-paste type at ILC, represented by 264 sherds. The paste is dissimilar to any reported at Comalcalco and was named after the lagoon by the PAILC. The paste is medium in hardness and colors ranged from yellowish gray to orangish and grayish brown. Few sherds have dark gray cores. No clouding was observed. The temper consists of a high density of angular particles of white quartzite ranging from 1 to 4 mm in size. There are no micaceous particles. As with Centla and Cimatán, a low percentage (9.8) of sherds are reddish, hard, and brittle compared to normal Mecoacán paste as a result of overfiring. Sherd thicknesses ranges from 4 to 12 mm, having a mean of 8.1 mm, a median of 8.5 mm, and a standard deviation of 2.1 mm.

Although 86.4 percent (n = 228) of the Mecoacán sherds are plain, Late Classic plastic decorative varieties include polishing (1.5 percent, n = 4), Soyataco (10.9 percent, n = 29), and Trinidad/Caobal (1.1 percent, n = 3) (Table 6.3). There are 12 sherds with a buff-colored slip, nearly all of which are thin (less than 7.5 mm), as was also the case with slip observed on Centla and Cimatán types. One body sherd has traces of red paint on its interior surface.

Fifty-seven Mecoacán rim sherds were collected. Of those, forms were determined for 55 (Table 6.4). Nearly 71 percent (n = 39) are from ollas—as with Centla and Cimatán types. However, there was a much higher percentage of plates (22 percent, n = 12) compared to those types. All or most morphological variables were observable on 52 rims (Table 6.5). These represent large plates, one large dish, medium-sized ollas, and two large jars. Nine of the plate rims are straight outflaring rims while the other has an outcurving rim. Orifice diameters range from 26 to 34 cm. All have rounded lips. The single dish rim has incurved sides, a D-shaped lip, and an orifice diameter of 28 cm. There were no bowls. Among the 39 rim sherds from ollas, 84.6 percent (n = 44) have vertical necks and

77 percent (n = 40) have D-shaped or otherwise everted lip forms. Olla orifice diameters range from 15 to 26 cm, with some having much larger diameters of 32 cm and over 40 cm. Both jars have outcurved necks and rounded lips. In addition to the rims, there are two flat bases.

Like Cimatán, the technological properties of Mecoacán paste are best suited for water storage in a hot climate but the majority of vessel morphologies are suited for cooking. The dense, angular, small to large quartzite temper would have created a porous wall, enabling evaporative cooling. However, the high percentage of ollas represented are morphologically suitable for cooking moist foods. The high percentage of lip forms suited for pouring liquids also suggest functionality for both uses. Yet the temper would have increased susceptibility to thermal fracturing from expansion and contraction when used for cooking. As with Cimatán ollas, the incongruence between technological and morphological suitability suggests that the local population did not receive the most adequate vessels for their cooking needs, thus resulting in short use-lives and more abundant olla discards.

The unusual percentage of large plates represented were best for serving dry foods. This suggests some variation beyond the moist-food cuisine. Because this type's medium hardness was not ideal for serving vessels—having a greater risk of breakage—the plates also likely had short use-lives.

Orange

This type was infrequent at ILC and was only present at El Bellote. The paste was similar to Centla but with far less temper and a distinct orange color. Forty-one sherds were classified into this category. Two sherds have cores: black and an unusual reddish gray. One sherd has zoned-incised cross-hatching. Except for the incised frame, the cross-hatching is the same as the Trinidad/Caobal variety. Nineteen sherds have vestiges of red surface paint. One has a band of red paint. Another has black paint (Figure 6.5). There are four rim sherds, but form was only identified for two. One is from a dish with straight flaring sides and a flattened lip. No orifice diameter or thickness could be measured. The other is from an olla with an outcurved rim, an everted lip, a 20-cm orifice diameter, and a thickness of 8.5 mm. There is also one shoulder of an olla or jar and one flat base sherd.

Type Y

This type, represented by 31 sherds found at El Bellote, was not identified in the regional literature but has a paste more common to traditionally defined Classic period wares in

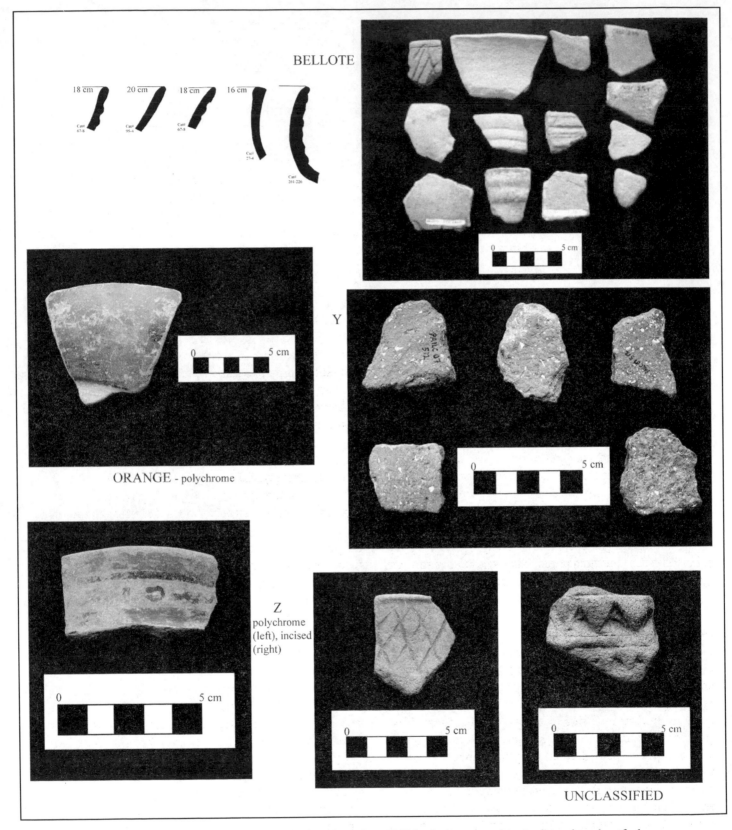

Figure 6.5. Other coarse-paste types: Bellote, polychrome orange, Y, Z (polychrome and incised), and unclassified. Prepared by the author.

the Usumacinta River region, and notably Golfo pottery from Aguacatal, especially Jilón (Matheny 1970:73). As such, type Y is considered to be a regionally intrusive, imported commodity. The paste is medium in hardness, has a color range from grayish yellow to orangish brown. Few specimens have gray cores. The temper is unusual for ILC: 1 to 4 mm-sized shell particles (Figure 6.5). Apart from its temper, the paste resembles the Mecoacán type. None of the sherds have plastic decoration or traces of surface paint. There is only one rim sherd, from a thick-walled (1.07 cm) bowl with rounded sides and a D-shaped lip. The orifice diameter could not be recorded. There are two flat base sherds.

Type Z

Type Z is represented by 38 sherds found at El Bellote, Like type Y, it is not identified in the regional literature and was likely imported. The paste is very hard. All sherds have thick black or dark gray cores with a contrasting yellowish-brown surface color. The temper includes abundant small angular quartzite and mica between 0.5 and 1.0 mm in size. One sherd has cross-hatched incisions characteristic of the Trinidad variety (Figure 6.5). Two have traces of bichrome paint: red over an orange background. Of the eight rim sherds found, vessel form was identifiable for six (Table 6.5). One medium-sized plate rim has outcurved sides and an everted lip. Two plate rims are large, with upcurved sides and rounded lips. Two large dish rims have rounded incurved sides with rounded lips. The single bowl rim has outcurved sides and an everted lip. The hard paste and the bias toward serving vessels illustrate technological and morphological congruence.

Late Classic Period Fine Paste Types

Despite receiving much attention in Mesoamerican literature, and even in regional literature (Armijo Torres, Gallegos Gómora, and Jiménez Alvarez 2005), fine paste pottery is infrequent at sites in the Chontalpa region. At ILC, these comprised only 5.8 percent (n = 503) of the sherds collected. They were, however, widely distributed across contexts and are useful for period associations. Socorro Jiménez Alvarez helped correlate the paste types to regional types, as per Armijo and colleagues (2005; Ensor and others 2006). Most of the fine paste vessel forms were for serving purposes, and possibly for symbolic displays. There were four regional types: Comalcalco, Jonuta, and Paraíso—considered "semi-fine" for having temper—and Huimangillo.

Comalcalco Fine

Named after the interior capital, this Late Classic type is found throughout the central Tabasco region (Armijo Torres, Gallegos Gómora, and Jiménez Alvarez 2005). Eighty-eight sherds were classified as Comalcalco Fine (Figure 6.6). The paste is soft and chalky. In all specimens, the surfaces and edges are highly eroded. Rubbing can remove a powder from the surface, requiring care in cleaning and handling. The paste contains very small but palpable temper particles that are less than 0.2 mm in size. Surface colors vary considerably: black, gray, cream, yellow, yellowish orange, and pink (thus giving the type names "Comalcalco Gray," Comalcalco Orange," and so on in other classification systems). Gray and Black have been suggested to indicate a "Middle Classic" date range (Armijo Torres, Gallegos Gómora, and Jiménez Alvarez 2005). Light to dark gray cores are common and of variable thickness. Many sherds' surfaces are entirely eroded away, leaving only the core to observe. All sherds are thin, ranging in thickness from 3.0 to 9.5 mm, with a mean of 5.3 mm, a median of 5.0 mm, and a standard deviation of 1.8 mm. Eighty-five percent (n = 75) were less than 7.0 mm in thickness. Though sherd-surface erosion partially accounts for this, the type is generally thin-walled. Although known to be painted, none of the Comalcalco Fine sherds from ILC have surviving remnants of paints or slips. Only one sherd has vestiges of plastic decoration: a Soyataco variety rim from an olla.

Eight identifiable rims were collected: one from a plate, one from a dish, two from bowls, and four from ollas. Although the rim shapes of the two bowls could not be determined accurately, these may have been straight-walled. One has an orifice diameter of 22 cm and the other 23 cm in diameter, indicative of medium-sized vessels. Most morphological and size attributes were recordable for six rims (Table 6.6). Lip shape could not be determined for four due to edge erosion. The small plate represented had outflaring sides. All four ollas represented had vertical necks. One sherd has a flattened lip, and another has a D-shaped lip. The orifice diameters indicate small vessels except for the two bowls (not included in the table) and the one medium-sized olla. Although a variety of functions are suggested by the range of forms, the poor paste quality and small to medium vessel sizes suggest limited utility other than for, perhaps, symbolic display.

Jonuta

Named for the site, this semi-fine paste pottery is also chronologically diagnostic of the Late Classic (Armijo

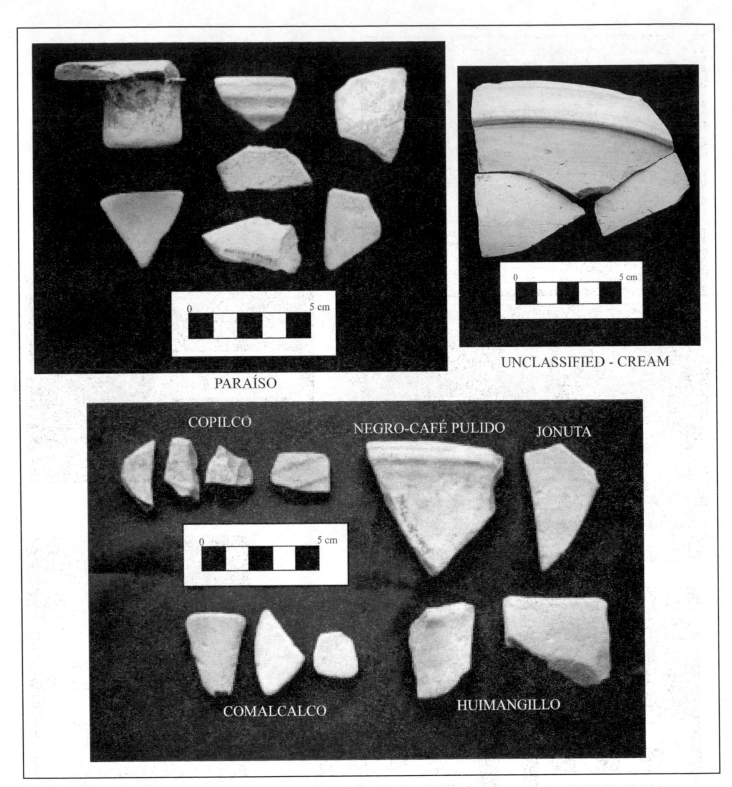

Figure 6.6. Late Classic fine paste types: Paraíso, Copilco, Comalcalco, Negro-Café Pulido, Jonuta, and Huimangillo. Prepared by the author.

Table 6.6. Fine Paste Vessel Morphologies and Orifice Diameters

Type	Morphology				Orifice Diameter (cm)		
	Form	Shape	Lip	Number of rims	Range	Mean	Standard deviation
COMALCALCO	Plate	B	–	1	12	–	–
	Dish	B	–	1	24	–	–
	Olla	A	–	2	14–22	18	5.7
		A	B	1	–	–	–
		A	G	1	15	–	–
			Total	6			
JONUTA	Plate	A	A	1	14	–	–
	Dish	E	B	1	32	–	–
	Bowl	B	B	1	18	–	–
		D	A	1	22	–	–
	Olla	A	A	2	30	–	–
		B	A	1	–	–	–
	Jar	A	A	3	12	12.0	0.0
		C	A	3	14–16	15.0	1.4
			Total	13			
PARAÍSO	Plate	A	A	1	–	–	–
		A	B	1	22	–	–
		B	A	2	26–28	27.0	1.4
		B	E	1	18	–	–
		C	A	1	28	–	–
		C	B	1	–	–	–
	Dish	C	E	1	22	–	–
		E	A	4	12–32	20.0	8.5
		E	H	1	–	–	–
			Total	13			
HUIMANGILLO	Dish	D	A	1	18	–	–
		E	A	1	14	–	–
	Bowl	E	C	1	32	–	–
	Olla	A	A	1	16	–	–
		A	G	1	20	–	–
			Total	5			

See Figure 6.1 for shape and lip keys.

Torres, Gallegos Gómora, and Jiménez Alvarez 2005). One hundred thirteen sherds were classified as this type (Figure 6.6). The paste is hard, which better resists erosion, and has very small but palpable temper particles less than 0.2 mm in size. Sherd surfaces are a dull yellowish to cream color, extending only 1.0 to 1.5 mm into a thick dark gray to very dark gray core. The combination of the hardness, semi-fine paste, surface color, and thick core are distinctive characteristics. Jonuta rims have a range in thickness from 2 to 9.5 mm, with a mean of 5.4 mm, a median of 5.0 mm, and a standard deviation of 1.9 mm. Seventy percent (n = 79) are thinner than 7.0 mm. Plastic decoration includes incising and grooves. Two that were collected from the same surface unit and may have come from the same vessel have a circumferential incision on the interior, just below the lip. Two body sherds have thick parallel grooves on the exterior surface. Three of the sherds have vestiges of paint on their exteriors. One body and one neck sherd have red paint. One is a polychrome, with red and black paint.

There are 16 rim sherds, 1 neck sherd, and 3 base sherds. Thirteen rims had most or all observable morphological and size attributes (Table 6.6). Represented were a small plate, a large dish, two mid-sized bowls, three ollas, and six medium-sized jars. The plate rim has straight outflaring sides with a rounded lip. The dish sherd has incurving sides with a flat lip. One bowl rim has straight outflaring sides with a flat lip and the other has rounded sides with a rounded lip. Two olla rims have vertical necks and one has an outflaring neck. All three have rounded lips. Three jar rims have vertical necks and three have outflaring necks. All six have rounded lips. The neck sherd was from a different jar with an outcurving rim. The three bases are flat. One body sherd has bitumen adhered to its interior surface.

The hard but non-brittle paste indicates technological suitability for serving and dry storage but not cooking or water storage. Though the plate, dish, and bowls are morphologically suited for serving and dry storage, more than half the vessels represented were morphologically suitable for cooking and liquid storage, which does not conform with the technological suitability, suggesting this type was also primarily used for symbolic display.

Paraíso

Named after the site, Paraíso (Figure 6.6) is another common fine paste pottery for the region associated with the Late Classic and possibly a "Middle" Classic period (Armijo Torres, Gallegos Gómora, and Jiménez Alvarez 2005). The collection includes 60 sherds of this type. The paste is moderately hard. Although temper particles occur, they are so small as to be barely palpable (0.1 mm in size and smaller). Sherd surfaces are typically orange or yellowish orange. Thin light gray cores are frequent but not universal. Paraíso sherds are thin: ranging from 3.0- to 8.0-mm thick, with a mean of 4.5 mm, a median of 4.3 mm, and a standard deviation of 1.4 mm. One body sherd has three parallel incisions. Three have deep parallel grooves. Although most sherd surfaces are eroded, eight have remnants of paint. Three have red paint—on the interior of two and on the exterior of one. Polychrome was likely common: two sherds have red over cream on their exteriors, one has red and white paint on its interior, and one has white or cream interior surface paint and red exterior surface paint. The interior painting suggests that the vessels represented were plates, dishes, and bowls.

There were 14 rims and three bases (two of which had supports). Most or all morphological and size data were recordable for 13 rims (Table 6.6). Vessels represented were medium-sized plates and medium-sized to large dishes. Eight rims are from plates: two with straight-flaring sides, three with outcurving sides, and three with incurving sides. In decreasing order of frequency, lips are rounded, flat, and D-shaped. The plate sherd with the D-shaped lip provided a complete vessel profile from lip to flat base. Six rims are from dishes. Seven have rounded sides. The other has outcurving sides. Most have rounded lips, one has a D-shaped lip, the other has an angular exterior thickened lip. The three bases are flat. Two have supports, one of which is hollow and spherical (Figure 6.6). The other is fragmented but appears to be part of a smaller, cylindrical support.

Unlike the other fine paste types, the technological and morphological suitabilities of Paraíso pottery conform with one another. The technological properties of the paste suggest suitability for serving purposes, which is also suggested by the interior painting, and the rims indicate functions limited to serving. The highly decorated serving vessels, including the ornamental supports, also suggest use for symbolic display.

Huimangillo

Named after the site, this is another regional fine paste type (Figure 6.6) that is represented at ILC by 20 sherds. The paste is distinctive for being very hard, lacking temper, and having very dark gray to black cores. Surface colors range from medium to dark brown (occasionally pinkish brown). Most sherds are thin, but thickness varied considerably: 3.0 to 11.5 mm, with a mean of 5.9, median of 5.0, and a standard deviation of 2.7 mm. Three sherds were polished. Two rim sherds from *ollas* had the Soyataco attribute. None of the sherds had remnants of paint.

There are six rims and two bases illustrating a variety of forms and shapes: two medium-sized dishes, one large bowl, and two small ollas (Table 6.6). One dish sherd has outcurving sides. The other has incurving sides. Both have rounded lips. The bowl sherd has straight-flaring sides and a beveled lip. Both olla sherds have vertical necks: one with a rounded and one with a D-shaped lip. Both bases are flat. Although the paste characteristics make the vessels more suitable for serving, this small sample indicates a diversity in thickness, vessel forms, and shapes that suggests a wide range of uses, but the vessels may have been used mostly for symbolic display.

Unclassified Fine Paste Pottery

Thirty-seven semi-fine and fine paste sherds were collected that could not be classified into recognized types with confidence, due either to excessive erosion or to one or more attributes that resembled but did not correspond well enough to described pottery types. Their surface colors are diverse: pinkish, orange, yellow, cream, light brown, and gray. Plastic decoration is limited to polishing on two sherds and grooves on another. Two sherds have red paint on their exteriors. A few sherds could be Copilco, Negro-Café Pulido, or Nonoalco—regionally-defined types that share paste similarities (Figure 6.6). Eight of the rim sherds represent two plates, two dishes, one bowl, two ollas, and one jar. Both plate sherds have straight outflaring rims and rounded lips. One plate represented was only 16 cm in diameter. The other was 26 cm in diameter. One of the dishes represented had rounded incurved sides with a flattened lip and was large (30 cm in diameter). One olla represented was also large (30 cm) but no additional morphological data could be recorded. The large jar (18 cm) had a straight-outflaring rim with a rounded lip. Like most of the fine paste types, a variety of functions are represented by the rims, yet their importance was more likely for symbolic displays.

TYPES OF UNKNOWN PERIOD AFFILIATIONS

Two types do not have known period affiliations. Each is represented by numerous sherds sharing uniform paste characteristics. The Bellote type and the yet unnamed Type X pottery have characteristics common to both Formative and Late Classic pottery. They might even be associated with an Early Classic or the proposed "Middle Classic." In addition to those categories, there are unclassified sherds without period assignments, though most appeared to be Late Classic.

Bellote

The Bellote type was assigned a local name because it did not match existing paste descriptions in the regional literature. Three hundred eighteen sherds were classified into this type. The paste is medium in hardness with an orangish-brown color and evenly distributed particles of fine quartzite and mica (less than 0.8 mm in size). None of the specimens have cores or clouding, suggesting a reduced oxygen firing environment. Bellote sherds are thin compared to most types: ranging from 2.5 to 8.0 mm in thickness, with a mean of 4.6 mm, a median of 4.5 mm, and a standard deviation of 1.42 mm. Nearly 74 percent (n = 235) were less than 5.0 mm thick.

Although most are plain, plastic decoration included polishing and incising and some have remnants of slips and paints. Among those with polished surfaces, 72.5 percent (n = 231) are burnished on both surfaces, 20 percent (n = 64) are polished only on exteriors, and the remainder are only polished on interiors. Although few have incisions, these are fine (less than 1 mm wide), resembling Guaytalpa Estriada, and one has cross-hatching, suggesting a Late Classic affiliation. Others have grooves more characteristic of Formative decoration (Figure 6.5). Vestiges of slips are noted on 17 sherds: 4 with interior and exterior buff-colored slip, 3 with interiors having an orange slip and exteriors with buff slip, 4 with buff-colored slip only on exteriors, and 6 with buff-colored slip only on interiors. Four sherds have traces of red paint on their exteriors. Two have faint traces of what appeared to be thin bands of red paint.

There are 27 rims, one neck, and one base. Most or all information could be recorded for 19 rims (Table 6.7), which represent large jars, large ollas, large wide-mouth *tecomates*, large to medium-sized bowls and dishes, and medium-sized plates. The neck sherd is from a large jar or an olla. The base has a slight curvature. Although the paste characteristics suggest suitability for cooking, the same properties lend themselves to a wide range of uses and there is no dominant form represented by the rims. This type would have performed well for cooking, storage, and serving. One body sherd had bitumen on its interior surface.

Type X

Type X is another paste category not recognized in previous literature for the region. A total of 121 sherds were classified into this type. The paste is distinct. It is hard, had light yellowish-brown surface colors extending only millimeters into a thick black or very dark gray core, and fine temper particles (less than 0.5 mm) of quartzite and mica. Traces of red paint were observed on two body sherds.

Plastic decoration most closely resembles Late Formative attributes. One bowl rim has circumferential parallel incisions on its interior. One *tecomate* rim and one plate rim have circumferential parallel grooves on their exteriors. One dish or bowl rim and one olla rim have striations. Four rim sherds are extremely everted thickened lip fragments without discernable forms. These also have circumferential grooves or incisions close to the lips, like Sierra Red despite the paste differences.

Among the X Type sherds are 18 rims, one neck, and three bases. The slightly thickened, curving rim style is also similar to the Formative coarse-paste styles. All or most of the morphological and size data were obtained for 13 rim sherds (Table 6.7). Two plate rims have straight-flaring

Table 6.7. Types of Unknown Periods: Vessel Morphologies and Orifice Diameters

Type	Morphology				Orifice Diameter (cm)		
	Form	Shape	Lip	Number of rims	Range	Mean	Standard deviation
BELLOTE	Plate	C	A	1	–	–	–
		C	B	1	22	–	–
	Dish	B	–	1	38	–	–
		B	D	1	20	–	–
		C	A	1	–	–	–
		E	A	1	–	–	–
	Dish/Bowl	B	A	1	–	–	–
	Bowl	D	A	1	20	–	–
		E	J	1	–	–	–
	Tecomate	–	A	2	32	–	–
		–	I	1	24	–	–
	Olla	B	A	1	22	–	–
		B	C	1	24	–	–
		C	A	1	36	–	–
		D	B	1	24	–	–
	Jar	A	G	1	16	–	–
		C	A	2	12–18	15.0	4.2
				Total 19			
X	Plate	C	A	2	> 40	–	–
	Dish	B	J	1	> 40	–	–
		E	A	1	–	–	–
	Dish/Bowl	B	A	1	38	–	–
		D	A	1	–	–	–
	Bowl	B	A	1	38	–	–
	Tecomate	–	A	1	–	–	–
	Olla	B	A	1	–	–	–
		C	A	2	24–32	28.0	5.7
	Jar	B	A	1	16	–	–
		C	A	1	16	–	–
				Total 13			

See Figure 6.1 for shape and lip keys.

sides with rounded lips. One plate represented was larger than 40 cm. One dish represented by a rim sherd was also very large and had straight-flaring sides. Another rim sherd has incurved sides. Two rims represent either dishes or bowls. One of the vessels represented was large, with straight-flaring sides, which matches the shape and size of the identified bowl rim. The other dish or bowl rim has rounded sides. Both have rounded lips. One olla rim exhibits a straight, outflaring neck. Two other olla sherds are outcurved necks. Two jar rims have the same orifice diameter. One has a straight, outflaring neck and one has an outcurved neck. All of the olla and jar sherds have rounded lips. The neck sherd (outcurving) is from a jar with a rounded shoulder. The bases are flat with rounded lower portions of the body. The uniformly distributed small temper would have been suitable for thermal expansion and contraction, but the hard paste was more suitable for serving or storage. The variation in vessel morphologies, with no dominant form category, conforms with these varied functions.

Unclassified Pottery

There were 271 sherds that could not be classified into the above types, either due to their conditions (most were small and highly eroded) or because what could be observed did not match the type descriptions. They were likely imported from outside the Mezcalapa Delta. Although having various paste characteristics and not encompassing a type on their own, some description is provided here on plastic treatment, painting, and form.

The plastic treatment includes polishing, incising, and striations. Only one body sherd has polishing (on its interior surface). Three are incised. One has curved parallel incisions on its exterior surface. One has zoned incisions but is too small to determine the design. Another small sherd has a single incised line. Five sherds have rough striations. One sherd with coarse reddish paste and a thick black core has a thickened band around its exterior lip with downward-pointing triangles, reminiscent of braziers, but is too small to determine its actual use (Figure 6.5).

Nine sherds have remnants of paint. Two are polychrome. One is flat but does not appear to be a base. It has vestiges of red, black, and orange paint on one side. The other has what would have been a thick red band over a buff-colored paint. Five have vestiges of red paint, which is on the exteriors of two sherds, the interior of one sherd, and on both surfaces of two sherds. One olla rim has black paint on its interior.

Eight rims provided little morphological information (Table 6.8). Two are from plates with incurving sides and rounded lips. Two are from dishes with incurving sides and rounded lips. Two are from ollas with straight-flaring necks and two are from ollas with outcurving necks. With the exception of one everted lip, the other olla sherds have rounded lips. Although not forming a type, the vessel shapes represented do reflect the preponderance of ollas at ILC.

REGIONAL COMPARISONS

The Formative Coarse pottery at ILC shares the fine sand temper characteristic of Formative pottery through much of the Gulf Coast and Isthmus regions, though the Sandy type has more abundant temper than usually described. Despite a difference in color, the NWAF Grayish Black type has similar paste (Piña Chan and Navarrete 1967:10). Their Polished Creamy type appears to be similar to the Type X paste, though the former has different rim styles and decoration. White-Rim Black and White-Rim Gray from San Fernando are primarily found as bowl forms (Piña

Table 6.8. Unclassified Vessel Morphologies and Orifice Diameters

Form	Morphology			Orifice Diameter (cm)		
	Shape	Lip	Number of rims	Range	Mean	Standard deviation
Plate	C	A	1	–	–	–
Dish	C	A	1	–	–	–
	E	A	2	14	–	–
Olla	B	A	1	–	–	–
	B	D	1	32	–	–
	C	A	2	22–32	27.0	7.1
		Total	8			

See Figure 6.1 for shape and lip keys.

Chan and Navarrete 1967:14–15). Although having similar decoration as those found at ILC, the White-Rim Black and White-Rim Gray sherds from San Fernando have fine sand temper rather than the ash temper usually associated with pottery from La Venta and the Tuxtlas region. This may suggest local production in the San Fernando area, whereas the Black and White pottery from ILC may have been imported from Southern Veracruz or extreme Western Tabasco. Elsewhere in the Lower Mezcalapa, a variety of temper types characterizes multiple Black and White wares of the Middle to Late Formative, many of which include ash like those at ILC (Sisson 1976:127–136). Thick parallel grooves on rim exteriors were found at multiple NWAF sites and are also found in Formative types like Aguatepec in the Lower Usumacinta (Ochoa and Casasola 1991). Interestingly, no pottery with paste characteristics like Sierra Red were described for the NWAF collection, yet the type is common to Late Formative contexts at ILC, Formative sites of the Lower Mezcalapa Delta (e.g., Cárdenas Red: Sisson 1976:120–121), and the Lower Usumacinta region (e.g., Laguna Red at Aguacatal: Matheny 1970). This suggests that interaction in the Chontalpa with the Chicanel sphere differed by location.

Among Late Classic pottery types, Centla resembles Sisson's (1976:137–138) descriptions of Ahualulco Red. Several of Piña Chan and Navarrete's (1967) descriptive types for the NWAF project are similar to the Late Classic pottery at ILC, though most of the NWAF project ceramics are described as being poorly fired. Although having dark cores, their Coarse Brownish type has similar temper as Centla but others are described as having larger temper and more grainy paste like Cimatán. They are predominantly ollas and include Soyataco and Trinidad/ Coabal decoration. Their Coarse Creamy type is similar to Mecoacán, which also includes Soyataco stylistic attributes. Their Coarse Reddish type, though having dark cores, may be similar to the reddish paste variants of Centla, Cimatán, and Mecoacán. They are also predominantly ollas and share Soyataco and Trinidad/Coabal decorations at multiple sites. Piña Chan and Navarrete's Fine Sandy Brownish type was like ILC's Type Z. Described for the NWAF collections but absent at ILC are vertical incisions and grooves, fabric or net impressions, and the crumbly, severely burned, Coarse Blackish type (Piña Chan and Navarrete 1967:13).

Several of Matheny's (1970) type descriptions for Aguacatal at the Laguna de Términos also suggest similarities with Late Classic pottery at ILC. Centla paste appears to be similar to Cuidadela unspecified. Cimatán paste is similar to the descriptions for Cuidadela unslipped, coarse-paste variety and Patano unslipped. Mecoacán paste is similar to that described for Hornos Smoothed. Importantly, the PAILC's Type Y pottery matches the descriptions for Golfo shell-tempered, which is abundant at Aguacatal, particularly Jilón (Matheny 1970:73). This indicates ILC connections to coastal regions to the east. No shell temper was described in the NWAF survey, which suggests that such pottery was primarily exchanged along the coastline (Piña Chan and Navarrete 1967) .

As at Comalcalco and ILC, fine pastes appeared toward the end of the Early Classic (closer to CE 600) in the Usumacinta region (Ochoa and Casasola 1991). Among the NWAF fine pastes, Fine Gray, Fine Creamy, and Polished Gray resemble Comalcalco Fine. They include mostly bowls (some with annular bases) and some plates. Their description of Creamy Gray bowls appears similar to Jonuta. Although most of the site-by-site descriptions of Fine Orange (also bowls and plates) share characteristics with Paraíso, the paste at San Fernando appears to be more similar to the Comalcalco type. Their Polished Brown and Polished Black types are similar to the Huimangillo type and some have Trinidad/Coabal cross-hatching.

A LATE CLASSIC POTTERY FREQUENCY SEQUENCE?

As noted in Chapter 2, a major limitation of the project was the difficulty in refining the local ceramic sequence due to the Late Classic recycling of earlier deposits to construct features. Stratigraphic analyses of Formative coarse types and their attributes were unlikely to identify a sequence

for those periods. It may be possible to identify a sequence in Late Classic pottery, assuming each mound-building deposit included earlier Late Classic pottery than the one above it. It is also possible, however, that earlier and later Late Classic deposits (themselves recycled from Formative deposits) were also mixed in the recycling of later mound-fill deposits. Nevertheless, paste and form were demonstrated to be useful chronological diagnostic tools in other Gulf Coast regions (Arnold 2003; Culbert and Rands 2007; Rands 1985; Stark 1989:88–93), so it was warranted to attempt an analysis of stratigraphic frequency for the PAILC collection. Collections from profiled walls of mines or erosional areas were too small for this purpose, so the analysis was limited to excavation data from three residential contexts that yielded larger stratigraphic samples: features 75 and 77-78 at Isla Chablé and composite Feature 32-34-35 at Isla Santa Rosita.

Table 6.9 compares the stratigraphic frequencies of the paste-based types in those contexts. Mecoacán and fine-paste types were rare and are not considered. In Feature 75 there were high percentages of Centla through all strata but with a general increase from lower to upper strata and levels. Meanwhile, the percentages of Cimatán decreased from lower to upper strata and levels. This observation suggests that Cimatán was more common earlier in the Late Classic, after which Centla became more frequent. In contrast, the percentages of Centla declined slightly from lower to upper strata in Feature 77 accompanied by increasing percentages of Cimatán. Centla was relatively uncommon in features 32-34 where Cimatán was the dominant type, the latter without a trend in frequency from lower to upper strata. Within the midden over platform Feature 35, Centla also declined in percentages from strata III to I while the percentage of Cimatán increased.

Seriating features into a relative sequence must assume one of these alternative frequency trends as a standard. If accepting the sequence indicated from Feature 75, then it is possible that features 77 and 32-34-35 were built and occupied earlier when Cimatán was more common. But the reverse would be the case if assuming the sequence suggested by Feature 77. Feature 75 could have been built and occupied earlier than features 77 and 32-34-35. The lack of one cross-feature sequence in frequencies to use as a standard prevents the use of seriation for sequencing features. Instead, access to different types might better explain the differences among these features.

Table 6.10 presents the numeric, stratigraphic distribution of varieties with plastic decoration. Although infrequent, there was an increase in the number of polished

Table 6.9. Stratigraphic Distribution of Late Classic Types in Percentages by Level

			FEATURE 75, UNIT 5				
Stratum	*Level*	*Number*	*Bellote*	*Centla*	*Cimatán*	*Mecoacán*	*Fine Pastes*
III	3	68	0	94	6	0	0
IV	4	34	0	100	0	0	0
	5	73	0	99	1	0	0
	6	47	0	94	4	0	0
	7	64	0	95	0	4	0
	8	68	0	77	15	3	6
	9	77	0	85	13	0	3
	10	32	0	69	28	0	3
	11	38	0	90	11	0	0
Feature 137		131	1	79	21	0	0

			FEATURE 77, UNIT 1				
Stratum	*Level*	*Number*	*Bellote*	*Centla*	*Cimatán*	*Mecoacán*	*Fine pastes*
I	2	8	0	38	50	0	0
II	3	23	9	35	47	4	4
II–III	4	51	8	47	26	14	6
III	5	132	0	80	17	2	2
IV	6a	0	0	0	0	0	0
V	6b	0	0	0	0	0	0
VI	7	18	6	83	12	0	0

			FEATURES 32 AND 34 (BLOCKS A AND B)				
Stratum	*Level*	*Number*	*Bellote*	*Centla*	*Cimatán*	*Mecoacán*	*Fine Pastes*
I	–	72	13	9	76	0	3
II	–	297	2	16	83	0	0
III	–	46	0	11	89	0	0
IIIa	–	0	0	0	0	0	0
IIIb	–	2	0	0	100	0	0
"IV"	–	2	0	50	50	0	0
IV	–	0	0	0	0	0	0
V	–	3	0	0	100	0	0

			FEATURE 35, UNIT 14				
Stratum	*Level*	*Number*	*Bellote*	*Centla*	*Cimatán*	*Mecoacán*	*Fine Pastes*
I	1	331	0	14	85	0	2
II	2–3	507	0	31	66	0	3
III	4–5	448	0	25	72	0	3
IV	6–7	35	0	6	93	0	0

**Table 6.10. Numeric Distribution by Strata of
Late Classic Sherd Varieties with Plastic Decoration**

		FEATURE 75, UNIT 5				
Stratum	Level	Polished	Fenix	Soyataco	Striated	Trin./Caobal
III	3	0	0	0	10	0
IV	4	1	0	0	0	0
	5	0	2	0	0	1
	6	0	0	0	0	0
	7	0	5	0	0	0
	8	0	6	0	1	2
	9	0	5	0	0	0
	10	0	7	1	0	2
	11	0	4	0	0	0
Feature 137		3	2	0	0	5

		FEATURE 77, UNIT 1				
Stratum	Level	Polished	Fenix	Soyataco	Striated	Trin./Caobal
I	2	0	0	0	0	0
II	3	11	0	0	0	0
II–III	4	12	0	0	0	0
III	5	1	0	0	0	0
IV	6a	0	0	0	0	0
V	6b	0	0	0	0	0
VI	7	3	1	0	0	0

		FEATURES 32 AND 34 (BLOCKS A AND B)				
Stratum	Level	Polished	Fenix	Soyataco	Striated	Trin./Caobal
I	–	11	1	0	0	9
II	–	10	1	2	2	61
III	–	0	0	0	0	0
IIIa	–	0	0	0	0	0
IIIb	–	0	0	0	0	0
"IV"	–	0	0	0	0	0
IV	–	0	0	0	0	0
V	–	0	0	0	0	1

		FEATURE 35, UNIT 14				
Stratum	Level	Polished	Fenix	Soyataco	Striated	Trin./Caobal
I	1	7	0	0	7	129
II	2–3	0	0	0	5	116
III	4–5	6	2	2	0	54
IV	6–7	4	0	0	0	4

Table 6.11. Stratigraphic Distribution of Late Classic Sherds Based on Vessel Morphology

	FEATURE 75, UNIT 5				
Stratum	*Level*	*Dishes*	*Bowls*	*Ollas*	*Jars*
III	3	–	–	1 6Ag	–
IV	4	–	–	–	–
	5	–	–	1 6Ab	–
	6	–	–	2 6Aj, 3 6Bj	–
	7	1 3Ea	–	1 6Aj, 1 6Bj	–
	8	–	–	–	1 7Ca
	9	–	–	–	–
	10	–	–	1 6Dj	–
	11	–	–	–	–
Feature 137		–	–	–	–
	FEATURE 77, UNIT 1				
Stratum	*Level*	*Dishes*	*Bowls*	*Ollas*	*Jars*
I	2	–	–	1 6Ba, 1 6Ca	–
II	3	1 3Ce	–	–	–
II–III	4	–	1 4Ba	–	–
III	5	1 3Ea	1 4Be,1 4Da	–	1 7Ca
IV	6a	–	–	–	–
V	6b	–	–	–	–
VI	7	–	2 4Da	–	–

Key: Shapes illustrated in Figure 6.1: Number = vessel form; upper case letters = shape, lower case letters = lip form.

sherds from the lower to upper strata in Features 77 and 32-34. There was a demonstrable decline in Fenix decorated sherds from the lower to upper strata in Feature 75. However, one must keep in mind that Feature 75 showed the opposite frequency trends in types compared to the other features and there were too few sherds of this variety (n = 31) in that feature to observe trends. Although rare, Striated occurred late in mound construction sequences at features 75 and 32-34, and in the midden over platform Feature 35. This is the best indication of a cross-feature sequence in varieties, yet the numbers are appallingly low (n = 25 for all features). Trinidad/Coabal variety sherds increased significantly from the lower to upper midden strata over Feature 35 and in mound fill strata in features 32-34. But there were too few from Feature 75 and none from Feature 77 to corroborate a chronological sequence. As with the distributional analysis of types, no discernible stratigraphic frequency trends could be concluded using varieties.

There were few rims from these excavations and the shape and lip categories were not observable for many sherds found in features 32-34 and 35. Table 6.11 shows the stratigraphic distribution of shapes and lips by form from features 75 and 77 (using the codes from Figure 6.1). There were no plate rims to observe and too few dish rims to consider. There were no bowl rims from the Feature 75 excavations to compare with the few from Feature 77. And no jars were represented in those contexts. Considering only the small sample of olla rims from Feature 75, there appears to be a trend from lower to upper strata and levels from varied shapes with consistent lips to predominantly vertical necks with varied lips. Only two olla rims were recovered from the excavation in Feature 77 and neither had vertical necks. Any interpretation of the sequence suggested from the Feature 75 data alone would be pure conjecture.

This attempted stratigraphic analysis of Late Classic pottery relied on limited comparisons available for cross-feature patterns and had too limited data on varieties or vessel morphology. A conclusion on the stratigraphic distribution of paste-types could not be made. A demonstrated decline in Cimatán and increase in Centla at Feature 75 contrasted with the opposite sequence at Feature 77. The only cross-feature pattern observed was a possible increase in the Striated variety, yet this was based on very few Striated sherds. There were no data from other features to compare with the increase in Trinidad/Coabal varieties at combined Feature 32-34-35 or with the vertical necks in olla rims at Feature 75, which were also based on only a few sherds.

Stratigraphic approaches have been unproductive for identifying a Late Classic pottery sequence at ILC. In Chapter 5, I demonstrated that Formative deposits, along with earlier Late Classic deposits, were recycled in the construction of Late Classic features. This analysis did not support the assumption that each mound-building deposit included later Late Classic pottery than the one beneath it. Ceramics and excavation data from other sites in the region may be more productive in this pursuit. Thermoluminescence dating of large samples of sherds from the types, varieties, and morphological categories may provide an additional, albeit costly, avenue.

A THERMOLUMINESCENCE DATING EXPERIMENT USING SURFACE COLLECTIONS

Because stratigraphic analyses were the proposed method for refining the ceramic chronology, I did not collect sediment samples along with the pottery. The growing awareness that stratigraphic sequencing would fail led to a subsequent consultation with James Feathers and a limited 2011 pilot experiment using surface-collected pottery for thermoluminescence dating (Ensor 2011c, 2013d). Funding was provided by Eastern Michigan University's Provost's Office for thermoluminescence and AMS dating of charcoal and one bone. If the results conformed with the dates for types having known period affiliations, then the use of surface collections might proceed on a larger scale and could also date pottery currently without period affiliations. Five sherds were selected from the 2001 surface collections (from features 2 and 5 at Isla Boca Grande). The sherds consisted of Formative Coarse, Centla, Cimatán, and Mecoacán, all of which have known period affiliations, and Bellote, which lacks a period affiliation. After selecting and documenting the sherds from the collection housed at the Centro INAH Tabasco, I returned to ILC to obtain surface sediment samples from the locations of the 2001

10- by10-m collection units. After obtaining INAH export permits, the sherds and sediment samples were submitted to the Luminescence Dating Laboratory of University of Washington (Feathers 2013).

In brief, the thermoluminescence technique reheats the minerals in objects to measure their luminescence—a product of the amount of radiation in the object, which indicates the amount of time that has passed since the object was last heated. It measures the duration of time since the electrons were emitted during the material's crystallization, specifically, the duration of time since a pot was fired. A sediment sample associated with a sherd is needed to compare its lumination with the luminescence of the location in the present to derive a duration in time since the firing of the vessel. The sediment samples are usually collected during excavations, whereby both the sherd and its associated sediment in an undisturbed context are collected in situ. The use of surface sediments collected a decade after the pottery was removed was experimental. Of concern was whether or not surface sediments from mixed Formative and Late Classic deposits that were collected *near* where the sherds were collected (rather than the precise place), would introduce methodological errors.

There were no errors detected in the analyses (Feathers 2013), but the results were still mixed. Although some results indicated slightly earlier or later dates than anticipated, one was dubious, and another was rejected.

Based on the presence at ILC of the Black and White and Sierra Red types, a Middle-Late Formative date range was expected for the Formative Coarse sherd from Feature 2. The thermoluminescence results were slightly earlier than expected, suggesting an Early to Middle Formative date: BCE 810 ± 560 (UW2612) (Feathers 2013). Accepting this result would expand the interpreted date range for the Formative occupations at ILC.

The Cimatán and Centla types are firmly affiliated with the Late Classic and possibly earlier. The two sherds representing these types were recovered meters apart at Feature 5. The results on the Cimatán sherd (UW2608) were slightly later than expected, suggesting a manufacturing date in the Mexican Epiclassic period or Maya Late-Terminal Classic period: CE 870 ± 60 (Feathers 2013). The resulting date for the Centla sherd (UW2610) was slightly earlier than expected: CE 490 ± 100 (Feathers 2013) in the late Early Classic (or the proposed "Middle Classic"). Accepting these dates would stretch their currently accepted range by a century in both directions.

The PAILC considered the Mecoacán type to be affiliated with the Late Classic given the decorative attributes and reddish paste variants, shared with Centla and Cimatán. The thermoluminescence analysis on the Mecoacán sherd (UW2611) from Feature 5 resulted in a much earlier date of CE 40 ± 120 (Feathers 2013), between the Late Formative and Early Classic periods. That result seems unreasonable given the paste similarities and decorative attributes to known Late Classic pottery, which differ considerably with those of the Formative periods.

The Bellote type shares some decorative attributes with Centla and Cimatán but has paste similarities with both the Formative and the Late Classic pottery, suggesting an Early Classic period affiliation. The thermoluminescence date on the Bellote sherd (UW2609) from Feature 2 was BCE 2600 ± 400 (Feathers 2013). This preceramic, pre-lagoon date represents either an astonishing find or a problem with the sediment used in the analysis. There were small mines or looter pits in Feature 2.

The results on the Centla and Cimatán sherds were not far from the expectations, offering some promise to the use of surface collections. Other results were highly questionable or rejected, leading to the decision not to expand the sample size using the 2001 collections. New collections with simultaneous adjacent sediment sampling—where there are no indications of disturbance—might better evaluate if surface collections are appropriate for this dating technique.

CONCLUSIONS

Given the problems with past culture historical complex-group-type-variety approaches to ceramic analysis and the sherd surface erosion requiring alternatives, the system that PAILC developed emphasized paste-based types and treated plastic decoration as varieties independent of types. This system conformed better to the materials at ILC. Morphological attributes were recorded for rim sherds: form, shape, lips, thickness, and orifice diameter.

Seventeen types were created. The descriptive Formative paste-types included the ubiquitous Formative Coarse along with Formative Sandy and Formative White. These likely spanned the Middle and Late Formative periods. Accompanying these were the rare Olmec-Horizon Black and White type and the Late Formative period Sierra Red type. There were more numerous types for the Late Classic period. The largest categories were the Centla and Cimatán types. These were accompanied by the less frequent regionally known semi-fine and fine paste types. Additional types were also created that may have been imported from Maya regions to the east. The paste-based classification also

resulted in three types absent in regional literature. These included the Bellote, Mecoacán, and Type X. Only 4 percent of the collection could not be classified into the 17 types.

Plastic decorative varieties differed between the Formative and Late Classic types. Thick grooves were present on a few of the Black and White sherds and parallel circumferential grooves were common for Sierra Red rims. Similar grooves were also associated with the undated Type X, suggesting a Late Formative affiliation. Apart from grooves and remnants of polished surfaces, other forms of plastic decoration were extremely rare among the Formative types. Also rare were vestiges of paint (usually black or red). The Late Classic plastic decoration or stylistic treatment was more diverse. Most could be classified as Fenix, Soyataco, Striated, or Trinidad (found on multiple paste types) but other incising, although rare, was more common than among the Formative types. Polishing was also relatively common across all Late Classic types. Where paint remnants were visible, they were typically red or black. White, cream, or polychrome paints were extremely rare.

One major observation on form is the absence of *comales* (griddles) in the collections. Although the 2001 season interpreted the possible presence of griddles at platform Feature 78 (Ensor 2002b), upon comparison and closer scrutiny, the slightly upcurved edges better indicated shallow plates. Subsequent seasons also failed to recover rims from *comales*. This is a significant finding. It demonstrates, in combination with the abundance of ollas, that local cuisine emphasized moist foods and generally lacked tortillas or other dry griddled-foods. This is corroborated by the paucity of ground stone (Chapter 7). Maize and other grains received into the local community could have been consumed as gruels, tamales, or as unground kernels and seeds added to stews (moist foods conforming with ollas).

Some Formative types had more specialized functions while two apparently fulfilled a wide range of functions. Although few, Black and White rims were from serving vessels, which conformed with the technological suitability of this type. There was also a bias toward serving vessels among the Sierra Red type, which was technologically more suited for cooking (alternatively viewed as an "average" performance characteristic for a variety of intended uses). The Formative Sandy type was dominated by cooking vessels, which conforms with its technological suitability. However, both the Formative Coarse type and the "X" type (suspected Formative pottery) had a wide range of vessel forms represented without a dominant form. These had pastes technologically suited for cooking, as well as having a range of "average" characteristics suitable for moderate performance in multiple uses. For most Formative types, morphological and technological suitability were generally congruent.

Congruence between morphological and technological suitability was more variable among the Late Classic types, suggesting that people had to use a good deal of pottery that was more susceptible to failure. The Late Classic coarse-paste Centla, Cimatán, and Mecoacán types had a range of forms but high percentages of ollas for cooking stews, soups, or gruels with imported maize or other grains, or even tamales with imported *nixtamal*. Among these, only the Centla type, the second most common, had paste attributes technologically well suited for cooking. The Cimatán and Mecoacán types had variably sized angular temper particles, making them susceptible to failure with thermal expansion and contraction. Because Cimatán was the most common, this suggests that a great many ollas used for cooking at ILC likely had short use-lives. In addition, the red-paste variants of these three types, also dominated by cooking forms, would have been too brittle for cooking vessels. Straight (2017) found that Maya cooking vessels had the shortest use-lives among household assemblages. Bellote, a possible Early or Late Classic type, had a wide range of morphologies without being dominated by any one functional category. These morphologies also had technological characteristics suited for cooking, which alternatively can be viewed as an "average" quality for numerous uses. Among the fine paste types, Comalcalco, Jonuta, Paraíso, and Huimangillo were technologically most suited for serving, though the Comalcalco Fine sherds at ILC were of relatively poor quality.

Uniformity in plastic decorative variants for the utilitarian coarse types suggests community-wide daily uses, a source of social cohesion through practice. As stated at the beginning of the chapter, symbolic display can include use for identity negotiation, gifting for alliances, and domestic to public food sharing and feasting. It is suggested that the Black and White and Sierra Red types—both highly decorated and in low frequencies—functioned primarily for symbolic display during Formative times. The fine paste types of the Late Classic were also suggested to have served primarily for social display. Comalcalco Fine had a wide range of small vessel forms without any dominant form. Jonuta vessels were dominated by cooking and liquid storage forms. Paraíso and Huimangillo vessels, in contrast, more frequently had serving-related forms, matching their technological suitability. Given the unsuitability of Comalcalco and Jonuta pastes for the functions implied by their

morphologies, these may have served more meaningfully for symbolic display. The distribution of Late Classic types across contexts is examined in Chapter 9 to better understand the character of social integration.

The stratigraphic analyses did not identify cross-feature diachronic trends in paste-types, decorative attributes, or morphological attributes for the Late Classic pottery. Due to the redeposition of Formative and earlier Late Classic deposits, it was assumed that each mound-fill stratum would have earlier Late Classic pottery than the one above it. Although the numbers of sherds by paste types were sufficient for the analysis, there were too few decorative and morphological attributes to determine this. The paste types showed opposite trends among different features, indicating that no chronological refinements to Late Classic pottery were possible through stratigraphic analysis.

The thermoluminescence-dating experiment using 2001 surface collections and sediment samples collected in 2011 had mixed results. The Formative Coarse sherd showed an earlier date than expected, placing it in the Early to Middle Formative periods. The result on the Cimatán sherd was slightly later than expected whereas that for the Centla sherd was slightly earlier than expected. Both, however, were not unreasonable and may suggest a longer date range for the Late Classic occupations. The result on the Mecoacán sherd was dubious and that for the Bellote sherd was rejected. More than likely, these results were influenced by the sediment samples from recently disturbed deposits. Future efforts to refine the ceramic chronology should consider less disturbed contexts or sites without the mixing of deposits so characteristic of ILC, alternative strategies, and much larger budgets.

Despite the inability to refine the ceramic chronology, it is hoped that the classification system and descriptions provide archaeologists with a useful guide toward understanding central coastal Tabascan pottery. The information presented significantly advanced the PAILC and provided essential data for a range of analyses in this book. The period affiliation of types were critical for demonstrating the recycling of earlier deposits that challenged prior assumptions about features at ILC (Chapter 5). The types, varieties, morphological attributes, congruity/incongruity in technological and morphological suitability, symbolic display types, and food sharing and feasting vessels also informed the analyses and interpretations of the prehispanic societies in chapters 8 and 9. But before proceeding to those subjects, the additional material culture at ILC needs consideration.

CHAPTER SEVEN

Other Artifacts and Materials

In addition to the ceramics discussed in the previous chapter, 1,462 other artifacts and samples of materials were collected. These included reworked sherds (mostly fish net sinkers), one figurine fragment, bitumen adhered to sherds, chipped stone (obsidian and chert), ground stone, waterworn stone, faunal remains, and architectural materials (daub, clay, mortar or plaster, sherds in mortar, and brick). This chapter describes these artifacts and materials, their attributes and conditions, and their chronological and functional interpretations. Vertebrate aggregate results and distributions are presented along with probable capture techniques. An analysis of screen mesh size effect on vertebrate specimen recovery is included, which should be applicable to other coastal projects. A comparison of vertebrate taxa with those from Comalcalco is also presented. Although not collected, the consumption, dating problems, and other uses of invertebrates—in particular the roles of oysters—are included in the discussion.

RE-USED SHERDS AND OTHER CERAMIC ARTIFACTS

A small number of sherds were reworked into net sinkers and discs. The only figurine fragment, found in Feature 100, dates to the Formative period and has implications for ritual at ILC. One miniature pot fragment was also recovered.

Twenty-two sinkers for fishing nets were collected. Sherds from a variety of vessel portions were ground into elliptical, oval, or semi-rectangular shapes with edge grooves on opposite ends for fastening (Figure 7.1). Fifteen were made from Late Classic sherds (Centla and Cimatán, and one Paraíso). Four were made from Bellote sherds (unknown period affiliation). Three were made from Formative Coarse sherds. The sinkers are a clear indication of net-fishing—implying the capture of schooling fish—during the Late Classic. The majority were found at the South Group of El Bellote and at Feature 77 on Isla Chablé, suggesting that net-fishing rights were restricted to certain groups (Chapter 9).

Two disc-shaped reworked sherds were found, both of which came from residential contexts on Isla Santa Rosita. One was a whole disk, made from a Centla sherd, and appears to have been an ornament. The other was a fragment made from an unclassified sherd.

There was one miniature vessel fragment made of an unclassified fine paste, indicating a Late Classic affiliation. Because only a small portion of the rim was recovered, the form and shape could not be identified. It had an orifice diameter of 3 cm.

The figurine fragment was recovered from the greatly disturbed Feature 100 in the South Group of Isla Chablé. The fragment was of the Formative Coarse type, although it has post depositional discolorations characteristic of the White type. Although greatly eroded, it presented a partial left side of an anthropomorphic face. From what little could be observed, the piece was not mold-made. It could not be determined if the face belonged to a larger figurine. That only one Formative figurine fragment was found across ILC signifies their general lack of importance to rituals during the Formative and Late Classic occupations.

BITUMEN

Processed bitumen was used in the Gulf Coast region as mortar, for architectural post and floor surfacing, as decorative pigment, as caulking for canoes (Wendt and Ciphers 2008:180–181), as decoration on spindle whorls (Stark,

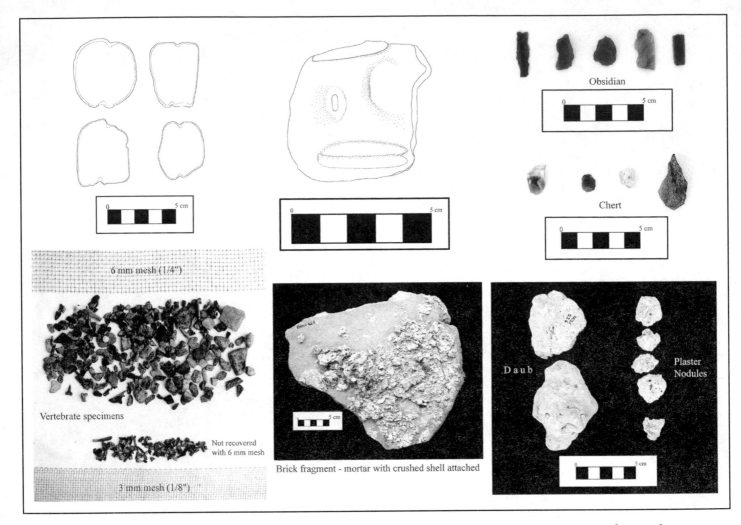

Figure 7.1. Miscellaneous artifacts and materials: top left = sherds used as fishing net sinkers; top center = figurine fragment; top right = chipped stone artifacts; bottom left = vertebrate remains and screen mesh sizes; bottom center = brick fragment with attached mortar and shell fragments; and bottom right = daub and plaster nodules. Prepared by the author.

Heller, and Ohnersorgen 1998:18), and even for defleshing bones (Argáez and others 2011). At the Olmec site of El Remolino, Veracruz, bitumen was concentrated around a hearth within a domestic area, suggesting domestic processing adjacent to dwellings (Wendt 2005:459). At Paso los Ortices, bitumen processing occurred both near dwellings and away from domestic areas, where plank-impressed slabs of bitumen appear to have been stored in a pit for recycling or exchange (Wendt and Ciphers 2008:183–184). Bitumen apparently was processed by heating it in large *tecomates* at Remolino and in large coarse-paste jars at Patarata, Veracruz (Wendt and Ciphers 2008:185; Stark 1989:71).

Despite bitumen's natural occurrence in offshore seeps along shorelines in the Gulf Coast region, it was rare at ILC.

The only bitumen encountered was adhered to the interiors of two Cimatán, one Bellote, and one Jonuta body sherds. The Cimatán and Bellote examples correspond to coarse-paste vessels used for processing bitumen. The Jonuta type, however, though it occurred predominantly in cooking and liquid storage forms, was more suitable for symbolic display. This suggests that the bitumen may have been used as a sealant on the vessel. The most likely use at ILC for processed bitumen, since no architectural uses are evident, was for caulking canoes. The two Cimatán sherds were from Feature 32—a commoner residential superior mound at Isla Chablé. The Bellote and Jonuta sherds with bitumen were both from ceremonial mounds at El Bellote (features 164 and 194, respectively), and presumably originated from recycled domestic deposits. Bitumen processing at ILC

Table 7.1. Obsidian Artifacts

Feature and Context	Source	Form	Portion	Length (cm)	Width (cm)
32 excavation	El Chayal	Prismatic blade	Distal	1.4	0.8
	El Chayal	Prismatic blade	Whole	4.1	1.2
	El Chayal	Prismatic blade	Proximal	1.5	0.8
35 excavation	El Chayal	Prismatic blade	Whole	3.1	1.0
40 excavation	Zaragoza	Prismatic blade	Whole	2.0	0.8
	El Chayal	Prismatic blade	Whole	2.5	1.3
77 excavation	Pachuca	Prismatic blade	Whole	2.9	0.8
122 excavation	Zaragoza	Flake	Whole	1.9	1.4
	Zaragoza	Flake	Whole	2.3	1.0
161 profile	Orizaba	Prismatic blade	Proximal	2.0	1.1
164 surface	Zaragoza	Prismatic blade	Medial	4.0	1.5
165 surface	Orizaba	Flake	Whole	2.2	1.1
170 surface	Unidentified	Flake	Whole	2.0	1.2
176 surface	Zaragoza	Prismatic blade	Distal	3.6	1.2
	Pachuca	Prismatic blade	Medial	1.2	1.1
195 surface	Unidentified	Flake	Fragment	1.2	0.8
Surface, on basal platforms at El Bellote	El Chayal	Prismatic blade	Proximal	3.3	1.0
	Unidentified	Prismatic blade	Proximal	1.5	1.3
	Unidentified	Core	Whole	3.2	2.1
	Unidentified	Flake	Whole	1.7	1.9

appears to have been a rare domestic activity across class contexts in the Late Classic.

STONE TOOLS

One distinctive characteristic of ILC was the paucity of stone tools. All observed stone was collected by the project, including obsidian, chert, and ground stone (metate and mano) fragments. Waterworn stones were also collected. They appeared to be unmodified but had potential uses. The following provides descriptions and functional interpretations for the stone artifacts, possible chronological affiliations, and a discussion about the scarcity of stone tools at ILC.

Obsidian

Obsidian is typically ubiquitous at Mesoamerican sites, including residential contexts, but it was among the rarest of materials found at ILC. Unexpectedly, no specimens were found on the islands during the 2001 survey or in the surface collections (Ensor 2002b). The lack of obsidian established the initial doubts about ILC having a port function and set expectations that little would be recovered in subsequent seasons (Ensor 2003b). Later excavations and profiling yielded nine pieces (Ensor and Tun Ayora 2004, 2011; Ensor and others 2006). The surface collections and profiling at El Bellote yielded an additional 11 pieces, indicating a higher density there than on the islands. The sources, forms, and evidence for retouching and use wear are summarized in Table 7.1.

Lewenstein (1995) and Lewenstein and Glascock (1996, 1997) provided the most comprehensive analyses of obsidian in the region to interpret Comalcalco's context in pan-Mesoamerican trade. To the east, Maya sites generally received very high percentages of obsidian from the El Chayal source in Guatemala (e.g., 96 percent at Palenque). The obsidian at Comalcalco was sourced through neutron activation and macroscopic analysis. Although the majority came from Maya sources in Guatemala, approximately 17 percent originated from the Zaragoza source in Puebla,

México, which is significantly higher than at Maya sites (Lewenstein and Glascock 1997). Assuming ILC received its obsidian through the same channels as Comalcalco, similar percentages were expected. However, the rareness of obsidian at ILC ruled out destructive analyses for sourcing or hydration dating.

For sourcing purposes, the project relied on macroscopic observations using previous descriptions (Braswell and others 2000; Lewenstein 1995; Lewenstein and Glascock 1996, 1997). Transparent obsidian with black veins or bands suggested an El Chayal source (Guatemala). Dark black obsidian may have originated from Zaragoza (Puebla) or Maya sources. Opaque gray obsidian may have been from Orizaba (Veracruz). There is also Pachuca obsidian (Hidalgo), representing a third source from central México. There are equal numbers of central Mexican and Maya obsidian pieces in the PAILC collection. Five transparent gray pieces were not provenienced but probably originated from the Maya highlands of Guatemala. There are six pieces of El Chayal obsidian. The central Mexican sources are represented by five pieces from Zaragoza, two from Orizaba, and two from Pachuca. If accurate, these identifications suggest that the central coastal Chontalpa was integrated with Mexican coastal and Maya riverine trade routes. The inclusion of western sources has been suggested to be a Late Classic characteristic (Lewenstein 1995; Lewenstein and Glascock 1996, 1997), though the Gulf Coast of Southern Veracruz already had greater integration with central Mexico by the Early Classic (Santley and Arnold 2005). This does not rule out Formative affiliations for some obsidian.

The forms include small prismatic blades and flakes (Figure 7.1). Five pieces are small whole (or nearly whole) prismatic blades. Eight are blade fragments: four proximal, two medial, and two distal portions. There are six flakes or flake fragments. In addition to these, there is one small exhausted prismatic core.

Retouching and possible use wear is evident on some pieces. Five of the blades or blade fragments have retouching scars, indicating reworking. Most blades show tiny scars along their edges. Those are either use wear or from post depositional damage, keeping in mind the recycling of fill for Late Classic mound construction.

Chert

Chert artifacts were equally scarce, only 14 pieces were recovered (Figure 7.1). The surface collection at Feature 5 yielded three specimens—the highest surface density of chert anywhere at ILC. None were sourced. The colors,

forms, and sizes were recorded and are summarized in Table 7.2. Chert colors vary considerably; it may be able to source these with further research. The closest possible sources are the mountainous areas of Oaxaca, Chiapas, Southeast Tabasco, and, possibly, limestone formations in Campeche. Most are whole flakes or flake fragments, although one prismatic blade fragment was also recovered. There is also one small exhausted core and one tip of a projectile point (no form or style was determined). There are no macroscopic indications of retouching or use wear.

Ground Stone

Only 11 pieces of ground stone were found at ILC (Table 7.3). One was from the South Group of Isla Chablé and the others were from El Bellote, concentrated at Subgroup A of the Northeast Group. All were for grain processing; there were no axes, adzes, or lapidary items. There were five metate fragments. One was from a trough-shaped metate. The other fragments had flat surfaces with rounded bottoms. There was one mano fragment with smoothed surfaces on opposite sides. The remaining pieces of ground stone were fragments of either manos or metates. All but two were basalt, the closest source for which is the Tuxtla mountains of Southeastern Veracruz, though they could also have come from the Maya Highlands.

The Functions and Paucity of Stone Tools

Limited cutting using blades and flakes took place at ILC. All of the whole blades are small and all of the blade fragments are thin and small (suggesting small whole sizes). Such sizes indicate that blades were not used for generalized cutting purposes, although these could have been inserted into wooden (or bone) implements for shredding. In the latter case, however, more small blades would be expected. Given the local resources available, a vertebrate-processing function for the blades seems most plausible. The flakes were likely tools, yet the minimal indications of use wear suggest the cutting of soft materials. The associations of chipped stone at features with net sinkers in some contexts support this interpretation (e.g., in the South Group of El Bellote). The only possible evidence for craft manufacturing was found at Isla Boca Grande, where three pieces of chert and one possibly incised piece of shell were collected from the surface of Feature 5. The two exhausted cores indicate that a very limited amount of core reduction took place at ILC. More likely, most blades and flakes were imported in finished form. The projectile point tip indicates some form of hunting, perhaps for turtles,

Table 7.2. Chert Artifacts

Feature and Context	Color	Form	Portion	Length (cm)	Width (cm)
5 surface	Grayish cream	Prismatic blade	Proximal	2.7	0.3
	Cream	Flake	Proximal	3.5	0.8
	Grayish cream	Flake	Distal	1.9	0.3
40 excavation	White & brown	Flake	Whole	2.0	1.2
77 excavation	Grayish brown	Core	Whole	2.7	2.0
	Grayish brown	Flake	Whole	1.3	1.0
	White	Flake	Whole	1.8	0.9
	Pink	Flake	Whole	3.6	1.8
122 excavation	Reddish orange	Flake	Distal	1.1	0.9
	White	Flake	Whole	1.3	1.0
152 surface	White & red	Flake	Whole	4.3	2.2
	Pale orange	Flake	Whole	3.9	3.3
200 surface	Orangish cream	Flake	Whole	2.6	1.6
Surface on basal platform at El Bellote	Orangish cream	Projectile point	Tip	3.8	1.6

Table 7.3. Ground Stone Artifacts

Feature and Context	Material	Description	Length (cm)	Width (cm)	Thickness (cm)
99 surface	Basalt	Metate fragment: one flat concave surface with rounded edge	10.0	5.0	–
152 surface	Basalt	Metate fragment: trough with smoothed concave interior and rounded edge	5.2	4.8	3.9
161 profile	Metamorphic	Mano fragment: rectangular cross-section with smoothed surfaces on opposite sides	5.7	5.7	4.5
183 surface	Basalt	Metate fragment: one flat side and one curved and smoothed side	12.2	9.1	5.6
183 surface	Basalt	Metate fragment: one flat side and one convex and smoothed side	5.9	4.1	3.9
183 surface	Basalt	Mano or metate fragment: one flat smoothed side and one convex smoothed side	4.3	4.0	4.5
186 surface	Basalt	Metate fragment: one flat side and one convex side	16.5	13.7	2.5
186 surface	Basalt	Metate fragment: quadrangular fragment	8.0	5.8	3.9
194 surface	Metamorphic	Mano or metate fragment: two adjacent smoothed sides and a curved lip	5.8	5.0	3.3
195 surface	Basalt	Mano or metate fragment: irregular shape with smoothed surfaces on adjacent sides	7.6	5.3	3.9
195 surface	Basalt	Irregular-shaped piece	4.8	3.6	2.2

sharks, or rays. The lack of more stone hunting tools may be because fish and other aquatic animals were captured in nets or by using wooden spears or shell points.

Alternative materials were most likely used for routine cutting purposes. The abundant shell provides the most obvious material that could have been used instead of chipped stone, although no modified shell with chipped or sharpened edges were identified.

The few pieces of ground stone were used for grain processing. The predominance of basalt, having voids to grip larger grains, suggests use for grinding maize. The local environment precludes cultivation (no artificially raised fields have been found), suggesting that small quantities of maize (as indicated by the low numbers of ground stone artifacts) were provisioned to ILC from interior agrarian areas. The maize was probably prepared as gruels and, perhaps, *atole*. Although there is no evidence for the preparation of moist foods other than the abundant *ollas*, already processed *nixtamal* for tamales (a common coastal cuisine) also could have been imported to ILC. Of course, perishable wooden mortars and pestles also could have been used for grain processing.

WATERWORN STONE

Because stone does not occur naturally in the mangrove sediments, all unmodified stones were collected (n = 106) as manuports—procured, unmodified natural objects (Table 7.4). One pumice stone was modified into a bead (1.0 cm in diameter, 0.2 cm thick, with a 0.2 cm perforation). The other stones are larger and have no macroscopic evidence for modification or use wear. They include a range of metamorphic rocks, pumice, and limestone, plus a small number of additional materials including igneous rock, possible cave-associated calcified pieces, and quartzite. In general, the stones are small: most are well under 10 cm in length. Their shapes vary, but nearly all were rounded with smoothed surfaces.

Pumice arrived naturally to the Mecoacán Lagoon. The area surrounding the lagoon is part of the recent Mezcalapa Delta, which had a high load that carried sediment and pumice from volcanic highland regions to the southeast (West, Psuty, and Thom 1969:38) before passing the Pleistocene terraces in southern Tabasco and through the coastal plain (Figure 1.1). Because pumice floats, its presence at the islands is no surprise—it did not require human agency to arrive at ILC.

The Mezcalapa, Grijalva, and Usumacinta deltas were all likely sources for the other materials (Figure 1.1). Limestone

Table 7.4. Waterworn Stone

Material	Number	Percentage	Mean Length (cm)	Size Range (cm)
Metamorphic	68	64.15	3.05	2.2 – 14.5
Pumice	22	20.76	3.38	1.8 – 4.3
Limestone	11	10.38	4.82	3.2 – 7.1
Other (calcareous & basalt)	5	4.72	7.99	5.0 – 14.0
Total	106	100		

is more associated with the low-load Usumacinta Delta much farther to the east (West, Psuty, and Thom 1969:38). But all three river systems originate in, or pass through, the Tertiary zones along the border of Southern Tabasco and Chiapas and could have transported the various metamorphic stones. Although they probably did not occur naturally within the mangrove sediments at ILC, they could have been obtained in the general area.

Given the paucity of chipped stone, it was not surprising that none of the waterworn stones had scarring, steps, or stress marks indicating use as hammerstones. Any use wear on pumice or limestone would have eroded away. The lack of evidence for use leaves only speculation on possible utility. Pumice could have been used for scouring any surfaces or for smoothing wood. Larger pieces of limestone could have been used as shaft straighteners, wood and shell sharpeners, presses, or hammers for crushing shell. The metamorphic and limestone rocks could have been used for polishing. For example, Jordan and Prufer (2017) illustrate similar waterworn pebbles used in pottery shaping and polishing. Although there were no indications of pottery manufacturing at ILC, other materials like wood, bone, shell, or even plaster stucco could have been polished with the stones. Another conceivable use was as hammers for breaking holes in gastropods such as whelks, though no extraction holes were recognized in the field. Alternatively, stones could have been used by children for play-hunting or by adults as gaming pieces or divination paraphernalia (Ember and Cunnar 2015).

The stones were widely distributed in small numbers across ILC. An unusual concentration of 15 stones was identified in the surface collection at Feature 152—a platform overlying the basal platform extending southeast from the Central Group of El Bellote. That residential feature also had high quality plaster, clay floor fragments, chert, and fauna (in addition to the shell), but these do not stand out as unusual for features at El Bellote.

Table 7.5. Vertebrate Remains by Recovery Technique

Taxon	Common Name	Excavated, Screened Contexts				Surface Collections				Totals	
		3–mm mesh		6–mm mesh		Insular		El Bellote			
		NISP	%	NISP	%	NISP	%	NISP	%	NISP	%
Aves (class)	Birds	2	0.21	2	0.27	0	–	1	0.76	3	0.27
Osteichthyes (class)	Boney fishes	290	30.49	185	25.34	0	–	0	–	290	26.29
Ariidae (family)	Barbs, catfish	1	0.11	1	0.14	0	–	0	–	1	0.09
Lamniformes (order)	Sharks	11	1.16	6	0.82	2	10.00	0	–	13	1.18
Rajiformes (order)	Rays	1	0.11	1	0.14	0	–	0	–	1	0.09
Crocodylia (order)	Crocodiles	9	0.95	8	1.10	0	–	0	–	9	0.82
Testudines (order)	Turtles	485	51.00	461	63.15	17	85.00	130	98.50	632	57.30
Unidentified	–	152	16.0	66	9.04	1	5.00	1	0.76	154	13.96
	Total	951	100	730	100	20	100	132	100	1103	100

VERTEBRATE REMAINS

The combined 2001, 2004, and 2007 field seasons collected 1112 vertebrate specimens. None were recovered in the 2005 excavations at residential features 32, 34, and 35. Most specimens came from the 2004 excavations in nonresidential contexts. A small number were recovered in surface collections and during profiling of disturbed features. Recovery methods, aggregated relative frequencies, contexts of vertebrate remains, and a comparison with vertebrate remains from Comalcalco are described in this section.

The bones, bone fragments, and other faunal remains such as scutes and teeth were classified by class, order, and family when possible. Due to the erosion of many specimens and the lack of an experienced zooarchaeologist, they could not be classified to lower-order taxa (with few exceptions) or to age or sex. The collection can, however, be accessed for future analyses. In the relative frequency analysis I used number of individual specimens (NISP), which provides a better comparative basis for fish than minimum numbers of individuals (MNI) (Reitz and Wing 1999).

Aggregated Results

The vertebrate taxa included birds, crocodiles, bony fishes, sharks, and rays. The aggregated relative frequencies are presented by recovery technique in Table 7.5. The single unclassified specimen from the surface collections on the islands was a small fragment of a possible manatee rib (dense and heavy). No terrestrial mammal bones were identified. Birds were identified primarily by long bones. Crocodiles, now locally extinct, were represented primarily

by their scutes. Bony fishes were represented by cranial bones and fragments, spines, vertebrae, and otoliths. Sharks and rays were represented primarily by their distinctive vertebrae and by a few sharks' teeth. Turtles were identified by carapace and plastron bones, as well as other parts of their skeletons.

Over half of the vertebrate specimens were from turtles and about one quarter were from boney fishes. All other identified taxa made up only 2.36 percent of the collection. Nearly 14 percent of the specimens were unidentified. From these observations, and considering the invertebrates that were recovered, it seems safe to conclude that shellfish (primarily oysters), boney fish, and turtles were the primary animals that were captured and consumed at ILC.

Screen Mesh Size Effect

Zooarchaeologists have long recognized the influence of archaeological recovery techniques on the interpretation of faunal remains. Surface collections, stratigraphic profiling, or any other technique that does not screen deposits, results in the recovery of larger specimens and specimens from larger animals compared to screened sediments from excavation. Furthermore, screen mesh sizes are known to influence recovery rates of smaller specimens, thus influencing interpretations about diet (Reitz and Wing 1999:145). Because the PAILC was the first systematic archaeological investigation at a coastal site complex in Tabasco, the first excavations (in 2004) included an analysis of the recovery of faunal remains by mesh size to guide subsequent excavation strategies and to inform future projects in the region (Ensor and Tun Ayora 2004). Customary screen sizes at

Table 7.6. Comparison of Faunal Specimen Recovery by Context

Feature	Feature Type	Number	Screen mesh size		Lost with 6-mm Mesh: Taxon (NISP)
			3-mm	6-mm	
40	Residential	58	100%	100%	None
75	Residential	0	–	–	None
77	Residential	1	100%	100%	None
92	Linear platform	116	100%	90%	Fish (7), turtle (1), indeterminate. (3)
122	Crushed shell deposit	780	100%	73%	Crocodile (1), fish (97), shark (5), turtle (23), unidentified (83)

Comalcalco and elsewhere in the region, if screening at all, typically relied on 10-mm or larger mesh sizes. The 2004 PAILC season used 3-mm (⅛-inch) mesh for screening all excavated deposits. The small mesh size consumed a great deal of field time for screening, especially in the residential mounds, which have compact clays, but the project did not want to risk a potential recovery bias. Rather than using unwieldy nested screens and having to bag remains from different mesh sizes separately in the field, all vertebrate remains recovered with the 3-mm mesh were later sifted in 6-mm (¼-inch) mesh at the lab to observe which specimens would not have been recovered with the larger mesh size. Figure 7.1 illustrates the differences in recovery for Level 1 in Unit 2 at Feature 122.

As seen in Table 7.5, surface collections recovered only specimens from large animals: predominately turtles but also sharks, and birds. In contrast, the vertebrate specimens recovered by screening had significantly lower percentages of turtle and shark remains, while boney fish, along with most other taxa, were better represented. If having used 6-mm mesh in the field, 221 specimens would not have been recovered. Furthermore, the smaller mesh size yielded a higher percentage of boney fish (30.6 percent) and a lower percentage of turtle specimens (51.0 percent) than would have been the case with 6-mm mesh. With the latter, boney fish specimens would reduce to 25 percent and those from turtles would increase to 63 percent. If having used only the 6-mm mesh size, fishing and the dietary contribution of fishes would appear slightly less significant.

Recovery rate differences were dependent on contexts (Table 7.6). During the 2004 season, excavations were conducted in three earthen residential features, the linear shoreline platform, and one crushed shell deposit. The 6-mm mesh would have recovered 100 percent of the faunal specimens from the residential features. No faunal remains were recovered from the 1.18 cubic meters excavated in residential mound Feature 75. Only one bone fragment was recovered from the 1.76 cubic meters excavated in residential mound Feature 77, which was large enough to have been recovered with 6-mm mesh. At residential platform Feature 40, 58 bones and bone fragments were recovered in the 1.08 m³ of excavated fill, all of which would have been recovered with 6-mm mesh.

Unlike the residential contexts, the specialized activity features did show different recovery rates by mesh size (Table 7.6). The excavation in Feature 92, the linear shoreline platform at Isla Chablé, had a high density of vertebrate remains. One hundred sixteen bones and bone fragments were recovered from only 0.79 cubic meters, 90 percent of which were from only one stratum (0.56 m³). Ten percent of the specimens would not have been recovered with 6-mm mesh. Of the total boney fish specimens, 24 percent would not have been recovered with 6-mm mesh. At Feature 122—the larger crushed shell deposit at Isla Chablé—mesh size had a much greater effect on vertebrate recovery. The 1.13 cubic meters of excavated sediment in Feature 122 had the highest density of vertebrate remains in any context at ILC. Most of the specimens were small or fragmented and presumably included with the crushed shell for use as temper for mortar. Approximately 27 percent of the 780 specimens would not have been recovered with 6-mm mesh (mostly of boney fish or unidentified taxa).

Because all vertebrate remains from residential contexts would have been recovered with 6-mm mesh, which takes less field screening time, the PAILC proceeded to use that mesh size in the 2005 excavations at the combined residential feature 32-34-35. No faunal remains were recovered in those much larger excavations, confirming once again that faunal remains are scarce at earthen residential mounds. Whether this is also the case for residential mounds with shell deposits has not been tested. Based on this analysis, however, the finer mesh (3 mm) is recommended for

**Table 7.7. Comparison of Vertebrate and
Crustacean Remains from ILC and Comalcalco**

Taxon	*ILC*		*Comalcalco**	
	NISP	*% NISP*	*NISP*	*% NISP*
Aves (Birds)	3	0.27	183	1.20
Mammalia (Mammals)	0	–	1026	6.74
Osteichthyes (Boney fishes)	290	26.08	66	0.43
Lamniformes (Sharks)	13	1.17	?	–
Rajiformes (Rays)	1	0.09	?	–
Crocodylia (Crocodiles)	9	0.81	144	0.95
Testudines (Turtles)	632	56.84	9679	63.62
Other Reptiles	–	–	4113	27.04
Gecarcinidae (Crabs)	9	0.81	?	–
Indeterminate	154	13.85	?	–
Total	1112	100	15,212	100

Comalcalco source: Hernández Sastre 1998.

Key: NISP = number of individual specimens.

excavations in all but earthen residential features at PAILC. For other projects along the Gulf Coast, finer mesh in early stages at multiple contexts is recommended to similarly evaluate which mesh sizes are optimal by context.

Capture Techniques

Capture techniques were likely similar to those used today. No hooks made of bone or other materials were found but the sinkers provide evidence for net fishing. Based on the sizes of the vertebrae recovered, no very large boney fish are represented. This also suggests that net fishing was the predominant method used. Today, rubber balls are tossed into the lagoon to attract fish to a location where the net is then thrown. Otherwise, the young men simply patrol the lagoon looking for schools at which to throw the nets. Larger nets could have been used along the shores of the gulf and in the river. Stationary nets are used around mangrove branches to capture shrimp. Stationary traps of perishable materials are also frequently used in the region. Given the low frequencies of sharks, rays, and crocodiles, these could have occasionally been trapped in nets, but they also could have been hunted with wooden spears. The turtles could have been trapped in nets, and those on shorelines could have been grabbed by hand. These capturing techniques require only one to two individuals to perform, rather than a collective effort.

Comparison with Comalcalco

Comparing the data on vertebrates from Comalcalco's elite palatial and temple contexts with ILC, there was only a 7 percent difference in turtle NISP (Table 7.7; Hernández Sastre 1997). In contrast, boney fishes at ILC comprised nearly 27 percent of aggregated NISP, the same percentage as reptiles other than crocodiles and turtles at Comalcalco. There were low percentages of birds and mammals in the elite contexts at Comalcalco. The large mesh sizes and less screening of sediments at Comalcalco undoubtedly influenced the different results. Fish and small bird specimens, if present in greater frequencies, were less likely to be observed or collected. Nevertheless, these data indicate a focus on local reptiles for nobility at Comalcalco whereas ILC had a broader spectrum of taxa. The elite contexts at Comalcalco also included rare items that most likely came from the ILC area. For example, the internment of one noble included stingray spines for autosacrifice, polished shell ornaments, and sharks' teeth (Armijo Torres 1999b). Unfortunately, no excavations with comparable screening have taken place in commoners' residential contexts near Comalcalco.

Dating Vertebrate Remains

Nearly all of the pottery found at shoreline platform Feature 92 and crushed shell deposit Feature 122 was Late Classic, suggesting that the fauna within those contexts, and presumably those found at Feature 89 (the other deposit of crushed shell), also primarily date to the Late Classic period. For most contexts, however, dating of vertebrate remains by association is problematic due to the recycling of earlier deposits in the Late Classic. One large sea turtle carapace bone from the profiled second stratum of ceremonial mound Feature 166 was selected for radiometric analysis (Beta Analytic 299882). The results indicated a Late Formative-Early Classic date (Cal. 40 BCE–130 CE [2σ, Cal. 1990–1820 BP]), which further indicates the re-use of early deposits for Late Classic mound building. The small sizes of most specimens prohibit radiometric dating. One of the original objectives of the PAILC—to analyze for changes in subsistence strategy over time—could not be realized.

In summary, the aggregated relative NISP frequencies suggest that boney fishes and turtles were the focus of consumption at ILC. Screen mesh size would have influenced the recovery of vertebrate remains at special use features 92 and 122 but the larger 6-mm mesh would have recovered all specimens from the earthen residential features. Recommended for other coastal projects in the region is the use of 3-mm mesh in early stages to similarly evaluate mesh-size optimums for different contexts. Net fishing was presumably the main capture technique. Turtles could have been captured by nets or by hand. Sharks, crocodiles, and rays were likely hunted opportunistically with spears but also with nets. The infrequent birds could also have been captured in nets, perhaps opportunistically. Comparing the aggregated collection from ILC with that of Comalcalco's palatial and ceremonial district, both appear to have focused primarily on local vertebrates: a broader spectrum including more fish at ILC and a focus on reptiles at Comalcalco. Because vertebrate remains could not be dated by stratigraphic associations with pottery, no comparison of Formative and Late Classic subsistence was possible.

INVERTEBRATE REMAINS

Oyster shell colored previous stereotypes of ILC. Perhaps due to overly brief shoreline visits during informal surveys, the mounds at the South Group of Isla Chablé—long mistaken to be Formative shell middens (*concheros*)—were used to characterize early coastal occupations in Tabasco (Fernández Tejedo and others 1988:51). That occupants in the Formative periods used oysters is not disputed. The Late Classic occupants also most certainly consumed shellfish. Because of the Late Classic recycling of earlier deposits, shell that originally accumulated in the Formative cannot be distinguished from that which was added in the Late Classic. The significance of shell goes beyond indicating a subsistence strategy. The shells were also processed at ILC for architectural materials used locally and at Comalcalco. It was an important commodity in the Late Classic regional political economy—restricted to some, processed collectively, and essential to constructing buildings in the capital. Yet shell and shell products were conspicuously absent at most of ILC.

The great majority of invertebrate remains observed were, of course, oyster shells (*Crassostrea virginica*). Also observed were quahogs (*Mercenaria campechiensis*) and at least two species of whelks (*Busycon* spp.). The capture techniques for harvesting oysters were likely the same as those used today. The principle technique probably consisted of people submerging themselves in the shallow lagoon and collecting the shellfish by hand. They would then use canoes or floating baskets for sorting and transporting oysters to shorelines where they were then shucked. Alternatively, pole rakes could also have been used, allowing the collector to remain standing in a canoe while rapidly piling the oysters for sorting and then transporting. Either technique could be done individually or collectively.

The paucity of oyster shells at most Late Classic residences at ILC suggest that most people in the class-based society did not have rights to exploit these local resources for their own domestic use. As described in chapters 4 and 5, most features at ILC were earthen and few, if any, shells were observed at those residential features. Practically none were recovered from the test unit in Feature 75 and in the much larger block excavations at combined feature 32-34-35. The greatest amount of shell recovered in excavations at earthen residential features was at Feature 40, where 4.5 liters of oyster shells and shell fragments were recovered (but not collected) within a total volume of 1.08 cubic meters of excavated sediment. At Feature 77, a total of 6.2 liters of oyster shells and shell fragments were recovered (also not collected) within 1.76 cubic meters of excavated sediment. Ninety-seven percent of that shell was in the uppermost level, however, accompanied by modern artifacts, and likely of modern origin.

During surface collecting, profile documenting, and excavating, shells were quickly evaluated for any signs of modification such as polish, grooves, perforations, retouch, use wear and other modifications (e.g., Jones O'Day and Keegan 2001; Feinman and Nicholas 1993). It is possible that cultural modification was mistaken for natural breakage, particularly on oyster shells that flake easily and whelk shells that thin considerably over time. However, sharpened edges, drilled holes, and incising should have been distinct on the harder quahog shells, yet no modifications were observed. Even extraction holes on whelk shells or fragments were not recognizable.

The only exception was one small fragment of a whelk shell with *possible* incisions. Although resembling small root grooves, two linear 5-mm long, 0.5-mm wide adjacent possible incisions were observed on the specimen, which was found in the surface collection unit at Feature 5—the same unit that yielded three chert artifacts (one blade fragment and two flake fragments). The surface unit—indeed the entire mound surface—was combed over a second time but no additional stone tools or possibly worked shells were found. No excavations took place at Feature 5 to investigate possible craft manufacturing because it subsequently was used as a nesting area for several years by a rare hawk.

It is certain that the Late Classic community crushed shell for construction materials. Evidence for this can be found in the deposits of crushed shell comprising features 89 and 122, in the mortar and plaster at ILC (most notably at El Bellote), and in the thousands of tons of mortar and plaster stucco at Comalcalco (Littman 1957). Shell was perhaps the most valuable commodity that ILC produced for the Late Classic tributary political economy but its scarcity at most residences indicate it was not equally available to all.

A scenario where crabs (family Gecarcinidae) were not harvested and eaten is difficult to imagine given their abundance in the environment. However, crab consumption is difficult to address. On the one hand, crab shells do not preserve well. On the other hand, their remains could have come from mangrove sediments used to construct the features, or, in the case of low platforms, crabs could have burrowed into the features where they died. Feature 92, for instance, was riddled with crab holes. Only 9 crab shell specimens were recovered—all small claws/fragments and all from screened excavated sediments. Only one was from Feature 92. One was recovered from the Feature 122 excavation. Seven were from the Feature 40 excavation, which was the only residential feature having more than one or few faunal remains. This is the best indication of crab consumption, though those remains could also have come from the mangrove sediment used to construct the platform.

ARCHITECTURAL MATERIALS

Twentieth-century indigenous houses in Tabasco were typically small, well-ventilated, and built entirely of plant materials. But unlike the traditional wood-plank housing at ILC described in Chapter 3, the indigenous houses were often built with vertical wall posts that hold in place horizontal canes for walls and narrow cross-beams over which A-frame roofs were made with thin beams covered by thick guano-palm roof thatching (Carrillo Salazar and González Lobo 1988; Vásquez Dávila, Solís Trejo, and Hipólito Hernández 1988). In some regions, these were built on earthen platforms. They were sometimes on stilts in coastal settings. Major activities took place outside the main house and were associated with smaller perishable structures (Carrillo Salazar and González Lobo 1988; Vásquez Dávila Solís Trejo, and Hipólito Hernández 1988). Of course, the reliance on these traditional materials and techniques among indigenous populations could be explained by their marginalization. Rural Mestizo and Creole housing more typically included cement floors and plastered walls. In a similar vein, there appears to have been unequal distributions of nonperishable, higher quality materials at ILC in the Late Classic.

The PAILC made a number of observations about architectural materials. Structures were described in Chapter 5. Here, more detailed descriptions of the construction materials themselves—mortar, sherds in mortar, plaster, brick, daub, and clay—are provided. These materials were associated with the Late Classic.

Mortar or Plaster

One hundred seventy-nine samples of mortar or plaster were collected. Much of this was likely plaster as opposed to mortar for setting bricks. The difference was not apparent from the materials themselves. Nevertheless, all were associated with architecture.

"Nodules" formed from the crumbling of a low-quality lime-based plaster followed by erosion that resulted in rounded forms. They were found in excavations at some earthen residential mounds on the islands (Figure 7.1). Within Feature 40, these were displaced in secondary contexts, not as part of an in-situ structure. Whatever structure did exist there was razed, and its materials were mixed into the mound fill. Similar nodules were associated with the Feature 75 mound fill overlying the in-situ structure (Feature 137). They are interpreted as having come from collapsed walls.

All nodules observed were collected (n = 129). These ranged in size from approximately 2 to 4 cm. In addition to the lime, the nodules typically contained temper materials (Table 7.8). Twenty (15.5 percent) had sand temper, which was recorded as "sand" (2-3 mm in size) or "fine sand" (<2 mm in size). The most common (79.1 percent) were nodules with fine shell particles (ca. 2 mm in size) or "very

Table 7.8. Characteristics of Mortar or Plaster Samples

Form & Quality	Temper	Number	Percent	Surface Treatments
Eroded Nodules	No temper	3	2.31	
	Sand	17	13.18	
	Fine sand	3	2.33	
	Sand and fine shell	2	1.55	
	Very fine shell	49	37.99	2 with one smoothed surface
	Fine shell	53	41.09	2 with one smoothed surface
	Small crushed shell (≤0.5 cm)	2	1.55	
	Total	129	100	
Thin or Fragile Slabs	Small crushed shell (≤0.5 cm)	2	50.00	1 with one smoothed surface
	Small-large crushed shell (0.5–2.0+ cm)	2	50.00	
	Total	4	100	
Hard or Durable Slabs	Fine sand	3	6.52	
	Fine sand and small shell (≤0.5 cm)	2	4.35	1 with one smoothed surface
	Small crushed shell (≤0.5 cm)	16	34.78	6 with one smoothed surface, 1 with groove on surface
	Crushed shell (0.2–1.0 cm)	18	39.13	8 with one smoothed surface, 1 with vegetal impressions on surface
	Small-large crushed shell (0.5–2.0+ cm)	5	10.87	1 with both surfaces smoothed and painted red
	Coarse sand and small shell (≤0.5 cm)	2	4.35	1 with one smoothed surface
	Total	46	100	

fine" shell particles (<2 mm in size). There were also combinations of sand and fine shell temper. Larger particles of crushed shell were uncommon. The nodules, therefore, appeared to be fragmented and eroded remains of plaster applied to walls or for flooring. Given the severe erosion to these soft materials, only four still had flat, smoothed surfaces.

Lime-based plaster was observed in additional contexts. A similar, albeit harder and better-preserved plaster covered the interior ceiling of Feature 196—the substructure of Feature 202 with the vaulted arch (Figure 4.5). Plaster was also observed lining pit Feature 159 in the Central Group of El Bellote (Figure 5.6).

Far more common than the nodules were concrete fragments made from a lime-based cement tempered with crushed shell or sand. The crushed shell had a mean size of 2 cm, which matches the observed crushed shell at features 89 and 122 on Isla Chablé. This material—far more common at El Bellote than the insular sites—was occasionally observed in situ from the mining and erosional cuts profiled, but also eroding from mound surfaces. It was used both as a material for floors, for mortar, and, apparently, occasionally in walls.

Ten sherds had mortar adhered to their surfaces or edges, indicating occasional inclusion in architecture. Seven were of the Late Classic Centla type and three were of Formative types (Coarse and Sandy). One had a fragment of oyster shell within the mortar adhered to its surface.

Samples of "slabs" were collected. All were loose fragments from surface collections. Their sizes ranged considerably but no samples larger than 15 cm in length were collected. The slabs exhibit differences in thickness and hardness indicating different degrees of quality (Table 7.8). Whether observed eroding out of mounds (and in one case, the backdirt from a looter's pit) this material at earthen residential mounds at the insular sites was thin and fragile. Typically, one surface was smoothed (presumably the floor surface) and the material appeared to have been applied as a thin layer over earthen sediments. More common at El Bellote and the South Group of Isla Chablé, the same material was thicker, harder, and more durable, indicating a higher quality. Feature 171—the exposed floor on the surface of mound Feature 150 in the Central Group of El Bellote (Figure 4.6)—was one example. Such floors were also observed in profiles: for example, the structure overlying the surface of inferior mound Feature 160 in

Table 7.9. Characteristics of Brick Fragments Sampled from the Top of Feature 196

Description	Length (cm)	Width (cm)	Thickness (cm)
Corner piece with black core, mortar attached with small crushed shell	5.0	4.5	2.6
Corner piece with light gray core, mortar attached with small crushed shell	5.1	3.6	2.6
Edge piece with gray and black core, mortar attached with medium crushed shell	26.7	23.5	2.4
Edge piece with gray core	8.9	6.2	2.8
Edge piece with gray core, mortar attached with small crushed shell	8.2	6.5	2.2
Edge piece with black core	7.3	6.0	2.1
Body fragment with no core	7.0	4.3	2.6

the North-Central Group of El Bellote (Figure 5.6) and the multiple floor fragments in mound Feature 156 in the South Group of El Bellote (Figure 5.2). The same materials appear to have been used for walls in those structures. One piece had smoothed and red-painted surfaces. Another had grooves on its smoothed surface, presumably a portion of a decorative treatment. The same material was used also as mortar for setting brick in El Bellote's ceremonial architecture (Figure 4.5).

In addition to these mortars and plasters, one portion of a structure had a lime-based cement for flooring that lacked temper and had completely disintegrated into a powder. This was the floor observed for Feature 137, which was built on the top of platform Feature 76, over which mound Feature 75 was constructed. It serves as another example of differences in the quality of architectural materials.

The observed differences in quality indicate social inequalities at ILC. The nodules, thin and fragile slabs, and the disintegrated floor of Feature 137 were all associated with the earthen residential mounds at the insular sites. The higher quality thicker and harder cements were only observed at El Bellote, at the South Group of Isla Chablé, and at one mound adjacent to, and possibly associated with, the latter. As described in Chapter 9, these are one of multiple differences in material culture between classes in the Late Classic.

Brick

In a region lacking local stone, brick was the typical Late Classic construction material for monumental architecture at Comalcalco (Álvarez Aguilar, Guadalupe Landa, and Romero Rivera. 1992; Andrews 1967, 1989; Littman 1957; Martinez Guzman 1973; Navarette 1967; Romero Molina 1987), elsewhere in the Chontalpa, and at Pomoná in the Lower Usumacinta region (López Varela 1994).

Within ILC, brick was only found at El Bellote, and only associated with ceremonial mounds. Although sizes differed, the bricks were typically rectangular in shape and approximately 2.0 to 3.0 cm in thickness. Bricks or brick fragments were noted where observed and inspected for epigraphy or art but only a sample of seven loose fragments were collected from the exposed roof of Feature 196: the vaulted substructure within ceremonial mound Feature 202 (Figure 4.5).

The observed bricks were light to dark reddish brown in surface color and had thick gray to black cores indicating a low firing temperature in an oxidized environment. All had fine sand temper. None had shell temper (as also observed in uncollected bricks). Several had mortar with fine to large crushed shell temper still adhering to their surfaces (Figure 7.1; Table 7.9).

Although used as a medium for writing and designs at Comalcalco (Alvarez Aguilar, Guadalupe Landa, and Romero Rivera . 1992; Navarette 1967; Romero Rivera 1992; Zender 1998), none of the bricks observed at El Bellote were engraved. All appeared to have come from the walls or roofs of substructures eroding from the larger ceremonial mounds built over them. Furthermore, the plaster over the brick and mortar architecture of Feature 196, and in Charnay's nineteenth-century descriptions of temple walls, suggests that the bricks were not meant to be visible.

Where and how bricks were made remains an important question for the region. Although produced on a massive scale for Comalcalco, no brick manufacturing areas have been found there or, to the author's knowledge, at any other site in the region. After hypothesizing domestic tributary production of cacao but finding no evidence for it at one residential area of Comalcalco, Gallegos Gómora (1995) instead interpreted domestic brick manufacturing but with little evidence. At ILC, there is as yet no evidence for ceramic manufacturing of any kind.

Daub

Daub was a less-frequently encountered wall material (Figure 7.1). There were eight pieces from excavated contexts in earthen residential mounds that also had plaster nodules. One was associated with the plaster nodules from the secondary deposition of a razed structure in the fill of Feature 40. Seven were associated with the floor fill of Feature 137. That fill also contained a large quantity of plaster nodules. The daub may have been a second material used in the construction of walls or roofs, where plaster was used for some sections and daub for others. Alternatively, the daub may have been used for patching or sealing holes in plaster walls and roofs. The specimens were hard, slightly reddish orange in color from burning (but not fired). They lacked temper. None had pole or plant impressions. Their sizes ranged from 2.0 to 8.0 cm in length, 1.0 to 5.2 cm in width, and 0.5 to 3.4 cm in thickness.

Clay

As described in Chapter 5, dense clay was used for floor materials at El Bellote (e.g., Figures 5.2 and 5.6), which is similar to successive floors observed in a house mound at Tierra Nueva in the NWAF study (Piña Chan and Navarrete 1967:30). Displaced dried chunks of clay were also observed in layers of earthen mound fill at the insular sites. Two chunks were recovered from the lower portion of Stratum I in Feature 40. Five displaced chunks were also recovered from different contexts in the excavations at combined Feature 32-34-35. There was also one burned chunk of clay directly overlying oven Feature 133, which was under superior mound Feature 77. These also likely originated from floor materials. Alternatively, they may have been primary materials for pottery manufacturing, but this seems doubtful given the lack of other indications for pottery production at ILC.

Clay used as wall material was observed in situ in at least one instance. Within Feature 137, an adobe wall base segment extended from the edge of the powdery lime floor (Figure 5.5). This wall segment was 27 cm tall. Only a small portion was visible within the test unit—no postholes were discerned within or adjacent to it. The wall portion was not formed of adobe blocks. Instead, the clay was modeled into shape. A lens of the same clay material overlay some of Stratum IV (above the floor fill of Feature 137)—likely a knocked-over portion of the same wall—at the same elevation as the top of the in situ wall base.

As described in Chapter 5, the compacted tops of some of the mound fill strata were identified as unprepared living surfaces by their association with pits. Inferior mound

Feature 34 had a compacted clay lens (Stratum IIIa; Figure 5.4) associated with two small pits (features 145 and 146) and the possible clay floor (Feature 144). Another lens of compacted clay (Feature 130) was found in the uppermost portion of Stratum I in Feature 77 but was associated with modern artifacts and not likely prehispanic.

SUMMARY

Although less abundant than pottery, the various materials described in this chapter offer additional insights on activities and social organization at ILC, along with its relationship to Comalcalco. The unequal distributions of Late Classic materials suggest that access to some materials (stone tools, faunal remains, and high-quality architectural materials) was determined by social class. Distribution analyses of pottery and these additional materials are presented in chapters 8 and 9.

The primary reuse of sherds from broken pottery vessels was for fish-net sinkers made by grinding edges into elliptical shapes with grooves on opposite ends. These were concentrated at the South Group of El Bellote and at Feature 77 on Isla Chablé, suggesting that fishing rights were specialized. The only figurine fragment—a portion of an anthropomorphic face—dates to the Formative. The only bitumen found was on the interior of body sherds, suggesting the material was processed by heating in vessels (perhaps for canoe caulking).

Stone tools were scarce. The 20 obsidian artifacts are mostly small blades or blade fragments. Their macroscopic characteristics suggest both Highland Maya and central Mexican sources. Most of the 14 chert artifacts are flakes. There are only two small exhausted cores indicating that most of the few stone tools arrived in finished form. Ground stone for grain processing is similarly scarce and was only associated with the South Group of Isla Chablé and El Bellote. If cultivated grains were consumed at ILC, it appears that most were provisioned in processed form, most likely from the agrarian areas around Comalcalco. None of the stone tools can be dated, though the central Mexican obsidian sources suggest arrival and use in the Late Classic. No shell tools were found.

Unmodified stones—mostly volcanic materials but also limestone—may have been manuports from the Mezcalapa Delta, adjacent Grijalva system, or the more distant Usumacinta Delta. Although there is no evidence for their use at ILC, they may have been scouring, scraping, smoothing, polishing, sharpening, straightening, and hammering tools.

The relative abundance of faunal remains (using NISP) indicates a broad spectrum of subsistence: boney fishes, turtles, and oysters, with less frequent opportunistic capturing of cartilaginous fishes, crocodiles, birds, and other shellfish. This contrasts with the elite consumption pattern at Comalcalco, which was dominated by turtles and other reptiles, though fauna from ILC was certainly present in small quantities there. Like many of the non-ceramic artifacts, however, most of the fauna and other materials described in this chapter could not be affiliated with specific periods.

There were a variety of Late Classic architectural materials. In addition to the consumption of oysters and other shellfish, shells were crushed at Features 89 and 122 to temper the mortar and plaster used locally at ILC and in vast quantities at Comalcalco. The mortar and plaster observed varies in quality: poor-quality materials associated with some earthen mounds on the islands and high-quality materials restricted to El Bellote and the South Group of Isla Chablé. The same material was used for floors, walls, and mortar. Brick with fine sand temper was only associated with ceremonial structures. Daub was less frequently used and may have served for architectural repair purposes. Clays were used for floors and for capping surfaces. In one case, clay was modeled into the lower portion of a wall.

CHAPTER EIGHT

The Formative Periods

Although all extant features at ILC were constructed in the Late Classic, the Formative pottery (28.7 percent of the entire ceramic assemblage) found in various features demonstrates a significant Formative occupation. A synthesis of previous research suggests that the Western Chontalpa was populated by widely dispersed small groups who moved into the area mostly after the decline of La Venta, and that those settlements, apart from coastal ILC, were concentrated in the lower Mezcalapa Delta along small distributaries. The percentages of Formative types indicate variation in the intensity and extent of occupations at ILC. Sherds diagnostic of the Middle Formative suggest a focus at El Bellote while diagnostics of the Late Formative suggest more extensive occupation. Displaced from their original contexts, the Formative pottery only allows for normative characterization of activities by general location. These spatial distributions, along with their associations with other material culture, enable some reasonable speculation on the kinds of features that may have existed, on subsistence, on social relations, and on trade and interaction. Although information on subsistence is very limited, I speculate about resource use based on the possibilities afforded by the environment. To address social relationships, I rely heavily on analogy with the more thoroughly researched Early Formative Olmec of southern Veracruz (Olman) and the southern Isthmus region.

THE WESTERN CHONTALPA

Very little is known about the Formative periods in the Chontalpa region east of La Venta. Early researchers working within a culture historical perspective sought to identify Olmec ethnicity, migrations, and influence, especially as the precipitator of Maya cultures. Drucker and Contreras (1953) sought Olmec traits east of La Venta to better define the Olmec Heartland, but Olmec stone monuments were found only in the Middle Usumacinta region (Fernández Tejedo and others 1988:17–19). Fernández Tejedo and colleagues (1988:51–52) considered the Formative occupations at Isla Chablé as representative of the earliest settlements of Tabasco, suggesting pre-Olmec or perhaps Early Formative affiliations (their treatment of "Olmec" largely considers Middle Formative La Venta). They also describe Late Formative Tabasco after the decline at La Venta around BCE 400 as a cultural vacuum except for the Lower Mezcalapa in the Western Chontalpa (Fernández Tejedo and others 1988:58–59).

A synthesis of surveys in the Western Chontalpa along the prehispanic Mezcalapa river provide a model for Formative settlement history and settlement patterns for the broader Chontalpa and to contextualize ILC. More surveys were conducted in the Western Chontalpa than any other Chontalpa region (Figure 1.1), though with different methods. The PAILC relied on pedestrian survey and was feature-oriented rather than site-oriented. Sisson's (1976) survey in the Lower Mezcalapa Delta combined aerial photography, pedestrian survey, and excavations. West, Psuty, and Thom's (1967) survey of the Middle Mezcalapa Delta relied on aerial photography alone for mound detection, with limited inspections at few, leaving most documented sites without chronological affiliations. The NWAF survey (Piña Chan and Navarrete 1967; Sanders 1962) in the Upper Mezcalapa Delta and Pleistocene terrace valley in southern Tabasco also relied on aerial photography for locating and defining sites, without inspection of many, yet was accompanied by mapping and excavations at few larger settlements.

Coast

As described in the following section, ILC was first occupied during the Middle Formative (at the earliest) with a small settlement at El Bellote. There were far more extensive occupations of the area during the Late Formative. No other Formative coastal sites are known in the Western Chontalpa, and if present, none were as extensive as those at ILC. Farther east, Aguacatal (Matheny 1970) in the Laguna de Términos was first established after La Venta's decline and was another example of a large, Late Formative lagoon settlement. Both ILC and Aguacatal had Chicanel sphere pottery matching Sierra Red, indicating Isthmus-oriented exchange and interaction. If a generalization can be made, this observation suggests the Chontalpan coastline was sparsely populated throughout the Formative periods with the exception of Late Formative settlements at lagoons.

Lower Mezcalapa Delta

Moving inland into the Lower Mezcalapa Delta, Sisson's (1976) survey indicates the presence of small settlements that were occupied from the Early to Late Formative (Figure 8.1). Early Formative sites were small, with dispersed residences largely on the western side of Sisson's (1976:586–603) survey. Campo Nuevo—interpreted as dispersed dwellings where only a few were occupied at any given time—was dated to ca. 1350–1050 BCE (Pellicer and Molina phases). Eight additional Molina phase (ca. 1250–1050 BCE) sites were also interpreted as small with dispersed dwellings. In the following Palacios phase (ca. 1050–900 BCE), 10 sites were occupied, most of which were also small. Throughout the Early Formative, pottery shared affinities with the Ocos sphere and the Tehuacán Valley. Central Mexican and Guatemalan Highland obsidian sources were both present. Pottery similarities and new obsidian sources suggest increasing interaction with Veracruz in the Palacios phase (Sisson 1976:586–603).

The Alameda site may have been occupied in the Molina and Palacios phases. If so, it is the only Early Formative settlement with three "large mounds arranged in a planned group," estimated between 12 and 15 m in height (Sisson 1976:668). This would clearly indicate an early settlement hierarchy in the region. The mounds, however, could be later constructions with recycled Early Formative deposits (Chapter 5).

Middle Formative sites dating after 900 BCE, chronologically affiliated with La Venta's growth, were generally small and widely dispersed, though few had mounds (Figure 8.1; Sisson 1976:605–627). In the Puente phase (ca. 900–700 BCE) there were eight small, non-nucleated settlements and two (Encrucijada and Naranjeño) with multiple conical mounds. If the mounds were indeed constructed in the Middle Formative, this would indicate a settlement hierarchy. In addition to residences, the San Felipe site had a midden with oyster shell, aquatic fauna, and terrestrial vertebrates, indicative of local to coastal resource exploitation. In the Franco phase (ca. 700–550 BCE), there was a settlement shift southward and a reduction to six occupied nucleated and non-nucleated settlements. Most were small but Limón and San Miguel had conical mounds that suggest continuity in the regional settlement hierarchy if the mounds were indeed constructed in the Middle Formative, despite the abandonment of Encrucijada and Naranjeño. In the subsequent Castañeda phase (ca. 550–300 BCE), six sites were occupied, including the mound sites of Limón and San Miguel and a reoccupied San Felipe (if it wasn't abandoned in the Franco phase). Middle Formative ceramics included differentially fired pottery, the introduction of incised white wares in the Puente phase, and stronger ceramic affinities with La Venta during the Franco phase. Many of these ceramics include ash temper. Sourced obsidian was from the Basin of Mexico, Guatemalan Highlands, and Oaxaca (Sisson 1976:605–627).

Sisson (1976) emphasized the Early and Middle Formative periods, but mentions a few settlements with Late Formative occupations, primarily those at ILC and others near the Mecoacán Lagoon. In addition, the site of Ahualulco (near the Machona Lagoon) and an unnamed site to the south were known to have Late Formative occupations. West, Psuty, and Thom (1969:93–94) documented 84 mounds on the western levee of the Seco River. These were widely dispersed, with few aggregates of two to three mounds. They appear to have been situated along deteriorating distributaries (Figure 8.1). West, Psuty, and Thom (1969:91) cite a personal communication by Sisson that pottery from many of these mounds included Late Formative types dating from ca. 200 BCE to CE 100. The mounds may have been built later, recycling Late Formative deposits. Though the information available does not rule out earlier Formative or later Classic occupations of these mounds, the overall impression suggests widespread Late Formative small settlements west of the Seco River.

Comalcalco was also occupied during the Formative. Though Peniche Rivero (1973) proposed a Los Pinos

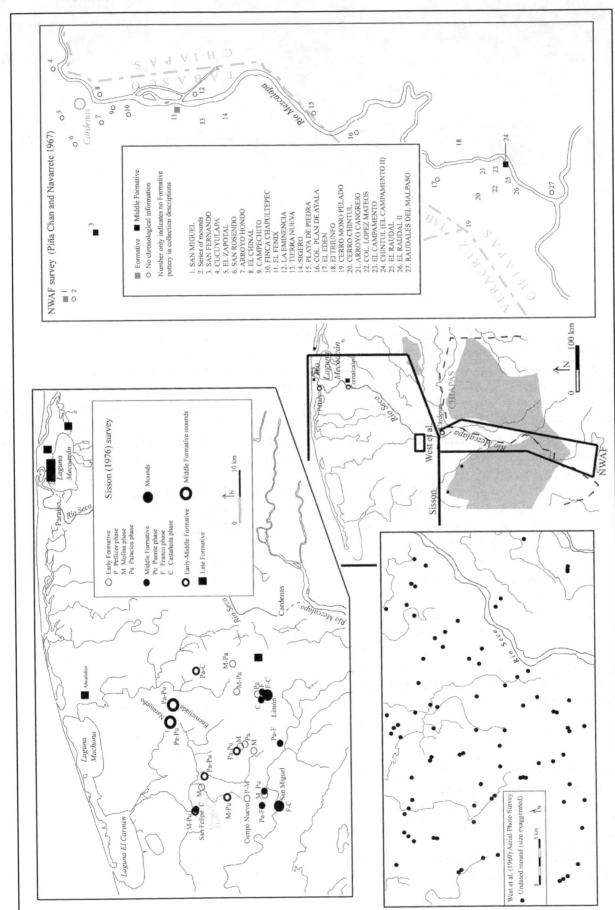

Figure 8.1. Formative settlements in the Western Chontalpa, from surveys by Sisson (1976), West, Psuty, and Thom (1969), and NWAF (Piña Chan and Navarrete 1967). Prepared by the author.

Complex (ca. BCE 800–CE 100) with ceramic similarities to Tres Zapotes, Martinez Guzman's (1973) thesis suggests that occupation dates from BCE 200 and later, which better conforms with the increase in Late Formative settlements along the lower Seco River. The data from Comalcalco on Formative occupations is from excavations at the site's center, however, and little is known about the extent of Formative pottery at the site. Although it is possible that Formative occupation of Comalcalco was extensive, adequate spatial analysis is not possible with the literature at hand to support or reject such a conclusion. Another complication is that, as with ILC, Formative deposits at Comalcalco were likely recycled to construct the Late Classic mounds.

Middle Mezcalapa and Terrace Valleys

Because the NWAF project did not include systematic inspections of sites defined by aerial photography, and because excavations were restricted to a few sites that had Late Classic occupations with larger mounds, there is limited information on the Formative settlement patterns farther upriver in the southern Mezcalapa alluvial plain and Terrace valley areas. Piña Chan and Navarrete (1967:15) identified White-Rim Black and Gray pottery at San Fernando, indicating influence from La Venta (although assuming Late Formative affiliation, this is now Middle Formative). Sand temper in that pottery may suggest that it was made locally, rather than being traded in from the La Venta area. Oddly, the NWAF collections lack Sierra Red pottery but do have other types with similar Late Formative plastic decoration (e.g., thick parallel grooves on outflaring and thickened bowl-rim interiors). These observations suggest local production of pottery with La Venta and subsequent Chicanel characteristics in the upper floodplain area, unlike the lower delta where tempers illustrate exchange with those spheres. This demonstrates active association with changing cultural identities. Figure 8.1 shows the locations of sites with Middle and Late Formative pottery, based on the above reinterpretations. Though most sites have no resulting Formative affiliations, and those with affiliations are probably under-represented, what can be gleaned is that these southern areas of the Mezcalapa were more sparsely populated than the lower delta areas.

Conclusions

From the information at hand, Western Chontalpa Formative settlements appear to have been small and dispersed, with a focus on the lower delta. Very few small sites had Early Formative occupations, which suggests that Gulf Coast populations gravitated toward the Oman to the west. The ceramic data indicates that those occupying the Mezcalapa Delta may have had a pan-Isthmus layer of identity or at least interaction. Perhaps because population was concentrated at La Venta in the Middle Formative, settlement in the Mezcalapa delta increased only slightly. There was continuity in the small, widely dispersed settlements, but there seems to have been a regional hierarchy (if the mounds indeed date to the Middle Formative). The Isthmus-wide interaction sphere was replaced by a La Venta sphere in the Middle Formative. Far more numerous small, yet still widely dispersed settlements were established in the Late Formative period when interaction and identities returned to a broader Isthmus sphere (Chicanel). ILC was by far the largest Late Formative settlement in the region. The upper delta and Pleistocene terrace valley areas were more sparsely populated throughout the Formative periods. Most of the occupation occurred along the riverine transportation corridor that linked the lower Mezcalapa Delta with the southern Isthmus.

The Formative settlement history in the Western Chontalpa may be linked to broader developments across the Isthmus. Inomata and coworkers' (2014) revision of the Kaminaljuyú sequence implies that there were social, political, and demographic "collapses" across the Isthmus around 400 BCE: at La Venta, in the Grijalva region of Chiapas, and in the Southern Maya region. The population growth in the lower Mezcalapa Delta occurred after this time. New sociopolitical complexity developed in the Southern and Lowland Maya regions around 100 BCE. Shortly thereafter, population appears to have declined in the lower Mezcalapa Delta. These developments suggest that there were demographic pulls toward La Venta and southeastern Mesoamerica at times when political complexity arose in those areas, with subsequent dispersals to areas like the Chontalpa during periods of sociopolitical decline.

ILC'S FORMATIVE SETTLEMENT HISTORY

The distribution of Formative pottery at ILC is used here to interpret the extent and intensity of occupations at ILC. This approach assumes that the Formative deposits that were displaced and reused in the Late Classic constructions were not moved far from their original locations. The representativeness of the surface collections are generally useful for this purpose. The results suggest that intensive settlement began at El Bellote, then spread to southern Isla Chablé, with less intensive occupations across most of the other islands.

Table 8.1. Comparison of Pottery from Surface Collections and Excavations or Profiles

Feature	SURFACE COLLECTION					EXCAVATIONS				
	Number	% Formative	Number BW/SR	% Late Classic	Number FP	Number	% Formative	Number BW/SR	% Late Classic	Number FP
34-35	11	0.0	0	100.0	2	1805	1.4	0	97.8	38
40	14	7.0	0	93.0	7	582	36.9	2	61.0	7
75	99	2.0	0	98.0	4	1568	0.3	0	98.7	7
77–78	40	5.0	0	95.0	7	521	33.8	0	64.7	5
122	6	50.0	0	50.0	3	369	29.5	0	70.5	19

Feature	SURFACE COLLECTION					PROFILE				
	Number	% Formative	Number BW/SR	% Late Classic	Number FP	Number	% Formative	Number BW/SR	% Late Classic	Number FP
93	8	38.0	1	63.0	4	43	65.1	0	14.0	1
96	5	20.0	0	80.0	4	45	60.0	0	40.0	1
97	7	29.0	1	71.0	3	43	13.9	9	86.1	3
99	12	42.0	0	58.0	6	21	47.6	0	42.9	1
100	13	76.9	1	23.1	1	5	100.0	0	0.0	0
151	277	74.3	5	16.6	5	26	11.5	1	88.5	1
156	25	56.0	0	44.0	1	3	33.3	1	66.7	0
157	35	77.0	0	23.0	0	24	50.0	0	41.7	1
160	26	81.0	1	19.0	0	16	43.8	0	56.3	2
167	304	63.0	0	32.0	18	11	27.3	0	72.7	0
196–202	63	20.7	0	79.4	4	5	20.0	0	80.0	0

Key: BW = Black and White; SR = Sierra Red; FP = Fine Paste.

Surface collections are impacted by postdepositional processes (Arnold and Stark 1997:320; Hendon 1992; Lewarch and O'Brien 1981:299-319). The recycling of deposits and low surface visibility at many ILC features prompt analysis of surface-subsurface representativeness. Table 8.1 compares the percentages of Formative and Late Classic pottery from surface collections with those obtained from excavations and profile collections at the same features. There were differences in percentages of Formative pottery among strata within features but the table pools pottery from multiple strata excavated or profiled within them. Except for Feature 122, the excavations were at earthen residential features. All profile collections were at features constructed with shell and earthen deposits (residential and ceremonial features).

Two major points can be made about the pottery distribution. First, even with vastly different sample sizes, the percentages of Formative pottery from surface collections were generally representative of subsurface percentages from excavations, and to a lesser degree those from profiles.

Low percentages of Formative pottery in surface collections were matched by low percentages (albeit different ones) in excavations at the same features (with a mean difference of 16.3 percent), and by low percentages (less than 50 percent) in three of five profile collections (with a mean difference among all five cases of 17.7 percent). However, high percentages of Formative pottery were matched by a high percentage in only one of six profile collections (with a mean difference of 34.8 percent). Although surface collection percentages do not predict the same percentages in subsurface deposits, low percentages in the former conform with different low percentages in the latter. Earthen features in particular have low frequencies of Formative pottery. The results also indicate the surface collections are reliable for examining the distribution of Formative occupations and for general approximations on their intensities.

The second point is that the absence of low-frequency, period-diagnostic types in surface collections predict the absence of those types in subsurface deposits. The absence

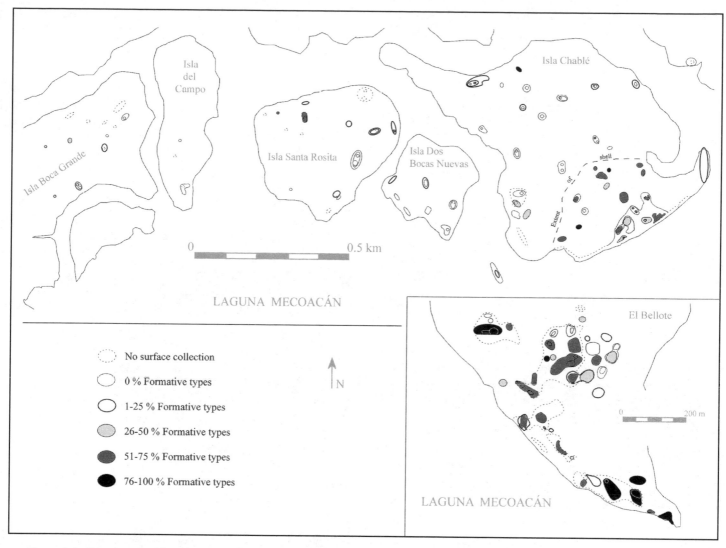

Figure 8.2. Percentages of Formative pottery in surface collections. Prepared by the author.

of the Black and White and Sierra Red types (BW/SR) in surface collections conforms with their absence (or very low frequency in one case) in excavation collections and in five of six profile collections. The presence of these types in surface collections is a less accurate predictor of presence in subsurface deposits. Nevertheless, the surface deposits contained them so they were present at least in those latest deposits. Therefore, these types are useful in determining the sequential extent of Middle and Late Formative occupations.

Figure 8.2 shows the spatial distribution of all Formative pottery (by percentage) from the surface collection units. The percentages were highest at El Bellote (with the exception of Subgroup B in the Northeast Group), in the south of Isla Chablé, and in the northwest portion of Isla Santa

Rosita. Formative pottery occurred in low frequencies or was absent from many of the surface collections across Isla Boca Grande, Isla del Campo, Isla Santa Rosita, Isla Dos Bocas Nuevas, and most of Isla Chablé. Based on the surface collections and the assumption that deposits were not moved far in the Late Classic, these distributions indicate that Formative occupations were concentrated at El Bellote and the southern half of Isla Chablé, along the southern end of the channel separating El Bellote and Isla Chablé, with much more limited use of most insular areas. These distributions beg the question of whether ILC's mangrove formations and islands were physically different than they are today (e.g., with "land-mass" only in the east) or more similar to today's configuration, but with differential preferences for occupation.

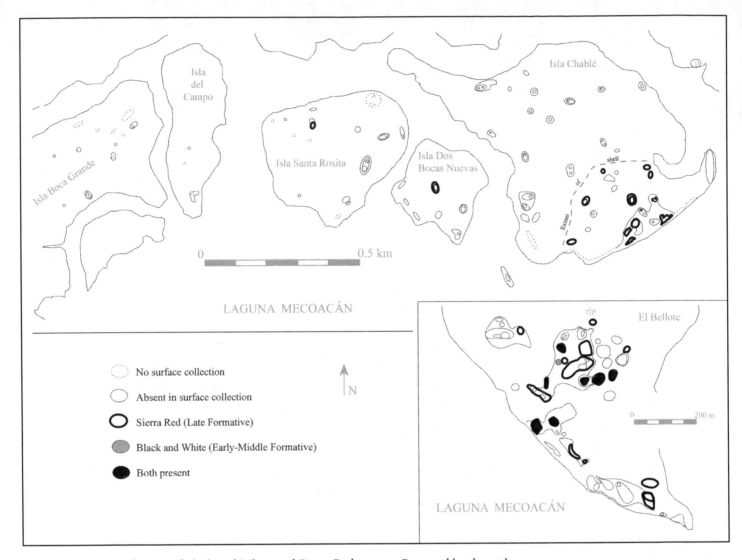

Figure 8.3. Distribution of Black and White and Sierra Red pottery. Prepared by the author.

The distributions of Black and White and Sierra Red pottery were used to define the extent of Middle and Late Formative occupations (Figure 8.3). The absence of Black and White pottery on the islands suggests that Middle Formative occupations were concentrated at El Bellote. Sierra Red had a wider spatial distribution, on both sides of the channel from El Bellote to southern Isla Chablé and at one feature on Isla Santa Rosita and Isla Dos Bocas Nuevas. The distribution of Sierra Red suggests a more extensive occupation in the Late Formative.

PROBABLE FEATURES

The Formative pottery from the surface collections allow for plausible speculation on what features may have existed during those occupations by comparing them with their associated deposits. With few exceptions, most of the surface collections at features constructed with shell and earthen deposits had higher frequencies of Formative types (over 50 percent) than in the collections from earthen features (Figure 8.2; Table 8.1). This pattern suggests a stronger association between shell deposits and Formative pottery. Although none of the extant features were shell middens, *concheros* may indeed have been present on both sides of Isla Chablé-El Bellote channel during the Formative periods. As demonstrated in Chapter 5, however, the Late Classic mounds and platforms containing shell also had earthen deposits (and many were mostly earthen) with Formative sherds. This suggests that earthen platforms may have been built and used during the Formative in addition to shell refuse areas.

Three possible scenarios for the original Formative features are entertained. First, earthen elevated areas (platforms or mounds) were constructed for habitation using the surrounding mangrove sediments. Through oyster consumption, shell trash deposits accumulated around and between those, a common practice that can be observed at modern residential areas. Second, extensive oyster shell refuse accumulated, over which earthen deposits taken from the mangrove sediments were used to level uneven surfaces for dwellings or workspaces. Similar practices have been interpreted for Archaic shell mounds in the Savannah River region in the US Southeast (Anderson and Sassaman 2012:81). Third, the earthen and shell deposits may have belonged to different classes of features dating to different periods. For example, *concheros* may have developed during the Middle Formative period whereas earthen platforms or mounds may have been built in the Late Formative period or vice-versa. Too few sherds diagnostic of specific Formative periods were observed in the profiling to test this third possibility.

The first scenario seems to be the most plausible interpretation. The use of mangrove sediments to prepare elevated living and working spaces makes sense to avoid the sharp edges of shell in living spaces. The numbers and thicknesses of earthen construction deposits containing Formative pottery in the Late Classic features suggest that significant earthen features were originally present alongside the probable shell middens. Furthermore, the remaining areas occupied across the islands in the Formative periods had to have used earthen platforms or mounds for habitation since those areas have no shell deposits. Viewed in this way, earthen platforms or mounds for habitation were likely the norm across ILC during the Formative periods but oyster shell middens accumulated off their sides or between them at El Bellote and on the southern portion of Isla Chablé.

Apart from elevated earthen habitation features and adjacent shell middens, any interpretations of architecture, storage features, and cooking features is even more speculative given that none survived destruction in the Late Classic. The project can safely conclude that all features and architectural materials observed date to the Late Classic. In the absence of evidence, the safest conclusion is that the architecture of the Formative periods included earthen floors and perishable walls and roofs. Of course, once the deposits they were constructed on were removed and redeposited, there would be no evidence for post holes or floors. The same would be the case for any pits, hearths, and other storage or thermal features but these presumably also existed at the Formative occupations.

SUBSISTENCE

ILC is part of a rich aquatic ecosystem. The channels provide well-sheltered environments with dense oyster reefs and natural mangrove nurseries. The open lagoon waters provide habitats for a diversity of fishes, including rays. Although now locally extinct, manatees and crocodiles presumably favored the channels while sea turtles and sharks also ventured into the open lagoon. Beyond the beach ridge on the north side of ILC, the Seco River provided a habitat for freshwater fishes and turtles until reaching the Gulf of Mexico where saltwater species were available. Rimming the south side of the lagoon, the marshes also provided habitats for freshwater species. And across all mangrove formations, blue crabs were once bountiful; smaller species are still abundant. Diverse bird species were also plentiful. Mangrove could have provided wood materials for architecture and other uses. Grasses, palms, and trees from the beach ridge and from the levee forest could have been procured for thatch, poles, and dugout canoes (*cayucos*). These different forests also would have provided a wide range of native fruits, legumes, and palm nuts and hearts, in addition to allspice (West, Psuty, and Thom. 1969:59–62, 67–69). Although the mangrove is unsuitable for farming, any elevated features created could have been used for tree crops and small gardens in addition to dwelling and workspaces, much as they are today. Other foods, including cultigens, and nonlocal materials could have been traded for with interior (upriver) populations or brought to the islands if occupation was seasonal during these early periods.

Among the 1,112 faunal specimens collected by the project from mixed Formative and Late Classic deposits only one was submitted for radiometric dating. This bone, part of a sea turtle carapace found in Feature 166, dated to the end of the Late Formative period (Cal. 40 BCE–130 CE [2σ, Cal. 1990–1820 BP]; Beta Analytic 299882). Nevertheless, it also seems reasonable to assume that the range of vertebrate taxa recorded by the project were exploited throughout the two Formative periods as well as during the Late Classic.

Although it is always assumed that oysters were exploited during the Formative periods, there is no evidence for this. The shell is associated with mixed Formative and Late Classic deposits but none has been dated radiometrically. Nevertheless, it seems entirely reasonable to assume that the oysters and the less common clams and whelks at El Bellote and southern portion of Isla Chablé were in part consumed by Formative-era occupants.

Any interpretation of diet for the Formative population is highly speculative. Although oyster shell appears abundant, it is not everywhere and we have no idea what proportion or which vertebrate and nonvertebrate taxa were exploited during those periods. Suffice it to say that oysters, although providing less meat individually than larger fishes and reptiles, likely contributed a substantial portion of the animal protein consumed. Among the larger taxa, turtles could have provided a major source of animal protein, while sharks, rays, and crocodiles were hunted less often. It is also quite possible that smaller fishes captured in nets may have contributed a significant proportion of meat. Few birds were represented in the faunal assemblage and virtually nothing is known about floral contributions to diet.

The procurement and capturing techniques used by Formative populations is speculative, but if all of the currently available local resources were at ILC in the Formative periods, people probably grabbed, speared, trapped, and netted vertebrates. Although there is evidence for net fishing in the Late Classic, it is not clear if the technique was used during the Formative period. Only 13.6 percent of the net sinkers were crafted from sherds of Formative types, and these also could have been made during the Late Classic. Oyster harvesting could have used any of the methods described in Chapter 3. No shell or stone axes were observed, leaving wood collection techniques unaddressed.

Ground stone was restricted to El Bellote and the South Group of Isla Chablé–another association with shell. As none of these were dated, their period affiliations also remain speculative. If some date to the Formative, then grains would have been traded for or brought seasonally, depending on whether or not the occupations at ILC were permanent or seasonal.

Oyster reefs were historically documented in most of the channels and across an extensive area south of the islands. This begs the question of why the shell deposits were restricted to El Bellote and southern Isla Chablé when areas adjacent to oyster reefs were occupied in the Late Formative. Access to local resources is variably organized across societies, and the variable presence of shell might suggest different subsistence strategies at Formative ILC. Alternatively, some of the earthen deposits from Formative features could have been transported away from a southern Isla Chablé-El Bellote origin in the Late Classic, leaving behind the shell but broadly distributing the earthen deposits containing Formative pottery. This alternative seems unlikely since it would be far easier to acquire platform and mound deposits from adjacent mangrove sediments. Thus, differential subsistence practices need to be considered for the Formative periods.

No interpretations on seasonality are possible. ILC could have been occupied permanently or seasonally, or both, during the Formative periods. If seasonal, then migration rounds could have provided the populations with agrarian and wild interior resources during portions of the year and fish and seafood during others. If permanently occupied, then nonlocal subsistence goods would have required trade relations and, likely, frequent river travel. The existence of Late Formative occupations around Comalcalco might suggest such trade for interior foods was possible yet does not rule out seasonal occupations at ILC. If accepting Arnold's (1999) suggestion that wide-mouth *tecomates* reflect mobility, then the low percentage of these vessels would indicate a more permanent occupation. On the other hand, the distributions of pot forms (below) may suggest both sedentary and mobile populations at ILC.

ACTIVITIES AND TECHNOLOGIES

Although Formative features were destroyed in the process of building the Late Classic features, the artifactual materials associated with the Middle and Late Formative periods enable some synopsis of activities that took place at ILC during those occupations. These include the speculative platform or mound-building and subsistence activities previously described and inferences derived from pottery analysis on cooking and food preparation, storage, serving, ritual or ceremony, and trade and interaction. Without the features, however, no distinction can be made between domestic versus public or collectivized activities. Given these limitations, a normative perspective is taken on activities across ILC. Spatial comparisons may indicate minor differences in activities by general location.

As discussed previously, Formative period platform or mound building most likely used mangrove sediments to construct elevated surfaces for perishable structures. Digging sticks and large pots, baskets, or perishable bags could have been used for that purpose. The range of structures is unknown but presumably dwellings were present. These could have been built with local materials: woods from mangrove, semi-deciduous and other trees from the beach ridge, rain forest, and river levees, along with beach ridge grasses and palms for thatch, which could have been transported in canoes. Although no axes were found, felling tools (of shell or stone) would have been required for wood harvesting. Those and waterworn stones could have been used for trimming and shaping. Platforms and mounds and their structures would periodically have needed maintenance, which would have required the reprovisioning of materials.

Food acquisition presumably involved fishing, hunting, and shellfish harvesting. For shellfish, either shallow diving and sorting or raking techniques could have been employed, although if the oysters grew closer to the water's edge than today, wading and hand-collecting would also have been a possibility. Turtles could have been captured by hand. Speculatively, fishing more commonly involved the use of traps or nets although there is little evidence to support or negate this interpretation. Nets also could have been used for hunting birds. Wooden spears could have been used for sharks, rays, and crocodiles (no whole stone spear or harpoon points were found). Although nothing is known about the dietary contributions of plants, any grasses, palms, or fruits could have been collected by hand. Many of these activities could have involved the use of bags, baskets, or pots.

ILC inhabitants presumably used hearths and other cooking features. Mangrove, other woods, grasses, and palms from the beach ridge, river levees, and rain forest could have been procured for fuel. More information on cooking can be derived from the pottery. The Coarse and Sandy paste types were technologically suitable for cooking (also viewed as an average performance quality for a variety of tasks) and ollas constituted the highest percentages of forms used. As the only cooking-related form category represented, the medium-sized to large ollas were likely used for wet cooking of stews, gruels, soups, or tamales (presumably stews were most common). To prepare animals for eating, scaling and butchering was likely done with unmodified bivalve shells. Although none of the obsidian and chert artifacts were dated, these were rare, and no modified shell was observed. Larger fish and reptiles could have been dry-cooked whole on spits over heathers, in coals, or in ovens, perhaps wrapped in *quentó*, arrowroot (*Thalia geniculata*), leaves. Turtles could have been cooked whole and served in their carapaces, as well as in stews. Although perishable, drying racks, placed in the open during the dry seasons, over hearths, or beneath ceilings could also have been used for preservation. Also without evidence, fermentation could have been practiced using jars or pits. With all these possibilities in mind, however, wet cooking is the only technique supported by artifactual evidence.

Any Formative storage features, formally lined or otherwise, also would have been destroyed in the Late Classic.

Dried plant and animal products could have been stored in pits, though sediment moisture might have necessitated plaster, clay, or plant material lining. Again, pottery provides the best evidence for storage. Large, wide-mouth *tecomates*, suitable for storage or cooking, were the second most common vessel form represented among the Coarse type, though these were less frequent for the Sandy type. There were no *tecomates* observed among the Black and White or Sierra Red types, indicating a reliance on coarse paste pottery for dry storage. If obtaining, or bringing, grains to ILC, these vessels were likely used for that purpose. Of course, foods could also have been stored and transported in perishable wraps and containers.

Infrequent liquid storage is indicated by the few medium to large sized jars of the Coarse type, although four medium-sized jars were represented among the Sierra Red sherds. Water would require only temporary storage, suggesting the possibility for storage of other, undetermined liquids. Secondary jar functions might include dry storage. Another possible use for the jars is fermentation. Ollas, *tecomates*, and bowls could have had secondary liquid or dry storage functions. Of course, perishable skin containers also could have been used for liquids.

Most serving vessels were medium-sized to large dishes and bowls, which also suggests stewed cuisines. Most belonged to the utilitarian Coarse and Sandy types. They were also present among the Black and White and the Sierra Red types. Infrequent serving vessels were plates for dry foods: only nine of the Coarse type, one of the Sandy type, two of the Black and White type, and six of the Sierra Red type were found. Dry foods could also have been served in perishable containers, including broad-leaf wrappings for fish and tamales in which they could also have been cooked. Turtle carapaces also could have been used for serving. Oysters could have been eaten raw or smoked and eaten in the shell, as they are today, without need for cooking and serving containers. Overall, however, the nonperishable artifactual evidence suggests that medium to large dishes and bowls were the most common serving vessels (for stews). The vessels were primarily utilitarian types but there were also types that could have been used for symbolic displays.

Speculation about a range of perishable materials can be entertained. Wood from the mangrove, beach ridge, and nearby rain forests and levee forests could have been used for fuel, architecture, spears, canoes and poles, serving or storage containers, and possibly mortars. Grasses and palms from the beach ridge could have provided seeds, nuts, hearts, fuel, cordage, roof thatch, and possibly packing

Table 8.2. Comparison of Formative Vessel Forms in Percentages by Location

Location	No.	Jars	Large Jars	Ollas	Large Ollas	Tecomates	Large Tecomates	Bowls	Large Bowls	Dishes or Bowls	Dishes	Large Dishes	Plates	Large Plates
El Bellote	117	2.56	0.0	22.22	9.4	17.09	2.6	10.26	4.3	16.24	21.37	8.6	10.26	5.1
Southern Isla Chablé	51	25.49	5.8	17.65	15.6	13.73	3.9	3.92	2.0	7.84	21.57	5.9	9.80	5.9
Dispersed Insular	34	17.65	0.0	26.47	5.9	35.29	5.9	8.82	2.9	2.94	5.88	0.0	2.94	0.0
Totals	202	10.89	–	21.78	–	19.31	–	8.42	–	11.88	18.81	–	8.91	–

material for transportation. *Quentó* from the southern and eastern margins of the lagoon could have been used for wrapping foods for cooking, serving, or transportation. Some marsh areas and lower edges of the beach ridge had reeds that could have been used in basketry and mats, as well as in architecture. The adjacent beach ridge and nearby levee forest, rain forest, and marshes also provided a wide range of native plant foods and medicines. With short forays, any of these materials could have been procured and efficiently transported back to ILC in canoes. Such harvesting forays were presumably an activity as common as fishing. Both, along with opportunistic hunting, could have been combined in day trips from ILC.

In this discussion of activities and their technologies I have attempted to paint a normative view of life at Formative ILC. Were there differences in activities by location, apart from the accumulation of shell deposits? Spatial analyses are problematic because the Formative deposits are known to have been moved during the Late Classic. However, the preliminary comparison of pottery by large areas suggests minor differences, which can be used to make interpretations on spatial variation in pottery-related activities. To explore this possibility, all Formative rim sherds with identified forms from El Bellote and southern Isla Chablé—the two more intensively occupied areas where shell deposits occur—can be compared with the dispersed locations across the islands (where shell is absent). Although the latter group lumps Formative deposits from across a broad area, further dividing these (e.g., by island) would result in too few rim sherds to compare for each area. The percentages of forms from these three spatial categories are presented in Table 8.2. All three had significant percentages of *ollas* for wet food cooking, although El Bellote had a much lower percentage of jars but higher percentages of dishes and bowls compared to the other groups, suggesting far less liquid storage and more frequent serving. Southern Isla Chablé had lower percentages of bowls but close to

average percentages of dishes compared to the other groups, suggesting shallower serving vessels. The pooled insular area with lower densities of Formative pottery had a much higher percentage of *tecomates* (for dry storage or cooking) yet had the lowest percentages of serving vessels of any kind, suggesting the possibility for relatively greater quantities of stored dry foods but also less use of pottery for serving foods. Assuming wide-mouth *tecomates* reflect mobility (Arnold 1999), this difference might suggest more mobile occupants in contrast to those at El Bellote and southern Isla Chablé. As stated, other materials could have substituted pottery but based only on the pottery to represent storage, cooking, and serving activities, this comparison suggests minor differences in liquid-use, culinary, and serving behaviors among the three arbitrarily defined groupings. Possible explanations for these differences are discussed in the following section.

SOCIAL RELATIONS

Three scenarios are entertained for settlement and social groupings at ILC based on the distribution of Formative pottery. Cultural historical, processualist, and agency theoretical perspectives provide nonmutually exclusive implications for each scenario. However, without intact Formative deposits to observe or large-scale sampling of pottery for thermoluminescence dating across ILC, none of the scenarios are testable.

The first scenario is that Formative settlement expanded from an original small occupation at El Bellote. At first, only one Middle Formative group occupied El Bellote, as indicated by the distribution of Black and White pottery (Figure 8.3). That group either expanded or was replaced by multiple larger groups occupying settlements on both sides of the El Bellote-Isla Chablé channel along with the smaller, dispersed groups across the rest of ILC in the Late Formative, as indicated by the distribution of Sierra Red pottery. From a culture historical standpoint, the early El Bellote group was eventually either replaced by a larger migrating population or grew locally while adopting the expanding Late Formative exchange sphere associated with Sierra Red pottery. From a processualist perspective, the development and stabilization of the lagoon and surroundings enabled more sedentary coastal settlement by the Late Formative, when the population expanded. An agency perspective might entertain the development of collective control over the local resources by the founding larger group that fissioned into two, yet those rights were denied to the dispersed smaller groups, which could also explain why those areas were less intensively occupied, possibly by more mobile groups.

A second scenario considers the more abundant Formative pottery that spans both periods. In this view, El Bellote, southern Isla Chablé, and the dispersed occupations were all established by Middle Formative times and there was continuity in settlement through the Late Formative. However, this scenario needs to explain the presence of Black and White serving vessels only at El Bellote. Treating those vessels from a culture historical perspective, this could be explained as migrants establishing an Olmec Horizon presence within an existing local community. A processualist perspective might entertain population pressure on lagoon resources, leading to hierarchical control over resources whereby elites were marked by Black and White pottery. The rest of the community had a different role in the system, which did not include rights to fauna or status displays. An agency perspective might emphasize elite manipulation of Black and White, and later Sierra Red pottery, as symbolic means to emphasize identities for regional alliances.

A third scenario is that the distribution of Formative pottery does not indicate settled groups. That is, there were no permanent settlements at ILC and numerous mobile groups, small or large, moved throughout the region, temporarily occupying the same locations. From a culture historical perspective, some mobile groups were culturally affiliated with Olmecs—establishing a minimal presence at ILC—while most were not. Later, ILC was occasionally occupied by mobile groups that were culturally affiliated with the Sierra Red-associated sphere while other visiting groups were not. A processualist explanation might entertain the need to seasonally augment inland cultigens with wild resources as a result of population growth there. The minor differences in vessel forms could be interpreted as groups' different seasonal uses. The notion that no groups would permanently claim the local resources and settle, from an agency perspective, might imply that ILC was a "commons" where groups could temporarily escape the unequal ownership or control over resources elsewhere or the area was used for seasonal shellfish harvest and feasting where groups convened to build reciprocal alliances and social memories.

Sedentary societies are routinely assumed for the Formative periods in the Gulf and Isthmus regions. Without evidence for or against the mobility in the third scenario, even if a logical possibility, I also lean toward sedentary Formative occupations at El Bellote and southern Isla Chablé. The range in pottery forms and their interpreted functions, although with different frequencies, mirrors the diversity in forms at Formative sedentary domestic sites elsewhere (Wendt 2010). Substantial deposits of shell presumably developed during those periods. This leaves the first and second scenarios to consider. Without intact deposits, a test of the first and second alternatives would require numerous thermoluminescence dates from the Coarse Paste and Sandy Paste Formative types. Earlier dates for those types only at El Bellote and later dates for those types elsewhere would support the first scenario. Similar date ranges spanning both periods from all locations across ILC would support the second scenario. Unless or until such a test can be done, I lean toward the first scenario because some amount of Olmec Black and White pottery could be expected at southern Isla Chablé if the second were accurate, even if distinctive groups were present. Although elements of the three scenarios are not necessarily mutually exclusive, accepting the first provides a plausible model with the data at hand.

Compared to the two Late Formative settlements at El Bellote and southern Isla Chablé, the dispersed locations were associated with less Formative pottery and a lack of faunal remains (vertebrate and invertebrate). They were also associated with lower frequencies of serving pottery but higher percentages of storage vessels (Table 8.2). The lack of local resources appearing in those areas generally suggests a more "impoverished" condition, which could also explain why the dispersed occupations had the lowest percentages of ceramic serving vessels and Sierra Red pottery for symbolic displays. The more intensively occupied areas at El Bellote and southern Isla Chablé may have been settlements for established sedentary groups claiming rights to local resources whereas those not occupying those settlements did not share affiliation with those groups or may have been temporary occupants, and thus had fewer rights to local resources.

Apart from that possible intergroup ranking, no interpretations can be made on the kinds of groups that occupied ILC in the Formative periods. Cross-culturally, an aggregated settlement may consist of only one descent group (e.g., a clan, lineage, or ramage); one descent group with subdescent groups (e.g., a clan with sub-clan lineages); segments from multiple descent groups cross-cutting settlements (e.g., lineages belonging to different clans, each with lineages at other settlements); or smaller numerous conjugal or extended residential groups (neolocal, unilocal, or bilocal) sharing only a network of bilateral descent relations or even nonkin-based relationships. To identify one of these patterns requires undisturbed residential contexts (Ensor 2013a, 2013b). Thus, the data on the Formative periods cannot be used to interpret the kinds of groups represented at El Bellote and southern Isla Chablé. The dispersed occupations suggest a *ranchería* settlement pattern, which is associated with bilateral descent (potentially combined with any form of residence). If each of the locations with reused Formative deposits reflects the original locations of those deposits, then bilateral descent with unknown residence practices is the best that can be interpreted.

Although a list of potentially exploited resources is extensive, suggesting economic autonomy, trade and interaction with other regional populations must have occurred. The Black and White and later Sierra Red pottery attest to the inhabitants' participation in wide-reaching spheres of exchange and the sharing of symbolic material. Even the coarse paste types are generally similar to those of the Formative periods throughout the Tabascan Gulf Coast, also indicating interaction in a wider cultural network. If some of the ground stone, chert, and obsidian dates to these early periods, then more evidence for trade could be concluded. Unknown is whether the local resources from ILC were traded outside the lagoon during the Formative periods. Although trade may not have constituted a major or frequent activity, it certainly occurred there or by the occupants when on forays or seasonal migrations. Just as the Early Formative Olman and other regions of the Olmec Horizon were not homogeneous (Arnold 2003; Pool 2009; Pool and others 2010; Santley, Arnold, and Barrett 1997; Reyes Gonzalez and Winter 2010), there is no reason to believe that such integration in broader interaction spheres by the occupants of ILC bound them or their identities within large-scale ethnic-linguistic groupings. Perhaps those broader exchanges simply indicate another layer of Formative culture over the local, in which Black and White and Sierra Red pottery were used in symbolic displays, as status markers or for negotiating social alliances (e.g., Blomster 2010; Joyce and Henderson 2010).

Only one Formative artifact indicates ritual or ceremony at ILC. The single figurine fragment, probably dating to the Late Formative, was presumably used in ritual. Blomster (1998, 2002) suggests that Olmec hollow figurines of the Early-Middle Formative were used by emerging elites in public ceremonies. In contrast, the more common solid figurines may have been used in a range of household rituals and non-elite personal ceremonies (Arnold and Follensbee 2015; Blomster 2002). Without the original context for the figurine fragment, we cannot distinguish whether it was used in household rituals or community ceremonies. When comparing the Formative occupations with other major sites of the Gulf Coast and Isthmus regions, those at ILC seem too small to have included ceremonial features. In short, little can be said of the ritual and ceremonial life of the Formative occupants at ILC.

Feasting appears to have been limited. There were low percentages of large storage jars, cooking vessels, and serving vessels (Table 8.2). Only four large storage jars were identified, and they were restricted to southern Isla Chablé. Wet-foods cooking vessels, represented by large ollas (and potentially large *tecomates*), were also more common at southern Isla Chablé, yet this was not matched by larger percentages of serving vessels in that area. El Bellote had the next highest percentage of large cooking vessels and did have the highest percentages of large serving vessels. Of note is that most large serving vessels in those two areas were of Black and White and Sierra Red types, which are known to have been used in symbolic displays. Even if considering *tecomates* as optional cooking pots, the dispersed groups had the lowest percentages of large cooking and serving vessels and no large dishes. Thus, although limited, feasting may have been more common among the groups at El Bellote and Isla Chablé, and more infrequent for those dispersed across the islands where perishable materials were probably more common for all serving and consumption activities. This conclusion conforms with the arguments for higher status and greater rights among the larger established southern Isla Chablé-El Bellote groups than those on the other islands. The southern Isla Chablê-El Bellote groups may have used their resources to engage more often in sponsoring feasts for gifting, symbolic displays, and alliance building.

Analyses of gender roles and status are best done with multiple lines of evidence: for example, burial accompaniments, iconography, and direct historical analogy. The latter provides a questionable source of data for all but late prehistoric societies as it rigidifies gender over hundreds or thousands of years. Speculating on gender in these earlier periods requires adopting rather than testing ideas or contributing new conclusions. Unlike trade, interaction, and social ranking, there has been limited research on Olmec gender roles. Nearly all research on Olmec gender emphasizes visual depictions on figurines and stone monuments. Although sex and gendered associations can be observed, there is sufficient gender ambiguity to reject gender binary roles and identities (Arnold and Follensbee 2015; Follensbee 2000, 2008; Blomster 2009; Joyce 2000a; Marcus 2009). In terms of status, women were frequently depicted as persons of status engaged in domestic ritual as well as public events suggesting relative gender equality among elites in ideology (Follensbee 2000; Joyce and Henderson 2010:197; Stone 2011). Applying these generalizations, gender roles and statuses at Formative ILC might have been overlapping.

SYNOPSIS

The Western Chontalpa, and likely the broader Chontalpa, experienced population growth in the Late Formative but in small, dispersed settlements. This growth took place after the "collapse" of La Venta and Southern and Lowland Maya centers and before the reemergence of sociopolitical complexity in the Maya regions. Assuming that the Formative pottery remained in the general locations where they were originally deposited, ILC was first occupied during the Middle Formative when settlement was likely limited and concentrated at El Bellote. In the Late Formative, areas of settlement expanded to encompass both sides of the channel separating El Bellote and southern Isla Chablé, while most of the other islands were occupied less extensively, less intensively, and possibly temporarily.

The features of the Formative periods were destroyed in the Late Classic period, but it is plausible that earthen platforms or mounds for elevated living and working spaces were built during the Formative. Where settlement was concentrated at El Bellote and southern Isla Chablé, shell middens (*concheros*) apparently accumulated adjacent to those earthen features. Though lacking any evidence for architectural materials, structures presumably had earthen floors and perishable walls and roofs. Because all Formative deposits were destroyed, there is also no evidence for storage or cooking features but presumably pits and hearths were once present.

Because all the Formative deposits were destroyed in the Late Classic, and, except for one turtle bone, no radiometric dates were obtained for shell and vertebrate remains, interpretations on Formative subsistence assumes that locally available taxa were exploited in those periods (the same for the Late Classic). Adding to this speculation, a variety of capturing techniques is also assumed, though none of the few net sinkers fashioned from reworked Formative sherds can be associated with the Formative periods. Differential subsistence strategies may, however, be evidenced by the restriction of shell to southern Isla Chablé and El Bellote. A wide range of plant foods and other materials were probably obtained from the beach ridge and nearby rain forest, levee forest, and marshes.

Nearly all imagined perishable materials, tools, and foods could have been acquired with short forays in canoes using mangrove, beach ridge, rain forest, river levee forests, and different aquatic environments. Platform and mound-building only required digging sticks and perishable or nonperishable containers. Wood materials for housing and canoes likely required stone or shell axes and adzes but none have been found. Although the pottery forms for cooking and serving suggest a focus on stews, larger fishes and reptiles could have been cooked and served dry or wrapped in leaves. Drying and fermenting is also possible but without evidence. Pottery also provides the only evidence for storage: coarse paste jars for liquids and *tecomates* for dry foods (plant and or animal, local or imported), although pits presumably existed. Some spatial differences in pottery forms were noted, suggesting less liquid storage and more serving at El Bellote, more shallow serving dishes at southern Isla Chablé, and more *tecomate* storage or cooking but less serving with pottery at the non-intensively used, dispersed locations across the islands (possibly suggesting more mobile groups occupying those areas).

Any discussion of social groupings in the Formative periods also requires the assumption that the original deposits were not moved very far during the construction of the Late Classic features. After considering the three alternative settlement scenarios, the favored one is that a single sedentary group occupied El Bellote in the Middle Formative. It grew into, or was replaced by, two larger Late Formative groups at El Bellote and southern Isla Chablé while additional smaller groups were spread across the rest of the islands. Those occupying El Bellote and southern Isla Chablé may have had rights to exploit local resources. The smaller, dispersed, and less-intensely (possibly temporarily) occupied locations lacked faunal remains, and appear more "impoverished," suggesting they did not have the same rights. Although the organizing principles and residence practices of the two larger groups are unknown, the dispersed smaller groups likely had bilateral descent. The presence of Middle Formative Black and White and Late Formative Sierra Red pottery indicates participation in successive broader interaction and exchange spheres through the use of pots in symbolic displays. These displays would have been related to identity formation or maintenance through local or regional alliances. There was no evidence for burials or ceremonial features, but the find of one figurine fragment indicates that some form of ritual took place. Infrequent feasting was common among the established groups at El Bellote and southern Isla Chablé. The paucity of research on gender in the Formative periods of the Gulf Coast and Isthmus regions prohibits linking the materials at ILC to gender roles, though studies of visual material culture suggest both binary and ambiguous gendered identities and some degree of gender equality in Formative society among elites.

CHAPTER NINE

The Late Classic Period

This chapter provides interpretations of the social lives and layered identities of the variably situated Late Classic actors within and across states in the Western Chontalpa, with an emphasis on those at ILC. Whereas my interpretations of the Formative societies at ILC are limited, the ability to socially contextualize and differentiate material culture for the Late Classic enables far more interpretation through political economic, practice, and agency perspectives. After some regional culture historical observations, settlement patterns are described to contextualize the different populations within the Western Chontalpa—the Mezcalapa drainage from the southern Terrace Valley in Chiapas to ILC at the coast—revealing three variably structured states. Next, the settlement history at ILC is interpreted through a reconstruction of the sequence of feature construction, which subsequently provides new insights on social classes and intra-class status. Although interpretations on classes and their kinship practices at ILC have been made previously (Ensor 2013b, 2017e; Ensor, Herrera Escobar, and Tun Ayora 2012), those analyses are buttressed here with new inter- and intra-class analyses on status and identities while providing new comparisons from the broader Western Chontalpa. Once contextualized by location, class, intra-class status, and kinship practices, the chapter presents plausible inferences on variation in gender and age relations (including children/childhood). Foodways and food sharing and feasting provide additional lines of inquiry into gender, practice, social memories, and identities within and across classes.

THE WESTERN CHONTALPA

The Late Classic occupations at ILC are discussed through a new synthesis on the Western Chontalpa. ILC was reoccupied in the Late Classic, after an Early Classic hiatus, which appears to have been a broader Chontalpa trend. A trait-based culture historical perspective suggests strong intraregional interaction and variable integration with the Maya and Veracruz regions. Settlement pattern comparisons suggest three differently structured tributary states.

A Chontalpa Early Classic Settlement Hiatus?

ILC was abandoned after the Late Formative and reoccupied in the Late Classic. None of the ceramic types are firmly associated with the Early Classic, though some are suspected to be earlier than CE 600. There were low quantities of Comalcalco Black or Gray and Paraíso types, which are suggested to represent a "Middle Classic" (Armijo Torres, Gallegos Gomora, and Jimenez Alvarez 2005), though that proposed period could use further testing. The Bellote type has attributes common to both Formative and Late Classic types and could be transitional but this argument is also unsubstantiated. The thermoluminescence date from one Centla sherd was slightly earlier than expected, around the late Early Classic (or possible "Middle Classic"). Regardless of whether a "Middle Classic" period is justified, and based on current knowledge of Chontalpa ceramic chronology, there is no evidence for continuity from Late Formative to Late Classic periods at ILC.

Although it has long been recognized that populations in the Northern Maya Lowlands grew only after declines in the Petén, that observation has been based only on the Usumacinta region within Tabasco (Rands 1969, 1973, 1985). A similar hiatus is suspected at Comalcalco. The parallel might indicate that there was a general depopulation of the Chontalpa or an Early Classic shift in settlement away from Late Formative sites. Although Sanders (1962:212–218) indicates many undifferentiated Classic period sites along the Mezcalapa, those he describes were more specifically associated with the Late Classic and Postclassic periods. Although Piña Chan and Navarrete (1967:15) describe continuity from the Late Formative to the Postclassic periods at San Fernando, this was preceded by descriptions of only two occupations: one with White-Rim Black and Gray (now known as Middle Formative), and another with regional Late Classic fine paste types, suggesting another Early Classic hiatus at that site. They also suggested Formative to Late Classic continuity at San Miguel but updated ceramic chronologies could suggest Formative and Late Classic, but not Early Classic, occupations. They did note an Early Classic hiatus at El Fenix. They noted that Tierra Nueva was not occupied until the late Early Classic, which would conform with the Late Classic (or the proposed Middle Classic) using an updated ceramic chronology. None of Sisson's (1976) site records indicate Early Classic pottery. South of Laguna Machona, in the western lower delta, the repopulation of mostly Late Formative sites occurred in the Late Classic (von Nagy's 1997). At Aguacatal, in the Laguna de Términos, Early Classic pottery is sparse compared to the abundance of Late Formative and Late Classic pottery (Matheny 1970), also suggesting an Early Classic population decline before the Late Classic. Thus, the Western Chontalpa was tied into the broader Northwest Maya Lowland pattern of low population densities in the Early Classic. This was followed by population growth in the Late Classic when abandoned or mostly abandoned Formative sites, including ILC, were reoccupied. In the broader picture, this may suggest commercial and population "pulls" to the west (implicating Teotihuacán influences) and to the southeast (implicating the Petén kingdoms), leaving the Chontalpa a frontier with low population densities until after CE 400.

Regional Integration

From outside the Chontalpa, twentieth-century Mesoamericanists speculated that the Chontal—the presumed "Mexicanized Maya" based on multilingualism noted in historical sources—played major roles in the sweeping interregional changes across Mesoamerica following the decline of Teotihuacán (Fox 1987; Morley, Brainerd, and Sharer 1983:157; Sabloff and Rathje 1975; Scholes and Roys 1968; Tourtellot 1988; Vargas Pacheco 1992). The Chontal were portrayed as the sources of mixed Mexican-Maya iconography that appeared at regional centers in both macroregions, the originators of fine paste pottery, and the purveyors of cacao. They were characterized as having a predatory segmentary social organization. They were

the hypothesized Itzá who expanded eastward and the Putún merchants of ethnohistoric fame. Arguments for or against Gulf Coast- Maya continuities were based on comparisons of material traits and Spanish contact-era languages among elites in Veracruz and the Usumacinta-Campeche zones, ignoring the extensive Chontalpa region that was in between (see Ochoa 2003; Parsons 1978; Pérez Suárez 2003).

The speculation of Veracruz-Maya continuity, or Chontal influence on both the Mexican and Maya macroregions, seems incredible when faced with Late Classic period Chontalpa material culture. Although obsidian was imported from both Mexican and Maya macroregions (Lewenstein 1995; Lewenstein and Glascock 1996, 1997), the majority of fine pastes appear to be regionally manufactured and preceded by those in the surrounding Veracruz, Oaxaca, and Yucatán peninsular regions. Little pottery appears to have been imported to the Chontalpa from surrounding regions. No trade ports have been identified to suggest a developing commercial focus. As yet, cacao production has only been assumed. This is a far cry from establishing the region as a major source for broader Mesoamerica. Nor does this lack of broader Mesoamerican integration bode well for interpretations of Nahua incursions during the Early to Late Classic transition (Dakin and Wichmann 2000; Macri 2005; Macri and Looper 2003).

From a trait-based perspective, there was strong intra-Chontalpa integration. Brick architecture at prominent sites like Comalcalco, Centla, Pomoná, and El Bellote spans the deltas. The same fine paste pottery was circulated across the Chontalpa as illustrated by their type names: for example, Centla, Cimatán, Comalcalco, Copilco, Huimangillo, Jilón, Jonuta, and Paraíso. Shared plastic decorative attributes (e.g., Trinidad/Coabal and Soyataco) appear throughout the region. Even with differences in coarse pastes in the Lower Mezcalapa, Middle Mezcalapa, and eastern Aguacatal areas that are indicative of localized production, those areas share plastic decorative attributes.

There is little trait-based integration with Veracruz. To the author's knowledge, no resist techniques for decorating pottery, Remojadas figurines, or other traits common to Central-Southern Veracruz have been identified along the Mezcalapa drainage. The only traits shared with southern Veracruz were ballcourts and quadratic plazas (rectangular plazas with monumental architecture on their ends and temples lining their sides; see Borstein 2005; Stark 1999). Both are less frequent in the Chontalpa but they are common Maya features to the east. Ballcourts in the Middle Mezcalapa (Piña Chan and Navarrete 1967) appear more similar to those in Veracruz (e.g., Stark 1999:209–210; Stark and Stoner 2017) but perhaps only because they were constructed of earthen deposits. The single ballcourt at Comalcalco is minuscule compared to the site's monumental architecture. Even the residential mounds (including discrete mounds and superior mounds) are most often small–supporting one dwelling each. This is similar to both the Maya and Veracruz regions. However, the larger mounds that accommodate multiple dwellings and even entire *plazuelas* in Central-Southern Veracruz (Stark 1999:209) seem absent in the Chontalpa.

There are more trait-based similarities to the Maya microregion but only in elite contexts. Though built of brick and mortar, the Late Classic monumental architectural designs, best evidenced at Comalcalco but also in the substructures at ILC, illustrate strong links to broader Maya architectural patterns. The architecture is matched by Comalcalco's iconography and linguistic attributes (Andrews 1967, 1989; Armijo Torres 1997; Zender 1998). Figurine styles in the Middle and Upper Mezcalapa were decidedly Maya (Piña Chan and Navarrete 1967). Unlike architecture and figurines, the majority of the pottery has Chontalpan characteristics, rather than shared traits across the Maya macroregion.

Settlement Patterns

Environmental zones, settlement distributions, and settlement hierarchies are considered here for the Mezcalapa drainage. There were four major environmental zones: the coast, the lower delta levees, the alluvial plains of the Middle Mezcalapa, and the Pleistocene terrace area along the Chiapas-Tabasco border. Although Chontalpa settlement patterns were previously assumed to follow the solar model (Gallegos Gómora 1995, 1998; Sanders 1962), this synthesis illustrates more differentiation explainable by intra- and interzonal political and economic relationships to resources. A model adopted from the Gulf Coast of Veracruz explains the coastal-lower levee relationships, which had the greatest degree of authoritarian structure. A dendritic solar model best characterizes the Middle Mezcalapa. A southern Terrace Valley settlement pattern resembled neither.

Coast and Lower Levees

Stark (1974, 1978, 1987) provides a generalizable model for coastal-interior settlement, interaction, and political integration. There were local community specializations in the early historical central-southern Veracruz Gulf Coast: fishing, pottery, and salt along the coast and food crops, cotton cloth, and cacao along interior levees. The "multisettlement tributary communities" spanned the different resource zones, with primary centers located near contrasting zones (Stark 1974, 1978). She characterizes coastal diets as heavily supplemented by terrestrial foods and cultigens from the levees (Stark 1987). Unless they had specialized roles such as salt production or trade, the coastal settlements had redundant resources, providing no political advantages for heavily populated centers of power. Centers that did control coastal populations were situated a short distance inland along rivers for easy transportation (Stark 1987).

Emphasizing only fish and shellfish for coastal zones would appear simplistic in light of the resource diversity described earlier in this book. In addition, tree crops on features could supplement aquatic resources. Likewise, depicting the levees as only agricultural areas ignores the diverse aquatic resources of the river, adjacent marshes, small distributaries, and terrestrial wild resources. The amount of levee available for cultivation near ILC was minimal unless one went several kilometers upriver. And south of the transition zone there were no estuarine or coastal resources. Thus, Stark's model for primate centers can be modified into a "diverse coastal-diverse levee" resource transition zone for complimentary specialized exchange.

ILC was uniquely large for a Late Classic coastal settlement. Other records indicate few mounds or mound groups within the coastal zone of the Mezcalapa Delta (Figures 1.1 and 4.1).

Comalcalco was 12 km south of ILC (via the Seco River) on the east levee close to the southwest corner of the Mecoacán Lagoon. It was the only Late Classic city anywhere in the region, with investments in monumental architecture far surpassing all others including palaces on acropolis. A dense population surrounded the city. All other sites in the western Chontalpa, including ILC, were dwarfed by comparison. At Comalcalco, Andrews (1975) estimated a residential mound density of 154 people per square kilometer (compared to 82 for Uaxactún and 280 for Tikal). The residential mounds were concentrated in the southeast sector, with a sudden decrease beyond. Romero Rivera's (1995) survey, however, indicated that the mounds continue along the east levee, extending from a ranch approximately 1.5 km east of Comalcalco's center to the Paraíso area. Gallegos Gomóra (1995, 1998) assumes that there was a solar settlement pattern and documented multi-mound groupings, also suggesting that Comalcalco's monumental center was surrounded by vast residential zones comprised of *plazuelas*.

As predicted in Stark's model, the primate center—Comalcalco—was indeed situated on the river levee near its transition with the coastal zone, facilitating tributary control of both zones. Though neither salt-producing nor a port, ILC supplied the thousands of tons of processed oyster shell for mortar and stucco for Comalcalco's monumental architecture. This important role fits with Stark's explanation for large coastal settlements. Other evidence for complimentary exchange between coastal ILC and levee agrarian zones includes the light presence of possibly Late Classic ground stone at ILC and marine and estuarine fauna in Comalcalco's elite contexts. Furthermore, Comalcalco's location along the Mezcalapa provided easy access to ILC and coastal exchange routes, access to the distributaries of the inland delta, and a transportation corridor upriver into Chiapas.

Lower Delta

Over half of Tabasco's archaeological sites are on the floodplains and levees just south of the coastal-lower levee transitional zones (West, Psuty, and Thom 1969:93). The Lower Mezcalapa Delta was characterized by alluvium-supporting rainforest (historically deforested for cacao plantations, cattle ranching, and lumber) intersected by distributaries. East of the Seco River (Mezcalapa), the deltaic floodplain was wide, until the river reached the marshlands of the Lower Grijalva Delta. This was also the area with the highest protohistoric population in the region (Figure 2.1). This portion of the delta was suitable for agriculture, the terrestrial hunting and gathering of a wide range of foods and medicinal resources, and large to small sources of timber. To the west, in contrast, the alluvial-rainforest associations were interspersed with marshlands and smaller distributaries creating a mosaic of environmental niches but also a more flood-prone area compared to the east side of the Seco River. In that western zone, there were few sites with ceremonial mounds along the mid-sized distributaries (Figure 9.1).

Sisson (1976:Appendix One) recorded Late Classic material at 26 sites, mostly on the western delta (Figure 9.1). Of the 209 sites scattered throughout that survey area, 98 lacked known period affiliations and many may also have Late Classic occupations. The site catalog is inconsistent in numbers and mound descriptions, either from lack of ground observation, destruction, or other problems. Nevertheless, there is sufficient information to claim a relatively high occupation density west of Comalcalco. Most of the 26 settlements apparently were small and dispersed. None were indicated as having more than three large mounds that could potentially be ceremonial. For Figure 9.1, I interpreted "large" mounds as possible ceremonial mounds. Most had a small number of mounds estimated to be less than a few meters in height, presumably residential mounds. The few clusters may suggest sprawling settlements with groups. South of Laguna Machona, von Nagy (1997) observed that Late Classic settlements were linear, with widely spaced residential deposits, along distributaries (a "*ribera*" settlement pattern).

The lower delta was an additional area under Comalcalco's control. Comalcalco was a primate center far overshadowing in size, population, and monumentality the next largest sites in the lower delta area. Given its specialized coastal role in the regional tributary economy, ILC was the only secondary center in the Comalcalco hinterland, with the inland delta sites forming lower tiers in the settlement hierarchy of a multi-settlement tributary community. In short, the settlement hierarchy involved one dominating super primate center with a sprawling surrounding population, only one significantly smaller secondary center (ILC), and dispersed small rural populations, not a dendritic solar pattern.

Middle Mezcalapa

Between the southern limit of the Seco River and the Pleistocene terrace formations near Cardenas lies the (pre-seventeenth-century) Middle Mezcalapa. The alluvial plains were covered by rainforest but were less subject to flooding compared to the lower delta. Well-watered soils support slash and burn horticulture. Piña Chan and Navarrete (1967) reported a wide range of cultigens (subsistence and cash crops, including tree crops), wild game, livestock, and wild palms.

Sanders (1962) concluded that there was a dendritic solar settlement pattern using the NWAF survey data from the Middle Mezcalapa area. At the apex was the elite ceremonial site of Tierra Nueva with its large plaza, multiple pyramids, a ballcourt, elite residences, and house mound clusters. Next were secondary sites like Sigero, having a plaza with one pyramid, an elite residence, and an area with three smaller pyramids and similar house mound clusters. Although he considered Sigero a Postclassic site (while indicating its similarities to Classic sites), Piña Chan and Navarrete (1967:35) concluded that it had a Late Classic affiliation with limited continuity into the Postclassic, which better conforms with the ceramic data. Finally, settlements surrounding the secondary sites were hamlets with one or two pyramids, small settlements with few house mound clusters, and sites with only small pyramids (Sanders 1962).

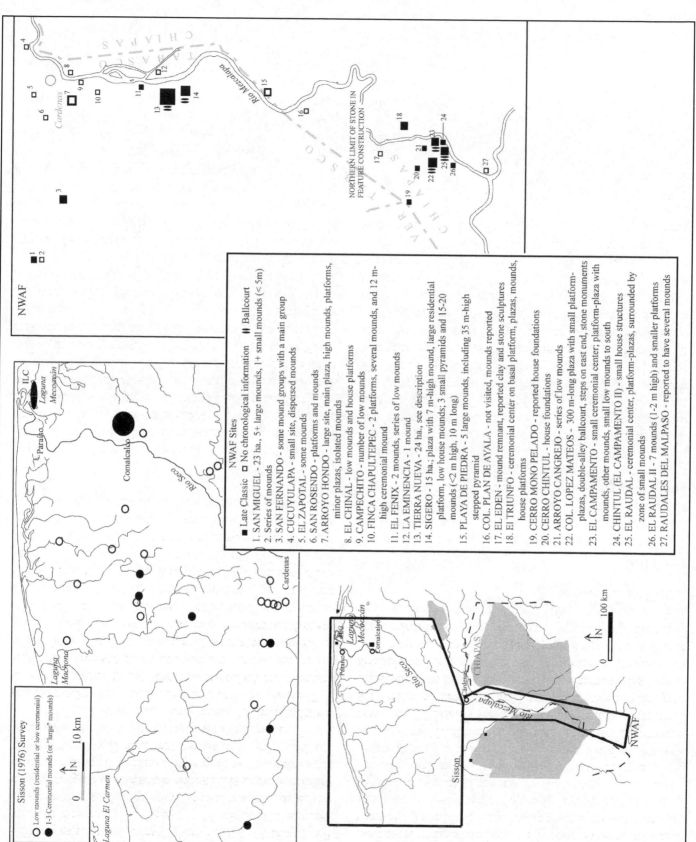

Figure 9.1. Late Classic settlements in the Western Chontalpa. Prepared by the author.

Sanders's model can be tested with the map and site information published by Piña Chan and Navarrete (1967). The NWAF survey area (Figures 1.1 and 9.1) included both the Middle Mezcalapa (referred to as the "Chontalpa") and the Terrace Valley areas (The "Las Palmas" area in Chiapas). The Chontalpa sites Sanders referenced are shown in the northern portion of the NWAF inset in Figure 9.1. Readers should keep in mind that the survey relied on aerial photography for site location, which could not detect mounds in forested areas. Given the project's culture historical orientation on pottery, they provided little and inconsistent information on site size, numbers of features, feature sizes, or settlement layouts. Another caveat is that a few Late Classic sites were occupied into the Postclassic periods, but my analysis assumes that most of the features mentioned are Late Classic. The site contents listed in the figure were all that were stated in the report. I could not employ site classification criteria due to inconsistencies in description; instead I used approximate relative differences in numbers of features recorded at each site. Those indicated as Late Classic conform with Piña Chan and Navarrete's conclusions or are my own assessments based on ceramic comparisons.

The resulting distribution of sites does suggest a dendritic solar model for the Middle Mezcalapa (Figure 9.1). There were at least three tiers: large sites with more abundant ceremonial features, ballcourts, and numerous residential features; secondary sites with fewer ceremonial and residential features; and smaller sites with one to two ceremonial features and even fewer residential features. To this, we can add that the larger two tiers were in the south of the cluster, with sites of the lower tier scattered to their north and concentrated along the river—an important fishing resource and transportation route connecting the area to Comalcalco. Just to the north of the NWAF survey area, the Sisson survey also documented a concentration of five sites—distinct from the more dispersed settlements on the Lower Delta—that should be considered part of the Middle Mezcalapa area (Figure 9.1).

Terrace Valley

From the Chiapas Highlands, the Mezcalapa winds its way northward, carving its way through the Pleistocene terraces at the Chiapas-Tabasco border before entering the Middle Mezcalapa alluvial plains. The river created a shallow meandering valley system within the terrace zone, with narrow floodplains flanked by foothills to the terrace summits. The valley and foothills also supported patches of rainforest and slash-and-burn farming. The

adjacent Pleistocene terrace surfaces have poor soils that support savanna vegetation. The terraces were largely used as hunting grounds; the few sites had low population densities even in historic times when they were largely used as hunting grounds (West, Psuty, and Thum 1969:94). Sites in this zone had access to stone that was used for square and rectangular stone-walled, earth-filled platforms and for sculpted artifacts and monuments (Piña Chan and Navarrete 1967). To the north, no stone was used for those purposes.

The Terrace Valley had a very different settlement pattern, as shown as the southern cluster in the NWAF survey inset (Figure 9.1). First, the settlement distribution was very compact and confined to the narrow valley areas, suggesting a high population density. Second, there was only a two-tier settlement hierarchy. At the top were three relatively compact sites, each having one plaza lined by ceremonial features and ballcourts, in turn surrounded by residential zones. The remaining sites surrounding those three only had residential features. This settlement pattern suggests that elites from three sites potentially allied or competed for power in a localized kingdom that lacked a primary center like those in the Middle Mezcalapa and Comalcalco states.

One settlement pattern model cannot characterize the Late Classic Western Chontalpa. The Comalcalco state had one super primate center with extensive residential zones, only one secondary center of much smaller size (ILC), and small residential sites extending along distributaries. That settlement pattern suggests the strong, centralized power of a regional state. Furthermore, as predicted in Stark's model, Comalcalco was situated in an agricultural zone immediately adjacent to the coastal and inland delta zones to maximize control over resource diversity. The more homogeneous Middle Mezcalapa alluvial plain had a second, much smaller kingdom with a dendritic solar settlement pattern. The Terrace Valley had an additional kingdom comprising tightly packed settlements with three possibly allied or competing elite groups that lacked a primate center. Based on culture historical trait comparisons, the Middle Mezcalapa and Terrace Valley states appear to have been less integrated with the Comalcalco state.

ILC'S LATE CLASSIC SETTLEMENT HISTORY

Returning the focus to ILC, this section considers ways by which the Late Classic settlement history—one of the original objectives of the PAILC—may be envisioned despite the failure to refine the ceramic chronology. First, percentages

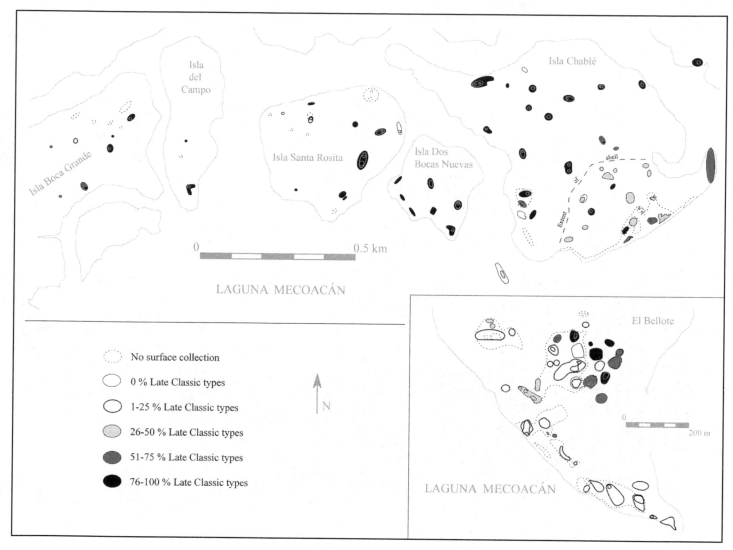

Figure 9.2. Percentages of Late Classic pottery in surface collections. Prepared by the author.

of Late Classic pottery are used, with the assumption that the earliest occupations will have larger percentages of Formative pottery because those were the first deposits to be recycled for mound building. Second, residence "duration categories" are created and used with the assumption that the whole local community was abandoned around the same time. This would indicate the relative order in which the locations were occupied. As a reminder, all extant features were constructed in the Late Classic.

Figure 9.2 illustrates the percentages of Late Classic pottery at ILC's features. The figure demonstrates differential access to Formative deposits for Late Classic feature construction. The percentages do not necessarily indicate a sequence. It is assumed that the earliest occupants in the Late Classic, the first to claim rights to resources, established

themselves at Formative deposits, which provided dry land and materials to recycle for constructing their own features. This resulted in lower relative percentages of Late Classic pottery at those features. The assumption also implies that subsequent generations who established new locations, made less use of substantial Formative deposits and mangrove sediments to construct their house platforms and mounds. Those features would therefore have less Formative pottery. As described in chapters 4 and 5, the earthen features across most of the insular areas had higher percentages of Late Classic pottery. If accepting the assumption, then the percentage distributions illustrated suggest that the earliest Late Classic occupations were concentrated at El Bellote and southern Isla Chablé, with few locations elsewhere on Isla Santa Rosita and Isla

Chablé. That first generation was followed by little population expansion, but there was, ultimately, a significant population expansion across the islands.

Residential platforms, like those at ILC, have been associated with lower-ranking classes in the Maya region (Webster and Gonlin 1988). Although the low residential platforms were all associated with commoners at ILC, not all commoners had platforms. Indeed, most had much taller mounds, mounds-on-platforms, and some of the largest residential features—multilevel mounds. As demonstrated in Chapter 5, the low residential platforms were not indicative of class, but rather, the first stages in long-term residential occupations.

Feature duration provides an alternative approach to interpret settlement history. Residential mounds-on-platforms and multilevel mounds represent longer occupation durations than discrete platforms and mounds. Structures were placed over platforms before mounds were built over them at mounds-on-platforms, and inferior mounds had structures before superior mounds were built over those at multilevel mounds. Profiles in tall discrete mounds indicate sequences of structures and mound-filling episodes. The excavated discrete residential platform (Feature 40) had only two strata built in one episode indicating a short occupation duration. Therefore, residential feature durations, in increasing order, are represented by (1) discrete platforms and low discrete mounds; (2) tall discrete mounds, mounds-on-platforms, and multilevel mounds; and (3) tall mounds or multilevel mounds on platforms. I defined tall mounds as 1.5 m or greater in height. Subdividing the second category into more duration categories would overlook the observation that much of the height of inferior mounds in multilevel mounds was achieved through labor investitures in a single episode of mound construction (Chapter 5).

Figure 9.3 shows the distribution of the three duration categories. The third category of features—representing the longest residential durations—were concentrated at the groups of El Bellote and the South and Southwest groups of Isla Chablé. There were also a few longer duration residences dispersed across the eastern islands: five in northern and western Isla Chablé, one on Isla Dos Bocas Nuevas, and three in eastern and northern Isla Santa Rosita. Features in the second duration category were more broadly distributed in intervening spaces of Isla Chablé, two additional locations at Isla Dos Bocas Nuevas, and two additional locations in northeastern Isla Santa Rosita but also at one location on Isla del Campo and three locations on Isla Boca Grande, most notably Subgroup B of

the Northeast Group at El Bellote along with two locations at the South Group of that site. The first category, which represented the shortest inferred occupations, filled more of the remaining spaces on the islands.

To interpret these distributions in a settlement history requires the acceptance of one of two alternative assumptions. The first is that colonization across ILC occurred simultaneously, in which case the occupation of all features began at the same time. That would suggest that many of the insular residences were short-lived, with few lasting throughout the Late Classic on the eastern islands and at El Bellote. This would also suggest depopulation over time. However, I prefer the alternative assumption—that occupations across ILC were abandoned around the same time at the end of the Late Classic. In this case, the duration categories suggest that the earliest and longest lasting occupations were concentrated at El Bellote and the South Group of Isla Chablé, as well as a few scattered locations on Isla Santa Rosita, Isla Dos Bocas Nuevas, and Isla Chable. New locations were then established elsewhere on those islands and expanded to a few locations on the western islands. Additional short-lived residences were established near those before the local community was abandoned. This suggests population increase over time. The three stages are a product of the three categories created but their distributions are independent.

Using the feature duration categories, the maximum number of conjugal (or nuclear) family dwellings may be used to estimate the population of ILC during the early, middle, and late Late Classic. All of the residential structures observed at ILC were for conjugal families (see kinship section below). Though the three stages in the settlement history are a product of the residential duration categories created, accepting the above-stated assumptions would result in an estimated 30 conjugal families in the early stage, 66 in the middle stage, and 115 in the late stage (Table 9.1). The conventional estimate of conjugal family size in Mayanist literature is 5.6, widely ranging alternatives notwithstanding (Haviland 1970c; Redfield 1950; Smith 1962). More convincingly, once differences between ethnographic and prehispanic populations are addressed, Haviland (1972) argued for a figure of 5.0 persons per family. Table 9.1 considers both to derive a range in maximum total population of 150 to 168 people in the early stage, 330 to 370 in the middle stage, and 575 to 644 in the late stage.

The two approaches to interpreting the settlement history at ILC converge, with minor differences. If accepting the assumptions, the pottery percentage distributions and

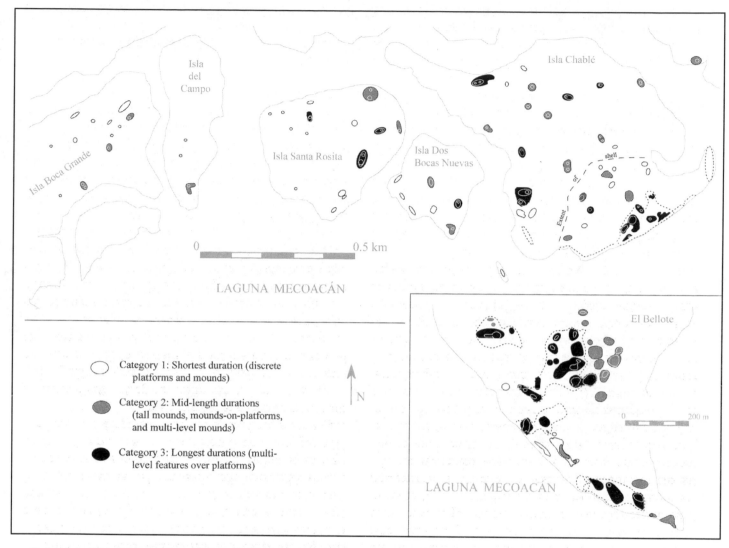

Figure 9.3. Distribution of occupation duration categories. Prepared by the author.

the residential duration categories both suggest that early occupation was concentrated at El Bellote and southern Isla Chablé. The two approaches produced differences in regard to settlement expansion across the islands, though neither negates the general interpretation. Based on pottery percentages, settlement growth outward from southern Isla Chablé and El Bellote would have been slow, followed by punctuated growth across the western islands at the end of the period. The residence duration categories suggest that an early concentration at Isla Chablé and El Bellote was followed by more growth there as well as expansions across all the islands. Ultimately more newly established residences filled more spaces across the islands. Although neither approach is entirely satisfying, they do paint a general picture of ILC's occupation history that I find

generally acceptable: first at El Bellote and southern Isla Chablé, with a few dispersed occupations on the eastern islands, followed by population expansion in the original locations filling more of the eastern islands and into the western islands. The discussion on kinship among classes in the following sections provides explanations for this interpreted spatial settlement history.

POLITICAL ECONOMY, CLASSES, AND IDENTITIES

The objective in this section is to synthesize previously published interpretations on Late Classic society at ILC (Ensor 2013b, 2016b, 2017e; Ensor Herrera Escobar, and Tun Ayora 2012) fortified with more substantial data, new analyses, and regional comparisons. Class interpretations

Table 9.1. Estimated Maximum Numbers of Late Classic Conjugal Family Dwellings by Stages, with Population Estimates

Stage	Number of Dwellings by Location									Population Estimates
	Boca Grande	del Campo	Santa Rosita	Dos Bocas Nuevas	Chablé	El Bellote	El Canal	La Islita	Total	
EARLY	0	0	3	1	Nongroup = 5 SW Group = 2 S Group = 7	NW Group = 1 NE Group A = 4 NE Group B = 0 NE Group C = 1 NC Group = 3 C Group = 1 S Group = 2	0	0	30	x 5.6 = 168 x 5.0 = 150
MIDDLE	3	1	5	3	Nongroup = 16 SW Group = 2 S Group = 7	NW Group = 3 NE Group A = 4 NE Group B = 6 NE Group C = 1 NC Group = 3 C Group = 3 S Group = 5 Other = 4	1	0	66 220% growth	x 5.6 = 370 x 5.0 = 330
LATE	13	3	17	7	Nongroup = 28 SW Group = 4 S Group = 8	NW Group = 3 NE Group A = 4 NE Group B = 6 NE Group C = 1 NC Group = 3 C Group = 7 S Group = 5 Other = 4	1	1	115 174% growth	x 5.6 = 644 x 5.0 = 575

are based on relations of production, rather than wealth differences. This requires discussion on the overlapping of class and "luxury" items and how the latter can be interpreted through class relations, intra-class agency, and identity negotiation. To provide regional contexts, the class-based tributary political economy of the Comalcalco state is discussed along with comparisons to the southern Mezcalapa states.

Political Economies of Western Chontalpa States

Without doubt, the vertical relations linking commoners to elites in the Late Classic Western Chontalpa were based on tribute. Although many Mayanists have imposed historical market systems onto ancient prehispanic societies, the identification of markets and, in particular, marketplaces, is fraught with difficulties. Although Dahlin et al.'s (2007) soil chemical patterns were concluded to indicate marketplaces, the same patterns could be expected for any public spaces where major festivities took place. Even the marketplaces at Classic Caracol (Chase and A. Chase 2014) could have alternative interpretations. Furthermore, tribute was the basis for class relations and conditions, even when markets were present. Speal (2014) indicates that linguistic terms for commerce and *possible* market-like exchanges among the Maya were minimal and are associated with "plazas" rather than formal marketplaces. The terms may have developed in the Late Classic at the earliest in the eastern Maya Lowlands. There was no concept of "money." In contrast, expressions of tribute for labor (corvée) were common and more deeply rooted across Mayan languages, in addition to other forms of forced labor, as well as reciprocity, and gifting (Speal 2014). So, despite obsessions with Spanish-interpreted, contact-period Chontal markets, there is no reason to assume that such a system was the basis for production and exchange in the Late Classic Chontalpa, especially at ILC, where few imported commodities even made it into the local community.

From the perspective of ILC, the local elites at El Bellote and the South Group of Isla Chablé likely serviced the royalty at Comalcalco by ensuring the flow of coastal tributary resources. For commoners at ILC, tribute probably included some of the fish, sea turtles, and crocodiles that made their way to Comalcalco, but was most visible in the thousands of tons of oyster shell products prepared for lime, mortar, and plaster. The vast majority at ILC did not have tools at their residences, suggesting those resources were largely exploited and processed in non-domestic settings, and quite likely collectively at the shoreline platform and large crushed sell deposit under the control of local elites (Ensor 2003b, 2013b, 2017d; Ensor and Tun Ayora 2011, Ensor, Herrera Escobar, and Tun Ayora et al. 2012). The specific class relations at ILC are described in more detail later in this section.

For commoners surrounding Comalcalco, tribute was probably in the form of agricultural surplus—foodstuffs and possibly cacao—in addition to other commodities from levee and freshwater resources (e.g., turtles and clay for bricks), not to mention conscription for construction and/or war. Although only one commoner residential context has been excavated near Comalcalco, no evidence for brick manufacturing was identified and possible evidence for cacao processing was limited (Gallegos Gómora 1994, 1995, 1997). If that one context characterized all commoners on the lower levee (a dubious assumption), then brick manufacturing (and possibly cacao orchards and materials processing spaces) may have been situated in nondomestic settings, whereby elites controlled corvée tributary production. But neither domestic nor public brickworks or cacao processing locations have been identified.

Whereas the Comalcalco state was situated for tributary extraction of resources from the sea, the beach ridges, the river, its distributaries, the levee rainforests, the lagoon, the mangroves, and the marshlands, and had access to both coastal and river trade, the smaller Middle Mezcalapa state headed by elites at Tierra Nueva commanded a more homogeneous territory and only had access to river trade. There, the alluvial plain for cultivation along with

the rainforest, river, streams, and ponds characterized each site's area—from the primary center itself to the secondary center of Sigero and to the smaller residential sites. The Middle Mezcalapa state had access to only a portion of the same tributary resources that the Comalcalco state commanded while having no tributary resources that Comalcalco lacked. Further upriver, the Terrace Valley kingdom had more limited floodplains for cultivation and its only other major tributary resources came from the forest, river, and terraces. All three states were situated along the Mezcalapa for inland travel and commerce, but only Comalcalco had access to coastal trade routes—a role denied even to its coastal secondary center (ILC). By comparison, the more extreme exploitative class-based relationships within the Comalcalco state were achieved by the royalty's command of diverse resources and trade, religiously legitimized through its ostentatious public monuments and spaces that were built, in part, through ILC commoners' shell-processing tributary labor.

Ceremony, Power, and Elite Identities

Prior generalizations on site structure for interpreted expansionist "Chontal" segmentary groups, or Chontal-influenced, sites (all outside the Chontalpa) suggest that civic-ceremonial architecture was built in nonresidential areas (Fox 1987; Tourtellot 1988). However, sites within the Western Chontalpa differ considerably from this characterization. The recent attention to Maya courts may shed light on Comalcalco's two acropoli but the courts also differ from the *patterns* found in Western Chontalpa elite contexts (Foias 2013; Inomata and Houston 2001a, 2001b; Jackson 2013). Instead, settlements along the Mezcalapa indicate two overlapping site structure patterns in elite contexts.

The first involves a Classic Maya acropolis-plaza association: a "triadic" plan having square to rectangular, or T-shaped plazas with a dominant structure supporting palaces or major temples at one end and flanked by a series of smaller ceremonial structures. The smaller structures may be built on a single U-shaped platform or on separate platforms around the plaza, and the entire group may or may not be on a raised platform (Velásquez Fergusson 2014). These sometimes included the royal palaces, or palaces were adjacent to the plaza-monument configuration. In addition, ballcourts were commonly incorporated into, or adjacent to, the triadic spaces. Velásqez Fergusson (2014) summarizes how triadic configurations across 59 Classic urban sites of the Maya Lowlands could function as ideological tools in an "architecture of power." They (1) reinforce vertical social ties, promoting the acceptance of precepts; (2) legitimize royalty through ancestral-mythical association with the monuments; (3) express distinctions to support hierarchy; and (4) identify royalty with an ancestral affiliation shared across regions since the Late Preclassic. This grants a practice or agency perspective on shared cultural historical traits, previously treated as indications of "ethnic" migration or expansion. Large public plazas served the same purposes of creating and negotiating power relationships (Tsukamoto and Inomata 2014). Plazas did not include palaces: royal residential areas were instead usually adjacent to them. Such plazas can be found at Epiclassic sites of the Tuxtlas (e.g., Borstein 2005) and across much of the Classic Maya macroregion. Ball games likely served for horizontal alliances, identities, and social memories, as only limited numbers of elites could witness the games, since the courts were restricted to elite contexts (e.g., Stark and Stoner 2017).

The triadic configuration is found at the three elite sites of the congested Terrace Valley state: Colonia López Mateos, El Campamento, and El Raudal (Figure 9.4). Farther east, this layout is shared with Tortuguero, which is situated in a similar southern terrace valley of the Chilapa River (Arellano 2006). Farther south, it was present at the aggressive state of Toniná (Taladoire 2015, 2016). It is also common along the Middle Usumacinta. Thus, as a *pattern*, the triadic-quadratic attribute can be associated with non-Chontalpa areas (south and above the alluvial deltas), and with the broader Maya macroregion. In the Lower Mezcalapa Delta, it is only found at Comalcalco's Great Acropolis and East Acropolis (Figure 9.4). Nevertheless, Comalcalco and Tierra Nueva share with the Terrace Valley sites large public temple-framed plazas (Figure 9.4).

The second pattern is usually overlooked when focusing on the largest monumental architecture and spaces at major centers. It involves ceremonial architecture incorporated into residential mound groups. Sometimes the groups were informally arranged clusters of residential mounds and one or more ceremonial mounds. In other cases, they were more formally arranged *plazuelas*—multiple residential mounds and one or more ceremonial mounds surrounding a small plaza space (Ensor and Tun Ayora 2011; Tun Ayora 2010). This arrangement is found in other Maya regions and in Veracruz (Becker 2004; Chase and Chase 2004; Freter 2004; Hageman 2004; Hutson, Magnoni, and Stanton 2004; Stark 1999). It is interpreted as a manifestation of elite extended families who are emphasizing relationships to their own ancestors (Ensor 2013b; Ensor, Herrera Escobar, and Tun Ayora 2012). This also implies the materializing of hierarchical and differentiating

identities among those multiple elite groupings through practice and symbolic displays in less public locations. The pattern is absent in the Terrace Valley area, but present in the Middle Mezcalapa, lower delta, and coastal zone. There were four such groups at Tierra Nueva (Figure 9.4 B1, C, F and G) in addition to the plaza-associated elite residential zone (Figure 9.4 A-B). "Pyramids" and ballcourts were also associated with residential mound clusters at Arroyo Hondo, Finca Chapultepec, El Fenix, and Sigero in the NWAF survey (Piña Chan and Navarrete 1967; Sanders 1962). At Comalcalco, in addition to palaces at the acropoli, there were at least three residential groups, possibly five, associated with a ceremonial mound (Figure 9.4 A, B, C, and possibly G and H). At ILC, the South Group of Isla Chablé and each residential group at El Bellote (with the exception of the South Group) incorporated at least one ceremonial feature (Figures 4.4 to 4.6).

Comalcalco, Tierra Nueva, and the three major sites in the Terrace Valley state, each had triadic or quadratic-plaza configurations. Comalcalco and Tierra Nueva also had ceremonial mounds incorporated into residential groups. In contrast, secondary centers in the Comalcalco and Middle Mezcalapa states *only* had residential groups with incorporated ceremonial mounds: the second pattern. Inductively, the implications on power and identities are interpreted as follows. The Comalcalco royalty and their less powerful counterparts at Tierra Nueva reinforced vertical social ties through large events at temple-lined plazas that were materially symbolic of broader royal Maya identities and networks outside the Chontalpa. This may be no accident in the case of Comalcalco, whose royalty, according to epigraphic accounts, identified themselves with royalty at Tortuguero, who in turn identified themselves with royalty at Palenque (Arellano 2006; Bíró 2011, 2012; Zender 1998).

The royalty at Comalcalco and Tierra Nueva also allowed lesser-ranking elites to emphasize their own ancestral affiliations through temples placed within their extended residential groups at primary centers, and at secondary centers where they were the highest-ranking elites. Royalty, whose power negotiations were far more public, sensational, and flauntingly identified with broader Maya royalty for horizontal alliances, imposed limitations on lesser elite expressions of power to ceremonies for each group's ancestors only. The two patterns expressed differences in status among the royalty and lesser elites while legitimizing their respective levels of power among one another and with non-elites.

In describing the monumental architecture at Comalcalco, George Andrews (1975) proposed the popular

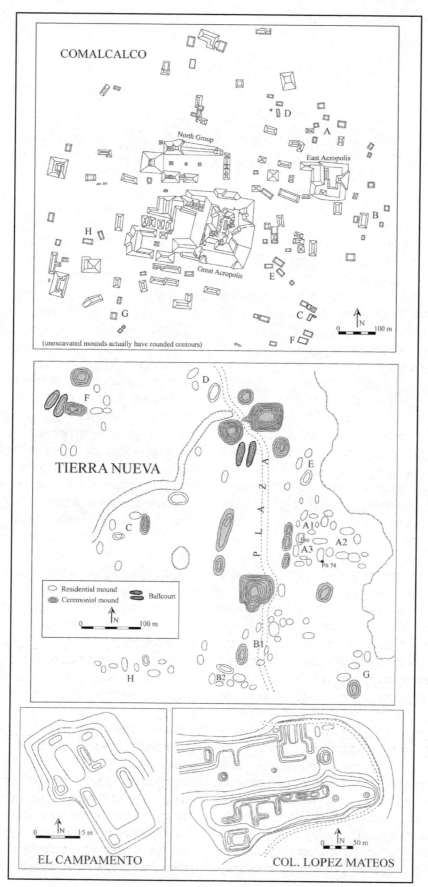

Figure 9.4. Comparisons of Late Classic site structures in the Western Chontalpa. Prepared by the author.

understanding that the architecture and stucco masks indicated a provincial tributary center for Palenque. Epigraphic translations have since provided a more detailed understanding of Comalcalco noble relations to other Maya centers, indicating ancestral identities with nobility at Tortuguero, which in turn emphasized ancestral identities with Palenque (Arellano 2006; Bíró 2011, 2012; Zender 1988). A practice-agency perspective instead suggests that whatever groups the Comalcalco royalty originated from, they used a Maya identity. They used the sensationalist public spaces at triadic configurations, the plaza, iconography, and language to negotiate vertical power within the local state while also establishing and maintaining alliances with other Maya royalty. In this perspective, Comalcalco need not be envisioned as under Palenque's, or even Tortuguero's, rule.

Classes at ILC

Previously presented class interpretations (Ensor 2013b, 2016a, 2017e; Ensor, Herrera Escobar, and Tun Ayora 2012) are expanded upon here. How to envision and categorize social classes is first discussed. Classes are defined by their *relationships* to production activities rather than on the distribution of exchange, "luxury," or "status" goods, which tend to obfuscate distinctions. Once classes are independently defined, however, the distributions of items used in symbolic displays can be explained through practice and agency perspectives on status and identities within and across classes.

Social Classification

One approach to defining classes is through direct historical analogy but this has two problems. First, archaeology does not contribute to the interpretations, instead consuming, projecting, and reifying an untested continuity that could be problematic—an example of "ethnological tyranny" (Ensor 2013b, 2013c, 2016b; 2017e; Maclachlan and Keegan 1990; Wobst 1978). Second, the Spanish descriptions of Maya classes were the same for practically all cultures they encountered across the Americas, which better reflects feudal Iberia than Mesoamerica (Sturtevant 1998:138–139). For these reasons, classes are best defined through archaeological means. Yet, there are different taxonomical philosophies behind approaches to define classes in Mesoamerican archaeology, which are often at odds with one another. The most common approach is based on income or wealth—a Weberian perspective masking social relationships between classes—that leads to analyses of luxury goods, foods, imports, grave accompaniments, and other traits to define classes (e.g., Charlton and Nichols 1992; A. Chase 1992; D. Chase 1992; Grove and Gillespie 1992; Haller, Feinman, and Nicholas 2006; Haviland and Moholy-Nagy 1992; Kowalewski, Feinman, and Laura Finsten 1992; Pendergast 1992; Robin and others 2014; Scherer, Wright, and Yoder 2007). Marcus (1992) correctly points out that this is a projection of contemporary North American ideology that also obscures relations of production today.

The production of different commodities has also served as a basis for class distinctions (e.g., Chase and Chase 1992). However, different commodities may be produced by the same classes with the same interclass relations (Marcus 1992). In addition, production and consumption of the same commodities may occur in different intensities across households of different classes, indicating "integration" but also obscuring class distinctions (Chase and Chase 2014; Haines, Feinman, and Nicholas 2004; Robin and others 2014). The questions should be what social relations of production took place, not simply what specific commodities were being produced. However, viewing only two classes—appropriators and the exploited (e.g., Marcus 1992)—also tells us little about the different elites and the different commoners, not to mention intra-class status and identity differences, which have multiple interrelationships (e.g., Aoyama 2007; Inomata and others 2002) in addition to varied domestic and craft producing roles. To be explicit, a political economic perspective on classes is used here: basing classification upon *relationships* in production, not on what was produced or how many "luxury" items were consumed (e.g., Ensor 2000, 2017b).

Identity Negotiation and Symbolic Display

Rather than indicators of "luxury" traits to define classes or, worse, as "ethnic markers," the distributions of symbolic display items are instead viewed here as reflecting the manipulation of identities. Through repetitive daily uses (practice), symbolic displays of homogeneous material culture may promote unity within and across classes for a mutual sense of community but also an important tool for elite power. These may link people to only a class or to local, regional, or international multiclass communities. Symbolic displays are also materialized expressions of differentiation, as argued previously for triadic or quadratic public spaces manipulated by royalty versus more private residential ancestor ceremonies of lesser elites. Therefore, the objective is to identify how materials were used to promote unity and differentiation across classes, and how they may have been used to negotiate prestige or rank identities within classes.

Material traits used in this sense include shell deposits, mound heights, plaster, fine paste pottery, and pottery performance characteristics. Shell deposits were valuable commodities in the tributary state economy but were instead used for nonproductive purposes to create less erodible residential mounds from earlier deposits (ancient limited resources). Exaggerated mound height investiture served no practical purpose for residential features yet symbolically differentiated residences. Architectural plasters (low and high quality) may be viewed as a material used to negotiate affiliation and differentiation. The distributions of fine paste pottery—useful only for symbolic displays primarily in serving foods—may indicate integration or differentiation with regional or interstate identities. Even the performance characteristics of utilitarian pottery can be used to infer practice-based identity—unity versus differentiation among and within classes.

Surface Collections

Before proceeding, the evidence for artifactual-based distributions of tools and the byproducts of production, and of symbolic displays need consideration. The surface collections are used for analysis because only a few features were excavated or profiled. This requires the assumption that even small surface collection yields were representative of the range of artifacts in subsurface deposits. In this study, the percentages of Formative versus Late Classic pottery from surface collections were found to be generally representative of subsurface proportions (see Chapter 8). Table 9.2 compares the percentages of Late Classic Centla, Cimatán, and fine paste pottery and the presence of chipped stone, ground stone, waterworn stone, vertebrate remains, and plaster found in surface collections with those obtained from excavations or profiles at the same features.

There are a few discrepancies. Some surface collections that yielded fewer than 10 artifacts predicted the percentages of subsurface pottery, but only in four of seven cases (57 percent). Where subsurface percentages differed significantly from surface percentages, five of nine cases involved a small-yield surface or profile collection. One reason for discrepancies may have to do with the strategy in the first season at insular sites, when only rims, bodies with decoration, or fine pastes were collected (features 35 to 100 in the table) whereas all sherds were collected in excavations or profiles. This may have increased the relative percentage of fine pastes found in those surface collections. This was not a concern for the collections at El Bellote (features 151 to 196 in the table) where all sherds were collected from surface units and where there were fewer surface-subsurface discrepancies in relative proportions of pottery.

On the more positive side, in only 4 of 15 cases (26.6 percent) did the surface collections fail to identify the *presence* of pottery types found in subsurface collections. In only one case did a surface collection fail to identify the *presence* of other materials found in subsurface deposits. This involved the abundant plaster nodules associated with the floor and floor fill of the buried structure beneath inferior mound Feature 75 that were not found in the general fill of Feature 75. In other words, the surface collections could not identify deeply buried and localized materials but did predict all cases of materials within fill deposits. As such, the Late Classic materials in the surface collections represent those in the fill deposits, which are assumed to originate from the activities at individual residences or, in the case of groups or subgroups, from the residences within them. When pooling the surface collections and the excavation or profile collections, there is greater similarity between the pottery type percentages in surface collections and excavations or profiles, though a higher percentage of Centla was obtained from the excavations compared to the surface collections. Otherwise, the pooled comparisons show predictability for subsurface pottery types and presence of other materials with the exception of the very rare items like chipped stone. The following analyses pool surface collections by class and by subclass categories.

The chipped stone, ground stone, waterworn stone, and vertebrate remains could be either Formative, Late Classic or both. Without item-by-item absolute dating there is no way to distinguish those of different periods due to the Late Classic recycling of Formative deposits. For present purposes, some of the undatable artifacts are assumed to have been Late Classic, the same assumption made in Chapter 8. This is an untested assumption but at least it allows a generalization that the reader can accept or not. In contrast, plaster, mound heights, and pottery are confidently associated with the Late Classic.

Class Interpretations

Ensor, Herrera Escobar, and Tun Ayora (2012) originally interpreted three social classes at ILC—elites, a managerial middle class, and a tributary class—when combining both production activities and the distribution of "status" items. This was revised when considering only relations of production because the consumption of goods may cross-cut classes. The resulting classes included ceremonial elites, resource-controlling elites, resource-accessing commoners, and resource-deprived commoners (Ensor 2013b).

Table 9.2. Comparison of Late Classic Pottery and Other Materials from Surface Collections and Excavations or Profiles

Feature	SURFACE COLLECTION									EXCAVATION COLLECTION								
	Pottery				Other Artifacts and Materials					Pottery				Other Artifacts and Materials				
	n	%CENT	%CIMA	%Fine	nCS	nGS	nS	nF	nP	n	%CENT	%CIMA	%Fine	nCS	nGS	nS	nF	nP
35	11	27.3	45.5	18.9	0	0	1	0	0	1305	24.3	72.7	3.0	1	0	0	0	0
40	11	9.1	9.1	72.7	0	0	0	5	1	312	17.0	45.5	2.6	3	0	0	58	26
75	96	27.1	64.6	4.2	0	0	0	0	0	1562	70.6	27.9	0.6	0	0	0	0	112
77–78	36	13.9	41.7	19.4	0	0	0	0	0	232	66.8	22.8	2.6	5	0	0	1	0
122	4	25.0	0.0	75.0	0	0	0	0	0	130	16.9	20.0	25.4	4	0	0	0	0
Pooled	158	22.8	52.5	15.2	0	0	1	5	1	3541	46.6	45.3	2.6	13	0	0	59	138

Feature	SURFACE COLLECTION									PROFILE COLLECTION								
	Pottery				Other Artifacts and Materials					Pottery				Other Artifacts and Materials				
	n	%CENT	%CIMA	%Fine	nCS	nGS	nS	nF	nP	n	%CENT	%CIMA	%Fine	nCS	nGS	nS	nF	nP
93	5	0.0	20.0	80.0	0	0	0	0	0	16	0.0	6.3	6.3	0	0	0	0	0
97	3	0.0	0.0	100	0	0	0	2	0	3	0.0	0.0	100	0	0	0	0	0
99	6	0.0	0.0	100	0	1	0	5	0	12	41.7	33.3	8.3	0	0	0	1	0
100	3	33.3	33.3	33.3	0	0	0	1	0	0	–	–	–	0	0	0	0	0
151	72	48.6	18.1	11.1	0	0	4	1	1	41	80.5	9.8	2.4	0	0	0	0	0
156	14	42.9	0.0	7.1	0	0	0	0	0	2	50.0	50.0	0.0	0	0	0	0	0
157	8	25.0	12.5	0.0	0	0	1	0	1	15	80.0	13.3	6.7	0	0	1	0	1
160	3	0.0	66.7	0.0	0	0	1	2	1	5	60.0	0.0	40.0	0	0	0	0	0
167	70	22.9	30.0	27.1	0	0	16	0	1	18	61.1	27.8	11.1	0	0	0	0	0
196–202	49	67.4	12.5	8.2	0	0	0	1	3	9	88.9	0.0	0.0	0	0	0	0	1
Pooled	233	39.9	21.8	18.5	0	1	22	12	7	121	71.1	17.4	9.9	0	0	1	1	2

Key: n = number; CENT = Centla; CIMA = Cimatán; Fine = fine paste; CS = chipped stone, GS = ground stone, S = waterworn stone, F = vertebrate remains, P = plaster

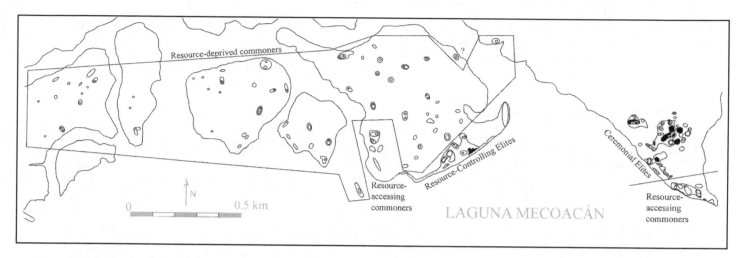

Figure 9.5. Interpreted social classes at ILC. Prepared by the author.

The ceremonial elites were not associated with large public production facilities but only with ceremonial mounds. They were considered the local nobility at ILC whose residential groups were located at El Bellote (all but the South Group). They had ceremonial mounds within residential groups characteristic of lesser elites as opposed to the public triadic or quadratic configurations distinctive of royalty. Their role in the political economy included the administration of and ideological justification for the tributary order that served their local power and that of Comalcalco's royalty.

The resource-controlling elites were represented by the South Group of Isla Chablé—another group that first occupied ILC and claimed resources in the Late Classic. Residents were associated with a ceremonial mound but also with the linear shoreline platform for collectivized fishing (Feature 92), which on one end connected to the large crushed shell deposit for collectivized shell processing (Feature 122). Their role in the political economy was to oversee collective tributary labor.

The resource-accessing commoners had residential groups associated with production activities as evidenced at the South Group of El Bellote with its fishing-related platform (Feature 176) and net sinkers in domestic contexts and the Southwest Group of Isla Chablé with its adjacent crushed shell deposit (Feature 89). Their position in the political economy granted them direct access to those resources for tributary production. Unlike these groups, Feature 77 (a residential mound-on-platform) also had an unusual amount of net sinkers in one stratigraphic context, which might suggest that a single conjugal residence (rather than an extended residential group) may have had temporary rights to access local resources.

The resource-deprived commoners, in contrast, had no features, tools, or byproducts at their residences apart from cooking (the last stage of food processing) and limited storage. They either produced nothing or they did so outside of domestic contexts, pointing toward the public collectivized activities exemplified by the shoreline platform and larger shell processing deposit. Given that those features and activities were associated with the resource-controlling elites, corvée labor is a logical inference.

Figure 9.5 illustrates the locations of the four distinguished classes. The discussion of settlement history and a comparison to Figure 9.3, suggests that (1) all four classes were present at the outset of the Late Classic occupations of ILC, with (2) some growth among the two elite classes and the two groups of resource-accessing commoners, but (3) significant growth over time among the resource-deprived commoner population.

Most Late Classic commoners at ILC differed considerably in access to resources, tools, and craft production compared to commoners elsewhere in Postclassic Mesoamerica who were able to negotiate their conditions and class-relations through production for markets (De Lucia and Overholtzer 2014; Haines, Feinman, and Nicholas 2004; Joyce and others 2014; King 2011). As a reminder, the vast majority of earthen mounds on the islands—associated with the resource-deprived commoners—had no shell, indicating they did not have rights to exploit those resources for their own benefit. Tools (chipped stone, ground stone, and waterworn stones) and byproducts (e.g., vertebrate remains), are presented in the four left columns of Table 9.3. The table clearly demonstrates disparities in tools but also in vertebrate remains among the features.

Regarding the vertebrate remains, five specimens from resource-deprived commoner contexts came from Feature 40, which was highly unusual. The conclusion is that access to tools and local resources for domestic labor in the Late Classic local community were generally denied to the resource-deprived commoners. These data suggest far more oppression in terms of economic rights compared to the Postclassic Mesoamerican cases.

The production-based relationships were characterized in the following manner (after Ensor 2013b). The resource-deprived commoners possessed no means of production other than for cooking already deboned fish, de-shelled shellfish, and other perishable foods. To meet basic needs, they were dependent on collective corvée labor controlled by the resource-controlling elites (South Group of Isla Chablé). The latter thus had power over the former. The surplus produced was undoubtedly collected as tribute (most notably in the processed construction materials but also presumably in fish and turtle) in exchange for foods, pottery, and other life-sustaining materials. The resource-accessing commoners, in contrast, had rights to their own means of production: shell to process into construction materials (Southwest Group of Isla Chablé) or fish nets and cutting tools (South Group of El Bellote) presumably also for tributary surplus production. The ceremonial elites may have directly appropriated the surplus of the resource-accessing commoners but also would have overseen transfers of surplus from the resource-controlling elites to themselves and to Comalcalco's royalty. Thus, the two commoner and two elite classes were defined by their different roles and relations in the tributary order.

Although the resource-accessing commoners at the Southwest Group of Isla Chablé processed oyster shell for crushing (and possibly for lime), there were no surface indications of plaster at those residential features, neither low- nor high-quality, which suggests that the commodities they produced were appropriated for tribute. The larger deposit of crushed shell (Feature 122) involved corvée labor yet few resource-deprived commoner residences had surface (or subsurface) evidence for plaster, and those cases always involved the poor-quality varieties. Based on the surface data in Table 9.3, the likely producers of plaster materials rarely had access to the finished product, and the few who did only had low-quality variants. Instead, the high-quality plaster was associated with ceremonial elite contexts (both at residences and ceremonial mounds) and less commonly with the resource-controlling elites and the resource-accessing commoners at the South Group of El Bellote. Plaster was appropriated from the producers but also serves as an indicator of integration and differentiation across classes.

Interclass Integration and Differentiation

As another example of how symbolic display items may cross-cut classes defined by social relations of production, the data presented in Table 9.3 indicate that fine paste types were associated with all classes at ILC, though in different percentages: very high among the resource-controlling elites (a strong display of regional identity), similar among the ceremonial elites and resource-accessing commoners, and lowest among the resource-deprived commoners. Though rare, pottery imported from farther afield was nearly exclusively associated with the ceremonial elites, yet two sherds of imported pottery were also recovered from resource-accessing commoner contexts in the South Group of El Bellote. Imported pottery is likely underrepresented for the ceremonial elite contexts. "Other" pottery consists primarily of Mecoacán but ceremonial elite contexts included more "unidentified" types, which could have been imported. Most of the identified imported pottery was Y-type (indicating connections to the Aguacatal area) and the Z-type (indicating connections to the Usumacinta region). This suggests that ceremonial elite identities were negotiated through a tapestry of regional relations and varying interstate networking. The distributions of symbolic displays show gradations in access and use rather than a basis for class definitions.

Another way to view class and access to goods is through the distribution of vessel performance characteristics. As with most utilitarian types, Cimatán pottery was dominated by cooking forms—specifically ollas—but had paste characteristics making it poorly suited for thermal contraction and expansion. Centla, also dominated by olla forms, was more technologically suitable for cooking. As indicated in Table 9.3, the proportions of Cimatán and Centla are similar within the ceremonial elite, resource-controlling elite, and resource-accessing commoner collections, though with different frequencies among them. In contrast, two-thirds of all utilitarian pottery in the resource-deprived commoner collection was of the Cimatán type, indicating that class mostly received the poor-functioning pottery for cooking. Interestingly, the resource-accessing commoners appear to have relied equally on Mecoacán (making up nearly all of the "other" pottery) and Cimatán for cooking (Table 9.3). Both commoner classes also had the highest percentages of the brittle, over-fired, poor-performing red paste variants (Table 9.3). In general, all classes defined by social relations of production shared

Table 9.3. Artifacts, Materials, and Pot Forms by Social Class, Derived from Surface Collections

Class		STONE ARTIFACTS, FAUNAL REMAINS, AND PLASTER SLABS					POTTERY											
		n Chipped stone	n Ground stone	n Waterworn stones	n Fauna	n w/ Plaster slabs*	Type	n	%	% Red	n Rims	% Serving Small	% Serving Large	% Tecomates Small	% Tecomates Large	% Ollas Small	% Ollas Large	% Jars Small	% Jars Large
Commoners: Resource–Deprived (44 collections)	Cimatán	3	0	8	9	0	Cimatán	458	67.0	76.3	147	5.4	4.1	0.0	0.0	83.7	4.8	2.0	0.0
							Centla	114	16.7	7.0	73	12.3	1.4	6.9	1.4	65.7	2.7	9.6	0.0
							Other	51	7.5	21.6	39	15.4	15.4	0.0	0.0	59.0	5.1	2.6	2.6
							Fine	61	8.9	–	18	44.4	11.1	0.0	5.6	33.3	0.0	5.6	0.0
							Import	0	0.0	–	–	–	–	–	–	–	–	–	–
Commoners: Resource–Accessing (11 collections)		2	0	3	4	2	Cimatán	15	23.8	70.6	12	0.0	0.0	0.0	0.0	91.7	8.3	0.0	0.0
							Centla	17	27.0	6.7	5	20.0	40.0	0.0	0.0	20.0	20.0	0.0	0.0
							Other	21	33.3	23.8	11	9.1	0.0	0.0	0.0	90.9	0.0	0.0	0.0
							Fine	8	12.7	–	2	50.0	0.0	0.0	0.0	50.0	0.0	0.0	0.0
							Import	2	3.2	–	0	–	–	–	–	–	–	–	–
Elites: Resource–Controlling (8 collections)		0	1	0	14	2	Cimatán	3	10.7	0.0	3	33.3	0.0	33.3	0.0	33.3	0.0	0.0	0.0
							Centla	3	10.7	0.0	2	50.0	0.0	50.0	0.0	0.0	0.0	0.0	0.0
							Other	1	3.6	0.0	1	100	0.0	0.0	0.0	0.0	0.0	0.0	0.0
							Fine	21	75.0	–	0	–	–	–	–	–	–	–	–
							Import	0	0.0	–	–	–	–	–	–	–	–	–	–
Elites: Ceremonial (28 collections)		14	9	85	108	11	Cimatán	236	30.4	19.4	25	36.0	0.0	0.0	12.0	36.0	8.0	0.0	8.0
							Centla	247	31.8	12.7	25	32.0	8.0	0.0	0.0	36.0	16.0	4.0	4.0
							Other	166	21.4	4.8	12	41.7	0.0	0.0	0.0	25.0	25.0	8.3	0.0
							Fine	107	13.8	–	14	57.1	7.1	0.0	0.0	7.1	0.0	21.4	7.1
							Import	20	2.6	–	7	85.7	14.3	–	–	–	–	–	–

Key: n = number; * = high quality plaster fragments only (see Chapter 7).

Table 9.4. Percentages of Fine Paste Pottery Types by Class, Derived from Surface Collections

Class	Fine Paste Pottery Type					Total No. of Sherds
	Comalcalco	Huimangillo	Jonuta	Paraíso	Other	
Resource-Deprived Commoners	31.1	11.5	24.6	27.9	4.9	61
Resource-Controlling Elites	38.1	4.8	33.3	9.5	14.3	21
Ceremonial Elites	20.0	6.7	38.1	23.8	11.4	105

the same poorer- and better-quality cooking vessels but the former were more concentrated among the commoner classes.

If the conditions for the resource-deprived commoners were so oppressive, then we need to make sense of their acquisition of goods like fine paste pottery (mostly serving vessels and small *ollas*) used for symbolic displays (Table 9.3). These pots were most likely acquired through elite provisioning (since they had nothing of their own to exchange, other than their labor). From an agency perspective, elite provisioning of regional fine paste pottery would strengthen vertical relations symbolically—embedding the two classes together with a common regional identity. Once possessed, such symbolic display items may also have been exchanged horizontally, as heirlooms across generations or even exchanges with other families symbolizing alliances for support or marriage, and thus integrating them with other members of their class.

Table 9.4 illustrates some class differences in the distribution of fine paste pottery. The resource-accessing commoners are excluded because the sample from those contexts is too small (only eight in total). The more local, low quality Comalcalco Fine was the most common symbolic display item among the resource-deprived commoner contexts. The resource-controlling elite contexts had the highest percentage of the poor quality Comalcalco Fine pottery. Among both classes of elites, Jonuta (from the eastern Chontalpa) was present in high percentages and was the most frequent among the ceremonial elites, suggesting a broader regional layer of relations and identity. These suggest that the resource-deprived commoners were more integrated with the resource-controlling elites than with the ceremonial elites who pursued broader relations and identities.

Internal Class Differentiation

Intraclass variation in material culture can also be interpreted through practice and agency. Feature characteristics and artifact distributions provide the basis for interpreting material negotiation of status (prestige or rank) and identities within each class.

Resource-Deprived Commoners

Residential durations are one source for viewing status among the resource-deprived commoners. If the oldest families had prestige as founding members of the class, then the multilevel mounds on platforms—indicating the longest intergenerational durations—could be viewed as markers of higher status. Support for this notion comes from feature height investitures. As indicated in Chapter 5, most of the mound heights of the inferior mounds in multilevel formations were achieved with one thick stratum to significantly increase their heights, rather than being a product of numerous sequential occupation layers. In this case, commoner agency is implied in negotiating status by investing in taller mounds than was necessary to support houses, far beyond the norm and need for residential features, even though it reduced functional space on the summits of those mounds. Those occupying multilevel mounds were inheritors of founding families' residential locations and they symbolically materialized that status distinction through mobilizing labor for, and living on, greater mound heights than most class members. Any within the class could have raised taller features at the time they established new residences and later with mounds-on-platforms, but most did not, suggesting social-symbolic differentiations were negotiated through residential feature construction.

Table 9.5 shows little difference among the residential feature types in chipped stone, waterworn stones, and fauna. These were scarce across all categories. Based on surface collections, only four residences of this class had poor-quality plaster, which did not correspond to a specific feature category or mound construction material (Table 9.3). Although possibly representing a desired architectural material, few residents of this class used plaster, possibly because whatever efforts it took them to acquire the cement was not worth the rapid decay in the poor-quality product available to them. Nevertheless, an agency perspective may

Table 9.5. Materials and Pot Forms by Feature Type: Resource–Deprived Commoners, Derived from Surface Collections

Feature Type	STONE, FAUNAL SPECIMENS, AND PLASTER				POTTERY												
	n Chipped Stone	n Waterworn Stones	n Fauna	n w/ plaster*	Type	n	%	% Red	n Rims	% Serving Small	% Serving Large	% Tecomates Small	% Tecomates Large	% Ollas Small	% Ollas Large	% Jars Small	% Jars Large
Platforms (7 collections)	0	0	5	0	Cimatán	14	40.0	28.6	9	0.0	0.0	0.0	0.0	88.9	11.1	0.0	0.0
					Centla	4	11.4	50.0	4	25.0	0.0	0.0	0.0	75.0	0.0	0.0	0.0
					Mecoacán	3	8.6	33.3	1	0.0	100.0	0.0	0.0	0.0	0.0	0.0	0.0
					Fine	14	40.0	–	1	0.0	0.0	0.0	0.0	0.0	0.0	100.0	0.0
Mounds: Earthen (14 collections)	3	2	0	0	Cimatán	28	49.1	39.3	11	9.1	0.0	0.0	0.0	63.6	9.1	18.2	0.0
					Centla	19	33.3	21.1	7	14.3	0.0	42.9	14.3	0.0	0.0	28.6	0.0
					Mecoacán	6	10.5	16.7	4	25.0	0.0	0.0	0.0	75.0	0.0	0.0	0.0
					Fine	4	7.0	–	1	100	0.0	0.0	0.0	0.0	0.0	0.0	0.0
Mounds: with Shell (8 collections)	0	2	0	1	Cimatán	1	4.3	0.0	0	–	–	–	–	–	–	–	–
					Centla	9	39.1	33.3	5	60.0	20.0	0.0	0.0	20.0	0.0	0.0	0.0
					Mecoacán	2	8.7	0.0	2	50.0	0.0	0.0	0.0	50.0	0.0	0.0	0.0
					Fine	11	47.8	–	4	75.0	0.0	0.0	0.0	25.0	0.0	0.0	0.0
Mounds-on-Platforms (20 collections)	0	1	1	1	Cimatán	53	46.9	34.0	41	9.8	7.3	0.0	0.0	75.6	7.3	0.0	0.0
					Centla	25	22.1	20.0	13	15.4	0.0	0.0	15.4	69.2	7.7	0.0	0.0
					Mecoacán	24	21.2	16.7	19	15.8	15.8	0.0	0.0	47.4	10.5	5.3	5.3
					Fine	11	9.7	–	5	40.0	0.0	0.0	20.0	40.0	0.0	0.0	0.0
Multilevel Mounds: Earthen (10 collections)	0	1	1	1	Cimatán	121	56.5	53.7	99	3.0	3.0	0.0	0.0	89.9	3.0	0.0	1.0
					Centla	58	27.1	31.0	38	5.3	0.0	2.6	7.9	84.2	0.0	0.0	0.0
					Mecoacán	22	10.3	40.9	19	0.0	5.3	0.0	0.0	94.7	0.0	0.0	0.0
					Fine	13	6.1	–	4	50.0	0.0	0.0	0.0	50.0	0.0	0.0	0.0
Multilevel Mounds with Shell (1 collection)	0	1	2	1	Cimatán	1	33.3	100.0	0	–	–	–	–	–	–	–	–
					Centla	0	0.0	–	–	–	–	–	–	–	–	–	–
					Other	0	0.0	–	–	–	–	–	–	–	–	–	–
					Fine	2	66.7	–	0	–	–	–	–	–	–	–	–

Key: n = number; * = poor quality plaster.

also consider this material an indicator of efforts by few resource-deprived commoners to differentiate themselves by emulating houses of other classes.

The sample sizes of pottery in Table 9.5 are small but some observations are useful. Most noticeably, there were higher percentages of fine pastes among the earthen platforms. Speculatively, the earthen platforms (for homes established late in the sequence) may have had higher percentages precisely because they were for newly established conjugal families. Upon marriage and establishment of a new home, these may have been gifts provisioned to them by elites. Over time, the quantity of utilitarian pottery would have increased, leading to reduced frequencies of fine paste pottery at the longer duration feature categories (mounds-on-platforms and multilevel mounds on platforms). However, this reasoning should also apply to the lower discrete earthen mounds, which are also assumed to have been established late in the settlement history.

The mounds including shell deposits were all near the elite residences of the South Group of Isla Chablé. Compared to the rest in their class, they also had higher percentages of fine pastes, just like their neighboring elites who emphasized a regional identity with the highest percentages of fine paste vessels. Interestingly, these same residences were provisioned with better performing cooking vessels compared to other resource-deprived commoners, which might indicate a special relationship to the resource-controlling elites. Yet another distinctive aspect to the pottery at the mounds with shell were much higher percentages of serving vessels—also more like elite assemblages (Table 9.5). Finally, they had rights to the less-eroding, more stable shell deposits for their residential features. Despite these differences, they remain classified here into the resource-deprived commoner class because they lacked means of production and therefore would have been just as dependent on corvée labor as the rest of that class. Yet through residential proximity, daily practice would have involved more interactions with resource-controlling elites, which might explain how they came to obtain higher percentages of fine paste vessels, more suitable cooking vessels, and shell deposits that would have reinforced commoner-elite vertical relationships through an ideology of unity masking class differences, which at the same time differentiated their identities from the rest of the resource-deprived commoners.

Resource-Accessing Commoners

Two mound groups were interpreted as belonging to this class—defined by access to local resources and production activities in special features and/or in domestic contexts associated with the groups. They differ considerably, however, in terms of status goods and pottery used in symbolic displays. The South Group of El Bellote and the Southwest Group of Isla Chablé were feature aggregates on basal platforms and were associated with production tools and features (fishing platform Feature 176 and crushed shell deposit Feature 89, respectively). This distinguished them from the resource-deprived commoners. They were not associated with ceremonial mounds, thus distinguishing them from the elite classes. Yet both groups were situated close to, but not adjacent to, elite groups. Both groups included platforms, mounds, mounds-on-platforms, and multilevel mounds, suggesting internal growth histories.

Despite these similarities there were several marked differences, as shown in Table 9.6. First, the South Group of El Bellote had access to the more stable, less-eroding shell deposits for their features, while the Southwest Group of Isla Chablé had none. Second, the surface collections indicate that the South Group at El Bellote had access to chipped stone, waterworn stones, and fauna, along with their net sinkers, while the Southwest Group of Isla Chablé did not. Third, the South Group of El Bellote was the only non-elite context to have high quality plaster for domestic architecture, while the Southwest Group of Isla Chablé had none, marking that group as more similar to the resource-deprived commoners. Fourth, the two groups' ceramic assemblages differed considerably. The surface collections from the Southwest Group of Isla Chablé, though a small sample, had high percentages of Cimatán (poor-performing cooking vessels) and more brittle, over-fired red pastes whereas the assemblage from the South Group of El Bellote had more Centla (better-performing cooking vessels). Both shared Mecoacán pottery (also with poor cooking performance characteristics yet dominated by ollas), though the South Group's "other" types also included the better-performing Orange cooking vessels. The South Group also had a modest percentage of fine paste types (symbolic display pots, emphasizing regional identity) and even a low percentage of imported types (Y and Z). The Southwest Group had no fine pastes or imports. Whereas the South Group of El Bellote shared material symbols of status and identities with elites, the Southwest Group of Isla Chablé appears to have been impoverished. The only interpretable status indicator at the Southwest Group of Isla Chablé was the height of inferior mound Feature 87, which elevated superior mound Feature 88's summit to the highest of any residential mounds at ILC. What the residents of that group lacked in tools and symbolic display pottery, they attempted to make up for in mound height.

Because neither group was associated with ceremonial mounds, neither was classed with the elites. Because neither controlled large-scale collective production facilities, neither can be considered a managerial class overseeing corvée labor. And, unlike the resource-deprived commoners, both had access to means of production. As such, they remain interpreted as two extended residential groups representing a distinct class having rights to access local resources for tributary production through their own labor yet with vastly different access to, and hence use of, materials and vessels for symbolic displays of status identities. One explanation for the difference may lie with what they had access to. The South Group of El Bellote had access to subsistence resources, while the Southwest Group of Isla Chablé only had access to shell for processing. Another piece of information that might explain the difference in status display is Feature 155 in the South Group of El Bellote.

Feature 155 was unique. Though low, it was the largest platform at ILC (except for the linear shoreline platform). Due to dense surface vegetation, the collection was limited to the eroded edge. That yielded another Late Classic net sinker, thick chunks of clay (associated with Late Classic structures), and Formative and Late Classic pottery demonstrating recycling of deposits for feature fill. There were only three Late Classic sherds—one Centla (body), one Mecoacán (body), and one Red-Paste Mecoacán rim from a small olla. Having no distinctive artifactual associations, only its morphology and size could be used to interpret its function—a platform accommodating unspecified collective activities, which may have contributed to the significant difference with the Southwest Group of Isla Chablé in symbolic display items. Perhaps the best way to perceive these two groups is that they occupied subtle differences in their relationships to production, potentially justifying splitting each into two separate classes that were still distinct from the resource-deprived commoners and the two elite classes.

Resource-Controlling Elites

This class, present at the South Group of Isla Chablé, was defined by its relationship to large collective production features. The group had one *plazuela* formed by two multi-level mounds and two mounds on the west side of its broad basal deposit (Figure 4.4). The single ceremonial mound was adjacent to this *plazuela*. Erosion and mining disturbance obscured the relationships between that subgroup and the additional mounds on the east side of the basal

platform. Regardless, the western *plazuela* subgroup was largest and formed the core extended residence within this class. It also had the only ground stone found on the islands. As stated previously, the resource-controlling elites had a high percentage of fine paste pottery (Table 9.3), indicating a more regional identity. There is, however, some internal differentiation in the distribution of fine paste sherds. Seventy-five percent came from the *plazuela* mounds, each having three to six sherds in the surface collections, compared to an average of only 1.3 from the other mounds in the group. That distribution also suggests intraclass status ranking. The mounds and the multilevel mounds of the *plazuela* had thick fill strata, which also suggests a concern for achieving unnecessary heights while other features were lower, which also suggests the materializing of intraclass status distinctions.

Ceremonial Elites

Distinctions in the materialization of status (interpreted as internal ranking) in this class is viewed through variation in numbers and sizes of ceremonial features, group basal platform materials and elevations, occupation durations, residential mound height investitures, plaster for domestic architecture, and symbolic display pottery. As indicated previously, all residential groups placed in this class were restricted to El Bellote (all but the South Group). Comparing the groups (Figures 4.5 and 4.6, Table 4.3), the Northeast Group was the largest (by number of residences and ceremonial mounds) and had the greatest investment in a basal platform, suggesting it was the highest ranking within the class. The Northwest Group was severely damaged but may have had the next largest number of residential mounds and it had the tallest extant ceremonial mound. The Central Group was likely the third largest in population, followed by the North-Central Group. The Central Group was also situated on a higher basal platform than that of the North-Central Group. In addition, the damaged ceremonial mound in the Central Group was larger than the small ceremonial mound in the North-Central Group. Thus, based on group populations and investments in basal platforms and ceremonial mounds, the sequence in intergroup hierarchy within the Ceremonial Elite Class can be interpreted (in declining order) as the Northeast, Northwest, Central, and North-Central groups.

The Northeast Group comprised two *plazuelas* incorporating residential and ceremonial mounds (Subgroups A and B), one residential-ceremonial mound pairing (Subgroup C), and additional residential mounds surrounding those subgroups (Figure 4.5). All ceremonial mounds had plaster and brick-and-mortar structural remains. High-quality plaster slabs were present in residential mounds of each subgroup (Table 9.7) indicating all had well-built dwellings, with the exception of the surrounding residences. Subgroup A had four residential mounds and three ceremonial mounds, including the suspected tallest temple (Charnay 1888; Blom and La Farge 1926; Berlin 1953b; and Stirling 1957). These features surrounded a small plaza space forming a *plazuela*. All three ceremonial mounds and the two largest residential mounds were constructed of the more stable shell and earth deposits whereas the others were of sediments only, suggesting later additions and possibly internal extended family ranking. Regardless, the subgroup's residences found in association with the most numerous ceremonial mounds suggest a high rank compared to other subgroups.

Subgroup A shared the same tall basal shell-and-earth platform as Subgroup C, the latter having only one residential mound paired with the tallest extant ceremonial mound in the group, which suggests a separate but also high-ranking nuclear family residence. Subgroup B formed another *plazuela*. It was situated on a low earthen basal platform, included six residential mounds (all earthen) and one ceremonial mound (with Feature 196, the vaulted substructure). The use of earthen deposits for the basal platform, set well below that of subgroups A and C, suggests that Subgroup B was an extended residential group that had been added to the Northeast Group. These attributes, combined with the low ceremonial to residential mound ratio, suggest a lower ranking for Subgroup B within the Northeast group. Three additional residences were located outside the subgroups but were still spatially aggregated with the Northeast Group (features 186, 193, and 203/204). These were situated on the low edges of the group adjacent to the mangrove, were not spatially incorporated into subgroups, lacked ceremonial features, and lacked plaster in domestic architecture, all of which suggests a lower rank than others within the Northeast group.

Supporting evidence for this internal ranking at the Northeast Group are the greater associations of chipped and ground stone, waterworn stones, and vertebrate remains at subgroups A and C. In addition to marking themselves with the largest ceremonial mounds, highest ceremonial-residential mound ratio, use of stable shell deposits, and literal placement above the rest on the highest platform, those of the highest rank (subgroups A and C) had greater access to and use of productive domestic tools (Table 9.7).

There were also differences in pottery types. Subgroups A and C had similar percentages of Cimatán, Centla, other (mostly Mecoacán and Orange), fine pastes, and imported pottery whereas Subgroup B had a very high percentage of Centla, low percentages of Cimatán, other (all Mecoacán), and fine pastes but no Orange or imported types (Table 9.7). Meanwhile, the mounds not affiliated with a subgroup had the highest percentage of the poorly functioning Cimatán. Another difference was that vessels were mostly for serving purposes at subgroups A and C whereas most were for cooking purposes at Subgroup B (Table 9.7).

Though severely damaged on the south side of its low basal platform where residential mounds may have been removed, the Northwest Group had three extant residential mounds and a large ceremonial multilevel mound. The features indicate residence by an extended family or lineage. The multilevel ceremonial mound with a ramp extending from the superior mound to the flat inferior mound's summit was the largest extant ceremonial feature at ILC, suggesting that, although of a lower rank than the Northeast Group, this elite group materially competed for a high-ranking identity within the class. Possible indications of internal ranking include the residential mound size differences (Figure 4.5, Table 4.3) and the distribution of plaster, which was found only at the taller residential mound.

The surface collections at the Northwest, North-Central, and Central groups (Table 9.7) yielded similar quantities of chipped stone, ground stone, waterworn stones, and fauna, which suggests that they conducted similar domestic activities and had similar access to tools and resources. Each had high-quality plastered architecture. There were, however, some differences in pottery frequencies among them. The Northwest Group had more Mecoacán and Orange than the more common Centla and Cimatán. This difference could be interpreted as symbolic display of distinctive relationships and identities.

This discussion on intraclass differentiation should be concluded with one final observation. As stated, there were no imported types among the areas occupied by resource-controlling elites, which suggests an emphasis on regional identity through fine paste types only. There were differences among the ceremonial elite groups in types Y and Z (from the Laguna de Términos and Usumacinta regions, respectively) (Table 9.7). Both were only present at Subgroup A in the Northeast Group and in the Central Group. The Northwest Group had only type Y. Subgroup C and the North-Central Group had only type Z. Subgroup B had neither. This variation suggests differentiation in terms of elite interstate relationships, identities, and social memories as embodied in vessels.

Table 9.6. Materials and Pot Forms by Feature Type: Resource–Accessing Commoners, Derived from Surface Collections

| Group | STONE ARTIFACTS, FAUNAL SPECIMENS, AND PLASTER SLABS | | | | | POTTERY | | | | | | | | | | | | |
	n Chipped stone	n Ground stone	n Waterworn Stones	n Fauna	w/ Plaster slabs*	Type	n	%	% Red	n Rims	% Serving Small	% Serving Large	% Tecomates Small	% Tecomates Large	% Ollas Small	% Ollas Large	% Jars Small	% Jars Large
Southeast Group, Isla Chablé (4 collections)	0	0	0	0	0	Cimatán	14	58.3	85.7	12	0.0	0.0	0.0	0.0	91.7	8.3	0.0	0.0
						Centla	2	8.3	0.0	2	50.0	0.0	0.0	0.0	50.0	0.0	0.0	0.0
						Mecoacán	8	33.3	50.0	8	0.0	0.0	0.0	0.0	100.0	0.0	0.0	0.0
						Fine	0	0.0	–	–	–	–	–	–	–	–	–	–
						Import	0	0.0	–	–	–	–	–	–	–	–	–	–
South Group, El Bellote (7 collections)	3	0	2	1	2	Cimatán	1	2.3	0.0	0	–	–	–	–	–	–	–	–
						Centla	17	39.5	5.9	1	0.0	0.0	0.0	0.0	0.0	100.0	0.0	0.0
						Other	15	34.9	6.7	3	33.3	0.0	0.0	0.0	66.7	0.0	0.0	0.0
						Fine	8	18.6	–	1	0.0	–	–	–	100.0	0.0	–	–
						Import	2	4.7	–	0	–	–	–	–	–	–	–	–

Key: n = number; * = high quality plaster fragments only.

Table 9.7. Materials and Pot Forms by Group: Ceremonial Elites, Derived from Surface Collections

| Group | STONE ARTIFACTS, FAUNAL SPECIMENS, AND PLASTER SLABS | | | | | POTTERY | | | | | | | | | | | | |
	n Chipped stone	n Ground stone	n Stones	n Fauna	w/ Plaster slabs	Type	n	%	% Red	n Rims	% Serving Small	% Serving Large	% Tecomates Small	% Tecomates Large	% Ollas Small	% Ollas Large	% Jars Small	% Jars Large
Northeast: Subgroup A (6 collections)	2	3	16	68	3	Cimatán	76	34.7	10.5	12	0.0	33.3	0.0	8.3	25.0	16.7	0.0	16.7
						Centla	47	21.5	21.3	2	50.0	50.0	0.0	0.0	0.0	0.0	0.0	0.0
						Other	41	18.7	0.0	3	33.3	0.0	0.0	0.0	0.0	66.7	0.0	0.0
						Fine	35	16.0	–	3	66.7	0.0	0.0	0.0	0.0	0.0	0.0	0.0
						Import	19	8.7	–	3	100.0	0.0	0.0	0.0	0.0	0.0	0.0	0.0
Northeast: Subgroup B (6 collections)	0	0	0	4	3	Cimatán	22	17.1	18.2	2	0.0	0.0	0.0	50.0	50.0	0.0	0.0	0.0
						Centla	88	68.2	5.7	7	14.3	0.0	0.0	0.0	57.1	14.3	0.0	14.3
						Other	6	4.7	50.0	0	–	–	–	–	–	–	–	–
						Fine	13	10.1	–	0	–	–	–	–	–	–	–	–
						Import	0	0.0	–	–	–	–	–	–	–	–	–	–

continued

Table 9.7. (continued)

| Group | STONE ARTIFACTS, FAUNAL SPECIMENS, AND PLASTER SLABS | | | | | POTTERY | | | | | | | | | | | | |
	n Chipped stone	n Ground stone	n Stones	n Fauna	w/ Plaster slabs	Type	n	%	% Red	n Rims	% Serving Small	% Serving Large	% Tecomates Small	% Tecomates Large	% Ollas Small	% Ollas Large	% Jars Small	% Jars Large
Northeast: Subgroup C (2 collections)	1	3	8	23	1	Cimatán	38	35.2	31.6	8	37.5	0.0	0.0	0.0	62.5	0.0	0.0	0.0
						Centla	17	15.7	29.4	2	0.0	0.0	0.0	0.0	100.0	0.0	0.0	0.0
						Other	26	24.1	15.4	3	33.3	0.0	0.0	0.0	66.7	0.0	0.0	0.0
						Fine	15	13.9	–	4	50.0	0.0	0.0	0.0	25.0	0.0	0.0	25.0
						Import	12	11.1	–	1	100.0	0.0	0.0	0.0	0.0	0.0	0.0	0.0
Northeast: Surrounding Mounds (2 collections)	0	2	2	0	0	Cimatán	17	50.0	17.6	1	0.0	100.0	0.0	0.0	0.0	0.0	0.0	0.0
						Centla	5	14.7	0.0	0	–	–	–	–	–	–	–	–
						Other	5	14.7	0.0	1	0.0	–	0.0	0.0	0.0	100.0	0.0	0.0
						Fine	6	17.7	–	0	–	–	–	–	–	–	–	–
						Import	1	2.9	–	0	–	–	–	–	–	–	–	–
Northwest (3 collections)	1	0	9	2	2	Cimatán	2	9.5	0.0	0	–	–	–	–	–	–	–	–
						Centla	3	14.3	0.0	2	50.0	0.0	0.0	0.0	0.0	50.0	0.0	0.0
						Other	10	47.6	0.0	3	33.3	0.0	0.0	0.0	33.3	33.3	0.0	0.0
						Fine	2	9.5	–	1	100.0	0.0	0.0	0.0	–	0.0	0.0	0.0
						Import	4	19.1	–	0	–	–	–	–	–	–	–	–
North–Central (3 collections)	2	1	6	3	1	Cimatán	23	33.8	21.7	0	–	–	–	–	–	–	–	–
						Centla	28	41.2	14.3	3	0.0	0.0	0.0	0.0	33.3	33.3	33.3	0.0
						Other	10	14.7	0.0	1	0.0	0.0	0.0	0.0	100.0	0.0	0.0	0.0
						Fine	5	7.4	–	1	100.0	0.0	0.0	0.0	0.0	0.0	0.0	0.0
						Import	2	2.9	–	1	0.0	100.0	–	–	–	–	–	–
Central (6 collections)	2	1	38	8	4	Cimatán	53	22.9	18.9	2	0.0	0.0	0.0	50.0	0.0	50.0	0.0	0.0
						Centla	60	25.9	10.0	8	37.5	50.0	0.0	0.0	12.5	0.0	0.0	0.0
						Other	66	28.5	1.5	2	100.0	0.0	0.0	0.0	0.0	0.0	0.0	0.0
						Fine	28	12.1	–	5	2	50.0	0.0	0.0	0.0	0.0	0.0	50.0
						Import	25	10.8	–	2	2	0.0	0.0	0.0	0.0	0.0	0.0	0.0

Key: n = number

KINSHIP, IDENTITIES, AND SOCIAL MEMORY

Kinship involves political economic relationships that influence the most important memberships, identities, alliances, and gender relations (Collier and Yanagisako 1987; Coehlo de Souza 2012; Dousset 2012; Dube 1997; Ellison 2009; Feinberg and Ottenheimer 2001; Friedman 1984; Godelier 1984; Hutchinson 1996; Mahalem de Lima 2014; McKnight 2004; Modjeska 1982; Moore 1988; Peletz 1995; Peregrine 2001; Sahlins 2013; Stone 2010; Tsing and Yanagisako 1983; Turner 2012). Archaeological kinship research can contribute long-term perspectives on social and subjective "relationality," identities, material embodiment, practice, and social memory (Ensor 2011b, 2013a, 2017d, 2018a; Ensor, Irish, and Keegan 2017; Johnson and Paul 2016; Keegan 1992, 2009, 2011; Morsink 2013; Souvatzi 2008, 2017). This section expands upon prior interpretations of Late Classic kinship at ILC (Ensor 2013b, 2016b, 2017d, 2017e; Ensor, Herrera Escobar, and Tun Ayora 2012) and introduces interpretations for the broader Western Chontalpa.

Approaches and Problems

Ancient Maya kinship has been approached through many perspectives (for a history see Ensor 2013b). Historical linguistics places modern/historic kinship terms into phylogenetic and unilinear evolutionary models to interpret ancient terminology, which then relies on structural functionalist assumptions to link those to social organization and marriage (e.g., Borodatora and Kozhanovskaya 1999; Hage 2003; Humberto Ruz 1997). Historic names and kinship terms were projected into antiquity and used for structural functionalist interpretations (e.g., Beals 1932; Eggan 1934; Roys 1940; Tozzer 1907). Ethnohistoric direct historical analogy uses multiple Maya societies to make normative generalizations (e.g., Gillespie 2000; Hopkins 1988; Izquierdo y De la Cueva 2004; Nutini 1961) or projects empirical observations based on specific historic communities (e.g., Haviland 1970a, 1970b, 1972, 1973; Thompson 1978; Witschey 1991). Twentieth-century ethnographic interpretations inform direct historical analogy (e.g., Holland 1964; Kintz 2004). Ethnographic analogy with other world regions also influenced interpretations (e.g., Carmack 1981; Fox 1987; Fox, Wallace, and Brown 1992). The same Classic epigraphic ruler successions informed competing interpretations (e.g., Haviland 1977; Thompson 1982; Joyce 1981). Inferences based on logic using archaeological settlement patterns were also common (e.g., Ashmore 1981; Becquelin 2002; Brainerd 1956; Bullard 1960; de Montmollin 1995;

Haviland 1963; Michels 1979; Sanders 1989; Voorhies 1972; Willey and Bullard 1956). Biocultural research is more limited due to intra- and intersite sample issues (Tiesler and Cucina 2012). More recently, there is a trend toward simply assuming *a priori* a lineage or a "house" model and then interpreting material culture accordingly (e.g., Hageman 2004; Hendon 2007; Hutson, Magnoni, and Stanton 2004; Joyce 2000b, 2007; McAnany 1995).

Problems with these approaches were described elsewhere (Ensor 2013b). Many assume universal Maya kinship terms and systems despite widespread differences. The structural functionalist leaps from kin terminology to social organization and marriage are untested, dubious, or otherwise problematic. Direct historical analogies, especially those that combine different Maya societies of different periods and places, assume static uniformity despite depopulations, dramatic colonial reorganizations, and equally profound postcolonial transformations (see also Haviland 1970a, 1972). Many assume one model for disparate classes when state political economies produce different class conditions and practices. Many analogies are inappropriate. Ethnological tyranny—the use of untested or problematic ethnohistoric and ethnographic ideas for archaeological interpretation—occurs with historical analogy and a priori assumptions. When inferring kinship from settlement patterns many of the interpretations are based on tradition of use rather than tested assumptions.

In addition, although internal variation is more common, typological normative models are often employed in the historical linguistic, naming or kin term, and archaeological approaches (Watanabe 2004). Typological assumptions are made on what kinship should be in chiefdoms versus states and "unitary" versus segmentary states when there exist no such correlations (e.g., Chase and Chase 1992; Sanders 1992) . Lineage versus "house" debates have led to the use of trait lists for interpreting kinship but those lists are never exclusive to any particular practice. Ancestor veneration (e.g., McAnany 1995), corporate property, group names and identities, exogamy, rank, and shrines (e.g., Hageman 2004) are not exclusive to lineages just as estates, heirlooms, and rebuilt dwellings (e.g., Gillespie 2000; Joyce 2000b, 2007) are not exclusive to "houses". Kinship cannot be approached through preconceived models, analogies, types, or laundry lists.

Mid-Level Theory

Because archeologists cannot observe behaviors, they need mid-level theories to link specific empirical patterns in material culture to specific practices (Trigger 2006).

Mid-level theories are independent of high-level models on how things are and how they change, and they allow archaeologists to avoid ethnological tyranny. They may be derived from logic (untested but seemingly persuasive), analogy, or cross-cultural ethnology. Direct historical analogy is problematic for assuming continuity rather than testing for continuity or change. Ethnographic analogy problematically assumes that one or few similarities equates to similarities in all behaviors. In contrast, cross-cultural ethnology provides *tested generalizations* that are more safely applied for *empirical analysis* of material culture (Peregrine 1996). The stronger the cross-cultural correlation between one specific material pattern and one specific practice, the greater the confidence in the mid-level inference (Ember and Ember 1995). In addition, empirical applications enable inference on variation in behaviors, thus avoiding typological perspectives. Different dimensions of kinship—descent, residence, marriage, etc.—need to be analyzed separately for any given ethnographic or archaeological community in order to observe the specific combinations of practices and how these differ among variably situated actors within their historically contingent contexts. Very strong cross-cultural correlations have produced reliable mid-level theories that archaeologists would be wise to use in empirical analyses if they ever hope to understand social relationships.

Beginning with residence, there are very strong cross-cultural correlations between dwelling patterns and residential groups. Ember (1973) first confirmed that conjugal family dwellings in patrilocal residential groups almost always had interior floor sizes less than 550 to 600 square feet and that dwellings for matrilocal residential groups were much larger (inclusive of interior conjugal family or storage spaces). The correlations were tested by Divale (1977), in Brown's (1987) intense scrutiny of cross-cultural data and methods, and by Porčić (2010) in using a different regression approach. Repeatedly, the cross-cultural pattern was supported except for some foraging societies. Removing ephemeral architecture from foraging societies, and noble palaces from states, results in cut offs of less than 43 square meters for conjugal family dwellings and 80 square meters or larger for matrilocal dwellings (Ensor 2013a). However, small dwellings are not exclusive to patrilocal residential groups. They also occur with bilocality, neolocality, ambilocality, virilocality, and avunculocality. Their spatial arrangements are key to distinguishing the practices (Ensor 2013a). Patrilocal residential groups are cross-culturally associated with conjugal family dwellings surrounding, and with entries facing, a small plaza—the *plazuela* ("patio group" or "courtyard") configuration that some Mayanists correctly associated with patrilocality through direct historical analogy (Haviland 1968; Rice and Puleston 1981; Sanders 1981). Yet this is not a "Maya" pattern, per se, but a cross-cultural pattern (Ensor 2013b:77). In contrast, bilocal and ambilocal residential groups are cross-culturally associated with unplanned, informal aggregations of conjugal family dwellings. Neolocality, in turn, is indicated by haphazardly dispersed conjugal family dwellings. The different organizations of residential space reproduce relatedness and identities through daily practice (Souvatzi 2008, 2017).

Residential groups are usually not the same as corporate kin groups, but the former implies the latter (Ensor 2013a). Matrilocality reproduces the membership (inclusive of rights, obligations, and "mutuality of being" [Sahlins 2013]) of corporate matrilineal extended families by keeping together sisters and, if large, their female matrilineal parallel cousins—the women through whom membership is passed—along with their children (the future of the corporate matrilineal family). Married men are dispersed to reproduce their wives' corporate matrilineal families using their wives' corporate group's resources, alongside unrelated men—the husbands of their wives' sisters. Patrilocality reproduces the corporate membership of corporate patrilineal extended families (sometimes confused with patrilineages in Mayanist literature) by keeping together brothers and, if large, their male patrilineal parallel cousins—the men through whom membership is passed—along with their children (the future of the corporate patrilineal family). Women who are dispersed after marriage either remain members of their patrilineal groups or, under extreme gender inequality, become members and subjects of their husbands' descent groups in order to reproduce the next generation of their husbands' groups (Ensor, Irish, and Keegan 2017). Only with bilocality (i.e., Lévi-Strauss' "houses" [1982:163–187; 1987])—are the residential and corporate kin groups one and the same because membership to the latter is through negotiated residence (Ensor 2013a:15–16). That is unique. Also unique is that any bilaterally based claims can be used to negotiate one's membership in corporate bilocal groups (presenting alternative opportunities while dividing loyalties), yet there are cross-cultural tendencies for patrilineal/patrilocal ideals associated with bilocality. Neolocality is the most common practice for Western societies, which has led to the West's naturalizing and universalizing beliefs on "family," the belief that kinship is biological relatedness (and hence that conjugal families are "nuclear"), and the difficulties for Westerners to understand other kinship systems. It is associated with populations who do not own productive resources and therefore base their survival on serfdom or wage labor (Ensor 2013b; Szołtysek 2015). With neolocality, there are no corporate groups because there are no estates, and the miniature residential group is impermanent, forming and dissolving within members' lifetimes. These differences should highlight the importance of distinguishing residential groups.

Mid-level distinctions for material patterns and corporate descent groups versus bilateral descent are also well-tested cross-culturally. Chang's (1958) world-wide study of non-Western agricultural villages demonstrated that (1) settlements for unilineal descent groups *always* had residential areas surrounding a large plaza and/or ceremonial structures, (2) settlements for multiple descent groups nearly always had segments—multiple aggregated residential groups—that spatially distinguished descent groups, and (3) bilateral descent was *never* associated with those community patterns but instead with haphazard arrangements of residential group locations or a dispersed *ranchería* settlement pattern. My cross-cultural study on 62 American cultures confirmed those mid-level associations: (1) settlements for exogamous unilineal descent groups were always planned (as per Chang) and (2) 97 percent of societies with bilateral descent had unplanned settlements or a *ranchería* settlement pattern (Ensor 2003a).

Although descent cannot be predicted from residence, a combination of a unilineal descent group community pattern with patrilocal dwelling arrangements unquestionably indicates a corporate patrilineal descent group. Likewise, a unilineal descent group community pattern combined with the large dwellings for matrilocal residential groups indicates a corporate matrilineal descent group. Bilateral descent, in contrast, can be combined with matrilocality, patrilocality, bilocality, and neolocality. Unlike corporate unilineal descent groups that can comprise hundreds of members (sharing rights, obligations, and "mutuality of being"), there are no analogous corporate kin groups above the corporate families with bilateral descent, only negotiable kindred and affinal networks of relations producing varied opportunities but divided loyalties (Ensor 2013a).

Identifying the strong cross-cultural indicators of corporate descent groups versus bilateral descent also has implications on safely inferring marriage practices. Unilineal descent groups *must be* exogamous to reproduce the principle upon which membership (conferring rights, obligations, and identities) is based (Fox 1967; Lévi-Strauss 1965, 1969). So the identification of a matrilineage or

patrilineage indicates alliances that link the exogamous corporate group to others (at the same settlement or elsewhere). Bilateral descent, in contrast, is always associated with "complex" marriage systems where there are no group-based prescriptions or proscriptions (Fox 1967; Lévi-Strauss 1969). Rather, individual-based taboos against culturally defined "close" biological relations results in potentially random marital alliances. Spouse pools could come from within a settlement or beyond. The former is favored to maintain local community control over resources while the latter is favored for alliances to gain access to resources elsewhere by casting bilateral networks across local communities. The "complex" system is the most common in Western societies, but it is only one practice and should not be naturalized or universalized. Moreover, marriage alliances are always associated with the production and exchange of material goods, which enables interpretations of marital alliances through exchange patterns (Fox 1967:175–239; Lévi-Strauss 1965, 1969; Mauss 1967; Rosman and Rubel 1971Abbott 2000; Douglas 2000; Ensor 2013a:230–231; Habicht-Mauche 2000). That some traded vessels or consumables at ILC must have been derived through marital alliances cannot be ignored. Speculation only enters the equation when trying to identify *which* items were obtained through those alliances versus other kinds of exchange.

Kinship at ILC

Late Classic kinship at ILC varied by class (Ensor 2013b, 2016b, 2017d, 2017e; Ensor, Herrera Escobar, and Tun Ayora 2012). The two elite classes practiced patrilineal descent with patrilocality and virilocality. The resource-accessing commoners used bilateral descent and practiced bilocality. The resource-deprived commoners emphasized bilateral descent and neolocality.

To begin, the residential features supported conjugal family dwellings and their distributions were determined by social factors. None of the residential platforms and mounds were large enough for matrilocal dwellings. Each could only accommodate a single conjugal family dwelling and all observed floors were small. Landform homogeneity across the mangrove formations permitted people to aggregate or not, in any way or anywhere they wished. This indicates that the community patterns were clearly guided by social factors. All extant features were constructed during the Late Classic, indicating that the residence distributions are products of social relations in that period.

The resource-deprived commoners clearly had a *ranchería* community pattern (Figure 9.5) indicative of bilateral descent. Though few multilevel mounds had more than one superior mound—indicating very small extended residences—the vast majority were neolocal. This mid-level interpretation based on strong cross-cultural correlations makes sense in light of the lack of production tools and features at those residences. Neolocality is associated with populations that lack means of production. The implications are that, upon marriage, some junior men and women replaced their parents at their natal locations while most would have established new neolocal residences elsewhere on the islands. Assuming class endogamy, their complex marital alliances could have been with any other resource-deprived commoners at ILC. The paucity of fine paste vessels (tables 9.2 and 9.3) might indicate that those items were provisioned by elites, probably rarely, and possibly for important occasions such as marriages. Once obtained, they could have been used with kin, exchanged through marital alliances, or even handed down to kin. As such, they were imbued with both vertical and kin-based histories (social memories) in addition to an elite-provided regional cultural identity.

The resource-accessing commoners had aggregated residential features, indicative of extended residential groups. This comes as no surprise since the class had access to resources, which are always associated with the formation of extended corporate groups in the absence of capitalism's private property. At both the Southwest Group of Isla Chablé and the South Group of El Bellote, there was no formal layout. The residential features were haphazardly clustered together (figures 4.4, 4.6, and 9.5), which matches the strong cross-cultural indicator for bilocal residential groups. The cross-cultural implications are that the corporate group memberships were defined by residence negotiated through affinal or bilateral descent claims but that members also had rights through those relations with other corporate groups, thus providing multiple avenues of opportunities while dividing loyalties. Given the larger size and accumulated "status" indicators at the South Group of El Bellote compared with that of the Southwest Group of Isla Chablé (Table 9.5), the former (speculatively) may have been more successful at attracting members and maintaining loyalties than the latter. The combination of bilocality and bilateral descent implies a complex marriage strategy. The South Group of El Bellote also had greater access to chipped stone, waterworn stones, Orange-type pottery (uncommon at ILC), and Y-type pottery (with coastal origins further east). If obtained through community-exogamous marital alliances, then their kin-based histories were enmeshed with broader regional identities.

The resource-controlling elites, with their residential groups and estate (including the shoreline platform and larger shell crushing location), exhibit the cross-cultural pattern for a small patrilineage. There was at least one *plazuela* on the west side of its basal platform (Figure 4.4). Although somewhat obscured by disturbance, the residential features on the east side of the platform may have formed a second *plazuela*. As an aggregate, these indicate a segment cross-culturally associated with unilineal descent groups. The *plazuela(s)*—cross-culturally associated with patrilocal residential groups—indicate an exogamous patrilineage. The implications are that memberships to the corporate patrilineal extended families at the smaller scale and to the patrilineage at the larger scale were through the localized men. Married women of the corporate group would have dispersed to their husbands' estates together with unrelated women, or, if under extreme gender inequality, also became members and subjects of their husband's corporate groups. The unrelated women residing at the South Group would have come from other corporate groups, either remaining members of those groups or becoming members and subjects of the men of the South Group. The paucity of chipped stone and ground stone, along with the lack of imported pottery other than regional fine pastes (Table 9.2), suggests more localized marital alliances (unless obtained through other exchanges). The exogamous marriages could have been with members of other elite groups within the local community or at Comalcalco. Although only one piece of ground stone was found, associating it with the Late Classic would also suggest access to grains meaning at least one (marital?) exchange relationship with a levee group at Comalcalco.

The four groups of the ceremonial elite class at El Bellote (Northeast, Northwest, North-Central, and Central) also represent distinct segments within ILC. They vary in size and spatial layouts. The Central Group was badly disturbed. No interpretations are offered other than as an unspecified extended residential group, and therefore some type of extended corporate group (Ensor 2013b:105). The North-Central group involves three residential superior mounds that shared a linear inferior mound. This also indicates that there was an extended residential group adjacent to a ceremonial mound but this layout is not associated with any of the cross-cultural patterns, so it, too, remains uninterpreted (Ensor 2013b:105–106). At best, it was the estate of another unspecified extended corporate family. Both groups had chipped stone, ground stone, waterworn stones, and imported pottery (Table 9.6) that, if associated with marital exchanges, would suggest that at least some of the marriages were with groups beyond ILC, and that some of the fine paste and imported vessels were imbued with kin-based histories enmeshed with nonlocal identities. Regarding the imported pottery, the Central Group had both Y (from coastal areas east) and Z (from the Usumacinta), which suggests relations with groups in both areas, whereas the North-Central Group had fewer and only Type Z, indicative of more limited interstate kin histories embodied in those vessels.

The Northwest Group was previously not interpreted due to the extensive disturbance to the south half of the basal platform (Ensor 2013b:105). The large multilevel ceremonial mound was clearly at the center of the group with extant residential mounds on the east and north sides (Figure 4.5). If extending that layout to encompass the destroyed southern half of the group, then the projected pattern would correspond to that of a small lineage consisting of residences surrounding a ceremonial structure. Conjugal family dwellings not aggregated into extended residential groups but surrounding a plaza or a ceremonial structure also indicate descent groups combined with virilocality or avunculocality, whereby conjugal families reside at the husband's patrilineage's or matrilineage's location. The pattern also implies identity with that larger scale of corporate group rather than with sublineage unilineal extended families (Ensor 2013a, 2013d, 2017b). Unlike the well-tested mid-level theories in this section, this is a logic-based mid-level hypothesis supported by a few selected analogies that need more rigorous cross-cultural testing (Ensor 2017a). Because avunculocality needs association with matrilineal descent, and given the absence of that elsewhere at ILC, I offer the interpretation of virilocality with a patrilineage's location. The implications are that corporate lineage membership was through men, identity was with the lineage only (not multi-scalar), marriages were exogamous, the group's women upon marriage dispersed to other groups' estates, and the married women residing at the Northwest Group were unrelated and belonged to other corporate groups. The chipped stone, waterworn stone, fine paste pottery, and imported pottery (all of Type Y from eastern coastal areas; Table 9.6) indicate broad regional identities. If these goods were acquired through marital exchanges, it suggests that they were imbued with intra- and interstate kin-based histories.

The Northeast Group of El Bellote was the largest segment at ILC (Figure 4.5). It included two *plazuelas*, each having residential and ceremonial mounds (subgroups A and B), one pairing of a residential and ceremonial mound (Subgroup C), and three additional residences not incorporated into those subgroups. The Northeast Group resembles a segment that cross-culturally corresponds with descent groups. The two *plazuelas* indicate patrilocality. The strongly supported mid-level theory for this pattern indicates an exogamous patrilineage. The corporate patrilineal families were ranked within the lineage. Subgroup A and C shared the same tall basal platform. Subgroup A had three ceremonial mounds, one of which was the largest at ILC before its destruction. Subgroup B, in contrast, was on a much lower earthen basal platform, had only one ceremonial mound, had only earthen deposits for residential features, and had no imported materials or pottery (Table 9.6), which were instead concentrated at subgroups A and C. Based on the duration categories for interpreting settlement history at ILC, the Subgroup B patrilocal residential group was a later addition to the lineage indicating the formation of a new, but lower ranked, patrilineal family that maintained its affiliation and identity with the local rulers of ILC rather than fissioning to establish its own corporate group. The one residence at Subgroup C and the additional residences not associated with the subgroups may reflect virilocality with the lineage location, perhaps also to maintain affiliation and identity with the ruling lineage. This suggests the negotiation of scales of membership identities: (a) with just the lineage or (b) with the lineage and sublineage patrilineal families. The implications are that memberships and identities with the most powerful group at ILC were through men. Marriages would have been exogamous to maintain those principles over the several generations the lineage was maintained. Married women of the lineage would have dispersed to reside at their elite husbands' locations along with unrelated women (barring sororal polygyny). The wives residing at the Northeast Group would have been unrelated women originating from other elite groups. Given the internal lineage ranking, we may also envision marriages with variously ranked elite groups— higher with marriages to Subgroup A and C members and lower for those of Subgroup B and the virilocal conjugal families.

A Tapestry of Kinship, Identities, Histories, Ancestors, Space, and Time

All were interwoven and embodied in Late Classic material culture at ILC. Building on the settlement history model, the local community was first occupied by elite patrilineages and bilocal resource-accessing commoners at El Bellote and southern Isla Chablé. At the same time, the first neolocal residences of the resource-deprived commoners were established on the eastern islands (Figure 9.3).

Kinship determines whether a next generation establishes new home locations, whether colonizing new territories or adding new residences adjacent to, or adjoining, natal ones (Keegan 2011). In corporate kin groups, each generation of members would be expected to reoccupy the collectively owned ancestral estate, replacing deceased members in the same homes, and, with population growth, adding new homes to the same group location. This pattern is seen in the additions to the South Group of Isla Chablé, as well as the South, Northwest, and, most remarkably, the Northeast Group of El Bellote (Figure 9.3). In contrast, with neolocality only one member of a neolocal residential group (and a spouse) would replace his or her parents at a natal residence. Other siblings and their spouses would establish new homes, explaining the greater territorial expansion over time among the resource-deprived commoners (Figure 9.3).

When considering Maya concepts of time and history, Mesoamericanists typically turn to classical archaeological research on the calendrics that are so famously recorded in stone. However, all cultures recognize multiple dimensions of time (Munn 1992), for example, cyclical or linear calendrical time, seasonal, lunar, and daily cycles establishing rhythms, capitalist clock-time to measure labor productivity (to name a recent addition), and other conceptualizations like Geertz's "static time" (Evans-Pritchard 1940; Malinowski 1927; Geertz 1973). Most relevant here is embodied "lineage time," where the ancestors and their descendants merge in both time and space (Burton 1983). Through repetitive communal group practices in ancestral spaces, living members and ancestors are joined—a kin-group "practice to collapse space-time" (Ensor 2018a). Within those singularities kin-based collective social memories (histories) are created, reproduced, and manipulated.

The residential feature duration categories, together with empirical kinship analysis, indicate that group memberships were embodied in ancestral spaces, creating social memories and reinforcing identities and relationalities through daily practice. This applies to the resource-deprived commoners who could negotiate the status of replacing their parents at natal residences or establish new residences. It applies to the corporate bilocal residential groups of the resource-accessing commoners whose successive generations occupied the same locations despite population growth, and particularly to those who

negotiated their occupation of the oldest ancestral residences. And it applies to the successive generations of members of the ranked elite lineages who expanded their populations at the same ancestral estates that included ceremonial mounds commemorating their patrilineal ancestors, and most particularly those who negotiated and embodied their rank by occupying ancestral residences within those corporate group estates. The tapestry of time, space, identities, histories, ancestries, class, and statuses can be read into ILC's kin-embodied landscape, which must have been perceived by the Late Classic community. Together with daily and seasonal cycles that established rhythms, descent time was likely far more relevant to most of the population than calendrical time (used, incidentally, to construct royal kin-based ancestral histories).

Kinship in the Broader Western Chontalpa

Less information is available for kinship analyses in other Western Chontalpa areas, but some mid-level interpretations are possible. Already described for the Comalcalco, Tierra Nueva, and Terrace Valley areas were the two elite site structure patterns. A closer look at those arrangements provide an opportunity to place the class-based kinship practices at ILC into a broader perspective.

The lack of detailed maps and dates of residential mounds around Comalcalco and the Lower Delta prevents an empirical analysis of class and kinship for the bulk of that population. Romero Rivera's (1995) and Andrews (1975) statements suggest dense rural settlement throughout the eastern levee. Gallegos Gómora (1994, 1995, 1997, 1998) reports *plazuelas*, indicating at least some patrilocal residential groups (and hence corporate patrilineal families) with access to tools and resources for their subsistence and tributary production. But informal groupings (indicating bilocality) and dispersed mounds (indicating neolocality) are also possible. Information on the distributions of residential groups to differentiate descent groups versus bilateral descent is also unavailable.

At Comalcalco's center were residences for at least two classes: the royalty in the two palace acropoli and the lesser nobility. Though few mounds have been excavated, the lower ones are interpreted here as residential mounds. One of the groups for lesser elites (Figure 9.4 Comalcalco A) is a *plazuela* including two ceremonial mounds, indicating a patrilocal residential group (and a corporate patrilineal family). Two groups approximate *plazuelas* (Figure 9.4 Comalcalco B and C), possibly indicating patrilocal residential groups (and corporate patrilineal families). Other groups were informally arranged (Figure 9.4 Comalcalco D, E, F, and G), suggesting bilocal residential groups. The implications are that some memberships of some extended groups were based on patrilineal principles and that daughters were replaced with wives, while other groups' memberships were based on residence negotiated through bilateral descent. Furthermore, apart from exogamy for the extended patrilineal families and (at least) sibling taboos among the bilocal groups, marriage alliances could be with other elite groups at Comalcalco or beyond. For access to diverse resources, alliances with elite groups at ILC would have been mutually beneficial. Because there are no cross-cultural mid-level theories to follow for palaces, I offer no interpretations on royalty other than to point out the obvious. There is one unspecified extended residential group with dwellings at the south end of the sunken plaza of the Great Acropolis (and presumably another at the East Acropolis). Epigraphic succession or marriage data may help but does not necessarily inform on social organization.

At least three classes comprised the Tierra Nueva state. Commoners were present at smaller hamlets, secondary centers, and Tierra Nueva. Sanders (1962:212) describes the most common sites as having 3 to 12 house platforms and no ceremonial mounds. Presumably these include Site 2, Cucuyulapa, El Zapotal, San Rosendo, El Chinal, and Campechito (Figure 9.1). Those "hamlets" represented extended residential groups though Sanders (1962:212) did not describe site layouts. The larger sites in this category may have had multiple residential groups. Assuming that Sanders (1962) and Piña Chan and Navarrete (1967) would have mentioned if central plazas were present, then their absence at these sites suggest bilateral descent combined with unspecified corporate extended families. Another common hamlet category described was the same but with residential platforms for elites and a pyramid or two (Sanders 1962:212). So with the exception of those elites, bilateral descent combined with unspecified corporate extended families should also characterize the commoners at sites like San Miguel, Finca Chapultepec, and Playa de Piedra (Figure 9.1). At Sigero, Sanders (1962:213) describes "some 15 to 20 low oval mounds, all less than one meter high, probably house structures, complete the surface architecture of the site." The latter were "small loosely planned clusters of two to four [mounds] that may represent extended family aggregations" (Sanders 1962:213). "Loosely planned" might suggest *plazuelas* but without clarification no interpretation is made here. For commoners, we are left with

unspecified extended residential groups for unspecified corporate families, and unknown descent.

At Tierra Nueva, only one commoner group can be identified in the southwest portion of the mapped central zone (Figure 9.4 Tierra Nueva H). That tightly packed linear cluster does not suggest a lineage. There is no formality expressed in the segment, nor were there internal *plazuelas* or large dwellings to indicate unilocality. It was a linear concentration of haphazardly arranged conjugal family dwellings suggesting one large bilocal residential group.

Lesser elites in the Tierra Nueva state were located at the hamlets with one or two ceremonial mounds, at Sigero, and at Tierra Nueva. As a generalization, Sanders (1962:212) states that one to two ceremonial mounds at those sites were associated with a large platform, "which might have been a residential platform of a local religious or political leader." At Sigero, Sanders describes a "formally oriented plaza with a pyramid on the north side seven meters high, a large residential platform to the west, which was probably the residence of the local cacique, a ball court on the east and two low platforms to the south." Again, with the available information on Sigero, all that can be concluded is that the lesser elites had extended residential groups, and thus unspecified corporate extended families.

When settlements are comprised of segments encircling a plaza or ceremonial structures, the cross-cultural correlations do not distinguish between multiple exogamous lineages versus one large exogamous clan with subclan lineages (Ensor 2013a). With this problem in mind, two alternative interpretations can be made for the elite classes at Tierra Nueva.

The first interpretation is that there were two exogamous lineages of different sizes, accompanied by multiple residential groups not forming lineages. Group A was the largest and had three subgroup *plazuelas* (Tierra Nueva A1, 2, and 3 in Figure 9.4) indicating a patrilineage. Piña Chan and Navarrete (1967:20) indicate this was the first and longest occupied sector of the site. This largest group was clearly associated with the plaza, monumental architecture, and the central ballcourt, indicating the highest ranking within the settlement, and hence a royal lineage. The implications are that membership (rights, obligations, and royal identity) was through patrilineal descent. Women members were dispersed to other groups, more likely among other centers' royalty, and the unrelated wives residing at this lineage's location were members of other groups, presumably royalty from elsewhere. The second lineage evident was Group B on the south, with two *plazuelas* (Tierra Nueva B1 and 2 in Figure 9.4) indicating a smaller patrilineage. Groups C, F, and possibly D, E, and G were separate *plazuelas* suggesting patrilocal residential groups for different exogamous patrilineal families. Group F was a *plazuela* incorporating three residences, two ceremonial mounds, and a ballcourt. Groups C and G had only one ceremonial mound each. Groups D and E had none. Though the elites of the smaller lineage and the individual patrilineal families had to have practiced exogamy, the implications are that they could have intermarried (or sought alliances with lesser elites at other settlements).

The second scenario that considers cross-cultural mid-level theory is that Tierra Nueva belonged to one exogamous clan comprising subclan lineages, which in turn comprised sublineage patrilineal families: that is, Omaha social organization (Ensor 2013a:121–122, 2013b: 39–41). Groups A, B, C, D, and E surround the central plaza, the largest monumental architecture, and the ballcourt. The largest and oldest segment—Group A—would have been the highest ranked subclan lineage comprising three sublineage patrilineal families, which suggests a "top-heavy" conical clan. Group B was the next largest subclan lineage—comprising only two sublineage patrilineal families. The other subclan segments were just patrilineal families. There were also two isolated conjugal family residences southwest of the ballcourt, which suggests virilocality with the clan's estate. Virilocality would indicate that either those families did not want to identify with a subgroup, or vice-versa. The implications are that membership and identities were negotiated among three scales: (a) with patrilineal families, lineages, and the clan; (b) with patrilineal families identifying with the clan but not with subclan lineages; and (c) virilocal conjugal families identifying with the clan but not with subclan lineages or patrilineal families. Marriages would require settlement exogamy, implying that married women members were dispersed to other settlements or states and that married women residing at Tierra Nueva were unrelated and from other settlements or states. Groups F and G could be interpreted as additional subclan extended family locations but their positioning away from the plaza and surrounding groups may also suggest they were not affiliated with the clan. If so, then the smaller concentration of ceremonial mounds and ballcourt at Group F would suggest that a much smaller exogamous patrilineal group competed with the large clan. The smaller group may have fissioned off but remained at their ancestral settlement. In either interpretation of Tierra Nueva, social organization involved patrilineal descent groups through which relationships and ranks were embodied in ancestral spaces.

GENDER AND AGE RELATIONS

In many ways, kinship is the subject of gendered strategies to form and perpetuate groups, which transcends domestic lives to maintain broader social institutions (Fox 1967; Stone 2010; Peletz 1995; Tsing and Yanagisako 1983). To approach gender without contextualizing relations within domains of kinship is to project universals onto the relationships of men, women, and others. At the same time, to ignore gendered relationships in a study of kinship is to ignore the "why," the "how," and the implications on socially constructed conditions and experiences of people. The same applies to age-set social dynamics (from children to adults), so the following develops these additional plausible implications of the kinship practices inferred in the preceding discussion, enriching the substance of those interpretations.

Humans have developed numerous ways to form social groups, which then must be perpetuated through marriages and other alliances (Fox 1967). The application of cross-culturally supported mid-level theories to ILC and the broader Western Chontalpa illustrates that the political economic conditions of different classes limited how commoners could form groups and perpetuate themselves (Ensor 2013b). For example, the resource-accessing commoners had means of production and rights to exploit resources, thus making corporate extended groups possible. Their bilocality would have offered flexibility. They could retain some natal members of any gender and recruit others of any gender through affinal and bilateral networks while negotiating the divided loyalties of individual members. Junior men and women who married needed to negotiate their group memberships. At stake was which corporate group they would belong to through residence, and all that entailed. The senior men and women heading those corporate groups had to view junior members as a means of productivity, group perpetuation, and alliances.

Without resources, by contrast, no corporate groups formed among the resource-deprived commoners, leaving only neolocal residential groups that were interrelated through networks of bilateral descent (Ensor 2013b). Though often viewed as "liberating" from the control of kin group elders, neolocality implies control by individual husbands if women's access to resources is dependent upon their husbands' labor, a different qualitative form of gender inequality.

Both elite classes at ILC had patrilineages. Patrilineal families were apparent among lesser elites at Comalcalco. Elite patrilineal families and patrilineages were obvious at Tierra Nueva, there may even have been a patriclan there. At whichever scale, the patrilineal groups restricted women's and men's membership to only their fathers' groups, making men the medium through which class, status, rights, and titles were transmitted. Elite children only belonged to their fathers' corporate groups, never their mothers', even upon death of a father. The solution to how to perpetuate the corporate patrilineal groups was patrilocality—retaining men and male children belonging to the estate while "exchanging" daughters for wives to reproduce the groups. The implications are that junior adult men resided with brothers and patrilineal male cousins of their groups at the estates they co-owned, under the authority of their group's higher-ranked and elder authorities, whereas women found themselves residing with unrelated women and reproducing the group of their husbands under the authority of that group's men. Under these conditions, enormous pressure and health risks are usually placed on wives to reproduce their husband's patrilineal groups. Cross-culturally, wives are valued by their husbands' groups, yet are a source of concern in dividing the loyalties of their husbands. This contradicts social relations that pit wives' agencies to influence their conditions against the agencies of senior men who are pressuring junior men into solidarity for the perpetuation of the patrilineal group (Stone 2010). If women's memberships were not transferred upon marriage (more common in the Americas before changes wrought by colonialism), then elite women maintained the membership and support of their own patrilineages among whom they were superior to wives (Stone 2010), which they undoubtedly exploited to their advantage. Indeed, the numerous accounts of elite Maya women engaged in high status offices or ceremonies (e.g., Josserand 2007; Joyce 2000a) could actually be images of sisters and daughters of noble groups rather than wives from other groups.

Succession does not indicate social organization, but the latter can provide structure to the former (Keegan 2006). Primogeniture is usually only a cultural preference. The only common "rule" covering all circumstances is that successors be members of the corporate group, opening the door to competition and negotiation of favor. Bilocality was exhibited among resource-accessing commoners at ILC and potentially some lesser elites at Comalcalco and Tierra Nueva. It is usually associated with patrilineal and androcentric biases (not rules) when it comes to titles

or successions for residential group leaders (Fox 1967; Keesing 1975:93–94), yet any natal or recruited loyal member could potentially become group leaders. Among the neolocal resource-deprived commoners, the only status succession would be the one sibling chosen to replace parents at an existing residence. Succession among the elite lineage members would have been altogether different. Cross-culturally, the only rule is that successors be members of the descent group, preferably within the highest ranked patrilineal family, in other words, the most direct descendants of the founding ancestors. Among the ILC elites, the individual patrilineal families were also likely internally ranked, in which case successions were needed at multiple scales. If lacking confidence in a first male born, then other patrilineal family members, men or their sisters, could potentially be candidates. In the case of women's group leadership (possibly with altered gender), they would need to separate with their husbands or transfer them to their group's estate as a compromise to maintain the rule of group member succession. Wives would be excluded from succession in their husbands' groups because that would transfer power to other groups.

In general terms, state development has long been associated with increasing gender inequality (Leacock 1972, 1978; Sacks 1975). Political centralization diminished women's status at Tikal, especially for elite women, yet possibly less so at other Maya centers (Haviland 1997). If this can be generalizable, we might expect greater gender status inequality among royalty at Comalcalco compared to ILC or the southern Mezcalapa states. When considering gender roles within the class and kinship contexts at ILC, however, gender inequality was more likely greatest among the resource-deprived commoners.

Gender roles are difficult to interpret due to the lack of archaeological contexts in the Chontalpa (e.g., burial accompaniments) and there are fewer investigations on roles in coastal settings. This circumstance necessitated the synthesis of direct historical analogy (problematic because the gender binary and gender division of labor could be Spanish perception or imposition) and analogies with agrarian Maya (e.g., Inomata and others 2002). New challenges to those models are the nuanced ways in which Mesoamerican gender, age, labor, and class intersections were manipulated in art, as well as indications of overlapping gender roles for what were long assumed to be strict gender divisions of labor (Stone 2011; Hoar 2009; King 2011).

Nevertheless, as a tentative, limited approach toward envisioning how disparate class-based kinship practices influenced men's and women's interrelationships, a direct historical binary engendered division of labor was adopted, wherein women processed food (indicated by hearths, cooking vessels, and storage vessels/features, ground stone, and faunal remains) and men fished and hunted (indicated by net sinkers, canoe landings, projectile points, and faunal remains) (Ensor 2013b). Next, the social contexts in which these took place were examined for interpretation (Ensor 2013b). Those contexts suggested that resource-deprived commoner women prepared the foods at neolocal dwellings but were dependent on their husbands' public corvée labor for access to resources—a circumstance cross-culturally associated with low status for women (Brown 1975; Brubaker 1994; Draper 1975; Ember 1983; Friedl 2004; Sacks 1975). Shellfish were apparently tributary commodities, but their harvesting could have been by men, women, or children. Despite the extended corporate residential groups among the resource-accessing commoners, women's labor was also largely restricted to conjugal family dwellings, but unlike other commoners, they sometimes engaged in collective production, thus mitigating gender inequality (Ensor 2000). They also had the support of kin within extended residences (some natal kin and others not). Men's labor also took place in domestic settings but more often collectively with other men of the group (some natal kin and others not).

Both men and women recruited through marriage would have been valued for the alliances they came with. Among the patrilineal elite, women (sisters/cousins not wives) and men likely had ceremonial roles that ideologically legitimized their power, though wives' (or servants' or slaves') domestic production was restricted to conjugal family dwellings. Sisters and patrilineal cousins may have held greater status as elders in the ceremonial affairs of their groups. The men of the resource-controlling elite patrilineage may also have overseen the corvée labor, granting them an important public role in the tributary order. This contextualizing of gender roles and contexts or scales of production by class-based kinship practices enabled a more dynamic interpretation of gender relations than normative characterizations (Ensor 2013b). Inferences on class-based masculine and feminine identities are discussed in the next section through the topic of foodways.

Through additional generalizations, some plausible inferences on class-based differences on children and childhood can be made. To do so, I apply the (1) universal condition that all infants are dependents and subordinates to adults (or youth), with (2) direct historical analogy suggesting that childcare was a female-engendered role (yet also considering a complementary role for men). Children belonged to the corporate groups. In the case of bilocal resource-accessing commoners, their biological mothers and other adult women and older siblings of the extended residential group were communal caretakers of infants and trainers of girls while all of the adult men of the group likely trained boys when they were of age. No child could become an "orphan" since they belonged to corporate groups, each with multiple care-taking adults.

In contrast, the investments in childcare and education among the neolocal resource-deprived commoners would have rested primarily on their individual biological mothers, lacking others in an immediate residential group for assistance, and frequently lacking men who labored away from homes. If a father died, as per cross-cultural generalizations, then the widowed mother would have no access to domestic resources without remarrying another corvée laborer. This made women and their children dependent on husbands' conditions. If a mother died, then the widower would need to remarry (unless children were old enough to replace the mother). If both died, then children would need to be absorbed into bilateral relatives' neolocal residences. Alternatively, elites could adopt them for servitude.

In the case of the elites, child-raising was primarily by mothers who were not members of the children's patrilineal descent groups. Though not belonging to their mothers' groups, children likely knew their mother's patrilineal relations. With an additional "Omaha" taboo on not marrying someone from the mother's group, then their interaction with the mother's group may have been guarded (e.g., non-joking relationships and avoidance). The wives of the descent groups' other men would have been socially equated as "mothers" by children and could have collectively assisted in childcare. Children's older, unmarried sisters and patrilineal cousins would also have assisted. And, we could envision senior women of the descent groups (residing elsewhere) as having a voice in the children's affairs when visiting. Again, assuming the non-overlapping gender division of labor, women collectively would have trained girls and men collectively would have trained boys. If a biological mother died, then one cross-cultural preference is the sororate to maintain the marriage alliance and replace the biological mother with the deceased mother's sister (or her socially equated patrilineal cousin). If a biological father died, then the levirate (replacement with the deceased husband's brother or socially-equated patrilineal cousin) would be the controlling elders' preference for the same reason. Because children belonged to their patrilineal families and lineages, widows or divorced women would need to remain at their former husband's estate if they wished to remain with their children (Ensor 2003b). Removing children from their descent group's estate would seem unlikely.

Ember and Cunnar (2015) provide generalizable cross-cultural inferences on play. Toys, primarily of perishable materials, are usually made by children and most play takes place away from dwellings with other children, unsupervised by adults. Playmates are almost always other children, rarely mothers and, less likely, fathers. Applying these cross-cultural generalizations to ILC, we could envision mobs of muddy children making toys of wood, grasses, and crabs in the mangrove, swimming themselves clean along shorelines, and creating life-long class- and kin-based identities. This would particularly be the case of resource-deprived commoner children who would have forged identities as bilaterally related neolocal mangrove dwellers. Children of different classes were probably segregated most of the time but interclass play, while creating local community unity would also unavoidably enculturate children into inequalities and guarded relations.

Bradley (1993) provided generalizable inferences on children's work, which is supported in another cross-cultural analysis by Ember and Cunnar (2015). Children's work is the same as adults' but boys also participate in women's work due to frequent time at home. Children also have additional tasks not done by adults like caring for small animals, though in foraging societies they do the least work. Children's subsistence work increases significantly between ages 6 and 10. Girls typically do more work than boys, especially childcare. From these, plausible inferences on children's work at ILC would include girls' enculturation into the food processing and childcare activities of adult women. Boys' work could have included small-scale fishing, short-distance canoe transport, and perhaps hunting, as well as the same work as their sisters. Shellfish harvesting and fishing would have been a tributary activity, enculturating them into those social relations of production through practice. Children's work would have differed considerably for the commoners of the interior settlements around Comalcalco and Tierra Nueva. There, girls' experiences might be similar to those at ILC, with the exception of living in extended residential groups with siblings and cousins and processing maíze. Boys' work would have been agriculturally associated, including shooing of birds (Ember and Cunnar 2015), along with hunting and turtle-raising.

Another plausibly interpreted generalization on childhood is on corporal punishment. Ember and Ember (2005) found a strong association between corporal punishment during child-raising in societies with high levels of power inequality and political integration (especially under colonialism), the use of nonrelative caretakers, or under conditions of frequent warfare. Power inequalities and political integration certainly would have characterized the Comalcalco state, and by applying the generalization, we could also envision corporal punishment in childraising in the Lower Mezcalapa.

FOODWAYS AND FEASTING

The study of foodways, ritual, and feasting in Mesoamerican scholarship is heavily influenced by indigenous and Spanish written sources (Staller 2010; Staller and Carrasco 2010); by ethnographic descriptions (Anderson 2010; Christenson 2010); and through archaeological analyses of pottery and zooarchaeological, paleobotanical, or skeletal stable isotope data (Goldstein and Hageman 2010; Straight 2017; Wendt 2010). Most commonly, these lines of investigation begin with subsistence strategies and end with interpretations of daily domestic cuisine preparation and consumption or communal feasting habits. Whereas foodways are commonly interpreted as a form of ethnic or local identity, feasting is commonly interpreted as an elite strategy to promote interclass cohesion (Herrera Flores and Marcus Götz 2014; Ochoa 2010; Staller and Carrasco 2010; Goldstein and Hageman 2010; Rosenswig 2007). Food and feasts justified social order, expressed identity, involved tribute, and marked the passing of seasonal time (Staller 2010:63). Feasting is also interpreted as a practice promoting horizontal cohesion through the production of shared identities and may be linked to ancestors and spirits or deities in the reproduction of collective memories (e.g., Straight 2017; Twiss 2007; Wendt 2010; Anderson 2010; Christenson 2010; LeCount 2010).

The sources of data for inferences—ethnographic, epigraphic or iconographic, and archaeological—influence how foodways and feasting are interpreted. Ethnographic accounts of the Maya are more often normative and emphasize horizontal cohesion due to the lack of class-based differentiation and relations because the ethnographic communities are *milpa*-owning peasant households from the same class and local community observed (e.g., Anderson 2010; Christenson 2010; Tuxill and others 2010). Social differentiation is usually limited to gender, for example, reproducing complementarity among men who get or grow food away from the household and women who process food into cultural forms at the household (e.g.,

O'Connor 2010). Gendered foodways in iconography, for example, men providing raw materials that women process into cultural materials in the home (e.g., Joyce and others 1993), are images from elite perspectives that also result in a normative perspective if not contextualized by class.

Archaeologists deal with all social segments in states and need to contend with classes as well as gender and intraclass horizontal relations in foodways and feasts. Not accepting the basic premise of the elite feast-sponsoring perspective on interclass cohesion, Freidel and Reilly (2010) argue that commoner food producers were not duped into granting elite power over them simply through religious ideological justifications and sponsored feasts but, rather, that elites' basis of power involved administrative control over the food the commoners produced and consumed. Though they emphasize late market systems, the salient point is that elites intervened in and appropriated foodways and feasting that helped to create social memories, collective identities, and gendered ideologies among commoners. The challenge in this section is to interpret the intersection of horizontal and vertical relations (e.g., Joyce and Henderson 2007) in the production of identities and collective memories through foodways and feasting at ILC and the broader Western Chontalpa.

Foodways

Foodways at ILC cannot be approached through agrarian comparisons and must consider a broader range of available materials (e.g., Goldstein and Hageman 2010; Parsons 2010). In addition to the local shellfish surrounding ILC, the wide range of foods from the mangroves, marshes, beach ridge, and closest levees were all accessible through short forays by *cayucos* or larger canoes. As indicated in Chapter 6, the only cooking vessels identified were ollas, wide-mouthed *tecomates*, and perhaps tall bowls, which suggests that their cuisine emphasized stews and possible tamales (see Ochoa 2010 for Gulf Coast examples), which would have been served primarily in dishes and bowls. Stew ingredients could have included wild plants, oysters and other shellfish, boney and cartilaginous fishes, turtles, and crocodile meat. Less commonly, these also could have been roasted without pottery and served in leaves or, for some but not most people, in shells. Turtles deserve some special mention. Their capture or breeding, their importance as a prehispanic food item, and their place in iconography indicate a pan-Chontalpan identity that was as important to inland populations as maize (Guevara Chumacero et al. 2017). This was also likely the case for those at ILC. Overlapping that broader, shared regional layer of

identity was the non-agrarian, predominantly aquatic emphasis in ingredients and coastal stews that distinguished the ILC in foods, place, and identity from their interior counterparts.

Maintaining the same interpreted gender division of labor, men of the resource-accessing commoners forayed for fishing and other purposes but transferred their acquisitions to women at residences. Those women (who may also have grown produce in small domestic gardens) processed those aquatic resources into the culturally patterned cuisine, thus completing the gender complementarity and gendered identities analogous to agrarian peasants (Joyce and others 1993; O'Connor 2010). Their tributary food surplus was produced without elite intervention into those gendered relations.

In contrast, the men and older boys of the resource-deprived commoner class were involved in the collective procuring, hunting, and fishing away from homes. These activities were overseen and controlled by elites who were also appropriating tributary surplus. Elites granted those men their gendered subsistence tasks but oversaw and hence denied some female-oriented food processing tasks such as milling and deboning or shucking. The same may have been the case for any women's foraging. Elites granted women and older girls of the resource-deprived commoners access to the ingredients obtained by men (and potentially women), in addition to any provisioned nonlocal ingredients (e.g., maíze or finished *nixtamal* for tamales). Moreover, elites provisioned those women mostly with Cimatán cooking vessels and the highest percentages of brittle red pastes, which were prone to failure (Table 9.2), for their gendered transformation of foods into cultural cuisine at dwellings. The gender complementarity, cultural cuisine, and shared foodway-based identities of the resource-deprived commoners were conditioned by the tributary-based intervention of elites.

Among the resource-controlling elites, men and boys had male-gendered roles in the acquisition of foods, but only as overseers of other men's labor. As such, men's foodways involved the appropriation of masculinity. However, the presence of faunal remains at dwellings suggest that women and girls controlled the entire range of feminine domestic transformations of foods into cultural cuisine. Moreover, the presence of ground stone suggests that female-gendered activity extended to processing maize, thus sharing in the broader Mesoamerican feminine practice.

Among the ceremonial elites, men and older boys were even further removed from masculinity in foodways as mere collectors of tribute. Women and girls, like their counterparts among the resource-accessing commoners and resource-controlling elites, were involved in the full range of feminine local and broader transformations of food materials into cultural cuisine. Though cuisine was the same across classes at ILC, thus creating a layer of common local identity, the layers of gendered identities through foodways varied by class. Masculine surplus products were appropriated by elite men who did not directly engage in masculine foodways and who limited the range of feminine foodways among women of the resource-deprived commoners.

How the classes consumed stews also varied. Table 9.2 indicates the differences in the percentages of cooking and serving vessels among the resource-deprived commoners and the ceremonial elites (the two classes with sufficient numbers for comparison). There were high percentages of serving vessels in ceremonial elite contexts and low percentages among resource-deprived commoner contexts. This may suggest that the latter more often ate out of perishable materials (e.g., gourds, wooden bowls, or leaves) or out of the cooking vessels themselves than out of ceramic serving vessels. The only resource-deprived commoners with some high percentages of serving vessels were those living at mounds with shell adjacent to the resource-controlling elites at Isla Chablé (Table 9.3), who in other ways also emulated their neighboring elites to differentiate themselves from the rest of their class. These differences suggest class-based etiquettes in eating, despite sharing the same cuisine, which would have created another dimension to identities through foodway practices.

More distinctions can be made based on serving vessels. For all classes, these included the fine paste vessels (Table 9.2) that, through practice, reinforced Chontalpan identities. For the ceremonial elites, eating stews from serving vessels involved not only identifying with the region through fine paste dishes and bowls, but also with imports emphasizing more distant relations and interstate identities (Table 9.2), which varied by patrilineal group (Table 9.6).

The NWAF investigations were oriented toward culture historical questions, so there are no intrasite group contexts for comparison (Piña Chan and Navarrette 1967). The described pottery at Tierra Nueva was all from Pit 74, which was associated with one of the *plazuelas* (A3) within the royal lineage's estate (Figure 9.4). The pottery types correspond to the Late Classic. The majority of vessels were of coarse pastes, which included ollas and deep bowls for cooking stews and *tamales*, and dishes and shallow bowls (referred to as "bowls and plates" by the authors) for serving wet foods. Except for some small ollas, most of the

highly decorated fine paste vessels were for serving—dishes and shallow bowls and "vases" or "cups" (Piña Chan and Navarrette 1967:23–25). There were no plates (in the classification used herein), nor were there *comales* for making tortillas. So, despite the agrarian subsistence orientation, the Tierra Nueva nobility mostly consumed stews, likely including turtle and possibly tamales—the regional cuisine—frequently using fine paste serving vessels that also expressed regional identity. Unless servants transformed the appropriated ingredients into that cultural cuisine, then the wives of the noble lineage participated in that feminine practice. The noble men would have either appropriated the masculine roles through oversight of commoner labor or were not involved in those masculine food-acquiring activities.

At Sigero, one of the secondary settlements in the Tierra Nueva state, Sanders (1962:213) indicates that one low mound (test-excavated with a trench) demonstrated a residential function. It appears that most of the sherds collected from the site came from that context (Piña Chan and Navarrette 1967:32). Unclear, however, is whether the residential mound was associated with the plaza and pyramid area or in one of the other mound clusters farther away, so no class contextualization is possible. Most pottery consisted of coarse paste ollas, along with some *tecomates* and some plates (in this case, conforming with plates used herein) whereas the majority of fine paste pots were bowls and dishes (Piña Chan and Navarrette 1967:33–34). These also suggest an emphasis on stews served in dishes and bowls, except for the rare plates for dry foods. The pottery from San Miguel and San Fernando—tertiary sites in the settlement hierarchy having few ceremonial mounds—similarly indicate that stews were served in bowls and dishes (Piña Chan and Navarrette 1967:8–10, 12–15). At a minimum, the information available from secondary and tertiary sites in the Tierra Nueva kingdom also illustrates participation in Mezcalapa-wide cuisine that was consumed by elites in regional fine paste vessels, which through practice provided a layer of Chontalpa identity.

The ceramic data for the Terrace Valley state is even more limited and lacks site distinctions (Piña Chan and Navarrette 1967:39–41). Ollas were dominant forms among coarse paste types, which suggests use for stews and tamales. Both coarse paste and highly decorated fine paste dishes and bowls were present, which also suggest wet food consumption. One notable difference in cuisine are *comales* reported from Chintul, but those are likely Postclassic in date (Piña Chan and Navarrette 1967:42-43).

No ceramic drinking containers were found at ILC. In the Comalcalco and Tierra Nueva states, vases were reported from nobility and lesser elite contexts (Piña Chan and Navarrette 1967). This may suggest more restricted access and thus a practice distinguishing elites from others. For most of the population in the Western Chontalpa, however, perishable containers or dippers may have been used for liquid consumption (e.g., from cultivated gourds or skins/organs of terrestrial animals). Such items could have been another item of tribute from interior populations.

Feasting and Food Sharing

Hayden (2014) makes the following cross-cultural points about feasts and food sharing. Though feasts can be classified by different criteria, the most productive approach for archaeologists is by the groups having them rather than by types of events. They are always held to create social bonds rather than to exclude and differentiate. They are always held to attract people to get something in return. Surplus is necessary and, for aggrandizers or elites, they require controlling ever-increasing surplus production through competition. With states, there were royal feasts in courts for networking and alliance-building, elite-sponsored religious festivals, and feasts for elite corporate descent groups. To Hayden's descriptions, we can add commoner feasting, which might better fall under the rubric of "food sharing," involving less surplus, fewer people involved, and domestic rather than public contexts. The vocabulary of reciprocity is prominent in prehispanic Mesoamerica (Speal 2014). Most importantly, horizontal food sharing establishes alliances and reciprocity that archaeologists can infer through material remains.

The large plazas of Comalcalco and Tierra Nueva were likely locations for major public feasts sponsored (after taking tributary surplus) by royalty for vertical social cohesion (Goldstein and Hageman 2010; Herrera Flores and Markus Götz 2014; Rosenswig 2007). There were no such spaces or features at ILC. Any commoners from ILC or from the Comalcalco levee hinterland likely attended feasts at Comalcalco.

Elite-exclusive feasting was also likely common for alliance-building. Royalty at Comalcalco likely hosted inter-elite feasts in exclusive palace settings. The vases reported for the Tierra Nueva state could have been used in food sharing episodes, as these were almost always of highly decorated fine paste types used for symbolic display (Piña Chan and Navarrette 1967). The local ILC elites focused on their own ancestors by incorporating ceremonial mounds within their individual group estates.

Their feasts, along with those of lesser elites at Comalcalco, Tierra Nueva, and elsewhere in the Western Chontalpa, were probably associated with individual patrilineal descent group ancestor ceremonies in nonpublic spaces. From a cross-cultural perspective, inter-elite feasting would have provided a source of competition to demonstrate relative status, ability to accumulate surplus, and to create alliances. In this sense, they would have created unifying identities among elites while creating collective and intergroup memories (Anderson 2010; Christenson 2010; LeCount 2010; Straight 2017; Twiss 2017; Wendt 2010). They were class-exclusive, in contrast with the large public feasts sponsored by royalty (those not directly involved in appropriating surplus from commoners) that were designed for vertical social cohesion.

Large cooking and serving vessels can be used as indicators of surplus food preparation for food sharing or feasts (Straight 2017; Wendt 2010). For the present purposes, food sharing—whether for special events or not—is defined as communal consumption involving any number of people beyond conjugal family members. The vessel size distinctions made in Chapter 6 are used for inferring food sharing at ILC. As Table 9.2 indicates, all classes had higher percentages of small ollas for cooking. However, larger vessels were present from which one can infer that larger quantities of foods were prepared. As indicated by Straight (2017), larger cooking vessels for feasting events should be lower in frequency because they are used less frequently. Following this logic, the classes with higher frequencies of large vessels—though low relative to small vessels—should indicate more frequent cooking of large batches of food. The same assumptions are made for small (individual) versus large (communal) serving dishes. Comparisons are made for the ceremonial elite and resource-deprived commoner contexts since those surface collections are larger.

The ceremonial elite contexts had more numerous and higher percentages of large ollas compared to commoner contexts (Table 9.2), indicating more frequent cooking for food sharing. Within the Northeast Group, Subgroup A had the highest percentages of large cooking vessels (Table 9.6)—the context for the highest ranked patrilineal family within the patrilineage. Although a small sample, there were also high percentages at the Northwest Group, which suggests that the patrilineal group may also have cooked in large batches more frequently than others. Continuing with the inferences on gender roles, wives more frequently cooked for the feasts of their husbands' elite patrilineal groups compared to other women at ILC (unless by servants), particularly for the higher ranked elite groups. Those large cooking vessels were all of utilitarian types. The tables also indicate fewer and lower percentages of large serving vessels among the ceremonial elites, which suggests that foods served communally were less common but present. After cooking in large vessels, food could have been consumed in individual serving vessels or presented in the communal but transferred to the individual for consumption. Unlike the cooking vessels, many of the large and small serving vessels were of fine paste and imported types signifying symbolic display during both routine and food sharing events.

In resource-deprived commoner contexts, there was less frequent cooking of large batches of food, which is indicated by lower percentages of large cooking vessels (all utilitarian types) compared to elite contexts (Table 9.2). The percentages of large communal serving vessels, however, suggests the opposite—that food sharing was not uncommon. A speculative interpretation may reconcile the difference: although food sharing was not infrequent, many women among the resource-deprived commoners made do with smaller cooking vessels to prepare those meals. Although the vast majority of serving vessels were of utilitarian types, the most common use of fine pastes was for serving, signifying symbolic display that would be most effective at expressing unifying identities. As entertained with the ceremonial elites, serving could have involved using the communal vessels for presentation and transferring contents to individual vessels for consumption.

If feasting was related to status among the resource-deprived commoners, then there should be greater percentages of large cooking and serving vessels at the elite-emulating residences with shell deposits and at the multilevel mounds, which were built as symbolic display with excess labor investiture. This, however, is not the case. Instead, the most frequent large cooking and serving vessels were associated with the mounds-on-platforms (Table 9.3). A speculative interpretation is that each person replacing their parents' platform emphasized their higher status vis-à-vis other siblings by investing both in mound construction over the platform and more food sharing. Those living at the mounds adjacent to the South Group and those at multilevel mounds were already more established in terms of status within the class.

SYNOPSIS

ILC's Early Classic occupation hiatus and settlement growth in the Late Classic appears to have been part of a broader Chontalpa pattern. The Late Classic material culture at ILC, and throughout the Western Chontalpa, suggests strong intraregional integration, sharing only with Southern Veracruz that which was also common to the Maya macroregion. The settlement distributions along the Late Classic Mezcalapa indicated three states. The Comalcalco state had one enormous capital, only one secondary center (ILC), and numerous smaller settlements. Comalcalco's lower levee in the coastal transition zone enabled tributary surplus from environmentally diverse areas and access to both coastal and river exchange. The Tierra Nueva kingdom had a more dendritic solar settlement pattern but with homogeneous resources, lacking some tributary surplus available to Comalcalco, and only had access to river trade. The congested Terrace Valley kingdom on the narrow valley floodplains and adjacent hills also had a homogeneous resource base but with access to terrace hunting. It had a two-tier settlement hierarchy with three compact centers for competing or allied elites and numerous commoner settlements.

The three states were based on tributary class relations among royalty, lesser elites, and commoners. The royalty at Comalcalco and at Tierra Nueva—both at primary centers within their respective states—built primarily pan-Gulf Coast quadradic plaza configurations (also shared with the Terrace Valley state, though those were more "Maya" in style), but Comalcalco also invested in Maya triadic temple/palace configurations. The quadratic and triadic configurations reinforced vertical social ties through spectacular public events, legitimated ancestry and identity with other Maya nobility, and expressed distinctions with lesser elites. Lesser elites were only permitted to materialize their group ancestral linkages by incorporating ceremonial mounds within their less-public residential spaces. At secondary centers like ILC, only the lesser elite pattern was practiced.

The analysis of classes at ILC was based on relations of production in the tributary order rather than on the distribution of "luxury goods," which tends to obfuscate distinctions because they cross-cut classes and instead serve as integrative media for local, regional, and interregional identities through practice. Four classes were distinguished at ILC. Resource-deprived commoners lacked productive tools or resources at residences and were dependent on corvée labor overseen by the resource-controlling elites. Resource-accessing commoners were granted rights to exploit local resources. And Ceremonial elites served as the local nobility who lacked roles in production but oversaw the flow of tributary commodities to Comalcalco. Based on the distribution of residences by duration category, all four classes were established early in the settlement history at El Bellote and southern Isla Chablé but expanded in population over time, with the resource-deprived commoners eventually occupying spaces across the islands.

Material displays of status identities overlapped classes. High quality plaster was found among the residences of both elite classes and one group of resource-accessing commoners. Fine paste pottery—mostly for serving vessels—was found at residences of all classes. It was, however, more common at the residences of resource-controlling elites and resource-deprived commoners, which suggests that strong vertical and horizontal regional identities were shared among those directly engaged in corvée relations. In contrast, both fine paste pottery and pottery from other regions were emphasized among the ceremonial elites, which suggests that more widespread horizontal identities and social memories were embodied in their vessels. Though the poorly performing Cimatán and over-fired red paste cooking vessels were present across all class contexts, their percentages were highest among the residences of resource-deprived commoners. Finally, the more stable shell deposits, which contained commodities for construction materials, were untapped resources when used for residential mound construction and can thus also be viewed as material symbols of status. These were common for the residences of all classes except for the majority of features associated with resource-deprived commoners.

Internal class differentiation in status negotiation was also apparent through symbolic material displays. Though impractically reducing the functional space of residential mound summits, only the oldest residential groups among the resource-deprived commoners invested labor in tall constructions, which would have materially accentuated their status vis-à-vis newer residential groups of their class. Some of the longest-occupied residential mounds were constructed with shell and earth deposits, also signifying a higher status within the class. Only four residences of the resource-deprived commoners had access to the plaster they processed collectively. Those cases involved only poor-quality materials yet may reflect agency to emulate elite architecture. Fine pastes were more common at the latest resource-deprived commoner residences, possibly due to elite provisioning at the time new residences or marriages were established. Overall percentages of fine pastes declined, as only utilitarian vessels were provisioned afterward. They were also more common at the commoners' residences that were adjacent to the resource-controlling elites, possibly from elite gifting due to spatial proximity, more intimate social integration

with, and emulation of that elite class. Status distinctions within the resource-controlling elite class were evident through mound heights and higher percentages of fine paste pottery at the western *plazuela* of the South Group of Isla Chablé. Among the ceremonial elites, status distinctions were evident through ceremonial-to-residential mound ratios in addition to ceremonial mound sizes. The local nobility at the Northeast Group of El Bellote also had internal ranking, which is evident through those ratios but also through basal platform heights and the presence of imported pottery. The latter varied in origins among the different groups of the ceremonial elites and within the Northeast Group, which suggests variation in regional and interregional relations, identities, and social memories embodied in imported vessels.

Rather than interpreting kinship through faulty direct historical analogy, other analogies, trait lists, or simply assuming a model and interpreting material culture accordingly, empirical analysis relied on cross-culturally-tested, generalizable mid-level theories on residential patterns. The resource-deprived commoners—like most populations lacking means of production cross-culturally—emphasized neolocality and bilateral descent. Neolocality also explained this class's expansion across the islands. Only one sibling could negotiate remaining at parents' residence while others needed to initiate new residences upon marriage. Rather than corporate groups, they had bilateral networks of kindred relations cross-cutting the neolocal residential groups. In contrast, through rights to resources the resource-accessing commoners established corporate extended residences that conformed with the cross-cultural pattern for bilocality. The implications are that membership to those corporate groups were negotiated using bilateral descent and affinal relations, which expands opportunities and identities but divides loyalties. Both classes of elites had local groups that conformed with the cross-cultural pattern for patrilocality, and, for some, patrilineages that practiced patrilocality and/or virilocality. The implications are that membership to the patrilineal families or larger lineages was through men who were localized whereas sisters were dispersed and replaced with recruited wives (nonmembers) to perpetuate the groups. Assuming some of the pottery used for symbolic display was obtained through affinal relations, the different distributions of regional and imported vessels suggests that there were varied marital alliances with elite groups at Comalcalco and beyond. The residences and estates were the material embodiments of status, group ancestry, time, and social memory written across the ILC landscape.

Lesser elite residential groups at Comalcalco and Tierra Nueva also exhibited patrilocality, though some had bilocality, indicating patrilineal and bilateral descent strategies for forming corporate elite groups. Although no interpretations were made for Comalcalco's royalty, those at Tierra Nueva formed a patrilineage with three sublineage patrilineal families whose estate included the public plaza and surrounding monumental architecture. Alternatively, the settlement belonged to a patriclan comprised of the royal lineage (the oldest segment), smaller lineages, multiple patrilineal families, and possible virilocal conjugal families, suggesting negotiated identities with the just the clan, with a lineage and the clan, or with patrilineal families and the clan. There was little information available for interpreting the kinship practices of other classes beyond ILC, yet patrilineal corporate organization was clearly the dominant pattern among elites in the Western Chontalpa.

Gender relations varied through kinship practices associated with the disparate class conditions. Because the resource-deprived commoners at ILC lacked rights to resources, men were dependent on corvée labor and, given neolocality, wives and mothers were dependent on being married and thus on their husbands for access to materials for their interpreted gender roles. Among the resource-accessing commoners, who had rights to exploit resources and could form extended bilocal corporate groups, junior men and women were likely valued and controlled for both labor and reproduction. Though placing greater demands on women, whose labor was mostly associated with private domestic contexts, women had kin both within and beyond their residential groups. Among both elite classes, and among the other patrilineal elite groups in the Western Chontalpa, wives likely found themselves laboring for and reproducing their husbands' and children's groups to which they did not belong and with unrelated women. At their husbands' and children's estates, high ranking elders valued them for reproducing the groups, but they were likely sources of conflicts for elders seeking junior men's solidarity over loyalty to wives. If their memberships were not transferred upon marriage, elite women could have retained rights and responsibilities, even in ceremonies, with their own patrilineal groups, despite patrilocality.

Childcare would have been the responsibility of mothers and older girls, men likely trained and socialized older boys, and play would have socialized children into their local and class identities. Among the resource-deprived commoners at ILC, neolocality would suggest dependence on biological mothers and older sisters. Because they lacked resource rights, both women and children were dependent on husbands' corvée labor. Among the resource-accessing commoners and both elite classes, the extended corporate groups would have provided a means for collective childcare with group rights to resources for those purposes. Based on cross-cultural patterns, young girls and boys would have assisted with women's roles in domestic settings but only girls would continue those into their youth and adulthood, as boys would have been trained into their roles by the men of their corporate group or by their biological fathers in the case of the resource-deprived commoners. Play—cross-culturally common away from home and unattended by adults—would have forged life-long relationships as bilaterally related people of the swamps among the resource-deprived commoner children, while occasional interclass play enculturated them into their class position.

Foodways provide additional insights into regional, local, class, and gendered identities. Ingredients like turtles and maíze were aspects of a broader Chontalpan identity. Though cuisine involved turtle, stews, and possibly tamales across the Western Chontalpa, the diverse coastal ingredients differentiated ILC's inhabitants from their interior counterparts. Masculine roles included obtaining ingredients whereas feminine roles transformed them into cultural cuisine. For resource-deprived commoners, men's roles in foodways were dependent on their relationship to the resource-controlling elite men who appropriated masculinity. The relationship with those elites also denied commoner women some of the feminine food processing characteristic of all other classes, and those commoner women were disproportionately burdened with cooking vessels that would have been prone to failure. Ceremonial elite men, in contrast, had little to do with masculine food acquisition. Consumption also differed among the classes: ceremonial elites more frequently ate from serving vessels compared to resource-deprived commoners. Most fine paste vessels were serving containers, which would have created unifying identities with social memories embodied in those vessels through horizontal food-sharing. For resource-deprived commoners, this would have included their relationship to the elites who provisioned those vessels. The ceremonial elites ate from the same vessels, but also had access to imported vessels through which they would have created broader identities and social memories. Though with more terrestrial and river ingredients, the cooking and serving vessels in the Tierra Nueva and Terrace Valley states also suggest that they were used for stews. Potentially, they had similar engendered roles in foodways including the appropriation of masculinity by elite men.

Only royalty would have provided public feasts for social cohesion as they were the only ones associated with the large public spaces at Comalcalco, Tierra Nueva, and the three elite contexts in the Terrace Valley state. Elites at those sites and at secondary centers like ILC engaged in class-exclusive, patrilineal group-sponsored ceremonies and feasting in their residential spaces, thus creating alliances and social memories with other elites. Elite wives or their servants at ILC cooked large batches of food more often than women of the resource-deprived commoners. This suggests that elites had more frequent feasting and food-sharing events. Resource-deprived commoner women relied on smaller cooking vessels for food-sharing events. Large communal serving dishes were present among both classes, but smaller vessels were more common, which suggests that food-sharing involved transferring contents to vessels for individual consumption. Only elite contexts were associated with vases, though there were none at ILC, which suggests that drinking from ceramic containers (possibly for cacao) was restricted only to the highest-ranking classes in Western Chontalpa kingdoms.

References Cited

Abbott, David R.
2000   *Ceramics and Community Organization among the Hohokam*. University of Arizona Press, Tucson.

Alejos García, José O.
2006   Identidad Maya y globalización. *Estudios de cultura Maya* 27:57–71.
2009   Los Itzaes y el discurso conservacionista. *Estudios de cultura Maya* 33:159–177.

Álvarez A, Carlos, and Luis Casasola
1985   *Las figurillas de Jonuta, Tabasco*. Universidad Nacional Autónoma de México, México, DF.

Alvarez Aguilar, L. F., M. Guadalupe Landa, and J. L. Romero Rivera
1992   Los ladrillos decorados de Comalcalco, Tabasco. In *Comalcalco*, edited by Elizabeth Mejía Pérez Campos and Lorena Mirambell Silva, pp. 239–251. Instituto Nacional de Antropología e Historia, México, DF.

Anderson, David G., and Kenneth E. Sassaman
2012   *Recent Developments in Southeastern Archaeology: From Colonization to Complexity*. Society for American Archaeology, Washington, DC.

Anderson, Eugene N.
2010   Food and Feasting in the Zona Maya of Quintana Roo. In *Pre-columbian Foodways: Interdisciplinary Approaches to Food, Culture, and Markets in Ancient Mesoamerica*, edited by John E. Staller and Michael Carrasco, pp. 441–465. Springer, New York.

Andrews, Anthony P.
1987   Puertos costeros del postclasico temprano en el norte de Yucatan. *Estudios de cultura Maya* 11:75–93.
1990   The Role of Trading Ports in Maya Civilization. In *Vision and Revision in Maya Studies*, edited by Peter D. Harrison and Flora S. Clancy, pp. 159–167. University of New Mexico Press, Albuquerque.
2008   Facilidades portuarias Mayas. In *El territorio Maya: Memoria de la quinta Mesa Redonda de Palenque*, edited by Rodrigo Liendo Stuardo, pp. 15–40. Instituto Nacional de Antropología e Historia, México, DF.

Andrews, Anthony P., and J. Fernando Robles Castellanos
1985   Chichen Itzá and Cobá: An Itzá-Maya Standoff in Early Postclassic Yucatan. In *The Lowland Maya Postclassic*, edited by Arlen F. Chase and Prudence M. Rice, pp. 62–72. University of Texas Press, Austin.

Andrews, George F.
1967   *Comalcalco, Tabasco, Mexico: An Architectonic Survey*. University of Oregon Press, Eugene.
1975   *Maya Cities: Placemaking and Urbanization*. University of Oklahoma Press, Norman.
1989   *Comalcalco Tabasco, Mexico: Maya Art and Architecture*. University of Oregon Press, Eugene.

Aoyama, Kazuo
2007   Elite Artists and Craft Producers in Classic Maya Society: Lithic Evidence from Aguateca, Guatemala. *Latin American Antiquity* 18:3–26.

Arden, Traci, T. Kam Manahan, Julie K. Wesp, and Alejandra Alonso.
2010   Cloth Production and Economic Intensification in the Area Surrounding Chichen Itza. *Latin American Antiquity* 21:274–289.

Arellano, Alfonso
  2006   *Tortuguero: Una historia rescatada*. Centro de Estudios Mayas, Universidad Nacional Autónoma de México, México, DF.

Argáez, Carlos, Erasmo Batta, Josefina Mansilla, Carmen Pijoan, and Pedro Bosch
  2011   The Origin of Black Pigmentation in a Sample of Mexican Prehispanic Human Bones. *Journal of Archaeological Sciences* 38:2979–2988.

Armijo Torres, Ricardo
  1997   Proyecto Arqueológico Comalcalco 1993–1994: Avances y Propuestas. *Los investigadores de la cultura Maya* 5: 167–183.
  1999a   Nuevo hallazgo en Comalcalco, Tabasco. *Arqueología Mexicana* 7:71–72.
  1999b   Proyecto arqueológico Comalcalco, Temporada 1998: Analisis de materiales arqueologicos. Ms. on file. Centro INAH, Tabasco.

Armijo Torres, Ricardo, and R. Hernandez Sastre
  1998   La fauna arqueológica de Comalcalco: Resultados preliminares. *Los investigadores de la cultura Maya* 6:120–145.

Armijo Torres, Ricardo, and Y. E. Millán Ruíz
  1995   Tecnología arquitectonica y uso de espacios en la Gran Acropolis de Comalcalco, Tabasco. Paper presented at the third International Congress of Mayanists, Chetumal.

Armijo Torres, Ricardo, Miriam J. Gallegos Gómora, and Socorro Jiménez Alvarez
  2005   La cerámica de pasta fina de Comalcalco, Tabasco y su periferia: Temporalidades y relaciones culturales. *Los investigadores de la cultura Maya* 13:189–208.

Armijo Torres, Ricardo, Miriam J. Gallegos Gómora, and Marc U. Zender
  1999   Urnas funerarias, textos históricos y ofrendas en Comalcalco. Paper presented at the IX Encuentro Internacional de Investigadores de la Cultura Maya, Campeche.

Armijo Torres, Ricardo, G. Fernández Martínez, Marc U. Zender, Miriam J. Gallegos Gómora, and A. Gómez Ortiz
  1999   Una ofrenda conmemorativa del katún 17 en Comalcalco, Tabasco. Paper presented at the third Mesa Redonda, Palenque.

Arnold, Phillip J., III
  1999   *Tecomates*, Residential Mobility, and Early Formative Occupation in Coastal Lowland Mesoamerica. In *Pottery and People: A Dynamic Interaction*, edited by James Skibo and Gary Feinman, pp. 159–170. University of Utah Press, Salt Lake City.
  2003   Early Formative Pottery from the Tuxtla Mountains and Implications for Gulf Coast Origins. *Latin American Antiquity* 14:29–46.

Arnold, Phillip J., III, and Billie J. A. Follensbee
  2015   Early Formative Anthropomorphic Figurines from La Joya, Southern Veracruz, Mexico. *Ancient Mesoamerica* 26:13–28.

Arnold, Phillip J., III, and Barbara L. Stark
  1997   Gulf Lowland Settlement in Perspective. In *Olmec to Aztec: Settlement Patterns in the Ancient Gulf Lowlands*, edited by Barbara L. Stark and Phillip J. Arnold, III, pp. 310–329. University of Arizona Press, Tucson.

Ashmore, Wendy
  1981   Some Issues of Method and Theory in Lowland Maya Settlement Archaeology. In *Lowland Maya Settlement Patterns*, edited by Wendy Ashmore, pp. 37–69. University of New Mexico Press, Albuquerque.

Ball, Joseph W., and Jennifer T. Taschek
  2003   Reconsidering the Belize Valley Preclassic: A Case for Multiethnic Interactions in the Development of a Regional Culture Tradition. *Ancient Mesoamerica* 14:179–217.
  2007   "Mixed Deposits," "Composite Complexes," or "Hybrid Assemblages?" A Fresh Reexamination of Middle Preclassic (Formative) Ceramics and Ceramic Assemblages from the Northern Maya Lowlands. In *Archaeology, Art, and Ethnogenesis: Papers in Honor of Gareth W. Lowe*, edited by Lynneth S. Lowe and Mary E. Pye, p. 173. New World Archaeology Foundation, Provo.
  2015   Ceramic History, Ceramic Change, and Architectural Sequence at Acanmul, Campeche: A Local Chronicle and Its Regional Implications. *Ancient Mesoamerica* 26:233–273.

Barrett, Jason W., and Thomas H. Guderjan
  2006   An Ancient Maya Dock and Dam at Blue Creek, Rio Hondo, Belize. *Latin American Antiquity* 17:227–239.

Beals, Ralph L.
  1932   Unilateral Organization in Mexico. *American Anthropologist* 34:467–475.

Becker, Marshall J.
  2004   Maya Heterarchy as Inferred from Classic-Period Plaza Plans. *Ancient Mesoamerica* 15:127–138.

Becquelin, Pierre
  2002   Linajes y poder político en la civilización Puuc: El ejemplo de la región de Xculoc. *Estudios de cultura Maya* 22:113–123.

Berlin, Heinrich
1953a   *Archeological Reconnaissance in Tabasco.* Current Reports No. 7. Department of Archaeology, Carnegie Institution of Washington, Washington, D. C.
1953b   Tabasco and Campeche [Report on Progress in Archeology]. *Yearbook* 52:284–287. Carnegie Institution of Washington, Washington, DC.
1954   Tabasco and Campeche [Report on Progress in Archeology]. *Yearbook* 53:293–295. Carnegie Institution of Washington, Washington, DC.
1955   Selected Pottery from Tabasco. *Notes on Middle American Archueology and Ethnography* 5-126:83–87. Carnegie Institution of Washington, Washington, DC.
1956   Late Pottery Horizons of Tabasco, Mexico. *Contributions to American Anthropology and History*, No. 59:95–153. Carnegie Institute of Washington, Washington, DC.

Binford, Lewis
1962   Archaeology as Anthropology. *American Antiquity* 28:217–225.

Bíró, Péter
2011   Politics in the Western Maya Region (I): *Ajawil/Ajawlel* and *Chʼen. Estudios de cultura Maya* 38:43–73.
2012   Politics in the Western Maya Region (II): Emblem Glyphs. *Estudios de cultura Maya* 39:31–66.

Blitz, John H.
1993   Big Pots for Big Shots: Feasting and Storage in a Mississippian Community. *American Antiquity* 58:80–96.

Blom, Frans, and Oliver La Farge
1926   *Tribes and Temples.* Tulane University, New Orleans.

Blomster, Jeffrey P.
1998   Context, Cult, and Early Formative Public Ritual in the Mixteca Alta: Analysis of a Hollow Baby Figurine From Etlatongo, Oaxaca. *Ancient Mesoamerica* 9:309–326.
2002   What and Where is Olmec Style? Regional Perspectives on Hollow Figurines in Early Formative Mesoamerica. *Ancient Mesoamerica* 13:171–195.
2009   Identity, Gender, and Power: Representational Juxtapositions in Early Formative Figurines from Oaxaca, Mexico. In *Mesoamerican Figurines: Small-Scale Indices of Large-Scale Social Phenomena*, edited by Christina T. Halperin, Katherine A. Faust, Rhonda Taube, and Aurore Giguet, pp. 119–148. University Press of Florida, Gainesville.

2010   Complexity, Interaction, and Epistemology: Mixtecs, Zapotecs, and Olmecs in Early Formative Mesoamerica. *Ancient Mesoamerica* 21:135–149.

Borodatora, Anna, and Irina Kozhanovskaya
1999   El protosistema de parentesco Maya: Tentative de reconstrucción. *Estudios de cultura Maya* 20:332–364.

Borstein, Joshua A.
2005   Epiclassic Political Organization in Southern Veracruz, Mexico: Segmentary Versus Centralized Integration. *Ancient Mesoamerica* 16:11–21.

Boucher, Sylviane
1981   Catálogo: Análisis y clasificación de la cerámica burda del lado sur, Templo III, Plaza Norte, Comalcalco. Ms. on file, Archivo del Archivo del Proyecto Arqueológico Comalcalco, Instituto Nacional de Antropología e Historia, Comalcalco.

Bradley, Candice
1993   Women's Power, Children's Labor. *Cross-Cultural Research* 27:70–96.

Brainerd, George W.
1956   Changing Living Patterns of the Yucatan Maya. *American Antiquity* 22:162–164.

Braswell, Geoffrey E., John E. Clark, Kazuo Aoyama, Heather I. McKillop, and Michael D. Glascock
2000   Determining the Geological Provenance of Obsidian Artifacts from the Maya Region: A Test of the Efficacy of Visual Sourcing. *Latin American Antiquity* 11:269–282.

Brown, Barton M.
1987   Population estimation from floor area: A Restudy of "Naroll's Constant". *Cross-Cultural Research* 21:1–49.

Brown, Judith
1975   Iroquois Women: An Ethnohistoric Note. In *Toward an Anthropology of Women*, edited by Rayna R. Reiter, pp. 235–251. Monthly Review Press, New York.

Brubaker, Pamela K.
1994   *Women Don't Count: The Challenge of Women's Poverty to Christian Ethics.* Scholar's Press, Atlanta.

Bullard, William R.
1960   Maya Settlement Pattern in Northeastern Peten, Guatemala. *American Antiquity* 25:355–372.

Burton, John
1983   Same Time, Same Space: Observations on the Morality of Kinship in Pastoral, Nilotic Societies. *Ethnology* 22:109–119.

Cabrera Bernat, Ciprián Aurelio
1997   Términos: El Territorio Perdido. In *Tabasco: Apuntes de frontera*, edited by Mario Humberto Ruz, pp. 43–55. Consejo Nacional para la Cultura y las Artes, México, DF.

Campbell, Constance E.
1996   *Forest, Field, and Factory: Changing Livelihood Strategies in Two Extractive Reserves in the Brazilian Amazon*. Ph.D. Dissertation, University of Florida, Gainesville.

Carmack, Robert M.
1981   *The Quiché Mayas of Utatlán: the Evolution of a Highland Guatemala Kingdom*. University of Oklahoma Press, Norman.

Carpenter, Lacey B., Gary M. Feinman, and Linda M. Nicholas
2012   Spindle Whorls from El Palmillo: Economic Implications. *Latin American Antiquity* 23:381–400.

Carrillo Salazar, Sonia, and Carlos González Lobo
1988   La vivienda rural en Tabasco. In *La vivienda rural en el sureste de Mexico*, edited by the Secretaría de Educación, Cultura y Recreación: Gobierno del Estado de Tabasco, pp. 58–83. Comite Regional de la Comision Nacional de los Estados Unidos Mexicanos para la UNESCO, Villahermosa.

Caso Barrera, Laura, and Mario Aliphat Fernández
2006   Cacao, Vanilla and Annatto: Three Production and Exchange Systems in the Southern Maya Lowlands, XVI–XVII Centuries. *Journal of Latin American Geography* 5:29–52.

Chang, Kwang-Chi
1958   Study of the Neolithic Social Grouping: Examples from the New World. *American Anthropologist* 60:298–334.

Charlton, Cynthia L. O.
1993   Obsidian as Jewelry: Lapidary Production in Aztec Otumba, Mexico. *Ancient Mesoamerica* 4:231–243.

Charlton, Thomas H., and Deborah L. Nichols
1992   Late Postclassic and Colonial Period Elites at Otumba, Mexico: The Archaeological Dimensions. In *Mesoamerican Elites: An Archaeological Assessment*, edited by Diane Z. Chase and Arlen F. Chase, pp. 242–258. University of Oklahoma Press, Norman.

Charnay, Desiré
1888   *The Ancient Cities of the New World* (English translation by J. Gonino and Helen S. Conant). Harper & Brothers, New York.

Chase, Arlen F.
1992   Elites and the Changing Organization of Classic Maya Society. In *Mesoamerican Elites: An Archaeological Assessment*, edited by Diane Z. Chase and Arlen F. Chase, pp. 30–49. University of Oklahoma Press, Norman.

Chase, Diane Z.
1992   Postclassic Maya Elites: Ethnohistory and Archaeology. In *Mesoamerican Elites: An Archaeological Assessment*, edited by Diane Z. Chase and Arlen F. Chase, pp. 118–134. University of Oklahoma Press, Norman.

Chase, Diane Z., and Arlen F. Chase
1992   An Archaeological Assessment of Mesoamerican Elites. In *Mesoamerican Elites: An Archaeological Assessment*, edited by Diane Z. Chase and Arlen F. Chase, pp. 303–317. University of Oklahoma Press, Norman.
2004   Archaeological Perspectives on Classic Maya Social Organization from Caracol, Belize. *Ancient Mesoamerica* 15:139–147.
2014   Ancient Maya Markets and the Economic Integration of Caracol, Belize. *Ancient Mesoamerica* 25:239–250.

Chávez Jiménez, Ulises
2007   Potonchán y Santa María de la Victoria: Una propuesta geomorfológica/archaeológica a un problema histórico. *Estudios de cultura Maya* 29:103–139.

Christenson, Allen J.
2010   Maize Was Their Flesh: Ritual Feasting in the Maya Highlands. In *Pre-columbian Foodways: Interdisciplinary Approaches to Food, Culture, and Markets in Ancient Mesoamerica*, edited by John E. Staller and Michael Carrasco, pp. 577–600. Springer, New York.

Clark, Jeffrey J.
2004   Tracking Cultural Affiliation: Enculturation and Ethnicity. In *Identity, Feasting, and the Archaeology of the Greater Southwest*, edited by Barbara J. Mills, pp. 42–73. University Press of Colorado, Boulder.

Collier, Jane F., and Sylvia J. Yanagisako (editors)
1987   *Gender and Kinship: Essays Toward a Unified Analysis*. Stanford University Press, Stanford.

Culbert, T. Patrick, and Robert L. Rands
2007   Multiple Classifications: An Alternative Approach to the Investigation of Maya Ceramics. *Latin American Antiquity* 18:181–190.

Coe, Michael D., and Richard A. Diehl
1980   *In the Land of the Olmec*. University of Texas Press, Austin.

Coehlo de Souza, Marcela
2012 The Making and Unmaking of "Crow-Omaha" Kinship in Central Brazil(ian Ethnology). In *Crow-Omaha: New Light on a Classic Problem of Kinship Analysis*, edited by Thomas R. Trautmann and Peter M. Whiteley, pp. 205–222. University of Arizona Press, Tucson.

Dahlin, Bruce H., Christopher T. Jensen, Richard E. Terry, David R. Wright, and Timothy Beach
2007 In Search of an Ancient Maya Market. *Latin American Antiquity* 18:363–384.

Dakin, Karen, and Søren Wichmann
2000 Cacao and Chocolate: A Uto-Aztecan Perspective. *Ancient Mesoamerica* 11:55–75.

Dance, Scott
2018 Crab Crisis: Maryland Seafood Industry Loses 40 Percent of Work Force in Visa Lottery. *The Baltimore Sun*. http://www.baltimoresun.com/news/maryland/bs-md-crab-visa-shortage-20180502-story.html. Accessed 27 July 2018.

de Haldevang, Max, and Daniel Wolfe
2020 Mexico is Illegally Destroying Protected Mangrove Trees to Build an $8 Billion Oil Refinery. *Quartz*, 5 March 2020. https://qz.com/1807407/mexico-is-illegally-destroying-mangroves-to-build-lopez-obradors-oil-refinery/. Accessed 5 March 2020.

De Lucia, Kristin, and Lisa Overholtzer
2014 Everyday Action and the Rise and Decline of Ancient Polities: Household Strategy and Political Change in Postclassic Xaltocan, Mexico. *Ancient Mesoamerica* 25:441–458.

Demarest, Arthur A.
2009 Maya Archaeology for the Twenty-First Century: The Progress, the Perils, and the Promise. *Ancient Mesoamerica* 20:253-263.

Demarest, Arthur A., Chloé Andrieu, Paola Torres, Mélanie Forné, Tomás Barrientos, and Marc Wolf
2014 Economy, Exchange, and Power: New Evidence from the Late Classic Maya Port City of Cancuen. *Ancient Mesoamerica* 25:187–219.

de Montmollin, Olivier
1995 *Settlement and Politics in Three Classic Maya Polities.* Monographs in World Archaeology No. 24. Prehistory Press, Madison.

Divale, William T.
1977 Living Floors and Marital Residence: A Replication. *Behavior Science Research* 12:109–115.

Douglas, John E.
2000 Exchanges, Assumptions, and Mortuary Goods in Pre-Paquimé Chihuahua, Mexico. In *The Archaeology of Regional Interaction: Religion, Warfare, and Exchange Across the American Southwest and Beyond*, edited by Michelle Hegmon, pp. 189–208. University Press of Colorado, Boulder.

Dousset, Laurent
2012 "Horizontal" and "Vertical" Skewing: Similar Objectives, Two Solutions? In *Crow-Omaha: New Light on a Classic Problem of Kinship Analysis*, edited by Thomas R. Trautmann and Peter M. Whiteley, pp. 261–277. University of Arizona Press, Tucson.

Draper, Patricia
1975 !Kung Women: Contrasts in Sexual Egalitarianism in Foraging and Sedentary Contexts. In *Toward an Anthropology of Women*, edited by R. R. Reiter, pp. 77–109. Monthly Review Press, New York.

Drucker, Philip, and Eduardo Contreras
1953 Site Patterns in the Eastern Part of Olmec Territory. *Journal of the Washington Academy of Science* 43:389–396.

Dube, Leela (editor)
1997 *Women and Kinship: Comparative Perspectives on Gender in South and South-East Asia.* United Nations University Press, Tokyo.

Eggan, Fred
1934 The Maya Kinship System and Cross-Cousin Marriage. *American Anthropologist* 36:188–202.

Ellison, James
2009 Governmentality and the Family: Neoliberal Choices and Emergent Kin Relations in Southern Ethiopia. *American Anthropologist* 111:81–92.

Ember, Carol R.
1983 The Relative Decline in Women's Contribution to Agriculture with Intensification. *American Anthropologist* 85:285–304.

Ember, Carol R., and Christiane M. Cunnar
1995 Cross-Cultural Studies and Their Relevance for Archaeology. *Journal of Archaeological Research* 3:87–111.
2015 Children's Play and Work: The Relevance of Cross-Cultural Ethnographic Research for Archaeologists. *Childhood in the Past* 8(2):87–103.

Ember, Carol R., and Melvin Ember
2005 Explaining Corporal Punishment of Children: A Cross-Cultural Study. *American Anthropologist* 107:609–619.

Ember, Melvin
1973 An Archaeological Indicator of Matrilocal versus Patrilocal Residence. *American Antiquity* 38:177–182.

Ember, Melvin, and Carol R. Ember

1995 Worldwide Cross-Cultural Studies and Their Relevance for Archaeology. *Journal of Archaeological Research* 3:87–111.

Ensor, Bradley E.

1994 *Morphological and Technological Suitability of Postclassic Maya Ceramics from Wild Cane Cay, Belize.* MA thesis, Department of Geography and Anthropology, Louisiana State University, Baton Rouge.

2000 Social Formations, Modo de Vida, and Conflict in Archaeology. *American Antiquity* 65:15–42.

2002a Archaeological Investigations at Islas de Los Cerros: Comalcalco's Main Tributary. Paper presented at the 67th Annual Meeting of the Society for American Archaeology, Denver.

2002b *Proyecto Arqueológico Islas de Los Cerros: Reconocimiento y recolecciones de la superficie.* Report to the Instituto Nacional de Antropología e Historia, México, DF.

2003a Disproportionate Clan Growth in Crow-Omaha Societies: A Kinship Demographic Model for Explaining Settlement Hierarchies and Fissioning in the Prehistoric U.S. Southeast. *North American Archaeologist* 23:309–337.

2003b Islas de Los Cerros: A Coastal Site Complex Near Comalcalco, Tabasco, Mexico. *Mexicon* 25:106–111.

2003c Kinship and Marriage Among the Omaha, 1886-1902. *Ethnology* 42:1–14.

2005a Late Classic–Epi-Classic Ceramic Chronology at Islas de Los Cerros, Tabasco, México. Foundation for the Advancement of Mesoamerican Studies, Inc. http://www.famsi.org/reports/05024/index.html. Accessed 7 January 2018.

2005b Preliminary Excavations at Islas de Los Cerros, Tabasco 2004. Paper presented at the 28th Annual Midwest Conference on Mesoamerican Archaeology and Ethnohistory, Bloomington.

2007 The Coastal Role of Islas de Los Cerros in the Chontalpa Region's Late Classic Political Economy. Paper presented at the 72nd Annual Meeting of the Society for American Archaeology, Austin.

2008a Crafting Classes and Kinship in the Late Classic Period Chontal Maya Social Formation at Islas de Los Cerros, Tabasco, México. Paper Presented at the 107th Annual Meeting of the American Anthropological Association, San Francisco.

2008b Preliminary Archaeological Investigations at El Bellote, Tabasco, México. Foundation for the Advancement of Mesoamerican Studies, Inc. http://www.famsi.org/reports/07019/index.html. Accessed 7 January 2018.

2011a The Crafting of Prehispanic Maya Kinship. Paper presented at the 76th Annual Meeting of the Society for American Archaeology, Sacramento.

2011b Kinship Theory in Archaeology: From Critiques to the Study of Transformations. *American Antiquity* 76:203–227.

2011c *Proyecto arqueológico Islas de Los Cerros 2011.* Report to the Instituto Nacional de Antropología e Historia, México, DF.

2013a *The Archaeology of Kinship: Advancing Interpretation and Contributions to Theory.* University of Arizona Press, Tucson.

2013b *Crafting Prehispanic Maya Kinship.* University of Alabama Press, Tuscaloosa.

2013c Kinship and Social Organization in the Pre-Hispanic Caribbean. In *The Oxford Handbook of Caribbean Archaeology*, edited by William F. Keegan, Corinne C. Hoffman, and Reniel Rodríguez Ramos, pp. 84–96. Oxford University Press, Oxford.

2013d *Proyecto Arqueológico Islas de Los Cerros 2011: Adendo.* Report to the Instituto Nacional de Antropología e Historia, México, DF.

2014a Ethnological Problems and the Production of Archaeological Kinship Research. Paper presented at the 113th Annual Meeting of the American Anthropological Association, Washington, DC.

2014b Modes, Classes, Gender, and Agency. Paper presented at the 79th Annual Meeting of the Society for American Archaeology, Austin.

2015 Evaluating Theoretical Models on Prehistoric Kinship: Two Case Studies in Archaeological Kinship Analysis. Paper presented at the Murdock and Goody Revisited: (Pre)history and Evolution of Eurasian and African Family Systems International Conference, Max Planck Institute, Halle, Germany.

2016a La arqueología como contribuidora al estudio etnológico de parentesco. Paper presented at the I Coloquiode Etnohistoria, Arqueología, y Etnografía: Interdisciplina y Praxis, México, DF.

2016b Ethnological Problems and the Production of Archaeological Kinship Research. *Structure and Dynamics* 9:80–109.

2017a A Call for Cross-Cultural Research Servicing Archaeological Kinship Analyses. Paper presented at the 46th Annual Conference of the Society for Cross-Cultural Research, New Orleans.

2017b Kin-Mode Contradictions, Crises, and Transformations in the Archaic Lower Mississippi Valley. In *Modes of Production in Archaeology*, edited by Robert Rosenswig and Jerimy J. Cunningham, pp. 123–143. University Press of Florida, Gainesville.

2017c The Mounds of Islas de Los Cerros, Tabasco, México. Paper presented at the 2017 Midwest Conference on Mesoamerican Archaeology and Ethnohistory, Detroit.

2017d Social Formations Analysis: Modes, Classes, Gender, and the Multiple Contexts for Agency. In *Modes of Production in Archaeology*, edited by Robert Rosenswig and Jerimy J. Cunningham, pp. 233-252. University Press of Florida, Gainesville.

2017e Testing Ethnological Theories on Prehistoric Kinship. *Cross-Cultural Research* 51:1–29.

2018a Prehistoric Histories of Hohokam Kin Groups. In *Problematising Time and History in Prehistory*, edited by Stella Souvatzi, Adnan Baysal, and Emma L. Baysal, pp. 172–191. Routledge, Abingdon.

2018b The Western Chontalpa: What's in the Archaeological "Black Hole" of the Mesoamerican Gulf Coast? Paper presented at the 83rd Annual Meeting of the Society for American Archaeology, Washington, DC.

2019 The Late Classic Islas de Los Cerros Landscape: A Tapestry of Kinship, Identities, Histories, and Ancestries. Paper presented at the 84th Annual Meeting of the Society for American Archaeology, Albuquerque.

Ensor, Bradley E., and David E. Doyel
1997 Trends in Subsistence, Settlement, and Land Use. In *Archaeological Survey in Districts 6 and 7, Gila River Indian Community*, Vol. 1: Research Orientation and Results, edited by David E. Doyel and Bradley E. Ensor, pp. 75–104. Report No. 98. Archaeological Consulting Services, Tempe.

Ensor, Bradley E., and Gabriel Tun Ayora
2004 *Proyecto Arqueológico Islas de Los Cerros, 2004.* Report to the Instituto Nacional de Antropología e Historia, México, DF.

2008 El Bellote: A Large Late Classic Chontal Ceremonial-Administrative Center at Islas de Los Cerros, Tabasco, Mexico. Paper presented

at the 73rd Annual Meeting of the Society for American Archaeology, Vancouver.

2011 The Site of El Bellote, Tabasco Mexico and Preliminary Observations on Late Classic Period Chontal Regional Integration. *Mexicon* 33:116–126.

Ensor, Bradley E., Marisa O. Ensor, and Gregory W. De Vries
2003 Hohokam Political Ecology and Vulnerability: Comments on Waters and Ravesloot. *American Antiquity* 68:169–181.

Ensor, Bradley E., Concepción Herrera Escobar, and Gabriel Tun Ayora
2012 La formación social del periodo Clásico Tardío en las Islas de Los Cerros, Tabasco: Una comparación del modo de vida entre clases sociales. In *VII Coloquio Pedro-Bosch-Gimpera: Arqueologías de la vida cotidiana*, edited by Guillermo Acosta Ochoa, pp. 185–214. Universidad Nacional de Mexico, Mexico, DF.

2018 Los rasgos de Islas de Los Cerros: ¿Concheros del Formativo o montículos del Clásico Tardío? Paper presented at the XXVIII Encuentro Internacional Los Investigadores de la Cultura Maya, Campeche.

Ensor, Bradley E., Joel D. Irish, and William F. Keegan
2017 The Bioarchaeology of Kinship: Proposed Revisions to Assumptions Guiding Interpretation. *Current Anthropology* 58:739–761.

Ensor, Bradley E, Gabriel Tun Ayora, and Concepción Herrera Escobar
2008 *Proyecto Arqueológico Islas de Los Cerros 2007.* Report to the Instituto Nacional de Antropología e Historia, México, DF.

Ensor, BE, Concepción Herrera Escobar, Keiko Teranishi Castillo, Gabriel Tun Ayora, and Socorro P. Jiménez Alvarez
2006 Proyecto Arqueológico Islas de Los Cerros. *Los investigadores de la cultura maya* 14: 211–226.

2006 *Proyecto Arqueológico Islas de Los Cerros 2005.* Report to the Instituto Nacional de Antropología e Historia, México, DF.

Ensor, Marisa O. (editor)
2009 *The Legacy of Mitch: Lessons from Post-Disaster Reconstruction in Honduras.* University of Arizona Press, Tucson.

Evans-Pritchard, E.
1940 *The Nuer.* Clarendon, Oxford.

Feathers, James
2013 Luminescence Analysis of Ceramics from Islas de los Cerros, Tabasco, Mexico. In *Proyecto Arqueológico Islas de Los Cerros 2011: Adendo,*

Feathers, James (*continued*)
by Bradley E. Ensor, pp. 9–14. Report to the Instituto Nacional de Antropología e Historia, México, DF.

Feinman, Gary M., and Linda M. Nicholas
1993   Shell-Ornament Production in Ejutla: Implications for Highland-Coastal Interaction in Ancient Oaxaca. *Ancient Mesoamerica* 4:103–119.

Feinman, Gary M., Linda M. Nicholas, and Helen R. Haines
2002   Houses on a Hill: Classic Period Life at El Palmillo, Oaxaca, Mexico. *Latin American Antiquity* 13:251–277.

Fernández Tejedo, Isabel, Margarita Gaxiola, Javier López Camacho, and Elisa Ramírez C.
1988   *Zonas Arqueológicas Tabasco.* Instituto Nacional de Antropología e Historia, México, DF.

Feinberg, Richard, and Martin Ottenheimer (editors)
2001   *The Cultural Analysis of Kinship: The Legacy of David M. Schneider.* University of Illinois Press, Urbana.

Foias, Antonia E.
2013   *Ancient Maya Political Dynamics.* University Press of Florida, Gainesville.

Folan, William J., Abel Morales, Rosario Dominguez, Roberto Ruiz, Raymundo Gonzalez, Joel D. Gunn, Lynda Florey, M. Barredo, José Hernandez, and David Bolles
2002   La ciudad y puerto de Champotón, Campeche: una encrucijada del Golfo de México y su corredor eco-arqueológico. *Los investigadores de la cultura Maya* 10:8–16.

Follensbee, Billie J. A.
2000   *Sex and Gender in Olmec Art and Archaeology.* Ph.D. dissertation, University of Maryland, College Park.
2008   Fiber Technology and Weaving in Formative-Period Gulf Coast Cultures. *Ancient Mesoamerica* 19:87–110.

Fox, John W.
1987   *Maya Postclassic State Formation: Segmentary Lineage Migration in Advancing Frontiers.* Cambridge University Press, Cambridge.

Fox, John W., Dwight T. Wallace, and Kenneth L. Brown
1992   The Emergence of the Quiche Elite: The Putun-Palenque Connection. In *Mesoamerican Elites: An Archaeological Assessment,* edited by Diane Z. Chase and Arlen F. Chase, pp. 169–190. University of Oklahoma Press, Norman.

Fox, Robin
1967   *Kinship and Marriage: An Anthropological Perspective.* Cambridge University Press, Cambridge.

Freidel, David, and F. Kent Reilly III
2010   The Flesh of God: Cosmology, Food, and the Origins of Political Power in Ancient Southeastern Mesoamerica. In *Pre-columbian Foodways: Interdisciplinary Approaches to Food, Culture, and Markets in Ancient Mesoamerica,* edited by John E. Staller and Michael Carrasco, pp. 635–680. Springer, New York.

Friedl, Ernestine
2004   Society and Sex Roles. In *Classic Readings in Cultural Anthropology,* edited by Gary Ferraro, pp. 48–54. Wadsworth, Belmont, California.

Freter, Ann Corrine
2004   Multiscalar Model of Rural Households and Communities in Later Classic Copan Maya Society. *Ancient Mesoamerica* 15:93–106.

Friedman, Jonathan
1984   Tribes, States, and Transformations. In *Marxist Analyses and Social Anthropology,* edited by M. Bloch, pp. 161–202. Malaby, London.

Gallegos Gómora, Miriam J.
1994   Entre el cacaotal y los popales: etnoarqueología de la vivienda tradicional de La Chontalpa. Paper presented at the 23rd Mesa Redonda of the Society of Mexican Anthropology, Villahermosa.
1995   La vida domestica entre los Mayas Chontales de Comalcalco. Paper presented at the Third International Congress of Mayanists, Chetumal.
1997   La relación entre el Rio Mezcalapa-Dos Bocas, con el sitio arqueológico de Comalcalco, y la fundación de San Isidro Comalcalco en el siglo XIX, a traves de documentos. Paper presented at the Annual Meeting of the American Society for Ethnohistory, México DF.
1998   Arquitectura y actividades tradicionales en la Region Chontal. *Los Investigadores de la Cultura Maya* 6:133–145.

Gallareta Negrón, Tomás, Anthony P. Andrews, Fernando Robles Castellanos, Rafael Cobos Palma, and P. Cervera Rivero
1989   Isla Cerritos: Un puerto Maya prehispánico en la costa norte de Yucatán. *Memorias del II Coloquio Internacional de Mayistas* 1:311–332.

Garza, Mercedes, Ana Luisa Izquierdo de la,
Maria del Carmen León, and Tolita Figueroa
1983   *Relaciones histórico-geográficas de la Gober-
        nación de Yucatán.* Centro de Estudios Mayas,
        Universidad Autónoma de México, México DF.

Geertz, Clifford
1973   Person, Time and Conduct in Bali. In *The
        Interpretation of Cultures*, edited by Clifford
        Geertz, pp. 360–411. Basic Books, New York.

Gerhard, Peter
1991   *La frontera sureste de la Nueva España.* Universi-
        dad Nacional Autónoma de México, México, DF.

Gillespie, Susan D.
2000   Rethinking Ancient Maya Social Organization:
        Replacing "Lineage" with "House." *American
        Anthropologist* 102:467–484.

Godelier, Maurice
1984   Modes of Production, Kinship, and Demo-
        graphic Structures. In *Marxist Analyses and
        Social Anthropology*, edited by Maurice Bloch,
        pp. 3–27. Malaby, London.

Goldstein, David J., and Jon B. Hageman
2010   Power Plants: Paleobotanical Evidence of Rural
        Feasting in Late Classic Belize. In *Pre-columbian
        Foodways: Interdisciplinary Approaches to Food,
        Culture, and Markets in Ancient Mesoamerica*,
        edited by John E. Staller and Michael Carrasco,
        pp. 421–440. Springer, New York.

González Lauck, Rebecca
1988   Proyecto Arqueológico La Venta. *Arqueología*
        4:121–165.

Grove, David C., and Susan D. Gillespie
1992   Archaeological Indicators of Formative Period
        Elites: A Perspective from Central Mexico.
        In *Mesoamerican Elites: An Archaeological
        Assessment*, edited by Diane Z. Chase and Arlen
        F. Chase, pp. 191–205. University of Oklahoma
        Press, Norman.

Guevara Chumacero, Miguel, Alejandra Pichardo Fragoso,
and Monserrat Martínez Cornelio
2017   La tortuga en Tabasco: comida, identidad y rep-
        resentación. *Estudios de Cultura Maya* 49:97–122.

Habicht-Mauche, Judith A.
2000   Pottery, Food, Hides, and Women: Labor, Pro-
        duction, and Exchange Across the Protohistoric
        Plains-Pueblo Frontier. In *The Archaeology of
        Regional Interaction: Religion, Warfare, and
        Exchange Across the American Southwest and
        Beyond*, edited by Michelle Hegmon, pp. 209–
        234. University Press of Colorado, Boulder.

Hage, Per
2003   The Ancient Maya Kinship System. *Journal of
        Anthropological Research* 59:5–21.

Hageman, Jon B.
2004   The Lineage Model and Archaeological Data
        In Late Classic Northwestern Belize. *Ancient
        Mesoamerica* 15:63–74.

Haines, Helen R., Gary M. Feinman, and Linda M. Nicholas
2004   Household Economic Specialization and Social
        Differentiation: The Stone-Tool Assemblage
        at El Palmillo, Oaxaca. *Ancient Mesoamerica*
        15:251–266.

Hall, Barbara A.
1994   Formation Processes of Large Earthen Resi-
        dential Mounds in La Mixtequilla, Veracruz,
        Mexico. *Latin American Antiquity* 5:31–50.

Haller, Mikael J., Gary M. Feinman, and Linda M. Nicholas
2006   Socioeconomic Inequality and Differential
        Access to Faunal Resources at El Palmillo,
        Oaxaca, Mexico. *Ancient Mesoamerica* 17:39–56.

Haviland, William A.
1963   *Excavations of Small Structures in the Northeast
        Quadrant of Tikal, Guatemala.* Unpublished
        PhD dissertation. Department of Anthropology,
        University of Pennsylvania, Philadelphia.
1968   *Ancient Lowland Maya Social Organization.*
        Publication 26:95–117. Middle American
        Research Institute, Tulane University, New
        Orleans.
1970a   Marriage and the Family Among the Maya of
        Cozumel Island, 1570. *Estudios de cultura Maya*
        8:217–226.
1970b   A Note on the Social Organization of the
        Chontal Maya. *Ethnology* 9:96–98.
1970c   Tikal, Guatemala, and Mesoamerican Urbanism.
        World Archaeology 2:186–198.
1972   Family Size, Prehistoric Population Estimates,
        and the Ancient Maya. *American Antiquity*
        37:135–139.
1973   Rules of Descent in Sixteenth Century Yucatan.
        Estudios de Cultura Maya 9:135–150.
1974   Occupational Specialization at Tikal, Guatemala:
        Stone-Working Monument Carving. *American
        Antiquity* 39:494–496.
1977   Dynastic Genealogies from Tikal, Guatemala:
        Implications for Descent and Political Organiza-
        tion. *American Antiquity* 42:61–67.
1997   The Rise and Fall of Sexual Inequality: Death
        and Gender at Tikal, Guatemala. *Ancient
        Mesoamerica* 8:1–12.

Haviland, William A., and Hattula Moholy-Nagy
  1992   Distinguishing the High and Mighty from the Hoi Polloi at Tikal, Guatemala. In *Mesoamerican Elites: An Archaeological Assessment*, edited by Diane Z. Chase and Arlen F. Chase, pp. 50–60. University of Oklahoma Press, Norman.

Hayden, Brian
  2014   *The Power of Feasts: From Prehistory to the Present.* Cambridge University Press, Cambridge.

Hegmon, Michelle
  2003   Setting Theoretical Egos Aside: Issues and Theory in North American Archaeology. *American Antiquity* 68:213–243.

Hegmon, Michelle, Jacob Freeman, Keith W. Kintigh, Margaret C. Nelson, Sara Oas, Matthew A. Peeples, and Andrea Trovinen
  2016   Marking and Making Differences: Representational Diversity in the US Southwest. *American Antiquity* 81:253–272.

Henderson, John S., Rosemary A. Joyce, Gretchen R. Hall, W. Jeffrey Hurst, and Patrick E. McGovern
  2007   Chemical and Archaeological Evidence for the Earliest Cacao Beverages. *Proceedings of the National Academy of Sciences of the United States of America* 104:18937–18940.

Hendon, Julia A.
  1992   The Interpretation of Survey Data: Two Case Studies from the Maya Area. *Latin American Antiquity* 3:22–42.
  2007   Memory, Materiality, and Practice: House Societies in Southeastern Mesoamerica. In *The Durable House: House Society Models in Archaeology*, edited by Robin A. Beck, pp. 292–316. Center for Archaeological Investigations Occasional Paper No. 35. Southern Illinois University, Carbondale.

Hernandez Sastre, Rutilo
  1997   *Analisis del material arqueozoológico procedente de las excavaciones de la zona arqueológica de Comalcalco, Tabasco, México.* Tesis de Licenciatura. División Academica de Ciencias Biologicas, Universidad Juarez Autónoma de Tabasco, Villahermosa.

Hernández Treviño, Ascensión
  2013   Chocolate: historia de un nahuatlismo. *Estudios de cultura Náhuatl* 46:37–87.

Herrera Escobar, Concepción
  2004   Etnoarqueología del sur Veracruz—norte de Tabasco: Elaboración de canoas, un medio económico para acercarnos a los ahualulcos del S. XVI. Paper presented at the Sociedad Mexicana de Antropologia Mesa Redonda, Xalapa.

Herrera Flores, David Alejandro, and Christopher Markus Götz
  2014   La alimentación de los antiguos Mayas de la península de Yucatán: Consideraciones sobre la identidad y la cuisine en la época prehispánica. *Estudios de cultura Maya* 43:69–98.

Hirth, Kenneth
  2012   Craft Production and the Domestic Economy in Mesoamerica. In *Arqueologías de la vida cotidiana: Espacios domésticos y áreas de actividad en el México antiguo y otras zonas culturales*, edited by Guillermo Acosta Ochoa, pp. 49–84. Universidad Nacional Autónoma de México, México, DF.

Hoar, Bryanne
  2009   Tlatilco: The Place Where Things are Hidden. In *Que(e)rying Archaeology: Proceedings of the 37th Annual Chacmool Conference*, edited by Susan Terendy, Natasha Lyons, and Michelle Janse-Smekal, pp. 163–170. University of Calgary, Calgary.

Hodder, Ian
  1982   *Symbols in Action: Ethnoarchaeological Studies of Materical Culture.* Cambridge University Press, Cambridge.

Holland, William R.
  1964   Contemporary Tzotzil Cosmological Concepts as a Basis for Interpreting Prehistoric Maya Civilization. *American Antiquity* 29:301–306.

Hopkins, Nicholas A.
  1988   Classic Maya Kinship Systems: Epigraphic and Ethnographic Evidence for Patrilineality. *Estudios de cultura Maya* 17:87–121.

Humberto Ruz, Mario
  1997   *Gestos cotidianos: Acercamientos etnológicos a los Mayas de la época colonial.* Gobierno del Estado de Campeche.

Hutchinson, Sharon E.
  1996   *Nuer Dilemmas: Coping with Money War, and the State.* University of California Press, Berkeley.

Hutson, Scott R., Aline Magnoni, and Travis W. Stanton
  2004   House Rules? The Practice of Social Organization in Classic-Period Chunchucmil, Yucatan, Mexico. *Ancient Mesoamerica* 15:75–92.

Inchaustegui, Carlos
  1987   *Las márgenes del Tabasco Chontal.* Instituto de Cultura de Tabasco, Villahermosa.

Inomata, Takeshi, and Stephen D. Houston (editors)
2001a *Royal Courts of the Ancient Maya*, Vol. 1: Theory, Comparison, and Synthesis. Westview Press, Boulder.
2001b *Royal Courts of the Ancient Maya*, Vol. 2: Data and Case Studies. Westview Press, Boulder.

Inomata, Takeshi, Raúl Ortiz, Bárbara Arroyo, and Eugenia J. Robinson
2014 Chronological Revision of Preclassic Kaminaljuyú, Guatemala: Implications for Social Processes in the Southern Maya Area. *Latin American Antiquity* 25:377–408.

Inomata, Takeshi, Daniela Triadan, Erick Ponciano, Estela Pinto, Richard E. Terry, and Markus Eberl
2002 Domestic and Political Lives of Classic Maya Elites: The Excavation of Rapidly Abandoned Structures at Aguateca, Guatemala. *Latin American Antiquity* 13:305–330.

Izquierdo, Ana L.
1997 *Acalán y la Chontalpa en el siglo XVI: su geografía política*. Universidad Nacional Autónoma de México, México, DF.

Izquierdo y De La Cueva, Ana L.
2004 Unidad y fragmentación del poder entre los Mayas. *Estudios de Cultura Maya* 25:57–76.

Jackson, Sarah E.
2013 *Politics of the Maya Court: Hierarchy and Change in the Late Classic Period*. University of Oklahoma Press, Norman.

Ji, Kun, Dapeng Zheng, Lambert A. Motilal, Michel Boccara, Philippe Lachenaud, and Lyndel W. Meinhardt
2013 Genetic Diversity and Parentage in Farmer Varieties of Cacao (*Theobroma cacao* L.) from Honduras and Nicaragua as Revealed by Single Nucleotide Polymorphism (SNP) Markers. *Genetic Resources and Crop Evolution* 60:441–453.

Jiménez Valdez, Gloria Martha
1989 Poblaciones costeras de Tabasco y Campeche. *Anales de Antropología* 26:99–105.
1993 Medios de comunicación y centros de intercambio en la Chontalpa y costa de Tabasco. In *Segundo coloquio Pedro Bosh Gimpera*, compiled by Maria Teresa Cabrero, pp. 366–375. Instituto de Investigaciones Antropológicas, Universidad Nacional Autónoma de México, México, DF.

Johnson, Kent, and Kathleen Paul
2016 Bioarchaeology and Kinship: Integrating Theory, Social Relatedness, and Biology in Ancient Family Research. *Journal of Archaeological Research* 24:75–123.

Jones O'Day, Sharyn, and William F. Keegan
2001 Expedient Shell Tools from the Northern West Indies. *Latin American Antiquity* 12:274–290.

Jordan, Jillian M., and Keith M. Prufer
2017 Identifying Domestic Ceramic Production in the Maya Lowlands: A Case Study from Uxbenka, Belize. *Latin American Antiquity* 28:66–87.

Josserand, Kathryn J.
2007 The Missing Heir at Yaxhilán: Literary Analysis of a Maya Historical Puzzle. *Latin American Antiquity* 18:295–312.

Joyce, Rosemary A.
1981 Classic Maya Kinship and Descent: An Alternative Suggestion. *Journal of the Steward Anthropological Society* 13:45–57.
2000a *Gender and Power in Prehispanic Mesoamerica*. University of Texas Press, Austin.
2000b Heirlooms and Houses: Materiality and Social Memory. In *Beyond Kinship: Social and Material Reproduction in House Societies*, edited by Rosemary A. Joyce and Susan D. Gillespie, pp. 189–212. University of Pennsylvania Press, Philadelphia.
2007 Building Houses: The Materialization of Lasting Identity in Formative Mesoamerica. In *The Durable House: House Society Models in Archaeology*, edited by Robin A. Beck, pp. 53–72. Center for Archaeological Investigations Occasional Paper No. 35. Southern Illinois University, Carbondale.

Joyce, Rosemary A. (editor)
2000 *Gender and Power in Prehispanic Mesoamerica*, University of Texas Press, Austin.

Joyce, Rosemary A., and John S. Henderson
2007 From Feasting to Cuisine: Implications of Archaeological Research in an Early Honduran Village. *American Anthropologist* 109:642–653.
2010 Being "Olmec" in Early Formative Honduras. *Ancient Mesoamerica* 21:187–200.

Joyce, Rosemary A., Julia A. Hendon, and Jeanne Lopiparo
2014 Working with Clay. *Ancient Mesoamerica* 25:411–420.

Joyce, Rosemary A., Whitney Davis, Alice B. Kehoe, Edward M. Schortman, Patricia Urban, and Ellen Bell
1993 Women's Work: Images of Production and Reproduction in Pre-Hispanic Southern Central America. *Current Anthropology* 34:255–274.

Joyce, Rosemary A, Marc N. Levine, Stade M. King, Jessica H. Balkin, and Sarah B. Barber
2014 Political Transformations and the Everyday in Postclassic Oaxaca. *Ancient Mesoamerica* 25:389–410.

Kaufman, Terrence, and John Justeson
  2007   The History of the Word for Cacao in Ancient Mesoamerica. *Ancient Mesoamerica* 18:193–237.

Keegan, William F.
  1992   "No Man [or Woman] Is an Island": Elements of Taino Social Organization. In *The Indigenous People of the Caribbean*, edited by Samuel M. Wilson, pp. 111–117. University Press of Florida, Gainesville.
  2006   All in the Family: Descent and Succession in the Protohistoric Chiefdoms of the Greater Antilles—A Comment on Curet. *Ethnohistory* 53:383–392.
  2009   Central Plaza Burials in Saladoid Puerto Rico: An Alternative Perspective. *Latin American Antiquity* 20:375–385.
  2010   Demographic Imperatives for Island Colonists. In *The Global Origins and Development of Seafaring*, edited by Atholl Anderson, James H. Barrett, and Katie Boyle, pp. 171–178. MacDonald Institute, Cambridge, UK.

Keesing, Roger M.
  1975   *Kin Groups and Social Structure*. Holt, Rinehart and Winston, Inc., New York.

King, Stacie M.
  2011   Thread Production in Early Postclassic Coastal Oaxaca, Mexico: Technology, Intensity, and Gender. *Ancient Mesoamerica* 22:323–343.

Kintz, Ellen R.
  2004   Considering the Ties that Bind: Kinship, Marriage, Household, and Territory Among the Maya. *Ancient Mesoamerica* 15:149–158.

Kowalewski, Stephen A., Gary M. Feinman, and Laura Finsten
  1992   The Elite and Assessment of Social Stratification in Mesoamerican Archaeology. In *Mesoamerican Elites: An Archaeological Assessment*, edited by Diane Z. Chase and Arlen F. Chase, pp. 259–277. University of Oklahoma Press, Norman.

Leacock, Eleanor
  1972   Introduction. In *The Origin of the Family, Private Property, and the State*, by F. Engels, pp. 7–67. International Publishers, New York.
  1978   Women's Status in Egalitarian Society: Implications for Social Evolution. *Current Anthropology* 19:247–275.

LeCount, Lisa J.
  2010   Ka'kaw Pots and Common Containers: Creating Histories and Collective Memories Among the Classic Maya of Xunantunich, Belize. *Ancient Mesoamerica* 21:341–351.

Lévi-Strauss, Claude
  1956   The Family. In *Man, Culture, and Society*, edited by H. L. Shapiro, pp. 261–285. Oxford University Press, New York.
  1965   The Future of Kinship Studies. *Proceedings of the Royal Anthropological Institute of Great Britain and Ireland* 1965:13–22.
  1969   *The Elementary Structures of Kinship*. Beacon Press, Boston.
  1982   *The Way of the Masks*. University of Washington Press, Seattle.
  1987   *Anthropology and Myth: Lectures, 1951–1982*. Basil Blackwell, Oxford.

Lewarch, Dennis E., and Michael J. O'Brien
  1981   The Expanding Role of Surface Assemblages in Archaeological Research. In *Advances in Archaeological Method and Theory*, Vol. 4, edited by Michael B. Schiffer, pp. 297–342. Academic Press, New York.

Lewenstein, Suzanne
  1995   La litica tallada de Comalcalco, Tabasco: Aspectos tecnologicos y culturales. Paper presented at the third International Congress of Mayanists, Chetumal.

Lewenstein, Suzanne, and Michael Glascock
  1996   Presencia del altiplano en la región de Comalcalco. Paper presented at the VI Encuentro de los Investigadores de la Cultura Maya, Campeche.
  1997   Obsidian Procurement at Comalcalco: Implications for Central Mexican-Lowland Maya Commercial Relationships During the Epiclassic. Paper presented at the 62nd Annual Meeting of the Society for American Archaeology, Nashville.

Littman, Edwin R.
  1957   Ancient Mesoamerican Mortars, Plasters and Stuccos: Comalcalco, Parts I and II. *American Antiquity* 23:135–140, 292–296.

López Varela, Sandra L.
  1994   Pomoná, Tabasco: Una ciudad puerta de entrada durante el Clásico. *Tierra y Agua* 4:33–42.

Maclachlan, Morgan D., and William F. Keegan
  1990   Archaeology and the Ethno-Tyrannies. *American Anthropologist* 92:1011–1013.

Macri, Martha J.
  2005   Nahua Loan Words From the Early Classic Period: Words for Cacao Preparation on a Río Azul Ceramic Vessel. *Ancient Mesoamerica* 16:321–326.

Macri, Martha J., and Matthew G. Looper
  2003   Nahua in Ancient Mesoamerica: Evidence from Maya Inscriptions. *Ancient Mesoamerica* 14:285–297.

Mahalem de Lima, L
2014   Kinship Producing Politics, Politics Producing
       Kinship in the Arapiuns River, a tributary of
       the Lower Tapajós (Amazon Basin, Brazil).
       Paper presented at the 113th Annual Meeting
       of the American Anthropological Association,
       Washington, DC.

Malinowski, Bronislaw
1927   Lunar and Seasonal Calendar in the Trobriands.
       Journal of the Royal Anthropological Institute.
       57:203–215.

Marcus, Joyce
1992   Royal Families, Royal Texts: Examples from the
       Zapotec and Maya. In *Mesoamerican Elites: An
       Archaeological Assessment*, edited by Diane Z.
       Chase and Arlen F. Chase, pp. 221–241. Univer-
       sity of Oklahoma Press, Norman.
2009   Rethinking Figurines. In *Mesoamerican Figu-
       rines: Small-Scale Indices of Large-Scale Social
       Phenomena*, edited by Christina T. Halperin,
       Katherine A. Faust, Rhonda Taube, and Aurore
       Giguet, pp. 25–50. University Press of Florida,
       Gainesville.

Mariaca Méndez, Ramón, and Efraim Hernández Xolocotzi
1992   Origen y domesticación del cacao (*Theobroma
       cacao* L.). *Tierra y agua* 3:7–19.

Marín-Mézquita, Lourdes, Lucely Baeza,
Omar Zapata-Pérez, and Gerardo Gold-Bouchot
1997   Trace Metals in the American Oyster, *Crassostrea
       virginica*, and Sediments from the Coastal
       Lagoons Mecoacan, Carmen, and Machona,
       Tabasco, Mexico. *Chemosphere* 34:2437–2450.

Martínez Guzmán, Lourdes
1973   *Poblamiento, arquitectura y ornamentación de
       Comalcalco, Tabasco*. Tesis de Licenciatura.
       Universidad Autónoma de Yucatan, Merida.

Martínez Paiz, Horacio, Arthur A. Demarest,
Chloé Andrieu, Paola Torres, Mélanie Forné
2017   Cancuén: Una ciudad portuaria en el Río de la
       Pasión. *Estudios de la cultura maya* 49:11–37.

Masson, Marilyn A.
1997   Cultural Transformation at the Maya Postclassic
       Community of Laguna de On, Belize. *Latin
       American Antiquity* 8:293–316.

Matheny, Ray T.
1970   *The Ceramics of Aguacatal, Campeche, Mexico*.
       Papers No. 27. New World Archaeological Foun-
       dation, Provo.

Mauss, Marcel
1967   *The Gift: Forms and Functions of Exchange in
       Archaic Societies*. W. W. Norton, New York.

McAnany, Patricia A.
1995   *Living With the Ancestors: Kinship and Kingship
       in Ancient Maya Society*. University of Texas
       Press, Austin.

McAnany, Patricia, and Satoru Murata
2007   America's First Connoisseurs of Chocolate.
       Food & Foodways 15:7–30.

McKillop, Heather I.
1987   *Wild Cane Cay: An Insular Classic Period to
       Postclassic Period Maya Trading Station*.
       Ph.D. dissertation, University of California,
       Santa Barbara.
1995   Underwater Archaeology, Salt Production, and
       Coastal Maya Trade at Stingray Lagoon, Belize.
       Latin American Antiquity 6:214–228.
1996   Ancient Maya Trading Ports and the Integration
       of Long Distance and Regional Economies:
       Wild Cane Cay in South-Coastal Belize. *Ancient
       Mesoamerica* 7:49–62.

McKillop, Heather I., and Paul F. Healy (editors)
1989   *Coastal Maya Trade*. Occasional Papers in
       Anthropology No. 8, Trent University, Peters-
       borough, Ontario.

McKnight, David
2004   *Going the Whiteman's Way: Kinship and Mar-
       riage among Australian Aborigines*. Ashgate,
       Aldershot, United Kingdom.

McNeil, Cameron L. (editor)
2006   *Chocolate in Mesoamerica: A Culture His-
       tory of Cacao*. University of Florida Press,
       Gainesville.

Michels, Joseph W.
1979   *The Kaminaljuyu Chiefdom*. Pennsylvania State
       University Press, University Park.

Millon, René
1955   *When Money Grew on Trees: A Study of Cacao
       in Ancient Mesoamerica*. Columbia University,
       New York.

Modjeska, Nicholas
1982   Production and Inequality: Perspectives from
       Central New Guinea. In *Inequality in New
       Guinea Highland Societies*, edited by Andrew
       Strathern, pp. 50–108. Cambridge University
       Press, Cambridge.

Moholy-Nagy, Hattula
1992   Lithic Deposits as Waste Management: Reply to
       Healan and to Hester and Shafer. *Latin Ameri-
       can Antiquity* 3:249–251.

Moore, John H.
1988   The Dialectics of Cheyenne Kinship: Variability
       and Change. *Ethnology* 27:253–269.

Morley, Sylvanus G., George W. Brainerd, and
Robert J. Sharer
    1983   *The Ancient Maya, Fourth Edition*. Stanford
            University Press, Stanford.
Morsink, Joost
    2013   Exchange as a Social Contract: A Perspective
            from the Microscale. In *The Oxford Handbook
            of Caribbean Archaeology*, edited by William
            F. Keegan, Corinne L. Hoffman, and Reniel
            Rodríguez Ramos, pp. 312–328. Oxford Uni-
            versity Press, Oxford.
Motilal, Lambert A., Dapeng Zhang, Pathmanathan
Umaharan, Sue Mischke, Vishnarayan Mooleedhar, and
Lyndel W. Meinhardt
    2010   The Relic Criollo Cacao in Belize—Genetic Diver-
            sity and Relationship with Trinitario and Other
            Cacao Clones Held in the International Cocoa
            Genebank, Trinidad. *Plant Genetic Resources:
            Characterization and Utilization* 8:106–115.
Munn, Nancy D.
    1992   The Cultural Anthropology of Time: A
            Critical Essay. *Annual Review of Anthropology*
            21:93–123.
Muñoz-Salinas, Esperanza, Miguel Castillo,
David Sanderson, and Tim Kinnaird
    2017   Geochronology and Landscape Evolution of the
            Strand-Plain of the Usumacinta-Grijalva Rivers,
            Southern Mexico. *Journal of South American
            Earth Sciences* 79:394–400.
National Public Radio
    2018   Trump Policy Leads to Worker Shortage in
            Crab Industry. *All Things Considered* transcript.
            https://www.npr.org/2018/05/05/608802924/
            trump-policy-leads-to-worker-shortage-in-
            crab-industry. Accessed 27 July 2018.
Navarette, Carlos
    1967   Los ladrillos grabados de Comalcalco, Tabasco.
            *Boletin de Insituto Nacional de Antropologia e
            Historia* 27:19–25.
Netting, Robert M., Richard R. Wilk, and Eric J. Arnould
(editors)
    1984   *Households: Comparative and Historical Studies
            of the Domestic Group*. University of California
            Press, Berkeley.
Nooren, Kees, Wim Z. Hoek, Tim Winkels, Annika Huizinga,
Hans Van der Plicht, Remke L. Van Dam, Sytze Van Heteren,
Manfred J. Van Bergen, Maarten A. Prins, Tony Reimann,
Jakob Wallinga, Kim M. Cohen, Philip Minderhoud, and
Hans Midelkoop
    2017   The Usumacinta-Grijalva Beach-Ridge Plain in
            Southern Mexico: A High-Resolution Archive of

River Discharge and Precipitation. *Earth Surface
            Dynamics* 5:529–556.
Nutini, Hugo
    1961   Clan Organization in a Nahuatl-Speaking
            Village of the State of Tlaxcala, Mexico. *Ameri-
            can Anthropologist* 63:62–78.
Ochoa, Lorenzo
    1997   En los límites de la imaginación. In *Tabasco:
            Apuntes de frontera*, edited by Mario Humberto
            Ruz, pp. 17–40. Consejo Nacional para la
            Cultura y las Artes, México, DF.
    2003   La Costa del Golfo y el área Maya ¿Relaciones
            imaginables o imaginadas? *Estudios de cultura
            Maya* 23:35–54.
    2010   Topofilia: A Tool for the Demarcation of Cul-
            tural Microregions: The Case of the Huaxteca.
            In *Pre-columbian Foodways: Interdisciplinary
            Approaches to Food, Culture, and Markets in
            Ancient Mesoamerica*, edited by John E. Staller
            and Michael Carrasco, pp. 535–576. Springer,
            New York.
Ochoa, Lorenzo, and Luis Casasola
    1991   Tierra Blanca y el Medio Usumacinta: Notas de
            su cerámica arqueológica. *Tierra y Agua* 2:7–28.
Ochoa, Lorenzo, and Ernesto Vargas
    1987   Xicalango. Puerto Chontal de intercambio: Mito
            y realidad. *Anales de Antropología* 24:95–126.
O'Connor, Amber
    2010   Maya Foodways: A Reflection of Gender
            and Ideology. In *Pre-columbian Foodways:
            Interdisciplinary Approaches to Food, Culture,
            and Markets in Ancient Mesoamerica*, edited
            by John E. Staller and Michael Carrasco,
            pp. 487–507. Springer, New York.
Oliver-Smith, Anthony, and Susanna M. Hoffman (editors)
    1999   *The Angry Earth: Disaster in Anthropological
            Perspective*. Routledge, New York
Ortega Peña, Elsa
    1999   Los ahualulcos de Tabasco: Una revisión
            histórica. *Antropológicas* 16:59–63.
Osland, Michael J., Laura C. Feher, Jorge López-Portillo,
Richard H. Day, Daniel O. Suman, José Manuel Guzmán
Menéndez, and Victor H. Rivera-Monroy
    2018   Mangrove Forests in a Rapidly Changing World:
            Global Change Impacts and Conservation
            Opportunities along the Gulf of Mexico
            Coast. *Estuarine, Coastal and Shelf Science*
            214:120–140.
Parsons, Jeffrey R.
    2010   The Pastoral Niche in Pre-Hispanic Mesoamer-
            ica. In *Pre-columbian Foodways: Interdisciplinary*

Approaches to Food, Culture, and Markets in Ancient Mesoamerica, edited by John E. Staller and Michael Carrasco, pp. 109–136. Springer, New York.

Parsons, Lee A.
1978 The Peripheral Coastal Lowlands and the Middle Classic Period. In *Middle Classic Mesoamerica: AD 400–700*, edited by Esther Pasztory, pp. 25–34. Columbia University Press, New York.

Peelo, Sarah
2011 Pottery-Making in Spanish California: Creating Multi-Scalar Social Identity through Daily Practice. *American Antiquity* 76:642–666.

Peletz, Michael G.
1995 Kinship Studies in Late Twentieth-Century Anthropology. *Annual Review of Anthropology* 24:343–372.

Pendergast, David M.
1981 Lamanai, Belize: Summary of Excavation Results, 1974–1980. *Journal of Field Archaeology* 8:29–53.
1992 Noblesse Oblige: The Elites of Altun Ha and Lamanai, Belize. In *Mesoamerican Elites: An Archaeological Assessment*, edited by Diane Z. Chase and Arlen F. Chase, pp. 61–79. University of Oklahoma Press, Norman.

Peniche Rivero, Piedad
1973 *Comalcalco, Tabasco: Su cerámica, artifactos, y enterramientos*. Tesis de Licenciatura, Universidad de Yucatán, Mérida.

Peregrine, Peter N.
1996 Ethnology versus Ethnographic Analogy: A Common Confusion in Archaeological Interpretation. *Cross-Cultural Research* 30:316–329.
2001 Matrilocality, Corporate Strategy, and the Organization of Production in the Chacoan World. *American Antiquity* 66:36–46.

Pérez Campos, Elizabeth Mejía, and Lorena Mirambell Silva (editors)
1992 *Comalcalco*. Antologias, Instituto Nacional de Antropología e Historia, México, DF.

Pérez Rodríguez, Verónica
2006 States and Households: The Social Organization of Terrace Agriculture in Postclassic Mixteca Alta, Oaxaca, Mexico. *Latin American Antiquity* 17:3–22.

Pérez Suárez, Tomás
2003 Hilos de un mismo tejido cultural: el área Maya y la Costa del Golfo. *Estudios de cultura Maya* 23:17–33.

Piña Chan, Roman, and Carlos Navarrete
1967 *Archaeological Research in the Lower Grijalva River Region, Tabasco and Chiapas*. Papers No. 22. New World Archaeological Foundation, Provo.

Plog, Stephen
1978 Social Interaction and Stylistic Similarity: A Reanalysis. *Advances in Archaeological Method and Theory* 1:143–182.

Pool, Christopher A.
2009 Asking More and Better Questions: Olmec Archaeology for the Next *Katun*. *Ancient Mesoamerica* 20:241–252.

Pool, Christopher A., Ponciano Ortiz Ceballos, María del Carmen Rodríguez Martínez, and Michael L. Loughlin
2010 The Early Horizon at Tres Zapotes: Implications for Olmec Interaction. *Ancient Mesoamerica* 21:95–105.

Porčić, Marko
2010 House Floor Area as a Correlate of Marital Residence Pattern: A Logistical Regression Approach. *Cross-Cultural Research* 44:405–424.

Psuty, Norbert P.
1967 *The Geomorphology of Beach Ridges in Tabasco, Mexico*. Louisiana State University Press, Baton Rouge.

Rands, Robert L.
1969 *The Ceramic Sequence at Trinidad, Tabasco*. Mesoamerican Studies No. 2. Southern Illinois University, Carbondale.
1973 The Classic Maya Collapse: Usumacinta Zone and the Northwestern Periphery. In *The Classic Maya Collapse*, edited by T. Patrick Culbert, pp. 165–205. University of New Mexico Press, Albuquerque.
1985 Ceramic Patterns and Traditions in the Palenque Area. In *Maya Ceramics*, edited by Prudence M. Rice and Robert J. Sharer, pp. 203–238. BAR, Oxford.

Redfield, Robert
1950 *A Village That Chose Progress: Chan Kom Revisited*. University of Chicago Press, Chicago.

Reitz, Elizabeth, J., and Elizabeth S. Wing
1999 *Zooarchaeology*. Cambridge University Press, Cambridge.

Reyes González, Liliana Carla, and Marcus Winter
2010 The Early Formative Period in the Southern Isthmus: Excavations at Barrio Tepalcate, Ixtepec, Oaxaca. *Ancient Mesoamerica* 21:151–163.

Rice, Don S., and Dennis E. Puleston
1981   Ancient Maya Settlement Patterns in the Peten, Guatemala. In *Lowland Maya Settlement Patterns*, edited by Wendy Ashmore, pp. 121–156. University of New Mexico Press, Albuquerque.

Rice, Prudence M.
1987   *Pottery Analysis: A Sourcebook*. University of Chicago Press, Chicago.

Robin, Cynthia, Laura Kosakowsky, Angela Keller, and James Melerhoff
2014   Leaders, Farmers, and Crafters: The Relationship between Leading Households and Households across the Chan Community. *Ancient Mesoamerica* 25:371–387.

Romero Molina, Javier
1987   Incrustaciones dentarias en forma de hongo. *Avances en antropología física* 2:149–164.

Romero Rivera, José Luis
1992   Tres tablillas de barro con inscripciones glíficas de Comalcalco, Tabasco. In *Comalcalco*, edited by Elizabeth Mejía Pérez Campos and Lorena Mirambell Silva, pp. 225–269. Instituto Nacional de Antropología e Historia, México, D. F.
1995   Un estudio del patrón de asentamiento de Comalcalco, Tabasco. In *Seis ensayos sobre antiguos patrones de asentamiento en el área Maya*, edited by Ernesto Vargas Pacheco, pp. 15–27. Universidad Nacional Autónoma de México, México, DF.

Rosenswig, Robert M.
2007   Beyond Identifying Elites: Feasting as a Means to Understand Early Middle Formative Society on the Pacific Coast of Mexico. *Journal of Anthropological Archaeology* 26:1–27.

Rosman, Abraham, and Paula G. Rubel
1971   *Feasting with Mine Enemy: Rank and Exchange among Northwest Coast Societies*. Columbia University Press, New York.

Roys, Ralph L.
1940   Personal Names of the Maya of Yucatán. *Contributions to American Anthropology and History* 31:31–48.
1957   *The Political Geography of the Yucatan Maya*. Carnegie Institution of Washington, Washington, DC.

Ruíz R., Jesús J.
2005   Untitled letter report in Appendix A of *Proyecto Arqueológico Islas de Los Cerros 2005*, by Bradley E. Ensor, Concepción Herrera Escobar, Keiko Teranishi Castillo, Gabriel Tun Ayora, and Socorro P. Jiménez Alvarez, p. 37. Report to the Instituto Nacional de Antropología e Historia, México, DF.

Rye, Owen S.
1981   *Pottery Technology: Principles and Reconstruction*. Taraxacum, Washington, DC.

SAGARPA
2013   *Cultivos de cacao en el sur-sureste de México*. https://www.gob.mx/sagarpa/prensa. Accessed 8 August 2017.

Sabloff, Jeremy A.
1976   *Excavations at Seibal: Ceramics*. Memoirs of the Peabody Museum of Archaeology and Ethnology, Vol. 13, No. 2. Harvard University, Cambridge, Massachusetts.

Sabloff, Jeremy A., and William L. Rathje
1975   The Rise of a Maya Merchant Class. *Scientific American* 233:72–82.

Sacks, Karen
1975   Engels Revisited: Women, the Organization of Production, and Private Property. In *Toward an Anthropology of Women*, edited by Rayna R. Reiter, pp. 211–234. Monthly Review Press, New York.

Sahlins, Marshall D.
2013   *What Kinship Is—and Is Not*. University of Chicago Press, Chicago.

Sanchez Caero, Oscar Fidel
1979   *Excavaciones arqueológicas en la zona de Jonuta, Tabasco*. Tesis de Licenciatura. Escuela Nacional de Antropología e Historia, México, DF.

Sanders, William T.
1962   Cultural Ecology of the Maya Lowlands. *Estudios de cultura Maya* 3:203–241.
1981   Classic Maya Settlement Patterns and Ethnographic Analogy. In *Lowland Maya Settlement Patterns*, edited by Wendy Ashmore, pp. 351–369. University of New Mexico Press, Albuquerque.
1989   Household, Lineage, and State at Eighth-Century Copan, Honduras. In *The House of the Bacabs, Copan, Honduras*, edited by David L. Webster pp. 89–105. Dumbarton Oaks, Washington, DC.
1992   Ranking and Stratification in Prehispanic Mesoamerica. In *Mesoamerican Elites: An Archaeological Assessment*, edited by Diane Z. Chase and Arlen F. Chase, pp. 278–291. University of Oklahoma Press, Norman.

Sandstrom, Alan R.
2000   Contemporary Cultures of the Gulf Coast. In *Ethnology*, edited by John D. Monaghan,

pp 83. Supplement to the Handbook of Middle American Indians, Vol. 6, Victoria Bricker, general editor. University of Texas Press, Austin.

Santillán, Patricia
1986   La vivienda en las tierras bajas mayas. In *Unidades habitacionales mesoamericanas y sus areas de actividad,* edited by Linda Manzanilla, pp. 399–424. Universidad Nacional Autónoma de México, México, DF.

Santley, Robert S.
2004   Prehistoric Salt Production at El Salado, Veracruz, Mexico. *Latin American Antiquity* 15:199–221.

Santley, Robert S. and Philip J. Arnold III
2005   The Obsidian Trade to the Tuxtlas Region and its Implications for the Prehistory of Southern Veracruz, Mexico. *Ancient Mesoamerica* 16:179–194.

Santley, Robert S., Philip J. Arnold, III, and Thomas P. Barrett
1997   Formative Period Settlement Patterns in the Tuxtla Mountains. In *Olmec to Aztec: Settlement Patterns in the Ancient Gulf Lowlands,* edited by Barbara L. Stark and Philip J. Arnold III, pp. 174–205. University of Arizona Press, Tucson.

Scherer, Andrew K., Lori E. Wright, and Cassady J. Yoder
2007   Bioarchaeological Evidence for Social and Temporal Differences in Diet at Piedras Negras, Guatemala. *Latin American Antiquity* 18:85–104.

Scholes, Frances V., and Ralph L. Roys
1968   *The Maya Chontal Indians of Acalan-Tixchel.* University of Oklahoma Press, Norman.

Shafer, Harry J., and Thomas R. Hester
1983   Ancient Maya Chert Workshops in Northern Belize, Central America. *American Antiquity* 48:519–543.
1986   Maya Stone-Tool Craft Specialization and Production at Colha, Belize: Reply to Mallory. *American Antiquity* 51:158–166.

Shepard, Anna O.
1976   *Ceramics for the Archaeologist.* Publication No. 609. Carnegie Institute of Washington, Washington, DC.

Simon, Arleyn W.
1988   *Integrated Ceramic Analysis: An Investigation of Intersite Relationships in Central Arizona.* Ph.D. dissertation, Arizona State University, Tempe.

Simon, Arleyn W., and James H. Burton
1989   Technological and Compositional Analyses of Patarata Ceramics. In *Patarata Pottery: Classic Period Ceramics of the South-Central Gulf*

Coast, Veracruz, Mexico, by Barbara L. Stark, pp. 113–128. University of Arizona Press, Tucson.

Simon, Arleyn W., and William A. Coghlan
1989   The Use of Indentation Testing for Obtaining Precise Hardness Measurements from Prehistoric Pottery. *American Antiquity* 54:107–122.

Simon, Arleyn W., Jean-Christophe Komorowski, and James H. Burton
1992   Patterns of Production and Distribution of Salado Wares as a Measure of Complexity. In *Developing Perspectives on Tonto Basin Prehistory,* edited by Charles L. Redman, Glen E. Rice, and Kathryn E. Pedrick, pp. 61–76. Roosevelt Monograph Series 2, Anthropological Field Studies No. 26. Arizona State University, Tempe.

Sisson, Edward B.
1976   *Survey and Excavations in the Northwestern Chontalpa.* PhD dissertation, Department of Anthropology. Harvard University, Cambridge, Massachusetts.

Smith, A. Ledyard
1962   *Mayapan, Yucatan, Mexico,* Part 3: Residential and Associated Structures at Mayapan. Publication No. 477. Carnegie Institution of Washington, Washington, DC.

Smith, Carol A.
1984   Local History in Global Context: Social and Economic Transitions in Western Guatemala. *Comparative Study of Society and History* 26:193–228.

Smith, M. F.
1985   Toward an Economic Interpretation of Ceramics: Relating Vessel Size and Shape to Use. In *Decoding Prehistoric Ceramics,* edited by Ben A. Nelson, pp. 254–309. Southern Illinois University Press, Tucson.

Souvatzi, Stella
2008   *A Social Archaeology of Households in Neolithic Greece: An Anthropological Approach.* Cambridge University Press, Cambridge.
2017   Kinship and Social Archaeology. *Cross-Cultural Research* 51:172–195.

Speal, C. Scott
2014   The Evolution of Ancient Maya Exchange Systems: An Etymological Study of Economic Vocabulary in the Mayan Language Family. *Ancient Mesoamerica* 25:69–113.

Staller, John E.
2010   Ethnohistoric Sources on Foodways, Feasts, and Festivals in Mesoamerica. In *Pre-columbian Foodways: Interdisciplinary Approaches to Food,*

Staller, John E. (*continued*)
> *Culture, and Markets in Ancient Mesoamerica*, edited by John E. Staller and Michael Carrasco, pp. 23–69. Springer, New York.

Staller, John E., and Michael Carrasco (editors)
2010   *Pre-columbian Foodways: Interdisciplinary Approaches to Food, Culture, and Markets in Ancient Mesoamerica*. Springer, New York.

Stanton, Travis W., and Tomás Gallareta Negrón
2001   Warfare, Ceramic Economy, and the Itza: A Reconsideration of the Itza Polity in Ancient Yucatan. *Ancient Mesoamerica* 12:229–245.

Stark, Barbara L.
1974   Geography and Economic Specialization in the Lower Papaloapan, Veracruz, Mexico. *Ethnohistory* 21:199–221.

1978   An Ethnohistoric Model for Native Economy and Settlement Patterns in Southern Veracruz, Mexico. In *Prehistoric Coastal Adaptations: The Economy and Ecology of Maritime Middle America*, edited by Barbara L. Stark and Barbara Voorhies, pp. 211–234. Academic Press, New York.

1987   Mesoamerican Gulf and Caribbean Coastal Adaptations. In *Coasts, Plains, and Deserts: Essays in Honor of Reynold J. Ruppe*, edited by Silvia W. Gaines, pp. 239–257. Anthropological Research Papers No. 38. Arizona State University, Tempe.

1989   *Patarata Pottery: Classic Period Ceramics of the South-Central Gulf Coast, Veracruz, Mexico*. University of Arizona Press, Tucson.

1991   Survey Methods and Settlement Features in the Cerro de las Mesas Region: A Comparative Discussion. In *Settlement Archaeology of Cerro de la Mesas, Veracruz, Mexico*, edited by Barbara L. Stark, pp. 39–48. Institute of Archaeology Monograph No. 34. University of California, Los Angeles.

1999   Formal Architectural Complexes in South-Central Veracruz, Mexico: A Capital Zone? *Journal of Field Archaeology* 26:197–225.

2006   Systematic Regional Survey in the Gulf Lowlands in a Comparative Perspective. In *Managing Archaeological Data: Essays in Honor of Sylvia W. Gaines*, edited by Jeffrey L. Hantman and Rachel Most, pp. 155–167. Anthropological Research Paper No. 57. Arizona State University, Tempe.

Stark, Barbara L. (editor)
1991   *Settlement Archaeology of Cerro de la Mesas, Veracruz, Mexico*. Institute of Archaeology Monograph No. 34. University of California, Los Angeles.

2001   *Classic Period Mixtequilla, Veracruz, Mexico: Diachronic Inferences from Residential Investigations*. Institute for Mesoamerican Studies, University at Albany, New York.

Stark, Barbara L., and Christopher P. Garraty
2004   Evaluation of Systematic Surface Evidence for Pottery Production in Veracruz, Mexico. *Latin American Antiquity* 15:123–143.

2008   Parallel Archaeological and Visibility Survey in the Western Papaloapan Basin, Veracruz, Mexico. *Journal of Field Archaeology* 33:177–196.

Stark, Barbara L., and Lynette Heller
1991   Cerro de las Mesas Revisited: Survey in 1984–1985. In *Settlement Archaeology of Cerro de las Mesas, Veracruz, Mexico*, edited by Barbara L. Stark, pp. 1–25. Institute of Archaeology Monograph No. 34. University of California, Los Angeles.

Stark, Barbara L., and Wesley D. Stoner
2017   Watching the Game: Viewership of Architectural Mesoamerican Ball Courts. *Latin American Antiquity* 28:409–430.

Stark, Barbara L., Lynette Heller, and Michael A. Ohnersorgen
1998   People with Cloth: Mesoamerican Economic Change from the Perspective of Cotton in South-Central Veracruz. *Latin American Antiquity* 9:7–36.

Stone, Andrea J.
2011   Keeping Abreast of the Maya: A Study of the Female Body in Maya Art. *Ancient Mesoamerica* 22:167–183.

Stone, Linda
2010   *Kinship and Gender: An Introduction*. Westview Press, Boulder.

Straight, Kirk D.
2017   A Houseful of Pots: Applying Ethnoarchaeological Data to Estimate Annual Ceramic Vessel Consumption Rates of Classic Maya Households. *Ancient Mesoamerica* 28:95–117.

Stirling, Matthew W.
1943   *Stone Monuments of Southern Mexico*. Bureau of American Ethnology Bulletin No. 138. Smithsonian Institution, Washington, DC.

1957   *An Archeological Reconnaissance in Southeastern Mexico*. Bureau of American Ethnology Bulletin No. 164, Anthropological Papers No. 53. Smithsonian Institution, Washington DC.

Stone, Linda
2010   *Kinship and Gender: An Introduction*. Westview Press, Boulder.

Sturtevant, William C.
1998　Tupinambá Chiefdoms? In *Chiefdoms and Chieftancy in the Americas*, edited by Elsa M. Redmond, pp. 138–149. University Press of Florida, Gainesville.

Szołtysek, Mikołaj
2015　*Rethinking East-Central Europe: Family Systems and Co-residence in the Polish-Lithuanian Commonwealth*. Peter Lang Press, Bern.

Taladoire, Eric
2015　Towards a Reevaluation of the Toniná Polity. *Estudios de cultura Maya* 46:45–70.
2016　Las bases económicas de una entidad política Maya: El caso de Toniná. *Estudios de cultura Maya* 48:11–37.

Tamura, Toru
2012　Beach Ridges and Prograded Beach Deposits as Paleoenvironment Records. *Earth-Science Reviews* 114:279–297.

Thompson, Phillip C.
1978　*Tekanto in the Eighteenth Century*. Ph.D. dissertation, Tulane University, University Microfilms, Ann Arbor.
1982　Dynastic Marriage and Successions at Tikal. *Estudios de Cultura Maya* 14:261–287.

Thompson, Raymond H.
1958　*Modern Yucatecan Maya Pottery Making*. Memoirs No. 15. Society for American Archaeology, Salt Lake City.

Tiesler, Vera, and Andrea Cucina
2012　Filiación, relaciones interpoblaciones y enlaces culturales en las tierras bajas Mayas durante el periodo clásico. *Estudios de cultura Maya* 40:97–112.

Tourtellot, G., III
1988　*Excavations at Seibal, Department of Peten, Guatemala: Peripheral Survey and Excavation, Settlement and Community Patterns*. Harvard University Press, Cambridge, Massachusetts.

Tozzer, Alfred M.
1907　*A Comparative Study of the Mayas and Lacandons*. Macmillan, New York.

Trigger, Bruce G.
2006　*A History of Archaeological Thought*, second edition. Cambridge University Press, Cambridge.

Tsing, Anna L., and Sylvia J. Yanagisako
1983　Feminism and Kinship Theory. *Current Anthropology* 24:511–516.

Tsukamoto, Kenichiro, and Takesi Inomata (editors)
2014　*Mesoamerican Plazas: Arenas of Community and Power*. University of Arizona Press, Tucson.

Tun Ayora, Gabriel
2010　*Antropología, arquitectura, y arqueología: Principios interpretativos para el estudio de unidades habitacionales Mayas prehispánicas desde la antropología arquitectónica*. Tesis de Maestría. Universidad Autónoma de Yucatán, Mérida.

Turner, Terence
2012　Schemas of Kinship Relations and the Construction of Social Categories among the Mebêngôkrê Kayapó. In *Crow-Omaha: New Light on a Classic Problem of Kinship Analysis*, edited by Thomas R. Trautmann and Peter M. Whiteley, pp. 223–239. University of Arizona Press, Tucson.

Tuxill, John, Luis Arias Reyes, Luis Latournerie Moreno, Vidal Cob Uicab, and Devra I. Jarvis
2010　All Maize is Not Equal: Maize Variety Choices and Mayan Foodways in Rural Yucatan, Mexico. In *Pre-columbian Foodways: Interdisciplinary Approaches to Food, Culture, and Markets in Ancient Mesoamerica*, edited by John E. Staller and Michael Carrasco, pp. 467–486. Springer, New York.

Twiss, Katheryn C. (editor)
2007　*The Archaeology of Food and Identity*. Center for Archaeological Investigations Occasional Paper No. 34. Southern Illinois University, Carbondale.

Vargas Pacheco, E.
1992　Arqueología e historia de los Maya-Chontales de Tabasco. In *Comalcalco*, edited by E. M. Pérez Campos, pp. 273–296. Instituto Nacional de Antropología e Historia, México, D. F.

Vásquez Dávila, Beatriz Solís Trejo, and Enrique Hipólito Hernández.
1988　La vivienda en la cultura Chontal de Tabasco. In *La vivienda rural en el sureste de Mexico*, edited by Secretaría de Educación, Cultura y Recreación : Gobierno del Estado de Tabasco, pp. 19–42. Gobierno del Estado de Tabasco, Villahermosa.

Velásquez Fergusson, Laura
2014　El patrón triádico en el contexto urbano e ideológico de los antiguos asentamientos Mayas. *Estudios de Cultura Maya* 43:13–40.

Von Nagy, Christopher
1997　The Geoarchaeology of Settlement in the Grijalva Delta. In *Olmec to Aztec: Settlement Patterns in the Ancient Gulf Lowlands*, edited by Barbara L. Stark and Philip J. Arnold, pp. 253–277. University of Arizona Press, Tucson.

Voorhies, Barbara
  1972   Settlement Patterns in Two Regions of the Southern Maya Lowlands. *American Antiquity* 37:115–126.

Voss, Barbara L.
  2015   What's New? Rethinking Ethnogenesis in the Archaeology of Colonialism. *American Antiquity* 80:655–670.

Watanabe, John M.
  2004   Some Models in a Muddle: Lineage and House in Classic Maya Social Organization. *Ancient Mesoamerica* 15:159–166.

Webster, David, and Nancy Gonlin
  1988   Household Remains of the Humblest Maya. *Journal of Field Archaeology* 15:169–190.

Weiss-Krejci, Estella, and Thomas Sabbas
  2002   The Potential Role of Small Depressions as Water Storage Features in the Central Maya Lowlands. *Latin American Antiquity* 13:343–357.

Wendt, Carl J.
  2005   Using Refuse Disposal Patterns to Infer Olmec Site Structure in the San Lorenzo Region, Veracruz, Mexico. *Latin American Antiquity* 16:449–466.
  2010   A San Lorenzo Phase Household Assemblage from El Remolino, Veracruz. *Ancient Mesoamerica* 21:107–122.

Wendt, Carl J., and Ann Cyphers
  2008   How the Olmec Used Bitumen in Ancient Mesoamerica. *Journal of Anthropological Archaeology* 27:175–191.

West, Robert C., Norbert P. Psuty, and Bruce G. Thom
  1969   *The Tabasco Lowlands of Southeastern Mexico.* Louisiana State University Press, Baton Rouge.

Whalen, Michael E., and Paul E. Minnis
  2012   Ceramics and Polity in the Casas Grande Area, Chihuahua, Mexico. *American Antiquity* 77:403–423.

Wilk, Richard R.
  1984   Maya Household Organization: Evidence and Analogies. In *Household and Community in the Mesoamerican Past*, edited by Richard R. Wilk and Wendy Ashmore, pp. 135–151. University of New Mexico Press, Albuquerque.

Willey, Gordon R., and William R. Bullard
  1956   The Melhado Site: A House Mound Group in British Honduras. *American Antiquity* 22:29–44.

Witschey, Walter R. T.
  1991   Maya Inheritance Patterns: The Transfer of Real Estate and Personal Property in Ebtun, Yucatan, Mexico. *Estudios de Cultura Maya* 18:395–416.

Wobst, H. Martin
  1978   The Archaeo-Ethnology of Hunter-Gatherers or the Tyranny of the Ethnographic Record in Archaeology. *American Antiquity* 43:303–309.

Wolf, Eric
  1972   Ownership and Political Ecology. *Anthropological Quarterly* 45:201–205.

Zender, Marc U.
  1998   *Epigraphic Research at Comalcalco.* Manuscript in the Archivo del Archivo del Proyecto Arqueológico Comalcalco, Instituto Nacional de Antropología e Historia, Comalcalco.

Index

Page numbers in *italics* indicate illustrations.

Acalán, 1, 11
acropolis-plaza association, 175–176. *See also* triadic plaza configurations
Aguacatal, 94, 151; pottery from, 121, 127, 128, 166, 182; recycled Formative deposits at, 95, 96(table)
Ahualulcos region, 4, 151
Alameda site, 151
alliances, 197; marriage, 193, 194–195, 197–198, 200
analogy, 162, 178, 191–192, 199, 200, 206
ancestor veneration, 59, 176, 178, 191, 195–96, 198–99, 201, 204–206
aquatic resources, 26, 29, 157–158, 159
archaeological sites: preservation of, 3, 6, 15, 21, 26, 30, 32–33
architecture: materials, 6, 16, 62, 144, 145–148, 149, 157, 160, 166, 186, 188, 206; monumental, 9–10, 18–19, 97, 167–168, 175–178, 197, 198, 207
Atlas Arqueológico projects, 10, 34

Bakal, kingdom of, 10
ballcourts, 166–168, 175–176, 197–198
beach ridges, 22, 23, 25, 30, 157–160, 163, 175, 202; modern settlement on, 26–27, 29, 31

Berlin, Heinrich, 9, 34, 52, 84, 88
bilateral descent, bilocal residence. *See under* kinship
bitumen, 6, 135–137, 148
Blom, Frans and Oliver La Farge, 9, 49, 83, 85, 88, 97
brick, 6, 9, 10, 19, 47, 49, 52–53, 56–57, 60, 83–84, 87, 88, 97, *136*, 145, 147, 149, 166, 175, 188

cacao, viii, 1, 10, 23, 30–31, 59–60, 147, 166–168, 175, 208
canals, possible, 14, 28, 37, 57
ceramics. *See* pottery
ceremonial mounds, 12, 37, *38*, 49, 54, 57, 60, 83–88, 95, 97, 176, 188, 195, 197
Charnay, Desiré, 8–9, 34, 49, 83, 84, 88, 97, 142
chert, 6, 14, 16, 138, 139(table), 148; at El Bellote, 56, 92
Chicanel Tradition/Isthmus sphere, 101, 108, 127, 151–153
childcare, children, 200–201, 207
chipped stone, 56, 70, *136*, 137–138, 188. *See also* chert; obsidian
Chontal Maya/Mayan, viii, 1, 3–4, 9, *11*–12, 166, 175
Chontalpa, 1, 2, 3–4; regional interaction, 166–167; trade in, 12–13
chronology, 3–4, 20, 58–59, 96, 100–101, 104, 128, 134, 137, 150–151, 165–166. *See also* pottery

classes, 2–3, 7, 19, 60–61, 88, 102, 137, 144, 148, 165, 172, 173–174; children and, 200–201; definition of, 178–182; interclass material display 182–184; intraclass material display 184–190; elite, 175–178, 208; feasting/food sharing and, 204–205; foodways, 201–203, 207–208; kinship and, 193–200, 206
Classic period, 7. *See also* Early Classic period; Middle Classic period; Late Classic period
clan. *See* kinship, patriclan
classification system. *See* features, pottery
clay: structural use of, 6, 15, 16, 17, 19, 54, 56, 66, 69, 75, 80, 85, 86, 88, 92, 93, 94, 104, 148, 149, 187. *See also* pottery
climate, 21
coastal settlements: Formative period, 151; Late Classic period, 167–168
coconut ranching, *27*, 30
Comalcalco, 4, 7, 8, 9, 12, 22, 31, 41, 128, 143, 145, 165, *177*, 194; architectural material at, 147, 149, 166; ceramic classification at, 100, 112; epigraphic information from, 10–11; Formative settlement of, 151, 153; monumental architecture at, 176, 178; obsidian at, 137–138; political economy of, 60, 174, 175;

pottery used at, 112, 204; regional settlement pattern and, 167–168, 170; kinship, 196–197, 207

commerce, 12–13. *See also* political economies

commercial development: modern, 31–33

commodity production, 179; and class, 178, 182

concheros (shell midden-mound), 2, 4, 6, 10, 12, 20, 36, 47, 58, 95, 99, 144, 156, 157, 162

construction materials: processing, 60, 168, 182; shell in, 144, 145

construction sequence, 60–61, 74–75, 98

cooperatives: fishing, 29, 59

corporate groups, 191, 192–196, 198–200, 204, 206–207. *See also* kinship

Cortés, Hernán, 1, 11

crabs (Gecarcinidae), 25, 29, 31–32, 41, 42, 89, 143, 145, 157, 201

craft production, 17, 37, 59, 60, 88, 97, 105, 138, 145, 158, 178, 181

dating, 9, 20; radiometric, 19, 76, 144; thermoluminescence, 6, 19, 132–133

daub, *136*, 148

demographics, Late Classic ILC, 172, 174

diet, 141–142, 157–158, 159, 167

discrete mounds, 68, 98, 172; collections and profiles of, 65–67; size range of, 64–65

discrete platforms, 172; characteristics of, 61–64

discs, sherd, 135

domestic activities, 3, 6, 10, 14, 16–17, 18, 20, 29–30, 37, 59–60, 71, 93, 96–97, 134, 136–137, 144, 147, 158, 161, 178, 182, 186, 188, 200, 201, 202, 204, 207

Dos Bocas, 4, 22, 31

dunes. *See* beach ridges

Early Classic period, 4, 7, 128, 144, 165–166

Early Formative period, 23, 151, 162

ecology, 3, 25–26, 104. *See also* theory, political ecology

economy, 162; tributary, 174, 200. *See also* theory, political economy

El Bellote, 4, 6, 10, 11, 12, 13, 18, 26, 27, 29, 30, 34, 57, 58, 93, 136, 137, 138, 140, 145, 175, 181; architectural materials at, 146–147, 166; Central Group, 51–52(table), 54–56, 80, 83, 86–87, 94, 140, 194, 195; ceremonial elites at, 187–188, 194–195; ceremonial mounds at, 83–88, 176; descriptions of, 49–56; discrete mounds at, 64, 65–67; early descriptions of, 8–9; elliptical platform at, 91–92; fishing-related activities, 97, 135, 182; Formative period pottery from, 107–108, 155, 156, 160; Formative period, 151, 153–164; Late Classic pottery from, 119, 121, 171; mangrove losses on, 32–33; mounds-on-platforms at, 68, 69; multilevel mounds at, 78–80, *81*; North-Central Group, 51(table), 54, 78–80, 86, 147; Northeast Group, 49, 51(table), 52–54, 64, 65, 83–86, 172, 195, 196, 206; Northwest Group, 51(table), 54, 64, 83, 86, 195, 196; occupation duration, 172, 173, 206; resource-accessing commoners at, 186, 194; South Group, 52(table), 56, 64, 65–67, 76, 78, 80–81, *82*, 68, 91–92, 97, 135, 148, 172, 182, 186, 194, 196, 206

El Bellote (modern town), 23, 26–27, 30–31

El Canal, 34, *43*, 48, 57

elites. *See* classes

environments, 6; and archaeological sites, 32–33; climate, 21; fauna, 24–25; flora, 23–*24*; hydrology and geomorphology, 21–23; and site locations, 25–26

Epiclassic period, 1, 4, 13, 132

epigraphic texts, 10–11, 100

ethnicity, 3, 104–105, 150, 162, 176, 178, 201. *See also* identity

ethnohistoric research, 1, 9, 11, 12–13, 166, 191

ethnological tyranny, 178, 191, 192

excavations: Isla Chablé, 69–71, 89; Isla de Los Cerros, 14–15, 17; Isla Santa Rosita, 62–63, 72–76; pottery in, 154–155

exchange: obsidian, 137–138; regional, 2, 3, 7, 8, 10, 11, 12–13, 16, 19, 20, 48, 60, 97, 100, 105, 128, 151, 153, 157, 158, 161, 162, 167, 168, 174–175, 178, 182, 184, 193, 194–195, 205

family. *See* kinship

faunal remains, 6, 14, 16, 19, 65, 97, *136*, 149, 158, 188; dating, 143–44; invertebrate, 144–145; on Isla Chablé, 48, 89; screen mesh-size effect, 141–143

feasting, 2, 3, 6, 7, 104–105, 134, 161, 162, 164, 201–202, 204–205, 208

features, 6, 13, 36, 39–40(table); El Bellote, 49–56; functions of, 96–97; hypotheses about, 58–61; at Isla Chablé, 44–48; at Isla del Campo and Isla Santa Rosita, 41–42; morphological classification of, 6, 37, *38*; and social class, 184–188

features by number (in **bold**): **22 and 23** (Isla Santa Rosita), 72; **30** (Isla Santa Rosita), 69; **31** (Isla Santa Rosita), 69; **32–34–35** (Isla Santa Rosita), 72–76, 93, 94, 95, 96, 128, 129–130(table), 131; **36–39** (Isla Santa Rosita), 71; **40** (Isla Santa Rosita), 62–63, *64*, , 65(table), 95, 96, 99, 112, 145, 172, 182; **73–76** (Isla Chablé), 72), 76, *77*, 78(table), 95, 96, 99, 128, 129–131(table), 145, 147, 179; **77–78** (Isla Chablé), 69–71, 93, 94, 95, 96, 99, 128, 129–131(table), 135, 148, 181; **87–88** (Isla Chablé), 186; **89** (Isla Chablé), 89–91, 92, 95, 97, 149; **92** (Isla Chablé), 89, 92, 95, 97, 143–144, 145; **93–94** (Isla Chablé), 76, 78, *79*, 93, 95, 96, 99; **95–96** (Isla Chablé), 80–81, *82*, 95, 99; **97** (Isla Chablé), 65, *66*, 95, 96, 99, 112; **98–99** (Isla Chablé), 80–81, *82*, 95, 99; **100** (Isla Chablé), 87, *88*, 95,

135; **102** (Isla Chablé), 68; **103** (Isla Chablé), 68; **104** (Isla Chablé), 68; **117** (Isla Chablé), 68; **118** (Isla Chablé), 68; **122** (Isla Chablé), 89–*91*, 92(table), 97, 142–143, 145, 146, 149; **127** (Isla Santa Rosita), 72; **130** (Isla Chablé), 69; **132–133** (Isla Chablé), 69, *70*, 71, 94; **134** (Isla Chablé), 69, *70*, 71, 93–94; **135** (Isla Chablé), 93; **137** (Isla Chablé), 76, 145, 147; **138** (Isla Chablé), 93; **140** (Isla Santa Rosita), 75, 93; **141** (Isla Santa Rosita), 93; **142** (Isla Santa Rosita), 75; **143** (Isla Santa Rosita), 75; **144** (Isla Santa Rosita), 75; **145** (Isla Santa Rosita), 75; **147** (Isla Santa Rosita), 75, 94; **150** (El Bellote), 80, *81*, 95, 96, 146; **151** (El Bellote), 86–*87*, 95; **155** (El Bellote), 92, 95; **156** (El Bellote), 65–66, *67*, 96; **157** (El Bellote), 66–*67*, 68(table), *81*, 96, 98; **158** (El Bellote), 93, 94; **159** (El Bellote), 80, 93, 146; **160–163** (El Bellote), 78–80, 96, 146–147; **164** (El Bellote), 86; **165** (El Bellote), 85, 88; **166** (El Bellote), 84, *85*, 95, 97; **167** (El Bellote), 72, 80, *81*, 93, 95; **170** (El Bellote), 84–85; **171** (El Bellote), 96, 146; **173** (El Bellote), 68; **174** (El Bellote), 68, 69; **176** (El Bellote), 91–92, 97; **185** (El Bellote), 84, *85*, 95; **194** (El Bellote), 85–86; **196–202** (El Bellote), 83–84, 88, 95, 146; **198–199** (El Bellote), 86, 88
figurine fragment, 135, *136*, 148, 164
fishing, 29, 59, 60, 96, 97, 139–140, 182; capture techniques, 143, 144, 158, 159
fishing rights, 7, 29, 59, 60, 97, 135, 144, 148, 161, 162, 163, 171, 181–182, 186, 187, 198, 205, 206–207
food processing, 96–97, 138, 140, 202
foodways, class and gender in, 201–204, 207, 208; pottery, 100, 104, sharing, 204–205
formation processes, 6; of features, 58–99 *passim*; recycled deposits,

59, 61, 65–66, 68, 70, 76, 83, 95–96, 128
Formative period, 3, 4, 7, 8, 20, 144, 148, 154–155; activities and technologies, 158–160; evidence for, 58, 59, 63; features associated with, 156–157; pottery, 6, 65, 67, 69–70, 71, 72, 102–112, 127, 128, 133–134; recycled deposits from, 61, 68, 76, 83, 95–96; social relations, 160–163; subsistence in, 157–158; in Western Chontalpa, 150–153; *See also* Early Formative period; Middle Formative period; Late Formative period

gender, 2, 3, 7, 19, 29, 164, 165; relations, 162–163, 194–195; roles, 28, 29, 31–32, 165, 191, 198; foodways and, 201–203, 204; and status, 165, 192, 199–200, 207
geomorphology, 10, 21–23, 25
globalization, 26, 31–32
González-Lauck, Rebecca, viii, 9, 12
Grijalva River/Delta, 4, 9, 10, 21, 23, 140, 153
ground stone, 19, 56, 97, 133, 138, 139(table), 140, 148, 158, 188

hearths, 69, *70*, 93–94
hydrology, 21–23

iconography, 1, 162, 166, 167, 178, 201–202
identity, 2, 3, 6, 7, 28, 100, 134, 161, 163, 164, 165, 174, 175, 176, 178–179, 182, 186–187, 188, 191, 192, 193, 194, 195–196, 197, 198, 200, 201, 204, 205–207; layered, 2, 3, 7, 104–105, 153, 162, 184, 202, 203
ILC. *See* Isla de Los Cerros
INAH. *See* Instituto Nacional de Antropología e Historia
Instituto Nacional de Antropología e Historia (INAH), viii, 10, 12, 13, 14, 16, 18, 19, 34, 36, 132,
Isla Boca Grande (E 15A-79-27-038), 34, 36, *39*, 57, 132, 138, 172; description of, 37, 41

Isla Chablé (E15 A-79-27-039), 4, 6, 10, *24*, *27*, *34*, 36, *43*, 57, 58, 112, 128, 150, 176, 194; description of, 14, 42, 44(table), 45, 46–48; artifacts at, 135, *136*, 138; commoners and elites on, 181, 186, 187; environment and features on, 25–26; features on, 44–46(table); fishing activities at, 29, 148; Formative period at, 153–164; landing at, 89, 92, 97; Late Classic period at, 171, 171–172; mangrove losses on, 32–33; mounds-on-platforms at, 68, 69–71; multilevel mounds at, 76–78, 80–81; occupation duration, 173, 206; plaster and mortar at, 145, 146; residential mounds on, 65, *66*; shell deposits at, 89–91, 97; South Group (Isla Chablé), 15, 16, 34, 36, 49, 57, 65, 68, 83, 87, 89, 97, 99, 135, 138, 146, 147, 148, 149, 158, 164, 176, 181, 186, 187, 189(table), 196; thermal features at, 93–94; vertebrate remains from, 142, 143–144; Southwest Group (Isla Chablé), 46–47, 172, 181, 182, 186, 194
Isla del Campo (E 15A-79-27-075), 34, 36, *39*, 40(table), 41, 57, 172
Isla de Los Cerros (ILC), 1, 2, 4, 6, 13, 167, 175, 197; ceramic classification system, 100, 101–102; classes at, 205–206; early descriptions of, 8–9; environment, 22–25; fieldwork at, 12–19; Formative period settlement, 151, 153–163; kinship at, 193–195; Late Classic settlement, 165, 170–173; social classes at, 179, 181. *See also various sites*
Isla Dos Bocas Nuevas (E15 A-79-27-074), 34, 36, 42, 43(table), 57, 156, 172
Isla San Andres García, 22, 23
Isla Santa Rosita (E15 A-79-27-073), 12, 15, *24*, 27, 34, 36, *39*, 40(table), 57, 69, 94, 128, 135, 171, 172; description of, 41–42; discrete platform at, 62–63; Formative period pottery, 112, 156; multilevel mound at, 72–76

Jonuta, 9, 10

kinship, 7, 11, 19, 165, 184, 186; archaeological inference (mid-level theory), 14, 191–193, 206; bilateral/bilocal, 162, 164, 192–194, 196, 197, 198, 200, 201, 206, 207; class-based systems, 7, 19, 165, 193, 199–200; conjugal (nuclear) families, 162, 172, 174(table), 186, 192, 193, 195, 197, 198, 200, 204, 207; and identity, 191, 194, 195–196, 200–201; matrilineal/matrilocal, 27, 192–193, 195; neolocal, 26–27, 162, 192–194, 196, 198, 199, 200, 201, 206, 207; patriclan, 162, 197, 198, 199, 207; patrilineal/patrilocal, 162, 188, 191, 192–193, 194–195, 196–198, 199, 200, 203, 204, 206, 207; patri-neolocal, 26; virilocal, 192, 193, 195, 198, 206, 207

labor, 61, 98—99, 175, 181, 182, 200, 207
Laguna de Términos, 19, 37, 95, 128, 151, 166, 188,
landing, at Isla Chablé, 48, 57, 89, 92, 97, 181
La Islita, 34, 43, 48
landownership, modern, 27
Late Classic period, 3, 4, 7, 10, 12, 13, 14, 15, 18, 20, 72, 95, 138, 165, 166, 180(table); ceramic chronology, 16–17; coarse-paste pottery, 112–121; commoners, 181–182; features associated with, 58–59; fine-paste pottery, 121–125; fishing-net sinkers, 135, 148; kinship, 193–195; mounds-on-plat-forms, 69–70; political economies, 174–175; pottery, 6, 15, 72, 105, 127–128, 133–134; pottery distri-bution and frequency, 128–132; recycled mound fill, 65–66, 95–96; residential platforms, 61–62; settlement patterns, 167–70; shellfish use, 144–145; vertebrate remains, 143–44
Late Formative period, 2, 4, 7, 15, 63, 144, 160–161; ceramics, 19, 108, 132,

133, 156; feature construction, 157, 158–159; Western Chontalpa, 151, 153, 163
Late Terminal Classic period, 132
levees, Late Classic settlement on, 167–168
La Venta, 4, 9, 127, 150, 151, 153
lineage time, 196
livestock, 30
looter's pits, 32, 42, 57, 84, 133, 166
Luminescence Dating Laboratory (University of Washington), 132

Machona Lagoon, 29, 151, 166, 168
mangrove (*Avicennia nitida*; *Rhizo-phora mangle*), 23–24, 25; loss of, 32–33
Maya, 153, 191; acropolis-plaza association, 175–176
Maya Lowlands, civic-ceremonial architecture, 175–176
Mecoacán Lagoon, 1, 4, 10, 22, 23, 31, 32, 134, 140, 151
Mezcalapa River/Delta, 4, 9, 10, 21, 140, 127, 150–153; Classic period, 166, 167, 168; Formative period, 150–153; Terrace Valley, 170, 176, 196, 203
middens, on platforms, 17, 75–76, 94, 98, 128, 131. *See also* concheros
Middle Classic period, 4, 121, 124, 125, 132, 165–166
Middle Formative period, 2, 4, 7, 23, 153, 156, 161, 163; at El Bellote, 19, 151, 160; feature formation, 157, 158–159; pottery, 132, 133, 164
miniature vessel, 135
monumental architecture. *See* architecture
mortar, 97, 136, 145, 146–147, 149
mounds, 6, 17, 48, 96, 179; catego-rization of, 37, 38; construction of, 15–16, 98; damage to, 32, 33; discrete, 64–68; collections and profiles of, 65–67; El Bellote, 18, 49, 52–54, 56; Formative period, 158–159; Isla del Campo and Isla Santa Rosa, 41–42; mounds-on-platforms, 6, 15, 37, 38, 46, 49,

56, 60–61, 68–69, 69–71, 98, 172; multilevel, 37, 38, 42, 46, 47, 49, 54, 60–61, 71–72, 72–76, 76–78, 78–80, 80–81, 82–83, 95, 96, 172, 186, 194; multilevel mound-on-platform, 37, 38, 46

Nahua, 4, 166
neolocality. *See* kinship.
New World Archaeology Foundation (NWAF), 10, 12, 203; Upper Mezcalapa Delta, 150–151; pottery types, 127–128
nobility. *See* classes

obsidian, 6, 14, 16, 75, 137–138, 148, 151, 166; at El Bellote, 56, 92
occupation duration, 61, 172, 173; and social class, 184, 205–206; strati-graphic data, 98–99
occupation surfaces, 15, 16, 17, 47, 60–61, 66, 68, 70, 73, 74–75, 78, 79, 93, 98–99
Olmec/Olman, 1, 2, 4, 8, 9, 11, 56, 104, 105, 107, 133, 136, 150, 161, 162, 163
oven, at Isla Chablé, 16, 69, 70, 78, 93, 94
oysters (*Crassostrea verginica*), 9, 14, 25, 144, 149; Formative period use, 157, 158; modern harvest of, 29, 30; reefs, 4, 158

Palenque, 9, 11, 137, 176, 178
Patarata, 101, 136
patrilineality, patrilocality. *See under* kinship
perishable materials, Formative period, 159–160
Peten-Ti'. *See* El Bellote
Petróleos Méxicanos (PEMEX), 31
Piña Chan, Roman and Carlos Navarrete, 10, 59, 127, 128, 153, 166, 168, 170, 197
pits, 75, 92, 93; at El Bellote, 54, 56, 80
plaster, 14, 62, 76, 96, 97, 136, 145–146, 149; in discrete mounds, 65, 66; social class and, 182, 206
platforms, 6, 37, 38, 41, 42, 57, 60, 95, 96; construction of, 15–16, 17; El Bellote, 18, 49, 52, 56, 91–92, 188;

Formative period construction of, 156, 158–159; Isla Chablé, 46, 47, 48, 89; residential, 61–64. *See also* mounds-on-platforms

plazas, 175–176, 204

plazuelas, 14, 176, 192, 194, 203; at Comalcalco, 167, 196–197; at El Bellote, 49, 54, 187–188, 195; at Isla Chablé, 47, 186; at Tierra Nueva, 197–198

political ecology, 3, 6; commercial development, 31–32; modern settlement, 26–28; modern subsistence, 28–31. *See also* theory

political economies, and class, 178, 181–182; Western Chontalpa, 60, 174–175. *See also* theory

Pomoná, brick at, 147, 166

population growth, 2, 12, 31, 163, 172, 174(table)

port of trade, 1, 4, 11, 12–13, 14, 16, 18, 20, 57, 60, 89, 97, 137, 166, 168

Postclassic period, 12–13, 168, 170, 203

Potonchán, 1, 11, 13

pottery types: classification of, 2, 6, 10, 15, 17, 18, 100, 102; Bellote, 101, 125, 126(table), 129(table), 132–133, 134, 135, 136; Black and White, 101(table), 107, 108, 127, 132, 133, 134, 154(table), 155, 156, 159, 160–161, 162; Centla, 101(table), 112–114, 116–117(table), 119, 127–128, 129(table), 132–133, 134, 135, 146, 165, 166, 179, 180(table), 182, 183(table), 185(table), 186, 187, 188, 189–190(table); Cimatán, 101(table), 112, 113, 114(table), 115–119, 127–128, 129(table), 132–133, 134, 135, 136, 166, 179, 180(table), 182, 183(table), 185(table), 186, 188, 189–190(table), 202, 206; Comalcalco fine, 101(table), 121–123, 128, 134, 165, 166, 184; Copilco fine, 132, 134, 166; Formative Coarse Paste, 108–111, 112, 127, 132–133, 134, 135, 146, 159, 161; Formative Sandy Paste, 101(table), 108, 110(table), 111, 112, 127, 133, 146, 159, 161; Formative White Paste, 101(table),

108, 111–112, 133, 135; Huimanguillo fine, 101(table), 121, 122, 123(table), 124, 128, 134, 166, 184(table); Jonuta fine, 101(table), 121, 122, 123, 128, 134, 136, 166, 184; Late Classic period reddish paste variants, 112, 113, 114(table), 115, 119, 127, 128, 133, 182, 186, 202, 206; Mecoacan, 101, 112, 113, 114(table), 118(table), 119, 121, 128, 129(table), 132, 133, 134, 182, 185(table), 186, 187, 188, 189(table); Orange, 101(table), 112, 119, 186, 188, 194; Paraíso fine, 101(table), 121, 122, 123(table), 124, 128, 134, 135, 165, 166, 184(table); Sierra Red, 13, 63, 66, 101, 105, 108, 109(table), 125, 127, 132, 133, 134, 151, 153, 154(table), 155, 156, 159, 160–161, 162, 164; X, 101(table), 125, 127, 133; Y, 101(table), 112, 119–121, 128, 188, 195; Z, 101(table), 112, *120,* 121, 128, 188, 195

pottery uses: class relations, 182–190; cuisine, 71, 111, 115, 134, 159, 202–203; feasting/food sharing, 104–105, 108, 116–117(table), 162, 164; feature dating, 58–59, 95–96; feature function, 59–64, 65, 72; formation processes, 67–68, 71, 81–82, 98–99, 154–155, 178, 180(table); technology and functional suitablility, 6, 102–104, 118–119, 124, 159, 179, 207; Late Classic period sequence, 128–132; mobility, 158, 160, 161, 163; settlement history, 154–156, 170–172; symbolic display/identity, 100, 121, 125, 136, 161, 162, 164, 179, 204–205, 206, 207; thermoluminescence dating, 6, 19, 132–133, 165

power, 3, 7, 11, 170, 175–176, 178, 181, 182, 195, 199, 200, 201, 202

projectile point tip, 138

Proyecto Arqueológico Isla de Los Cerros (PAILC), 1, 8, 20, 57; fieldwork, 12–19

Proyecto Arqueológico La Venta, 9

Puerto Ceiba, 30, 31

pumice, 14, 17, 36, 41, 140

Putún merchants, 1, 2, 166

quadratic plaza configurations, 166, 168, 170, 175, 176, 178, 181, 197, 204, 205

quahog (*Mercenaria campechiensis*), 14, 25, 144, 145

ramp, 54, 86

Rancho El Bellote, 27, 30

rancheria settlement pattern, 46, 57, 162, 193; resource-deprived commoners, 193–194

rays, 25, 141, 143, 144, 158, 159

recycled deposits, 61, 68, 70, 76, 83, 95

Registro Público de Monumentos y Zonas Arqueológos (INAH), 14, 34, 36

residence. *See* kinship

residential features, 6, 14, 37, 46, 128, 142, 172, 173(table), 176, 192; commoners, 184, 186–187; defining, 59–60; discrete mounds, 64–68; discrete platforms, 61–64; functions of, 96–97; mounds-on-platforms, 68–71; multilevel mounds, 71–83

residential groups, 181, 192–193; Comalcalco, 196–197; occupation duration, 205–206

residential mounds, 2, 12, 176, 179; at El Bellote, 49, 54, 56, 195; at Isla Chablé, 46, 47, 65, 66; occupation duration, 61, 172

residential platforms, 61–64, 172, 188

roasting pit, at El Bellote, 93

San Fernando, 127, 128, 153, 166, 203

San Lorenzo, 9

San Miguel, 95, 151, 166, 197, 203

Sanders, William, 10, 165–166, 168, 170, 191, 196, 203,

screen mesh size effect. *See* faunal remains

Seco River, 4, 10, 22, 23, 24, 25, 26, 151, 153, 157, 167, 168,

sediment mining, mines, 6, 15, 18, 32, 33, 42, 47, 49, 52, 56, 57, 65, 67, 78, 80, 83, 84, 85, 166, 187

settlement history, 2, 3, 7, 14, 15, 98, 150, 152–156, 170–173; classes and,

181, 184, 205–206; influence of kinship, 195–196

settlement patterns, 57; ecology and, 25–26; kinship and, 192–195, 196; Late Classic period, 167–170; modern and historical, 26–28

shell deposits, 14, 16, 142, 149, 156, 158, 179; Isla Chablé, 48, 57, 60, 89–91, 97, 181, 182; materials processing, 60, 97, 144

shellfish, 14, 25, 29, 149, 200; Formative period use, 156, 157–158, 159; processed, 96, 97, 175, 187; use of, 144–145

Sigero, 168, 176, 197, 203

sinkers, fishing net, 6, 16, 56, 70, 92, 97, 135, *136*, 148, 158, 181, 187

Sisson, Edward, 9, 10, 12, 21, 34, 36, 37, 41, 42, 48, 52, 56, 95, 127, 150, 151, 166, 168, 170

social class. *See* classes

social memory, 2, 3, 7, 100, 105, 165, 176, 188, 190, 194, 196, 201–202, 204, 206, 207, 208. *See also* embodiment, identity, lineage time, and pottery uses

social organization. *See* classes and kinship

Spanish contact, viii, 1, 2, 10, 166, 175, 178, 199, 201

specialized features, descriptions of, 88–94, 97

status, 2, 3, 7, 61, 99, 104, 105, 161, 162, 163, 165, 176, 178, 194, 196, 199–200, 204, 205, 206; materialization of, 61, 172, 179–190

Stark, Barbara, 167–168, 170

Stirling, Matthew, 9, 34, 49, 83, 85, 88

stone tools, 6, 138, 140, 148. *See also* chert; ground stone; obsidian

storage features, 159

substructures, in ceremonial mounds, 83, 84, 97

subsistence: Formative period, 157–158, 159; modern, 28–31

surface collections, 37, 63(table), 69, 72, 142, 179, 188; at discrete mounds, 65, 67; at discrete platforms, 61–62; Isla de Los Cerros, 13–14, *171*; material culture in, 180(table), 183(table), 189(table); pottery in, 154–155, 156

surveys, archaeological, 1, 9–10, 12, 13, 18, 19, 34, 36–37, 57, 58, 61, 95, 97, 128, 137, 150–151, 167, 168, 170, 176

symbolic display, 6, 7, 176, 178–179, 182, 184, 186–187, 196. *See also* pottery uses

Tabasco, 2, 5(map), 127, 138, 150

Teotihuacán, 9, 166

Terminal Classic period, 4

theory, 1, 2, 3; agency/negotiation, 99, 102, 134, 140, 160–161, 165, 176; mid-level cross-cultural ethnology, 4, 105, 162, 190–193, 194, 195, 196, 197, 198; culture historical, 6, 7, 9, 10, 100, 101, 132, 150, 165, 170, 203; embodiment, 7, 99, 188, 191, 195–196, 198, 206, 207; political ecological, 6, 21, 26–32; political economic, 7, 10, 12, 14, 18, 21, 26, 57, 59–60, 102, 144, 145, 167, 168, 173–175, 178, 179, 181, 182–184, 187, 192, 196, 198–199, 200, 201, 202, 204–205; practice, 104, 105, 134, 186

thermal features, 93–94

thermoluminescence dating, 19, 132–133, 134, 165

Tierra Nueva, 148, 166, 168, 175, 176, *177*, 196, 197, 199, 207; pottery associated with, 203, 204

time, Maya concepts of, 196

tombs, possible, 97

Tortuguero, 10, 11, 176, 178

tourism, 31, 32, 33

trade. *See* exchange

transportation, 25, *28*

tree crops, 23, 26, 29–30, 167

triadic plaza configurations, 175–176, 178, 181, 205

turtles, 25, 141, 143, 149, 158, 159; radiometric dating, 144, 157

Tuxtla Mountains, 127, 138, 176

United States: crab harvesting, 31–32

Usumacinta River, 4, 9, 10, 19, 21, 23, 101, 119–121, 127, 128, 140, 147, 148, 150, 165, 166, 176, 182, 188, 195

vases, 203, 204

Veracruz, 1, 8, 9, 11, 16, 31, 41, 78, 101, 127, 136, 138, 151, 165, 166–167, 176, 204

Villahermosa, 4, 13, 18, 31

virilocality. *See under* kinship

waterworn stone, 137, 140, 158, 179, 181, 183(table), 184, 185(table), 186, 188, 189(table), 194, 195

West, Robert, Norbert Psuty, and Bruce Thom, 10, 11, 12, 22, 24–25, 34–36, 40, 56, 150, 151, *152*

Western Chontalpa, 1, 3, 4, 7; Formative period, 150–153, 163; kinship in, 196–198; Late Classic period, 165–170; monumental architecture in, 175–178; political economies, 174–175

whelks (*Busycon* sp.), 14, 25, 144, 145

Xicalango, 1, 11, 13

Yucatéc Maya/Yucatán, 4, 8, 11, 16, 89, 104, 166

ABSTRACT

For archaeologists and ethnohistorians, the Chontalpa region of Tabasco, Mexico, has conjured multiple images. One is of an intermediary zone between the Mexican and Maya macroregions. Another is of a periphery to broader Mesoamerican developments. Yet another is of cultures that shaped broader Mesoamerica (e.g., as part of the Olmec Heartland, the origins of cacao, the homeland of expanding Itzá and Putún, and a multiethnic region with Nahua intrusions). Despite attention to Olmec La Venta, the Late Classic Comalcalco elite, and ethnohistorical interest in contact-period Chontal kingdoms and trade centers, however, the region remains archaeologically under-investigated (especially coastal areas), speculated upon from afar, and misinterpreted. This volume seeks to balance past perspectives with the first systematic investigation and analyses of material culture at a large coastal settlement—Islas de Los Cerros—contextualized within a new regional synthesis of the Western Chontalpa. Going beyond descriptions, the analyses test alternative hypotheses on the material culture and an alternative pottery classification is introduced that is more appropriate to the material and contemporary questions. The regional synthesis indicates a sparsely settled frontier in the Early and Middle Formative, with significant population growth in the Late Formative. Contrary to a widespread assumption, the features at Islas de Los Cerros were not Formative era shell middens but were Late Classic constructions mostly built with earthen deposits, which has implications on interpreting Formative developments throughout the region. Explicit assumptions and different theoretical perspectives enable new interpretations on Formative settlement history, adaptations, features and technologies, social groups, their lifeways, and identities. After an Early Classic hiatus, the region experienced population growth in the Late Classic when there was strong intra-regional integration but little influence from Veracruz or the Maya region (with the exception of elites). Settlement patterns indicate three differently structured kingdoms. The most powerful was headed by royalty at Comalcalco who controlled the most diverse resources, including those of Islas de Los Cerros, which was not a trade port. Using diverse methods, some of which are original, the study indicates that the Late Classic tributary political economy

RESUMEN

Para los arqueólogos y etnohistoriadores, la región Chontalpa de Tabasco, México ha hecho surgir múltiples imágenes. Uno es como una región intermedia entre las macroregiones mexicanas y las mayas. Otra es como una zona periférica al desarrollo mesoamericano. Otro más es como un conjunto de culturas que contribuyeron decisivamente a la formación de mesoamérica (e.g. como parte del núcleo olmeca, el orígen del cacao, los orígenes de los itzá y putúnes expansionistas, y como una región multiétnica en donde habían intrusiones nahuas). Sin embargo, a pesar de la atención que se le ha prestado al centro olmeca de La Venta y a la élite de Comalcalco del clasico tardío, y del interés etnohistórico a los reinos chontales y centros comerciales del período de contacto, la región permanece insuficientemente investigada arqueológicamente (en particular los sitios costeros), el subjeto de especulaciones desde afuera, y malinterpretada. Este volumen complementa las perspectivas prevalentes aportando la primera investigación sistemática y los correspondientes análisis de la cultura material de un extenso poblado costero—Islas de Los Cerros—contextualizados dentro de una nueva síntesis regional de la Chontalpa occidental. Yendo más allá de descripciones, los análisis aportados prueban hipótesis alternativas sobre la cultura material; asi mismo se introduce un sistema de clasificación de la cerámica que es más apropiado para el material y a las temas contemporáneas. La síntesis regional sugiere la presencia de una frontera escasamente poblada durante el period formativo temprano y medio con crecimiento demográfico en el period formativo tardío. En contra de lo que se assume generalmente, los rasgos de la época formativa no eran concheros sino montículos construidos en el clásico tardío, mayoritariamente con depósitos de tierra, lo cual tiene implicaciones importantes con respecto a la interpretación del desarrollo formativo de la región en términos más amplios. Suposiciónes explícitas y diferentes perspectivas teóricas permiten nuevas interpretaciones sobre la historia de poblamiento en la época formativa, sus adaptaciones, rasgos y tecnologías, sus grupos sociales, sus modos de vida, y sus identidades. Después de una interrupción en el clásico temprano, la región experimentó un crecimiento demográfico regional en el clásico tardío cuando hubo una integración intraregional fuerte pero poca influencia por

differentially structured intra- and interclass social relations, conditions, kinship practices, settlement expansion, statuses, identities, associations with ancestors, gender relations, and foodways. This study offers new approaches to Mesoamerican archaeology, provides much needed revisions to Chontalpan prehistory, and demonstrates the significance of coastal settlements in the Gulf Coast region.

parte de Veracruz o de la región maya (a excepción de la élite). Los patrones de asentamiento indican la existencia de tres reinos diferentemente estructurados. El más poderoso de ellos estaba encabezado por los realeza de Comalcalco la cual controlaba los recursos más diversos, incluidos los de Islas de Los Cerros que no era un puerto de intercambio commercial. Utilizando métodos diversos algunos de los cuales son originales, el estudio indica que la economía política tributaria del clásico tardío estructuraba de manera diferente las relaciones sociales dentro de y entre clases las sociales, las condiciones, las prácticas de parentesco, la expansion de los asentamientos, los estatuses, las identidades, las asociaciones con los ancestros, las relaciones de género, y las prácticas alimentarias. Este estudio ofrece nuevos enfoques de la arqueología mesoamericana, proporciona revisiones muy necesarias de la prehistoria de la Chontalpa, y demuestra la importancia de los asentamientos costeros de la región de la Costa del Golfo.

ANTHROPOLOGICAL PAPERS OF THE UNIVERSITY OF ARIZONA

1. **Excavations at Nantack Village, Point of Pines, Arizona**
   David A. Breternitz. 1959.

2. **Yaqui Myths and Legends**
   Ruth W. Giddings. 1959. Now in book form.

3. **Marobavi: A Study of an Assimilated Group in Northern Sonora**
   Roger C. Owen. 1959.

4. **A Survey of Indian Assimilation in Eastern Sonora**
   Thomas B. Hinton. 1959.

5. **The Phonology of Arizona Yaqui with Texts**
   Lynn S. Crumrine. 1961.

6. **The Maricopas: An Identification from Documentary Sources**
   Paul H. Ezell. 1963.

7. **The San Carlos Indian Cattle Industry**
   Harry T. Getty. 1963.

8. **The House Cross of the Mayo Indians of Sonora, Mexico**
   N. Ross Crumrine. 1964.

9. **Salvage Archaeology in Painted Rocks Reservoir, Western Arizona**
   William W. Wasley and Alfred E. Johnson. 1965.

10. **An Appraisal of Tree-Ring Dated Pottery in the Southwest**
    David A. Breternitz. 1966.

11. **The Albuquerque Navajos**
    William H. Hodge. 1969.

12. **Papago Indians at Work**
    Jack O. Waddell. 1969.

13. **Culture Change and Shifting Populations in Central Northern Mexico**
    William B. Griffen. 1969.

14. **Ceremonial Exchange as a Mechanism in Tribal Integration Among the Mayos of Northwest Mexico**
    Lynn S. Crumrine. 1969.

15. **Western Apache Witchcraft**
    Keith H. Basso. 1969.

16. **Lithic Analysis and Cultural Inference: A Paleo-Indian Case**
    Edwin N. Wilmsen. 1970.

17. **Archaeology as Anthropology: A Case Study**
    William A. Longacre. 1970.

18. **Broken K Pueblo: Prehistoric Social Organization in the American Southwest**
    James N. Hill. 1970.

19. **White Mountain Redware: A Pottery Tradition of East-Central Arizona and Western New Mexico**
    Roy L. Carlson. 1970.

20. **Mexican Macaws: Comparative Osteology**
    Lyndon L. Hargrave. 1970.

21. **Apachean Culture History and Ethnology**
    Keith H. Basso and Morris E. Opler, eds. 1971.

22. **Social Functions of Language in a Mexican-American Community**
    George C. Barker. 1972.

23. **The Indians of Point of Pines, Arizona: A Comparative Study of Their Physical Characteristics**
    Kenneth A. Bennett. 1973.

24. **Population, Contact, and Climate in the New Mexico Pueblos**
    Ezra B. W. Zubrow. 1974.

25. **Irrigation's Impact on Society**
    Theodore E. Downing and McGuire Gibson, eds. 1974.

26. **Excavations at Punta de Agua in the Santa Cruz River Basin, Southeastern Arizona**
    J. Cameron Greenleaf. 1975.

27. **Seri Prehistory: The Archaeology of the Central Coast of Sonora, Mexico**
    Thomas Bowen. 1976.

28. **Carib-Speaking Indians: Culture, Society, and Language**
    Ellen B. Basso, ed. 1977.

29. **Cocopa Ethnography**
    William H. Kelly. 1977.

30. **The Hodges Ruin: A Hohokam Community in the Tucson Basin**
    Isabel Kelly, James E. Officer, and Emil W. Haury, collaborators; Gayle H. Hartmann, ed. 1978.

31. **Fort Bowie Material Culture**
    Robert M. Herskovitz. 1978.

32. **Wooden Ritual Artifacts from Chaco Canyon, New Mexico: The Chetro Ketl Collection**
    R. Gwinn Vivian, Dulce N. Dodgen, and Gayle H. Hartmann. 1978.

33. **Indian Assimilation in the Franciscan Area of Nueva Vizcaya**
    William B. Griffen. 1979.

34. **The Durango South Project: Archaeological Salvage of Two Late Basketmaker III Sites in the Durango District**
    John D. Gooding. 1980.

35. **Basketmaker Caves in the Prayer Rock District, Northeastern Arizona**
    Elizabeth Ann Morris. 1980.

36. **Archaeological Explorations in Caves of the Point of Pines Region, Arizona**
    James C. Gifford. 1980.

37. **Ceramic Sequences in Colima: Capacha, an Early Phase**
    Isabel Kelly. 1980.

38. **Themes of Indigenous Acculturation in Northwest Mexico**
    Thomas B. Hinton and Phil C. Weigand, eds. 1981.

39. **Sixteenth Century Maiolica Pottery in the Valley of Mexico**
    Florence C. Lister and Robert H. Lister. 1982.

40. **Multidisciplinary Research at Grasshopper Pueblo, Arizona**
    William A. Longacre, Sally J. Holbrook, and Michael W. Graves, eds. 1982.

41. **The Asturian of Cantabria: Early Holocene Hunter-Gatherers in Northern Spain**
    Geoffrey A. Clark. 1983.

42. **The Cochise Cultural Sequence in Southeastern Arizona**
    E. B. Sayles. 1983.

43. **Cultural and Environmental History of Cienega Valley, Southeastern Arizona**
    Frank W. Eddy and Maurice E. Cooley. 1983.

44. **Settlement, Subsistence, and Society in Late Zuni Prehistory**
    Keith W. Kintigh. 1985.

45. The Geoarchaeology of Whitewater Draw, Arizona
Michael R. Waters. 1986.

46. Ejidos and Regions of Refuge in Northwestern Mexico
N. Ross Crumrine and Phil C. Weigand, eds. 1987.

47. Preclassic Maya Pottery at Cuello, Belize
Laura J. Kosakowsky. 1987.

48. Pre-Hispanic Occupance in the Valley of Sonora, Mexico
William E. Doolittle. 1988.

49. Mortuary Practices and Social Differentiation at Casas Grandes, Chihuahua, Mexico
John C. Ravesloot. 1988.

50. Point of Pines, Arizona: A History of the University of Arizona Archaeological Field School
Emil W. Haury. 1989.

51. Patarata Pottery: Classic Period Ceramics of the South-central Gulf Coast, Veracruz, Mexico
Barbara L. Stark. 1989.

52. The Chinese of Early Tucson: Historic Archaeology from the Tucson Urban Renewal Project
Florence C. Lister and Robert H. Lister. 1989.

53. Mimbres Archaeology of the Upper Gila, New Mexico
Stephen H. Lekson. 1990.

54. Prehistoric Households at Turkey Creek Pueblo, Arizona
Julie C. Lowell. 1991.

55. Homol'ovi II: Archaeology of an Ancestral Hopi Village, Arizona
E. Charles Adams and Kelley Ann Hays, eds. 1991.

56. The Marana Community in the Hohokam World
Suzanne K. Fish, Paul R. Fish, and John H. Madsen, eds. 1992.

57. Between Desert and River: Hohokam Settlement and Land Use in the Los Robles Community
Christian E. Downum. 1993.

58. Sourcing Prehistoric Ceramics at Chodistaas Pueblo, Arizona: The Circulation of People and Pots in the Grasshopper Region
María Nieves Zedeño. 1994.

59. Of Marshes and Maize: Preceramic Agricultural Settlements in the Cienega Valley, Southeastern Arizona
Bruce B. Huckell. 1995.

60. Historic Zuni Architecture and Society: An Archaeological Application of Space Syntax
T. J. Ferguson. 1996.

61. Ceramic Commodities and Common Containers: Production and Distribution of White Mountain Red Ware in the Grasshopper Region, Arizona
Daniela Triadan. 1997.

62. Prehistoric Sandals from Northeastern Arizona: The Earl H. Morris and Ann Axtell Morris Research
Kelley Ann Hays-Gilpin, Ann Cordy Deegan, and Elizabeth Ann Morris. 1998.

63. Expanding the View of Hohokam Platform Mounds: An Ethnographic Perspective
Mark D. Elson. 1998.

64. Great House Communities Across the Chacoan Landscape
John Kantner and Nancy M. Mahoney, eds. 2000.

65. Tracking Prehistoric Migrations: Pueblo Settlers among the Tonto Basin Hohokam
Jeffery J. Clark. 2001.

66. Beyond Chaco: Great Kiva Communities on the Mogollon Rim Frontier
Sarah A. Herr. 2001.

67. Salado Archaeology of the Upper Gila, New Mexico
Stephen H. Lekson. 2002.

68. Ancestral Hopi Migrations
Patrick D. Lyons. 2003.

69. Ancient Maya Life in the Far West Bajo: Social and Environmental Change in the Wetlands of Belize
Julie L. Kunen. 2004.

70. The Safford Valley Grids: Prehistoric Cultivation in the Southern Arizona Desert
William E. Doolittle and James A. Neely, eds. 2004.

71. Murray Springs: A Clovis Site with Multiple Activity Areas in the San Pedro Valley, Arizona
C. Vance Haynes, Jr., and Bruce B. Huckell, eds. 2007.

72. Ancestral Zuni Glaze-Decorated Pottery: Viewing Pueblo IV Regional Organization through Ceramic Production and Exchange
Deborah L. Huntley. 2008.

73. In the Aftermath of Migration: Renegotiating Ancient Identity in Southeastern Arizona
Anna A. Neuzil. 2008.

74. Burnt Corn Pueblo, Conflict and Conflagration in the Galisteo Basin, A.D. 1250–1325
James E Snead and Mark W. Allen. 2011.

75. Potters and Communities of Practice: Glaze Paint and Polychrome Pottery in the American Southwest, A.D. 1250–1700
Linda S. Cordell and Judith Habicht-Mauche, eds. 2012.

76. Los Primeros Mexicanos: Late Pleistocene and Early Holocene People of Sonora
Guadalupe Sánchez. 2015.

77. The Ceramic Sequence of the Holmul Region, Guatemala
Michael G. Callaghan and Nina Neivens de Estrada. 2016.

78. The Winged: An Upper Missouri River Ethno-Ornithology
Kaitlyn Chandler, Wendi Field Murray, María Nieves Zedeño, Samrat Clements, Robert James. 2016.

79. Seventeenth-Century Metallurgy on the Spanish Colonial Frontier: Pueblo and Spanish Interactions
Noah H. Thomas. 2018.

80. Reframing the Northern Rio Grande Pueblo Economy
Scott G. Orman, ed. 2019.

81. Oysters in the Land of Cacao: Archaeology, Material Culture, and Societies at Islas de los Cerros and the Western Chontalpa, Tabasco, Mexico
Bradley E. Ensor. 2020.